Down Home

Down

Published in association with

THE JEWISH HERITAGE FOUNDATION OF NORTH CAROLINA

by THE UNIVERSITY OF NORTH CAROLINA PRESS

Chapel Hill

JEWISH LIFE IN NORTH CAROLINA

Home

LEONARD ROGOFF

© 2010

The Jewish Heritage Foundation of North Carolina

All rights reserved

Designed by Richard Hendel

Set in Caecilia, The Serif, and Scala Sans

by Tseng Information Systems, Inc.

Manufactured in Canada

The paper in this book meets the guidelines for
permanence and durability of the Committee on
Production Guidelines for Book Longevity of the
Council on Library Resources.

The University of North Carolina Press has been
a member of the Green Press Initiative since 2003.

Library of Congress Cataloging-in-Publication Data

Rogoff, Leonard.

Down home : Jewish life in North Carolina / Leonard Rogoff.

  p. cm.

Includes bibliographical references and index.

ISBN 978-0-8078-3375-9 (cloth : alk. paper)

1. Jews—North Carolina—History. 2. Jews—North Carolina—Social life
and customs. I. Jewish Heritage Foundation of North Carolina. II. Title.

F265.J5R64 2010

975.6′004924—dc22   2009039478

14 13 12 11 10 5 4 3 2 1

To the memory of

ANNA LOU DOCTOR CASSELL,

a matriarch of her family and

community

CONTENTS

Down Home

INTRODUCTION

"I thought my stories were going to die with me," said Lena Gordon Goldman, a ninety-eight-year-old resident of a Greensboro retirement home. Relative to Virginia and South Carolina, North Carolina is often thought to have no or little Jewish history. Biographies, dissertations, and local histories have focused on individuals and communities. Some extraordinary archives and oral histories have been collected, but they have not yet been assembled into a whole. *Down Home* gathers North Carolina Jews into a community.

The stories recounted here are many and speak with different and sometimes contradictory voices. *Down Home*, in both format and contents, reflects the diversity of its subject. At its core is a narrative history spanning North Carolina's past and present, from Roanoke Island in 1585 to the Research Triangle in 2009. To bring that history to life, interpolated into the narrative are exemplary stories, portraits, and texts. Stories present oral history in original voices; portraits offer profiles of significant personalities or organizations; and texts present primary documents from newspapers, memoirs, and public or synagogue records. Collectively, these gatherings of history comprise a Jewish heritage, a folklore that roots Jews in North Carolina.

Down Home joins a growing list of state Jewish histories. Typically, these books argue for the uniqueness of their state's Jewish community. Mark Bauman in *The Southerner as American: Jewish Style* argues that the story of southern Jews is but a variation on an American theme, more closely attuned to the national story of immigrant acculturation than to the specific history of the largely Protestant South. He further suggests that even more significant than regional identity is local environment. Much in *Down Home* supports these arguments.[1] There are many Souths, but there are many North Carolinas, too.

North Carolina often seems more a gathering of localities than a unified state. Appalachian Asheville is quite different from the Old South port of Wilmington, and Charlotte's Sunbelt skyline little resembles Mount Airy's main street. North Carolina divides into three geographical zones—coast, piedmont, and mountain—that developed distinct cultures and economies. English settlers created a plantation society on the coastal plain, importing African American labor. The Piedmont drew Scotch-Irish and Germans. From its hardscrabble agrarian roots, it grew into the state's industrial heartland. The mountains, settled by Germans and Scotch Highlanders, sheltered fiercely independent Appalachians. North

Carolina in its early days was a polyglot immigrant society. Native Americans and African Americans added to the ethnic mix. A welter of religious sects—Baptist, Methodist, Lutheran, Catholic, Presbyterian, Anglican, Quaker, and Moravian—made it welcoming to religious diversity even as its Protestant character led it to suspect those who did not share the faith.

North Carolina largely lacked the entrenched social hierarchies of its northern and southern neighbors. North Carolina was the proverbial "vale of humility between two mountains of conceit." For much of its history, its representative citizen was the yeoman farmer in contrast to the cavalier of Virginia or the Low Country aristocrat of South Carolina. The log cabin and the wood-framed farmhouse, not the plantation manse, are its iconic dwellings. North Carolina's motto is "To be, rather than to seem." North Carolina has been a place of small towns. When historian Lee Shai Weissbach did a comparative study, *Jewish Life in Small-Town America: A History*, he documented that North Carolina in 1927 was the most extreme of all states in its profile, with thirteen communities of more than 100 Jews but none with over 1,000.[2] North Carolina's small-town character explains much of its politics and social values—as well as the Jewish acculturation there. In contrast to most states, North Carolina lacked a Jewish urban capital, an Atlanta, Baltimore, or New York.

State borders mark political boundaries, not social or cultural ones, but North Carolina displays distinct contradictions that describe its people as well as its geography. Religiously orthodox and socially conservative, North Carolinians have also been libertarian and progressive. A self-made man or woman, a hard worker, a person who respected family and religion was admired, Jews among them. In the antebellum and postbellum eras, North Carolina ranked among the poorest states, but with the New South and Sunbelt it has moved into the economic vanguard. The Southeast's leading industrial state also held the most farms. North Carolina was the least resistant of southern states to integration but remained the most segregated. Its elections are the most closely contested in the South. Today, it is the tenth-most-populated state, but its largest city, Charlotte, ranks only twentieth. Observers speak of two North Carolinas: the prosperous, high-tech Sunbelt along interstate corridors and a poor agrarian region in its rural corners and inland eastern counties.[3]

The title *Down Home* suggests Jews were rooted in North Carolina, although their history demonstrates mobility. Often Jews did not remain in a community through a second generation. If the yeoman farmer is the representative North Carolina pioneer, then the peddler is the typical early North Carolina Jew. At almost any time in a North Carolina Jewish community, recently arrived residents outnumber native born. Certainly, cores of multigenerational families persist as southern Jews, but they are subcommunities in their hometowns.

Jews have their own complexities, too. As immigrant people, Jews transcend borders. A very few Spanish-Portuguese from colonial days were followed by far larger numbers of German-speaking Jews in the nineteenth century and then by even greater numbers of East Europeans in the late nineteenth century. Typically, southern Jewish communities bifurcate between a temple and a synagogue, an older German Reform and a newer East European traditional congregation, but most North Carolina communities were East European. Mixed in were Jews from other countries and continents—Egypt, Iraq, Greece, Syria, Israel, South Africa. Most often, North Carolina was not their first place of American settlement. If, as Eli Evans eloquently writes, southern Jews were provincials to northern Jews, they were cosmopolitans to southerners.[4] A North Carolina Jew may thus claim many homelands tracing to national origin and paths of immigration. A Rocky Mount Jew may speak of Bialystock, Baltimore, and Jerusalem as home. Jews were diverse both among and within themselves.

State histories tend to emphasize accommodation, how Jews became Americans. As historian Stephen J. Whitfield argues, the story is also one of how Jews retained their difference, how they remained Jews. As an immigrant people, Jews confronted choices of "assimilation, resistance, and hybridity." Although at the extremes some Jews wholly assimilated into southern Christian society and some Jews resisted any compromise with Orthodox tradition, most Jews partook of all three responses. They negotiated constantly between Old World and New. A synagogue in the religiously devout South was a Jewish church, which took its civic place in the faith community even as it maintained Jewish difference in religion and peoplehood. As cultural hybrids, Jews both "braided" and blended their various identities.[5]

Adding southern to American Jewish identity complicates the mix. The South itself has differed from America, especially on issues of race. Yet most North Carolina Jews as migrants lacked multigenerational southern histories, and their memories extended less to Appomattox than to Auschwitz. Southerners did not always see Jews as Jews saw themselves. Journalist W. J. Cash described southern Christianity as "essentially Hebraic." Southerners welcomed Jews as patriarchs and matriarchs, the people of Jesus. Jews themselves, immigrants from European poverty and persecution, ventured south seeking economic opportunity, a place where they could find security for themselves and futures for their children. Jews aspired to become Americans even as, Cash observes, southerners saw the Jew as the "eternal Alien."[6]

Jews felt themselves members of a global as well a local community. "A concern for Jewries abroad virtually defines the American Jewish persona," observes historian Henry Feingold.[7] Jews remained attached to families they had left behind through letters, packages, and visits. As a community, they organized to assist Jews trapped by World War I, endangered in Nazi Europe, and oppressed in the Soviet Union. Rooted in North Carolina, they helped build and defend a Jewish homeland in Israel.

Most Jews thus resisted a complete assimilation. Cultural pluralism, popularized by the philosopher Horace Kallen, sanctioned a hyphenated Jewish-American identity. But Jews renegotiated its terms, fearing both an accommodation that would mean a loss of Jewishness and a separation that would isolate them from their neighbors. Identities are fluid and unstable. Today, North Carolina is redefining itself as a multicultural society with the arrival of new Asian, Arab, African, and Hispanic immigrant peoples, but the Jewish place on that spectrum is not fixed. Jews have become white Americans even as they continue to view themselves as a victimized minority. Their southern identity has evolved with the South itself, which is now a more generically American place of highway strips, shopping malls, and suburban subdivisions.

The Jewish presence has always been more outsized than census data suggest. Without necessarily having a North Carolina address, Jewish peddlers, salesmen, drummers, students, soldiers, tourists, schnorrers (transient beggars), labor organizers, and civil rights activists constantly flowed through the state sometimes in numbers larger than the native Jewish population. The country peddler trekked to the remotest farmhouses, and mill workers and farmers spilling into downtowns saw storefronts advertising Leder, Schulman, Stadiem, Brody, Kramer, Fleishman, or Finkelstein. Revered statesmen across three centuries—William Gaston, Zebulon Vance, Frank Graham, Kerr Scott, Josephus Daniels, Terry Sanford, and Jim Hunt—identified with Jews and publicly advocated their causes. The 1776 state constitutional convention spent a third of its time debating whether Jews qualified for public office, although few lived there. In 1918, when the state's Jews appealed to Christians on behalf of a national Jewish War Sufferers Campaign, its citizens supported it so heartily that the North Carolina Plan became a national model. Even now, North Carolina ranks among the first to have a Judaica Gallery in its state art museum, a state-sponsored Holocaust Council, and an Israel partnership. Jews have been present in the minds of North Carolinians beyond their numbers.

The North Carolina experience is not unique among American Jews, but an argument can be made for its difference in degree if not in kind. Southern Jewish histories tend to emphasize the antebellum and Civil War eras, and Sephardic and German Jews predominate. The North Carolina story features the New South and the Sunbelt, and the East European migration is more significant. The story of community creation and growth focuses on the urbanizing and industrializing that accelerated in the 1880s when mill and market towns spread across the landscape. The state claimed one congregation in 1880, but twenty-two by 1927. With the advent of the Sunbelt, Jewish migration has grown at unprecedented rates. Today, the state claims more than forty congregational groups.

The presence of Jews historically has been an index of the state's change. Just as the New South welcomed the Jewish peddler, merchant, and industrialist, so too has the Sunbelt invited the doctor, professor, engineer, lawyer, and entrepreneur. With their links to centers beyond the state's borders, Jews brought new material and intellectual capital. The routes of commerce—extending to Baltimore and New York, and abroad to Europe—also served as channels of cultural transmission. Today, North Carolina presents itself as a multicultural society competing in a global marketplace. Jews have been harbingers of that change.

The unprecedented growth and vibrancy of North Carolina Jewry today offer counterevidence to an American Jewry supposedly in demographic decline and assimilating through intermarriage and attenuation of religious belief and practice. Observers of American Jewry debate whether its narrative is one of declension or reinvention. Fears are expressed of Jewish survival even as a Jewish renaissance is proclaimed. The growing numbers and institutions of North Carolina's Jews seemingly justify a celebratory history—with, as is usual with Jews, dissenting opinions. Jews have indeed remained Jews, but their American accommodation also raises questions as to the depth and durability of that commitment. Their varied, reinvented American Judaisms are both loyal to and discontinuous with the Jewish past. If immigrant Jews aspired to blend Americanism onto their Jewish identities, their grandchildren face the challenge of grafting Jewishness onto their American identities.[8]

The Jewish rise from immigrant poverty to middle-class prosperity, from marginality to the American mainstream, parallels the North Carolina story. A historically poor state is now counted among the most prosperous. If Jews are distinguished by educational achievement, they are coming to a state now noted for the excellence of its universities. An economy built on farms and textile mills now features high technology and global finance. A state that historically struggled to stem the outflow of its people to more inviting places now ranks among the fastest growing. Jews are coming down, and they are making North Carolina home.

1 **THE COLONY** POOR MAN'S COUNTRY
1585-1776

When Joachim Gans set foot on Roanoke Island in 1585, he became not only the first Jew to arrive in Carolina but the first in a British colony in the New World. Gans, a native of Prague, was the lead "mineral man" on Sir Walter Raleigh's second expedition to what was then the Virginia Territory. The 108 colonists intended not just to plant England's flag but to find new wealth for the crown. Facing starvation and hostile Indians, the colonists, Gans among them, returned to England in 1586 when Sir Francis Drake's privateer fleet sailed unexpectedly into the inlet.

Roanoke Island, where Joachim Gans arrived in 1585. (North Carolina Collection, University of North Carolina Library at Chapel Hill)

Despite his short stay, Gans was a prototype of Jewish settlers for generations. His origins were cosmopolitan. He had left a traditional European Jewish community for an uncertain New World where his talents in commerce were valued more than his religion was despised. In his search for economic opportunity, Gans was highly mobile, emigrating from Bohemia to Saxony to England and then to America. He was living in an England that had been unwelcoming to Jews since their massacre and expulsion in the late thirteenth century. Indeed, the several hundred Jews who lived in Elizabethan England were virtually all Spanish-Portuguese who practiced Judaism secretly, if at all.[1] Yet, with the rise of global capitalism, religious prejudice was becoming less significant than economic gain. Jews—excluded from guilds and landowning—had a history as merchants and moneylenders. Through commerce, Jews left the ghetto and entered the modern, secular world.

Poverty and persecution pushed Jews from the Old World, and economic opportunity and religious liberty pulled them to the New. Although Gans was an Ashkenazi Jew from Central Europe, the earliest migrants were Sephardic Jews. Jews on the Iberian Peninsula had flourished under Moslem rule in the Middle Ages, but after the Christian conquest and the establishing of the Roman Catholic Inquisition, they faced the choice of massacre or conversion. Many Jewish converts, or New Christians as they were called, practiced Judaism secretly at the risk of prison, torture, or the stake. In 1492 Jews were expelled altogether, fleeing mostly to Portugal but also to the Ottoman Empire. With the Inquisition established in Portugal in 1536, they fled again. In the seventeenth century, they arrived in a relatively tolerant Holland, where many openly embraced Judaism. Holland was also the meeting place for Ashkenazi Jews who were emigrating westward from villages in German and Polish lands. They sought haven from the Thirty Years' War, a Catholic-Protestant conflict dating to 1618. Cossack rebellions and massacres in the mid-seventeenth century pushed Ukrainian and Polish Jews westward. After the creation of the British Commonwealth, Dutch rabbi Manasseh Ben Israel personally petitioned Oliver Cromwell in 1655 to open doors for Jews. Valued for their commercial skills, Jews established themselves in London, numbering some 6,000 by 1730.[2]

Jewish investors in the Dutch East India Company in Amsterdam secured rights for Jews to settle and trade in American lands. From Holland, Jews followed colonial trade routes that extended to Brazil, Surinam, Cayenne, Curaçao, and New Amsterdam. From England, Jews created mercantile links to Jamaica and Barbados, and to Newport, New York, Savannah, and Charleston. Recife, Brazil, in the 1640s had more than 1,000 Jews, and in 1679 54 of the 404 householders in Barbados were Jews. More Jews lived in Barbados than in all of North America. From

PORTRAIT: JOACHIM GANS

For Joachim Gans, the bare, sandy shores of Roanoke Island contrasted starkly to the metropolitan world that he had left behind. His native Prague was verging on a golden age for Jews. By 1600 some 7,000 Jews lived there including learned rabbis and wealthy merchants. The Gans family was among its luminaries. David Gans (1541–1613)—whose relation to Joachim, if any, is unclear—was known for both rabbinical and scientific learning, and he, like Joachim, collaborated with Christian scholars.[1] Joachim Gans was employed as a metallurgist in the Ore Mountains of Saxony when at the bequest of Queen Elizabeth herself German "workmasters" were recruited to locate mines and smelt ore in England for the Society of the Mines Royal. In 1585, when Sir Walter Raleigh undertook his second expedition to Virginia, Gans led a group of German metallurgists to investigate native minerals and Indian artifacts. Gans built an assayer's oven at Fort Raleigh, the first scientific laboratory in America.

Returning to England, Gans settled in London and resumed his work in the mines. In 1589, at a Bristol inn, the company carpenter was astounded to hear Gans deny the divinity of Jesus. He summoned a minister, Richard Curteys, who conversed with Gans in Hebrew. Needing witnesses to the alleged blasphemy, Curteys turned to English, and Gans responded, "What need has Almighty God for a son? Is he not almighty?" Gans was taken to the mayor and town council where he affirmed that he was a circumcised Jew, never baptized. He was sent to the Queen's Privy Council in London as "a most wicked infidel." Prison, torture, and death awaited heretics in Elizabethan England, but Gans's fate is unknown. During his ordeal, Gans wrote a manual on saltpeter, which was needed to manufacture gunpowder. He dedicated it to his sponsor, Sir Francis Walsingham, secretary of state and governor of the Mines Royal, "hoping thereby to be defended from all adversaries." Historians speculate that he returned to Europe.[2]

1. "Gans, David Ben Solomon," *Encyclopedia Judaica*, vol. 7 (Jerusalem: Keter, 1972), 310–11. The Gans name is spelled variously as Ganz or Gaunz. In expedition documents, Joachim Gans is Dougham Gannes.

2. An extensive discussion of Gans, with historic documents, can be found in Gary Grassl, *The Search for the First English Settlement in America* (Bloomington: AuthorHouse, 2006), 221–43. See also Gary Grassl, "Joachim Gans of Prague: The First Jew in English America," *American Jewish History* 86, no. 2 (June 1998): 195–217. Gans is also discussed in James Shapiro, *Shakespeare and the Jews* (New York: Columbia, 1996), 74, 180.

the Caribbean, Jews worked the North American coast as traders and agents. A Sephardic Jew appears in Jamestown in 1621, and several settled in Maryland in 1657, one of whom traded Virginia tobacco. A boatload of twenty-three Dutch Jews, fleeing Brazil after the Portuguese conquest, settled in New Amsterdam in 1654. American Jewish *communal* history begins with this colony. The South Carolina Jewish community traces to 1695, and by 1749 enough Jews arrived to organize a congregation in Charleston. London's Bevis Marks congregation in

1733 sponsored a boatload of indigent Jews—thirty-four Spanish-Portuguese and seven German—to the new Savannah settlement.[3]

America's Jewish population rose from 200 in 1700 to 2,500 by the Revolution. By the 1720s Ashkenazi immigration to America outnumbered Sephardic.[4] Of America's five synagogues before the Revolution, two were southern: Savannah and Charleston. North Carolina's early Jews, like other settlers, tended to be the overflow of Virginia and South Carolina. Colonial Jews were mobile, and their settlements were often transitory. Early congregations in New York, Newport, and Savannah expired before being revived by new arrivals. Often settlers were single young men, who moved on.

Unlike colonies to its north and south, North Carolina was not inviting for Jews—or for anyone else. North Carolina's shallow, heavily shoaled coast was the graveyard of the Atlantic. A 1657 colonial map of the Albemarle warns, "This is A Swampy wilderness." The colony's inland waterways were treacherous, and few rivers were navigable. Drought and hurricane ravaged early coastal colonies. Puritan merchants from Massachusetts and planters from Barbados, "upheld by Negroes," attempted colonies in Cape Fear in the early 1660s but soon returned home. The first large number of Jews to set foot in North Carolina did so accidentally in 1733 when their Savannah-bound ship, buffeted by gales, was "forced to seek safety . . . for some weeks" in New Inlet.[5]

North Carolina lacked the deepwater port—Annapolis, Norfolk, or Charleston—to draw Jews in numbers sufficient to create communities, although ports like Edenton, Beaufort, New Bern, and Wilmington periodically had Jews present. These ports handled ships by the dozen while Charleston harbored hundreds. Nor did the thickly forested Piedmont and mountain backcountry offer opportunity. Towns were few and isolated, as a corrupt, indifferent government failed to finance the roads, bridges, or ferries to create transportation networks. Geography was not the only barrier to European progress. Iroquoian tribes, the Tuscaroras and Cherokees, resisted the settlers, who had plundered Indian lands and property. In 1711 the Tuscarora began two years of bloody reprisals. On the coast pirates and smugglers flourished, including the notorious Blackbeard.

Early North Carolina was ungovernable. In 1663 Charles II granted a charter for the Province of Carolina to eight Lords Proprietors. The Proprietors proposed the Fundamental Constitutions of Carolina, which, although authorizing slavery, endorsed civil and political rights, but colonial assemblies never enacted it. Governance yielded to infighting, corruption, and rebellions on such issues as taxes, boundaries, prerogatives, and leadership. Gentrified neighbors in Virginia and South Carolina disdained North Carolinians as lawless, uncouth, and ill bred. In 1689 and 1712, lines were drawn dividing North from South Carolina. In 1729 the Lords Proprietors, excepting Earl Granville, abandoned their claims. North Carolina became a royal colony, but rebellion and contempt for government persisted.

Colonizing of North Carolina occurred by land rather than by sea as settlers moved into Albemarle from Virginia and into Cape Fear from South Carolina. Virginia marketed tobacco, and South Carolina proffered indigo, cotton, and rice, but North Carolina lacked a commercial crop. Virginia had its cavaliers and South Carolina its Low Country aristocrats, but in North Carolina yeomen set the colony's character. Small, self-sufficient farmers struggled to raise corn and tobacco on hardscrabble land while their hogs and cows foraged field or forest. They dwelled in log homes, not plantation houses. Although a landed gentry arose on the coast and later in the backcountry, the colony, relative to its neighbors, lacked a plantation slave society. The towns held a small elite of wealthy planters, attorneys, and merchants. The colony's economic importance grew after 1705 when the British passed a Naval Stores Act to supply the British fleet. Timber plantations, supported by slaves imported from South Carolina, extracted tar, pitch, and turpentine from pine forest.[6]

POOR MAN'S COUNTRY

In 1730 the colony's population was less than 35,000, but by 1775 it exceeded 200,000, the fourth most populous of the thirteen. A settler in 1770 described North Carolina as the "best poor man's Country I Ever heard of." Land-hungry migrants from Virginia, Maryland, New Jersey, and Pennsylvania headed south down the Great Wagon Road, which began outside Philadelphia and ended in North Carolina, where it fanned across the Piedmont. New towns like Charlotte arose in the frontier. The colony was a quilt of ethnicities: English on the coastal plain; Welsh in Cape Fear; Scotch Highlanders in the backcountry; Germans and Scotch-Irish in the Piedmont. Some 400 settlers from the Swiss and German Palatine founded New Bern in 1710. Pockets of Roman Catholics, mostly of English origin, settled the coastal plain. In 1753 Moravians named their settlement Wachovia after their Bohemian homeland. French Huguenots spread in the Pamlico region. Cherokees were pushed into western mountains. From 1720 to 1767 the number of Africans is estimated to have risen from 3,000 to 39,000.[7]

One Scotsman saw potential for Jewish colonization. Sir Alexander Cuming had ventured to the North Carolina mountains in 1730, returning to England with seven Cherokee chiefs whom he presented to King George. In 1750 he was in prison for debt. Seeking solace, he opened the Bible to the prophet Isaiah and felt "a call to the Jews." He contemplated visiting Poland but instead wrote Lord Halifax with a "scheme" to settle "300,000 families of Jews" in the North Carolina mountains for the "improvement of the lands." Jews, he believed, would generate enough income for the crown to repay 80 million pounds of national debt. Although Cuming later died "deranged in intellect," he reflected popular folklore in believing that Jews had magical powers in trade. Utopian Jewish colonization schemes arose globally, including seventy years later in Florida, New York, and the American West.[8]

More modest evidence of a Jewish presence appears in a petition that Carolina merchants presented to the House of Lords in London in 1705. "Complaining of great Abuses and Oppressions," the petitioners contended that "all sorts of people, even servants, Negroes, Aliens, Jews and Common sailors were admitted to vote" for the General Assembly in 1703. In 1740 a servant, claiming to be underfed, filed a complaint in Wilmington against his employer Moses Gomez. The Gomezes were Sephardic New York merchants with roots in Jamaica. In 1740 Aaron Moses witnessed a will in Perquimans County. In 1758 Jacob Franks, whose family were purveyors to the British army, was paid seven shillings for providing provisions to Indians and twenty pounds for "Looking after Fort Dobbs by the Governour's Order." From 1759 to 1784, Mr. Laney, identified as a Jew, appears in colonial records as a business partner of Mr. Haryon at Cabin Point. In 1765 Moses Levy, Michael Judah, and Napthali Hart Jr. contested court cases in Craven County. Levy and Hart were merchants in Newport, where Levy served as synagogue trustee. In 1780 Frances Sheftall wrote her husband from Charleston, "There is a Jew gentleman gone from here to North Carolina" to purchase gold coins.[9]

The most significant Jew in North Carolina's early history never resided there. Aaron Lopez of Newport, Rhode Island, sent some thirty-seven ships to North Carolina from 1761 to 1775 laden with consumer goods including rum, axes, mules, desks, fiddles, English cutlery, New England cranberries, Madeira wine, and slaves. The merchandise was sold or bartered in Edenton, New Bern, or Wilmington for naval stores—staves, lumber, tar, and turpentine—and produce, including corn, pork, tobacco, and herring. Lopez's triangular trade extended to Lisbon, London, and the West Indies. In the off-season, his whaling ships were enlisted in North Carolina commerce. Among his clients was the prominent Edenton merchant, Cullen Pollock, a native Scot, who addressed Lopez as his "dearest friend" and who was his guest in Newport. Judge James Iredell, upon learning of Lopez's drowning, eulogized him as "a very respectable man."[10] Lopez enjoyed a high reputation, a necessary asset at a time when commerce relied on a merchant's honor. Neither Pollock nor Iredell ever commented on Lopez's public Judaism.

Lopez dispatched commercial agents, often relatives, along the east coast and

Aaron Lopez, a Sephardic merchant of Rhode Island, established trade routes to colonial North Carolina. (American Jewish Historical Society, New York, N.Y., and Newton Centre, Mass.)

as far south as Jamaica. Several early Jews in Wilmington—Gomez, Lopez, and Rivera—were members of his extended family.[11] A pattern was set: North Carolina Jewish communities would long serve as colonial outposts of mercantile centers and metropolitan Jewish communities outside its borders. These ties of commerce intertwined with relations of family, religion, and culture.

JEWS, HEATHENS, AND OTHER DISSENTERS

With a patchwork of ethnicities, North Carolina was religiously diverse. Colonial governors, as authorized by the Carolina charters, attempted to establish the Church of England but failed. Anglican missionaries struggled with a frontier people who, they lamented, were more given to drink and carousing than to holy vows. William Byrd observed that North Carolinians "are not troubled with any Religious Fumes."[12] North Carolina hosted numerous Protestant sects: English Anglicans, German Lutherans, Pennsylvania and New England Quakers, Scotch Presbyterians, and Moravian United Brethren, among them. Quakers dominated colonial government until the early 1700s. The First Great Awakening, a religious revival of the 1730s, won converts for Baptists, Methodists, and Presbyterians.

North Carolina's religious environment would not have discouraged Jews. In other colonies, Jews were not permitted public worship but could do so privately at home. Colonial religious establishments, whether Puritans in Massachusetts or Dutch Reformed in New Amsterdam, protected their privilege by denying or restricting the rights of other dissenting sects. The Fundamental Constitutions of 1669 had expressed the hope that "heathens, Jews, and other dissenters from the purity of Christian Religion may not be feared and kept at a distance." The Lords Proprietors thought that tolerance rather than coercion would lead unbelievers "to embrace and unfeignedly receive the truth" of the Gospels.[13] Protestantism was the religion best suited for an independent people.

North Carolinians, like other Americans, viewed Jews through a European cultural lens. Their frames were the Bible and classical literature. Americans saw themselves as both republicans drafting a new social contract and Israelites receiving a new covenant. America was a New Eden, and Revolutionary rhetoric was rife with biblical imagery. Thomas Jefferson saw the yeoman, independent and self-sufficient, as the ideal New American: "Those who labor in the earth are the chosen people of God, if ever he had a chosen people." A North Carolinian echoed, "We are a favoured people."[14]

If America was the New Zion, Jews were dispossessed. European anti-Semitic prejudices emigrated from the Old World to the New. To Christians, Jews were various evils incarnate. In 1774 a Northampton County reverend complained that Protestant dissenters were rending the Anglican Church no less than the "cruelty of the Jews" tore "the body of the blessed Jesus." The *New Berne Gazette* saw the British as "blind" as the Jews of old.[15] Jews were less living persons than abstractions and mythic figures lumped in an outsider category with other peoples who were affronts to public morality and civic peace like atheists, Quakers, and Roman Catholics. At times "Hindoos" or "Mahotmeans" were added as if tolerating Jews led to absurdity.

In North Carolina, anti-Jewish sentiment was less significant than the animosity against Quakers and more especially against Roman Catholics. Nor would North Carolinians have feared Jewish worship. No place had the ten male Jews then required for a communal prayer quorum. Moreover, Sephardic Jews with their experience of presenting themselves publicly as Christians could not have been an affront to civic order or the dominion of Christianity. The habit of outward conformity but inward difference was engrained in early American Jews.[16]

In embarking to the New World, to the North Carolina frontier especially, Jews broke from the rabbinic authority and communal mores that had governed their daily lives. European Jews had lived in self-governing communities as "'a people apart.'" The Kahal, the European community's ruling authority, imposed taxes, regulated religious observance, fined violators, and negotiated with governments to secure rights and privileges. Jews suffered from economic restrictions that limited their ability to own land, enter trades, or conduct commerce. As feudal monarchies fell and secular, enlightened societies arose, individual rights were valued over group identity. In America, Jews enjoyed an unusual freedom. When Aaron Lopez arrived in America in 1752, he cast off his New Christianity and reinvented himself as an American Jew. He shed his Portuguese name Duarte for the Hebrew Aaron, underwent circumcision, and remarried his wife in a Jewish ceremony.[17]

In America, the synagogue-community assumed the responsibilities of the Kahal, governing life in both home and synagogue. Without rabbis, lay leaders, men of wealth, assumed authority. In a free, modern society, where religious affiliation was voluntary, Jewish dissenters rebelled against the Kahal's efforts to regulate their ritual practice, Sabbath adherence, or even marital choices. Synagogue attendance was poor. Social, linguistic, and religious differences divided America's early Jews by nationality even as small numbers united them. Jews were too few to sustain separate Sephardic and Ashkenazi synagogues as they did in London or Amsterdam. Sephardic Jews looked upon the newly arriving Germans as unrefined, while Ashkenazi Jews saw the Spanish-Portuguese as religiously lax. Even as Ashkenazi Jews grew more numerous, Sephardic Jews dominated synagogue ritual and governance. The parnas (president) served as lay leader, and the hazzan (cantor) chanted prayers with Iberian accents and melodies. A mutual concern for kosher meat united them, and Lopez's cargoes included "Casher beef." What bound Jews spiritually was a sense of peoplehood and a belief in one God. Jews, like the Puritans, came to America with feelings of messianic expectation, and early synagogues bore names like Mikveh Israel (Hope of Israel) or Shearith Israel (Remnant of Israel), as if exiles were being ingathered for redemption.[18]

THE COLONIAL LEGACY

North Carolina was too agrarian and too economically backward to draw significant numbers of Jews, who were an urban, mercantile people. In a society that lived largely off the land, Jewish traders found few opportunities. Colonial Jewish communities tended to rise in port cities, and Jews who appeared in North Carolina's coastal towns were commercial agents from Charleston, Newport, and New York.

North Carolina's colonial legacy was not unwelcoming. Early North Carolina, historian Harry Watson notes, was characterized by a "remarkable human diversity" and "a basic reliance on the outside world for a variety of cultural and commercial necessities." Ports were cosmopolitan places, and the backcountry was a frontier society open to new peoples. With its traditions of yeomanry, its people were stubbornly independent. North Carolina lacked the social, economic, or religious hierarchy to block the Jews' progress or to exclude them from the company of respectable people. William Byrd observed that, "in North Carolina, every One does what seems best in his own Eyes."[19] Religious dissent meant a toleration of difference, although underlying this tolerance was a conviction of the truth of Protestant Christianity. North Carolinians, like colonists elsewhere, divided on whether they were creating a secular republic, where one's religion or irreligion was a private matter, or a Christian nation. As North Carolinians sought to define the character of their new state and their relation to the nation, the presence of Jews and the question of their rights became significant beyond their small numbers.

1776-1835

"You will think with me that we are the Wandering Jews," Judith Myers Mordecai wrote in 1792 on her journey to North Carolina, "but I still hope that when we get there we shall be settled . . . the object we have so long pursued in vain." Judith and Jacob Mordecai had begun their wanderings from New York after a depressed economy had left them bereft of cash and prospects. The young family headed south to Richmond, where Jacob had once worked in his stepfather's mercantile house. Jacob opened a country store, but farmers were too few and poor to support it. While Judith and his children went to her brother in Petersburg, Jacob continued south to Warrenton, a county seat and market town across the state line. There, in the village center, he opened another store, and his family rejoined him, moving to a house next door.[1] Although North Carolina was a rare choice for Jews, the Mordecais were very typical in their failures and ambitions, in their mercantilism, and in their reliance on family networks.

The Mordecais' southward journey followed a popular migratory path. From 1770 to 1790 North Carolina's population doubled, and it grew into the third most populous state as land-hungry immigrants flowed from the north. Unlike these other newcomers, the Mordecais did not intend to farm, although their livelihood depended on the rural economy. North Carolina remained an agrarian state, having little more than two dozen communities worthy of being called towns. Excepting a few isolated merchants in the backcountry, Jews were found mostly in the ports of New Bern and Wilmington or in river towns like Halifax or Fayetteville. With 2,500 residents, New Bern, at the mouth of the Neuse River, remained the state's largest town until the 1840s, when Wilmington, located in the Cape Fear River basin, surpassed it.

Jews in North Carolina were colonists from more abundant communities in Virginia and South Carolina. Warrenton was an offshoot of Richmond, which by 1820 had 200 Jews. The very year that the Mordecais arrived, congregation Beth Shalome organized there. Wilmington was linked commercially to Charleston, which by 1820 hosted the nation's largest Jewish community of nearly 700 per-

PORTRAIT: JACOB MORDECAI

The Mordecai family was the most distinguished among early North Carolina Jews. Jacob's father Moses, a native of Germany, had arrived from England in 1760 as an indentured servant and, as did many Jews, started as a peddler. On his travels, he met Elizabeth Whitlock, an English-born Christian, who adopted Judaism, creating a precedent of religious conversion that marked the family history. Jacob was born in Philadelphia in 1762.

Jacob was largely self-taught. At Philadelphia's Mikveh Israel congregation, he was known as a Hebrew and biblical scholar. He was also an American patriot. Sergeant of a rifle corps, he escorted the First Continental Congress into Philadelphia in 1774.

After working in the mercantile house of David Franks, a Tory, he left for New York and later for Richmond, failing in his efforts to trade commodities or open stores. Jacob Mordecai was twice married, first to Judith Myers and, after her death in Warrenton in 1796, to her half sister Rebecca. Both were daughters of Myer Myers of New York City, a celebrated colonial silversmith whose candlesticks, Kiddush cups, and Torah finials are still valued.

In Warrenton, the Mordecais were isolated as Jews, but family visits to Richmond, Charleston, and New York and their habitual letter writing kept them Jewishly connected. Warrenton was a country town of several hundred, a place where farmers gathered to attend court, enjoy some grog, and purchase soap, seed, candles, or smoked beef at the Mordecai's store. Like many backcountry places, its people were not especially churchgoing, and those who were tended to piety. Although Jacob, Judith, and Rebecca remained observant Jews, they were accepted into Christian social circles. Jacob was elected master of Warrenton's Masonic Lodge. As his son Alfred wrote, "I believe that no serious embarrassment ever ensued, in social or other relations from this difference of religion, in our retired village."[1] Christian southerners who enrolled their daughters at Mordecai Female Academy, established in 1809, entrusted a Jew with the moral and intellectual education of their daughters. Jacob's own daughters Ellen, Carolina, and Rachel taught there. In its nine years, the school educated 544 students.

Jacob Mordecai settled in Warrenton in 1792. (Mordecai-Lane House)

When Jacob and Rebecca retired to Spring Farm in Virginia in 1818, the family became stalwarts at Richmond's Beth Shalome. As parnas, Jacob delivered the speech in 1822 dedicating the synagogue. Mordecai children achieved distinction. Rachel ranks among the state's first literary women. West Point graduate Alfred was known internationally for his expertise in ordnance. Solomon was a physician in Mobile. George served as president of the North Carolina Railroad and the Bank of North Carolina. Ellen, Emma, and Samuel were published authors. Historic signposts mark Mordecai homes in Raleigh and Warrenton.

Through conversion, intermarriage, and low birth rates, the Mordecais' Judaism expired over several generations. Today many of North Carolina's leading Christian families descend from devoutly Jewish Jacob, Judith, and Rebecca Mordecai.[2]

1. Jacob Rader Marcus, *Memoirs of American Jews: 1775–1865* (Philadelphia: Jewish Publication Society of America, 1955), 1:219.

2. David Goldberg, "An Historical Community Study of Wilmington Jewry, 1738–1925" (History Seminar, University of North Carolina at Chapel Hill, Spring 1976), 13.

sons.[2] Of America's five synagogues in 1800, three—Richmond, Charleston, and Savannah—were in the South.

AMERICAN JEWS

By the 1820s, historian Malcolm Stern observes, "a truly American Jewry" emerged. From 1820 to 1840 the number of Jews in America increased from an estimated 2,750 to 15,000. Overwhelmingly, Jews were engaged in retail and wholesale trades, mostly as storekeepers. In contrast to other Americans, who were largely rural, some 90 percent of the Jews were city dwellers concentrated in New York, Philadelphia, and Charleston. Their countries of origin were diverse. The migrations before 1830 included Jews from France, Holland, Britain, and Germany but also from Poland, Hungary, Bohemia, Morocco, Ireland, and the Caribbean. North Carolina naturalization lists before 1830 include Jewish-sounding names from Bavaria, France, Germany, Great Britain, and Saxony.[3] American Jews were mostly foreign born, although this was less true in the South. Both Judith and Jacob Mordecai were second-generation Americans.

Citizenship in the American nation required allegiance only to the democratic creed, not to a race or religion. In America, Jews secured rights as individuals rather than as members of a group. Not beholden to their rabbis or governed by their Kahal, they were free to choose their religious allegiances and marry outside their faith. Many immigrants were Jewishly uneducated and religiously lax. In 1791, in Petersburg, Virginia, a Jewish woman—bemoaning the absence of rabbis, kosher food, and Sabbath observance—complained, "Anyone can do what he wants."[4]

Jews reflected national divisions when revolution came. Although some cast their lot with the Tories—as merchants, their livelihoods were at stake—larger numbers chose the cause of independence. Scant as they were, North Carolina Jews identified with the Revolution. In 1774 Jacob Mordecai as a twelve year old had marched with a rifle corps that had escorted the First Continental Congress into Philadelphia. Aaron Cohen of Albemarle, Joe Nathan of Charlotte, and Sigmund Freudenthal of New Hanover all served in Brevard's Company of the North Carolina Battalion. Moses Cohen's name was engraved on a Revolutionary War monument in Monroe. Abraham Moses enlisted in 1781 in the Halifax district, and his cousin Solomon Simons was a member of Captain Liggett's Mecklenburg militia.[5]

Jews supplied and underwrote the Revolution. Joseph Laney of New Bern provided beef and furnishings for the Continental army. In 1780 Michael Levy of Edenton was conducting "bisnis" in rum and coffee with Colonel John Walker, a prominent patriot. Levy warned Walker that "the enemy are landed in Virginia." Levy feared for his safety because he was lodging with a "vidue" (widow), who was "a great Tory." Mordecai Myers of Georgetown, South Carolina, bartered indigo for "captured goods" in "Nerbern" (New Bern). Colonel Benjamin Hawkins, a state agent (and later a U.S. senator), personally intervened with financier Haym Salomon of Philadelphia to obtain loans for the militia in 1783, and a year later Richard Spaight, member of the Continental Congress (and future governor), corresponded with Lieutenant Colonel David Salisbury Franks, who was entrusted with diplomatic missions to Europe. Savannah merchant Philip Minis loaned some $11,000 to help pay salaries and buy provisions for North Carolina troops.[6]

The Revolution left North Carolina broke, its currency worthless. Most North Carolinians struggled as subsistence farmers. North Carolina still lacked commercial appeal for any merchant, Jew or gentile; historian Jacob Rader Marcus noted that "there were more attractive opportunities elsewhere." The British imposed taxes on imported goods, reducing the demand for North Carolina's naval stores. North Carolina's ports were now mostly engaged in a coastal trade extending to the West Indies rather than with London. Corn, lumber, and increasingly tobacco remained the chief exports. After 1793, when Eli Whitney's gin came into common use, cotton production rose in economic significance. The state's first cotton mill opened near Lincolnton in 1813, the number quickly increasing until 40,000 looms spread across the state. Even as its slave population grew to 100,000 by 1790, North Carolina did not develop the plantation economy and slave society of states deeper in the South. Perhaps one-quarter of the state's population was black.[7]

Port cities like New Bern, Edenton, and Wilmington were motley communities of merchants, artisans, seamen, traders, lawyers, planters, and storekeepers. At river fall lines grew towns like Halifax, Kinston, Tarboro, Lumberton, and Fayetteville, where farmers brought hogs, cows, sheep, hides, or tobacco to be shipped on flatboats to coastal ports for export. Boats returned upriver with imported European goods to supply country stores. In 1818 the first steamboat sailed Cape Fear from Wilmington to Fayetteville. In the backcountry were nascent towns consisting of little more than a county courthouse and a few stores, taverns, and artisan shops where a cash-strapped farmer might obtain credit or barter corn, hides, or tobacco for salt, sugar, tea, coffee, fabric, molasses, and shoes. The store was a grog shop, a social center where neighbors gathered for smoke, drink, and gossip. Reports of Jewish traders invariably list rum among their merchandise. For rural people, the store offered a taste of the cosmopolitan world.[8]

THE RIP VAN WINKLE STATE

In the early Republic, Virginia and South Carolina flourished, and Jews prospered there, but North Carolina went into hibernation, isolated culturally as well as geographically. Political rivalries between the gentrified east and the backcountry west stifled progress. On the coastal plain, planters of tobacco in the north and of cotton in south, like their more numerous counterparts in Virginia and South Carolina, aspired to aristocracy and high culture. Port cities were home to an educated, well-traveled elite. Imbued with republican values and conversant in the philosophical debates of this enlightened age, the eastern gentry built homes, churches, and public buildings in the manner of London, Jamaica, or Charleston. Their children were tutored in French, and at parlor gatherings their daughters sang Donizetti arias. They sent their sons to the University of North Carolina to learn practical sciences and classical literature.

Although the eastern gentry controlled the state's politics and economy, they were hardly characteristic North Carolinians. Inland North Carolina was a vast forest. From the swamps of its east to the mountains of its west, the terrain hindered transportation and communication. "Towns we have none," wrote one Piedmont resident. And where towns existed, Joseph Caldwell, president of the university, lamented that they were "places of wildness and rudeness, intemperance, ferocity, gaming, licentiousness, and malicious litigation." Carolina yeomen were proudly individualistic, distrustful of authority, and militantly uneducated. North Carolinians identified more with their families and localities than with the civil society of their state. From the clothes they wore to the whiskey they drank, subsistence farmers were more given to homespun than to store-bought. This "yeoman's paradise" resisted taxes and regulations. A state report on education from 1819 to 1835 observed that half the population "received no education," and the general assembly refused every bill to create public schools. In 1840 a third of the white adult population was illiterate. To impose taxes or compel school attendance went against the grain of North Carolinians. The state's per capita wealth was the smallest of any state in the Union. A legislative committee in 1828 referred to the "moral and intellectual darkness which now broods over" the state.[9]

In the early 1800s, North Carolina earned the sobriquet of the "Rip Van Winkle State." Its soils depleted by farming and clear-cutting, its inland rivers mostly unnavigable, its people uneducated, its legislature refusing taxes to build canals, roads, or schools, North Carolina was asleep. Capital that might have financed industry or improved agriculture was invested in slavery. Between 1815 and 1850, a third of its people, totaling 400,000, left for richer soils in the west, emptying farms and towns.[10]

PORT JEWS

Jews settled in those places where they could find opportunities for commerce — mostly in the coastal ports. Jews were overwhelmingly involved in mercantile trades. Jewish commerce was global, and merchants maintained links to England and the Caribbean. Sea-lanes were coastal highways. Given North Carolina's location between Newport and Charleston, Jewish traders constantly passed through its ports. As one Savannah Jew wrote, Jewish communities were marked by "comings & goings." When Charleston journalist Isaac Harby estimated that 400 Jews lived in North Carolina in 1826, he reported a number that *seemed* true.[11]

Public records document a Jewish presence. In 1790 the *North-Carolina Gazette* of New Bern reported, "Died On Tuesday last, in an advanced age, the Rev. Mr. JACOB ABROO, a Jewish Rabbi." The name derives from the Spanish river Ebro. "Rabbi" suggests that he was learned or observant. He was likely the Jacob Abbo who appeared in New York in 1768 with a map guiding him to the Ten Lost Tribes. New York Jews paid him to leave town. Downriver from New Bern in Beaufort, Joel Henry, a native of Fuerth, Germany, was listed in the 1790 census as heading a household of three. Henry's friend was Michael Levy, the Edenton merchant, with whom he shared South Carolina roots. In 1826 another Edenton merchant Simon Oliveira, from a Charleston Sephardic family, contracted to purchase cotton for five years from a Bertie County farmer. That Jewish peddlers traveled the state

by 1822 is confirmed by New Bern memoirist Stephen Miller, who recalled an old German Jewish trader named Davis who visited town with jewelry, watches, and an elegant dressing case allegedly made for Napoleon. He guaranteed it to contain forty ounces of silver and asked $300. As Davis knew little English, he asked Miller to write letters on his behalf to New York merchants.[12]

More suggestive of Jewish community is a New Bern deed dating to 1809 that cites "a lot used as the burying place of the Jews." As Jewish communities develop, a cemetery typically precedes a congregation. The "burying place" might have held graves of transient Jews who met untimely ends during yellow fever epidemics or in the locally treacherous seas. Genealogies of early American Jewish families list members lost "at sea," and traders faced constant perils. In 1787 New Bern merchant Abraham Nathan, "of the Jewish nation," was sailing his merchant sloop *Betsey* from Bath to Charleston laden with shingles and barrel staves. Off the South Carolina coast, the shipmaster and two crewmen clubbed him with a sassafras root, tied an iron pot to his wrist, and tossed him overboard. Nathan carried $500 in French crowns and Spanish gold. In Charleston, a mercantile agent became suspicious when he saw the bloody root. The shipmaster

On Monday,

The 17th of December,
Precisely at TWELVE *o'clock,*
WILL BE SOLD
The SLOOP

BETSEY,

WITH all her rigging, tackle and apparel, as she now lies at Cochran's wharf.
At the same time and place,
WILL BE SOLD,
A NUMBER OF
Shingles and Staves,

The cargo of said sloop, formerly the property of Mr. Abraham Nathan, merchant, of Newbern, North-Carolina, deceased.
A L S O,
Some Wearing Apparel,
Of the deceased.
By order of the Administrator,
JACOB JACOBS,
Vendue Master.

37

and crewmen confessed to murder and were arrested, convicted, and hanged. In 1837 sisters Sarah, Frances, and Olivia Levy drowned when their ship wrecked at Ocracoke Island.[13]

Wilmington was home of a budding Jewish community, the state's first. These Jews were branches of families and commercial networks that extended to Newport, New York, and Charleston. In 1795 Aaron Lazarus, son of a Charleston merchant, arrived to open an auction and commission house. His wife Esther Sarzedas Cohen came from a Caribbean Sephardic family that had settled in Savannah and Charleston. After she died in 1803, leaving him with seven children, Lazarus married Jacob and Judith Mordecai's daughter Rachel. His store sold "Jacob Turks Island salt, prime green coffee, West Indian and New England rum, sugar, crockery, glassware, padlocks, Negro cloths, calicoes, and assorted articles." In 1799, according to the *Wilmington Gazette*, Abraham Isaacs and Jacob

Levy dissolved a partnership. Isaacs went to Charleston, but Levy replaced him with Aaron Lopez Gomez, who came from New York to be his manager. In 1801 Jacob Levy "informs his friends and the public" that "he has on hand for sale, on low terms, a few puncheons of St. Croix old Rum, one trunk of Calicoes, and two casks of Hard Ware." Levy was also a lottery agent. Before 1800 Joseph Jacobs of Hingham, Massachusetts, Lewis Gomez of New York, and Judah Mears of Newport resided in town. Ship captain Benjamin Jacobs also arrived around 1800. Philip and Rebecca Benjamin, a Sephardic family with roots in London and the West Indies, moved from Savannah to Wilmington by 1813, drawn there by her uncle, Jacob Levy, with whom they resided. The Levy, Gomez, Lopez, and Rivera families were bound by kinship and commerce. Levy's wife Maria was the granddaughter of Newport merchant Aaron Lopez. These Sephardic families had achieved wealth and social prominence.[14]

Like other North Carolinians, Jews moved westward from port towns into the backcountry. Cousins Abraham Moses and Solomon Simons von Grol had arrived from Surinam before the Revolution. By 1790 Moses had a store in the Halifax District, not far from Warrenton, while Simons located in the Hillsboro District of Chatham County. They, too, had Charleston ties. By 1798 the cousins formed a partnership and—known locally as "the jewes"—opened a store near Charlotte between Waxhaw and Monroe. Other Jews in Charlotte came from Charleston. Daniel and Isaac Hyams of England were naturalized in Mecklenburg County in 1811, as was Jonas Cohen in 1820. English-born Aaron Cohen settled in Charlotte in 1824, where he was a gold- and silversmith. His trademark was a colonial hat in the center of a Star of David. In 1830 Nathan and Benjamin Cohen, also of English origin, were living in Mecklenburg County. After a fire destroyed Jacob Levy's Wilmington store in 1819, he moved up the Cape Fear River to Fayetteville. He was followed by his relatives, Phillip and Rebecca Benjamin, including their son Judah, who enrolled at the Fayetteville Academy. The family lived on the second floor of its Hay Street store.[15]

North Carolina's commercial worth lay in the extractive potential of its land. Barnard and Michael Gratz, from an eminent Philadelphia family, and Polish-born Mordecai Cohen of Charleston purchased North Carolina timberlands. The Richmond firm of Cohen & Isaacs, which speculated in real estate, including the Great Dismal Swamp, hired Daniel Boone in 1781 to survey tracts. Merchants Jacob Levy and Aaron Lazarus also bought timberlands, and Lazarus owned a plantation.[16]

Commerce integrated Jews into civil society. Upwardly mobile Jews rose from the trading and shopkeeping most characteristic of Jews in the early Republic. Mordecai children included two attorneys, a physician, a banker, an army officer, a farmer, and several railroad executives. Four were published authors. Jews were leaders in two emerging national enterprises that created a modern economic state: banking and railroading. When North Carolina chartered the Bank of the Cape Fear in Wilmington, the state's first, Aaron Rivera was cashier while Aaron Lazarus was a director. One week in 1833 the Lazarus firm had fourteen ships unloading at its docks, and its trade extended to the West Indies. With New York investors, Lazarus built the city's first steam-operated planing mill, where he manufactured shingles and naval stores. Lazarus owned a city block downtown and in 1816 built there an Italianate style house, which still stands among the city's oldest and grandest. Notably, Lazarus formed partnerships with non-Jews. Lazarus & Whitemore until 1850 ranked as the city's chief import and export house. Jacob Levy and Abraham Isaacks formed a partnership with Isaac Bishops as auctioneers, and in 1802 the broker Mears Levy dissolved his partnership with William Nutt and formed a new firm with A. Jocelin and Thos. N Gautier.[17]

North Carolina's commerce ranked among the smallest of any state. Cycles of depression—in 1785 and 1819—jeopardized merchants. In 1785 the *Gazette* published a letter by "Anonymous" warning that Americans needed a tariff on imported goods to protect them from "enriching the shop keepers and Jews at the ruin of others." The Panic of 1819 provoked anger against the federal Bank of the United States that grew into resentment against northern economic domination. Southerners "asserted that the excessive purchase of unnecessary goods had drained money from the South to the North, and from the nation to England." Much of this wrath was directed against peddlers, who brought goods into the state and took money out. North Carolina passed laws in 1817 and 1821 that doubled the tax on any peddler who proffered goods grown or manufactured out of state.[18] Given the predominance of peddling among Jews, they may have felt reluctant to head there.

The economic system jeopardized storekeepers. Merchants, who were often planters, extended credit to farmers by taking crop liens, settling in winter after harvest when wheat, corn, and tobacco were marketed. Fluctuating prices could ruin the merchant who held the lien. With few roads or rivers, high transport costs meant that rural stores had to price goods as high as 100 percent of their value. Jacob Mordecai's Warrenton store prospered until 1807 when a competitor and a failed investment bankrupted him. Mordecai had speculated in tobacco, but when President Jefferson imposed a trade embargo on Britain, his investment failed. A widower with six children, he was reduced to accepting a position as a dormitory and dining hall steward at the Warrenton Male Academy. The Mordecais were financially ruined again in 1819 after an economic panic and in 1826 after a bad crop year.[19]

ENLIGHTENED JEWS

Although living in a frontier tobacco town, the Mordecais were conversant with a wider intellectual world. North Carolina Jews very much identified with the state's cosmopolitan eastern gentry. As historian Holly Snyder notes, Jews followed the path of other immigrant groups—Scots, Scotch-Irish, and Huguenots—who aspired to literary culture as a portal into polite society. They assumed the guise and garb of English ladies and gentlemen. In 1818 Jacob Mordecai wrote to John C. Calhoun recommending his fifteen-year-old son Alfred to West Point: "he is a good english [sic] Scholar has read the Latin & Greek classics has made considerable progress in the French language and lately commenced Euclid." Alfred graduated first in the West Point class of 1823 and joined the faculty. Marx Lazarus, Aaron's son, attended Hillsborough Academy before entering the University of North Carolina in 1837, the first Jew to enroll.[20]

Alfred Mordecai, portrait by English artist Thomas Sully. (American Jewish Historical Society, New York, N.Y., and Newton Centre, Mass.)

Although one wit quipped that "the only culture North Carolina has is agriculture," town elites were cosmopolitan. When Archibald DeBow Murphey—a planter, professor, and legislator—reported on education for the state, he cited Swiss and English models. Plantation names like Somerset and Toby Hall, which was purchased by Aaron Lazarus, evoked the English countryside and the novels of Jane Austen and Laurence Sterne. With family and business ties to Boston, New York, and London, Jews, like other members of the coastal gentry, were well traveled and negotiated in the marketplace of ideas as well as commerce. George and Alfred Mordecai toured Europe, and Solomon summered in Saratoga. English-born artists John Wesley Jarvis and Thomas Sully were commissioned to paint portraits of Jacob and Alfred Mordecai. Southern Jews identified with an emerging global Anglophone community.[21]

A meeting place for Jews and town elites was the Masonic Lodge, a secret society founded on Enlightenment principles of reason, tolerance, and brotherhood. In contrast to England, where Jews were excluded and formed their own societies, America's lodges welcomed Jews. Over centuries lodges were agencies of Jewish civic integration. In Wilmington's St. Tammany Lodge were Aaron Lazarus, Abraham Isaacs, J. M. Levy, Aaron Gomez, and Philip Benjamin. A 1781 roster of Masons meeting in Philadelphia listed Simon Nathan of Charlotte as deputy grand inspector general for North Carolina. In 1797 Jacob Mordecai was elected master of the Warrenton Masonic Lodge. The New Bern Lodge included at least four Jews. Jacob Levy had the singular distinction of being a "prominent member of the Wilmington Whistling Society," which met at Dorsey's Tavern. Another sign of their Americanism occurred during the War of 1812. Although the war was unpopular in North Carolina, when fears arose of a British invasion, Samuel Mordecai and Jacob Henry joined the militia.[22]

Christian neighbors respected Jacob Mordecai's learning and character. His failed financial speculations did not arouse any anti-Semitism. Prominent citizens prevailed upon the school steward to open the Mordecai Female Seminary (later the Warrenton Female Academy). With his children as teachers—most notably Rachel and Solomon—Jacob served as principal and proprietor. Jacob and Solomon wrote the textbooks. Rachel, well versed in the classics, was especially admired at a time when women were often regarded as lacking rational capacity. Other teachers included Frenchmen from the Caribbean. The academy's curriculum was intended to educate plantation daughters in the social graces. Rachel was counted among the emerging class of southern literary women, which included Jews like Clara Solomon of New Orleans and Phoebe Yates Pember of Charleston. The school focused on girls aged nine to fifteen. In addition to drawing, music, and dancing, the students learned history, geography, Greek, Latin, and history. Although education was commonly suffused with Christianity, Mordecai offered no instruction in the Bible. The school's fame spread, and students came from the Carolinas, Virginia, and Georgia. The initial student body of 30 grew to 110 by 1814, including Jewish girls. Mordecai children were joined by the daughters of Cohen, Lazarus, and Myers from South Carolina and of Elcan, Marx, Myers, and Etting from Virginia. Philah and Rachel Lazarus of Wilmington introduced their father Aaron to their teacher Rachel, who became their stepmother.[23] By 1818 Jacob was sufficiently wealthy and tired of school mastering that he retired to a farm near Richmond.

As lead teacher, Rachel Mordecai had been enamored of a book, *Practical Education,* by Irish writer Richard Lovell Edgeworth and his daughter, novelist Maria. The Edgeworths had promulgated what historian Emily Bingham calls an "enlightened domesticity" that encouraged collaborative family education in the sciences and literature. Their intellectual circle included Enlightenment thinkers Jean-Jacques Rousseau, Joseph Priestley, and Josiah Wedgwood. Rachel was discomfited to read Maria Edgeworth's 1812 novel *The Absentee*, which featured an unscrupulous Jew named Mr. Mordicai. Indignant, Rachel penned a letter to Maria, which her brother Sam took to England, accusing Edgeworth of being "biased by prejudice." Rachel feared that this libel of a people, so inconsistent with the Edgeworths' liberality, would corrupt youth. In Europe, Jews may be the "the subject of scorn and derision," Rachel wrote, but "in this happy country . . .

where religious distinctions are scarcely known . . . we find the Jews to form a respectable part of the community."[24]

In time, Rachel received apologetic letters from the Edgeworths promising to correct the wrong. A year later her brother Sol, visiting a New York bookshop, came across Maria Edgeworth's new novel *Harrington*. In a preface, her father noted that his daughter had been inspired by "an extremely well-written letter . . . from a Jewish lady complaining of the illiberality which the Jewish nation had been treated" in earlier works. One character in *Harrington* was an American Jewess named Berenice who responds to English bigotry by quoting Rachel's very words, "in this happy country . . ." Sol wrote to his brother Sam, "At that moment I could have felt pride in saying, 'I am a Jew.'" Rachel's fame spread to New York and Philadelphia. For the next decade, Rachel and Maria corresponded. Among the gifts Rachel sent Maria were botanical specimens, *The Last of the Mohicans*, and Mordecai Noah's Address on Ararat, in which the Jewish diplomat and journalist advocated a new Zion in America.[25]

PESTILENCE OF SLAVERY

As slaveholders, Jews did not differ from other southerners of their class, location, and occupation. About one-quarter of southern Jews owned slaves, but very rarely in significant numbers. The Lopez, Gomez, and Rivera families of Newport and New York had imported African slaves, but they did not rank among the leading slavers of Newport, which dominated the American trade until it was abolished in 1808. As Jews were urban dwellers—and very rarely planters—they owned mostly household servants or hirelings and were less likely to own more than ten slaves. Historian Bertram Korn notes that "any Jew who could afford to own slaves and had need for their services would do so." Thus, 83 percent of Charleston's Jewish families owned slaves in 1830 compared to 87 percent of the city's Christian families.[26]

Slaveholding divided the poor from the wealthy; ownership of more than twenty slaves distinguished a prosperous farmer from a rich planter. North Carolina census data do not demonstrate extensive Jewish slaveholding. In 1800 Joel Henry of Beaufort was listed as the owner of ten slaves. In 1830 Aaron Lazarus owned thirteen slaves, but this number declined to seven in 1840. His son Gershon, a business partner, owned five in 1830, but three in 1840. The largest slave owners in 1830 were Isaac Hyams & Co. of Mecklenburg County, which owned thirteen, and Washington Lazarus of New Hanover County, who owned thirty. They were absentee slave owners, suggesting that they owned plantations and likely lived in town. The numbers imply that slaves were employed as household servants or as workers in stores, warehouses, or factories. As part of their merchandise, mercantile slave owners hired out a craftsman as a cook or carpenter, with the slave keeping half of his or her wages.[27]

Like most southerners, the Mordecai family—which prided itself on its enlightened views—accepted slavery as an entitlement. Just as Protestants wanted religious freedom only for themselves, southern Jews who advocated for Jewish emancipation did not extend their concern for civil liberties to African Americans. Slaves worked in the Mordecai household, and as Emily Bingham observes, gave the family the liberty to pursue the intellectual and literary pursuits that they regarded as a birthright. Rachel Mordecai Lazarus complained that "servants are the pest of Wilmington." She deplored the practice of allowing hired slaves to keep their wages because it left them with "notions of independence" and "all the time complaining." Rachel found her cook Sarah so disagreeable that her husband Aaron sold her. The cook's discontent, Rachel felt, owed to "the great difference in our religions."[28]

North Carolina was less broadly a slave society than its neighboring states. By 1825 the North Carolina Manumission Society had twenty-eight branches, and the American Colonization Society claimed to have emancipated 2,000 slaves between 1823 and 1836. Their ambition was the return of slaves to Africa. In the 1820s, fear of slave rebellions turned public attitudes against manumission, especially after the Nat Turner insurrection of 1831 just across the Virginia state line. When rumors of a slave revolt struck Wilmington, the Lazaruses bunkered in their home, while other whites sought refuge in banks and churches. Aaron Lazarus patrolled the streets as a captain in the civic guard. Rachel desired to leave a place where "soon or later we or our descendents will become the certain victims of a band of lawless wretches who will deem murder and outrage just retribution" for their enslavement. The alleged "ringleaders" of this abortive rebellion were lynched, their heads cut off and impaled in public places. Three of Aaron's warehouse slaves were accused. His son Washington, recently admitted to the bar, defended two of these slaves, Adam and Billy, but they were convicted, shot by firing squad or hanged. The state compensated Aaron partially for his lost property.[29]

DEISM, EVANGELISM, AND JEWS

From the Revolution until the 1820s, American Jewry scarcely grew in either numbers or institutions, but it was being transformed by the new American ethos. Jews negotiated between their obeisance to tradition and rabbinic authority and their allegiance to the republican values that gave them liberty as citizens. They were free to worship, or not, as they chose. North Carolina Jews found friends and defenders among an enlightened gentry who held Jeffersonian principles

on personal and religious liberty. An educated elite held to a deism that revered reason more than revelation. According to its standards of honor, a person was to be measured by conduct, not by belief.

Accommodating to the new nation, Richmond's Beth Shalome congregation had a "constitution" that derived authority from "We, the subscribers of the Israelite people." Congregants were enfranchised as voting members who elected officers. Haskalah, the Jewish enlightenment, reinterpreted traditional Judaism by the lights of reason, philosophy, and history. The German Jewish philosopher Moses Mendelssohn advocated freedom of conscience. He called upon Jews to follow the commandments but sought also to liberate them from the chastising authority of the rabbis. The worth of a religion, Mendelsohn philosophized, is found in ethical conduct. He advocated secular education for Jews, which would emancipate them and integrate them into modern society.

When Judith Mordecai died, Jacob gathered his children to read them an ethical will. A Jewish genre dating to the Middle Ages, the ethical will left survivors not a material inheritance but moral guidance. The Mordecai will, in the form of a letter, offered little religious instruction but was intended, as Bingham observes, "for intellectual cultivation, family solidarity and dedication to useful work." This family "covenant" evoked Mendelssohn in its emphasis on reason, social utility, and citizenship.[30] Without forsaking their Judaism, the Mordecais were expanding their identities. Mordecai children bore names—Moses, Augustus, and George Washington—that embraced a hybrid heritage—Hebrew, Roman, and American.

North Carolina Jews were conversant with the international discourse on religious reform and political emancipation transforming the larger Jewish world. In 1824 twenty-four young Jews, led by playwright Isaac Harby, split from the Orthodox K. K. Beth Elohim in Charleston to organize the Reformed Society of Israelites. They wanted to bring Protestant decorum, "English discourse," to Hebrew worship. Their concern was not rabbinic commandments but Judaism's universal moral law. The Charlestonians cited the "reformation which has recently been adopted by our brethren in Holland, Germany and France," but they were also responding to the local challenges presented by Christian evangelizing and the new Unitarian movement. Jacob Mordecai answered the Charleston reformers by writing a defense of Orthodoxy. He sent it to his daughter and son-in-law in Wilmington, Aaron and Rachel Lazarus, who both advised against its publication. They feared that Christians would "think this reform one step towards the accomplishment of their much desired conversion" of the Jews.[31]

Rachel's fears were real. If a rational Enlightenment undermined traditional belief and theology, Jews also confronted a Second Great Awakening that preached Christian piety and religious fervor. Distant from synagogues and community, North Carolina's Jews lived among evangelical Christians who worked and prayed for their conversion. The Second Great Awakening swept across the state as it did the nation in the early 1800s. Backcountry camp meetings drew large crowds and new adherents to the Baptists, Methodists, and Presbyterians. Religious revivalism arose in the 1830s with renewed fervor, crossing from the countryside into towns. Church membership defined a social circle as well as a theology. The reigning religiosity among all classes of North Carolinians—merchants, planters, and hardscrabble farmers alike—according to historian Milton Ready, was "a Protestant evangelical folk identity." In their correspondence, North Carolina Jews, too, spoke a Protestant language replete with appeals to a "merciful providence" and the "goodness of your heart."[32]

Adopting Protestant Christianity was part of the process of becoming American, and African and Indian peoples, like the Jews, faced the challenge of negotiating between native traditions and modern, Christian society. Although slaves professed Christianity in church balconies, they "still had faith in evil genii, charms, spirits, philters," a doctor visiting a North Carolina plantation observed. On Christmas Day, slaves danced to drums. Christian Cherokees consulted conjurors and sang their own "Amazing Grace." Ethnic white Protestant sects were blending, too, as German, English, Scotch, and Scotch-Irish peoples intermarried. German-speaking Moravian, Lutheran, and Reformed churches adopted English.[33]

Jews were also undergoing an ethnic and religious American blending. Sephardic and Ashkenazi intermarriages became commonplace in the early 1800s, giving birth to ethnically American Jews. Both Alfred and Rachel Mordecai married into Sephardic families. Younger, native-born Jews especially wanted English worship in a Protestant setting. Although American Jewry was by now largely Ashkenazi, the Sephardic ritual, regarded as more dignified, prevailed in Charleston and Richmond. North Carolina Jews were linked to these synagogues.

Evangelical religion appealed especially to women. Filled with heartfelt zeal, Christian ladies sought to win souls. Men might control institutions, but women were more likely to be church members. The Awakening stressed not liturgical performance, which was man's domain, but inner feeling. Believers spread the word through religious schools and missionary and benevolence societies. This spiritualism was felt in the Jewish community, too. Jewish women responded in new and openly religious ways. Both Penina Moise of Charleston and Rebecca Gratz of Philadelphia offered models of personal piety and duty. Moise was a poet and teacher whose devotional hymns were printed in prayer books. Rebecca Gratz, inspired by Protestants, created a Jewish Sunday School movement in 1818. Emma Mordecai, who knew Gratz through family ties, wrote guides for Jewish teachers and founded a Sunday School at Richmond's Beth Shalome, and her niece Ellen Lazarus established one in Boston in 1848.[34]

The absence of congregations gave North Carolina's Jewish women the opportunity to express their piety, even to become prayer leaders, in ways denied them in larger, traditional communities. The home and family, rather than the synagogue, became the setting of Jewish life. One Yom Kippur, visiting her brothers George and Augustus in Raleigh, both of whom were married to Christians, Emma did "eat not a mouthful and read the prayers through, repetitions and all, without interruption." Her brothers neither prayed nor fasted. Later that winter, Emma observed that her brother's sister-in-law, Harriet Lane, had Augustus read aloud Isaac Leeser's *The Jews and the Mosaic Law*. Emma believed that Harriet, a Christian, is "half inclined to the Jewish faith herself." For Yom Kippur in 1821, Rachel Lazarus wrote her sister that Wilmington services were led by women, including her sister Eliza and stepdaughter Philah:

Philah and myself were readers of the day. . . . Eliza fasted the whole day and she was desirous to do so and as the other two girls were making their first attempt, I made no objection. . . . I am always willing to pass the day thus, and should think it natural to pass one day a year so, even it were not commanded.[35]

Throughout Jacob Mordecai's life in Warrenton, he negotiated among the intellectual Enlightenment, evangelical Christianity, and Jewish traditionalism. After his wife Judith died in 1796, Jacob inscribed a blessing in Hebrew to his mother Esther Cohen. Contrarily, to his "Dear & Respectable Brethren" of the Masonic Lodge, he sought guidance from the "Architect of the Universe" to "bear this affliction with a Rational Composure." When queried by Methodist ministers, Jacob explained that he accompanied his students to church on Sundays. In Warrenton in 1810, a curious and skeptical Jacob joined Christian friends at Baptist and Methodist camp revivals, giving rise to rumors that the schoolmaster, as Rachel wrote, "has become one of the elect." Jacob admitted to feeling estranged from Jews, but he declared his fidelity to Judaism. As a man of reason, he honored "virtue in whatever garb it appeared."[36]

For centuries, small-town, southern Jews would speak of *fitting in* as a social necessity. The Mordecais knew the lesson of accommodation well. At their academy, younger Mordecai children teased "kosha" Jewish students who did not fit in. After having dinner in Warrenton with Mordecai Cohen of Charleston, who expressed interest in enrolling his daughters, Rachel feared being "well stocked . . . with Yehooda." Fitting in was such a social obligation that when Judith Mordecai lay dying, she planned a funeral that would "omit such parts 'as from their novelty will make my Mordecai appear ridiculous'" to neighbors "unaccustomed to our religious rites."[37]

Wilmington Jews joined St. James Episcopal Church, where they had pews. Aaron Lazarus was a subscriber and trustee in 1815, as was Jacob Levy. Rachel Lazarus, a member of the St. James woman's society, had her son Gershon baptized at the church, although she raised him as a Jew. Joseph Jacobs attended services at St. James, but when he died "of Bilious Fever" in 1829, church records noted that he was "not a parishioner." Church membership suggests that Jews aspired to Christian society if not faith. Inevitably, Jews and Christians intermarried. From 1776 to 1840, 28.7 percent of marriages known to involve American Jews were intermarriages. Outside Jewish communities, rates were higher. Jews confronted the choice of remaining in the hinterlands without a Jewish future or removing to viable, urban communities. George Mordecai wrote of the "disagreeable and unfortunate situation" of his sisters: "They are either obliged to lead a life of seclusion and celibacy, marry a man whom they cannot admire or esteem . . . or they must incur the certain and lasting displeasure of their parents by marrying out of the pale of their religion." In 1830, when Aaron Rivera of Wilmington married a Mrs. Pierce, Rachel Lazarus felt that his "very strict" mother in Newport will never reconcile herself to the match of her hitherto "exemplary son." Bachelors and spinsters were common in early Jewish families. Of Jacob Mordecai's thirteen children, four did not marry, three married Jews, and six married Christians. That Jews married into elite Christian families, or at least highly educated ones, was a sign of Jewish social acceptance. Dr. Simon Gratz of Philadelphia married the socialite Mary Porter Ashe at Wilmington's St. James Church. George Mordecai, president of the Bank of North Carolina, wed Margaret Cameron, daughter of his predecessor at the bank and heir to perhaps the state's greatest fortune. Moses Mordecai's wedding to Margaret Lane brought him into Raleigh's founding family. Their home, located on what was once a 5,000-acre plantation, is now a historical site known as the Mordecai-Lane House.[38]

Jews constantly balanced their social reality and their Jewish loyalties. In explaining his membership at St. James Church, Aaron Lazarus avowed that he "could worship Jehovah in any temple." Along with other Jewish members of St. James—Judah Mears Levy and Abraham Isaacs—Lazarus also joined Beth Elohim synagogue in Charleston. When Beth Elohim laid its cornerstones in 1792, Abraham Moses, a North Carolina storekeeper, purchased an honor for five pounds, seven shillings. His intermarriage did not imply a loss of Jewish identity. When he died, he left five dollars each to the Baptist and Methodist churches but twenty dollars to the Charleston synagogue. Joel Henry of Beaufort had Christians witness his 1803 will, but he wrote it "in the name of the God of Israel" and signed it in Hebrew as Joel, son of Rabbi Hirsh Eiger, "may his memory be a blessing," and dated it, 23rd of Kislev, 5564.[39]

For North Carolina Jews their community extended beyond state borders. Rachel Lazarus's letters are full of gossip about Charleston's Jews whom she labels "our crowd." When the War of 1812 threatened Richmond, the Marx and Myers families moved in with their Warrenton relatives. The state's Jewish dead were sent for burial among their own in Charleston, Richmond, Norfolk, and New York. When Rachel and Aaron Lazarus married in Wilmington in 1821, Isaac Judah, lay prayer leader of Richmond's Beth Shalome, performed the ceremony. Samuel Mordecai in Richmond kept a Jewish calendar, reminding his Warrenton family of approaching holidays. For Passover, he provided them with matzot. In 1814 Rachel hoped that her brother was "enabled to sleep with tolerable comfort & safety in" a booth during Sukkot. Family correspondence suggests visits to Richmond or New York during Jewish High Holidays. In Philadelphia, Rachel and Aaron attended services at Mikveh Israel.[40]

The relentless missionary spirit of the Second Great Awakening made inroads on Jews. In the early 1800s, Joseph S. C. F. Frey toured the South on behalf of the

TEXT: THE WILL OF ABRAHAM MOSES

The will of Abraham Moses draws a portrait of the merchant as a Jew and a southerner.

State of North Carolina, Mecklinburg [*sic*] County, 8th October 1821

Be it remembered that I Abraham Moses of the State & County afore Said being weak in Body, but of sound and perfect mind & memory, blessed be the Almighty God for the Same, do make & publish this my last will & testament, in manner & form following that is to day. I give bequeath and devise unto my beloved Wife Nancy Moses my plantation on Lanes Creek Anson County, also my Negros John & Betty together with my Horses, Cattle, Household furniture & farming utensils during her widowhood & in order to raise Educate & Clothe my Children . . .

I also will that the Negro Wench Violet now in possession of my Daughter Esther Continue with her until such time as my Executors have an opportunity of replacing her by a younger Wench of about twelve or thirteen . . .

I also will that fifty Dollars be remitted to my Brother Isaac Moses in Germany & Twenty Dollars to the Hebrew Synagogue in Charleston which money to be deposited in the Hands of Mr. Solomon Simons for that purpose. Also five Dollars to the Baptist Church & five Dollars to the Methodist Church, and that One Hundred & Ten Dollars be paid to my said Wife Nancy to buy provisions & for her & my Children. And lastly I nominate and appoint my Worthy friends David Cuthbertson, Esq. Of Anson County & State aforesaid & Alexander McLarty of Mecklenburg C. whom I request to have my Grave made round with Brick & a small tomb laid over it . . .

Signed seal'd published declared by the above Abraham Moses to be his last will & testament in the presence of us. Who at the request & at his presence do the herewith Subscribe our names as witnesses to the Same.

Tho L Dillon
William L McLuer
Levi Preslar[1]

1. "Moses, Abraham," Mecklenburg County Wills, 1749–1967, NCSA.

American Society for Meliorating the Condition of the Jews. A German-born Jew who had converted to Christianity, he was supported in his efforts by English and American dispensationalists who believed that the conversion of the Jews was the prelude to messianic times. Rachel Lazarus found a social circle among the Ladies Working Society of St. James. The church was fired with missionary zeal. The genteel, born-again ladies pressed evangelical literature upon Rachel, introduced her to clergy to resolve her doubts, and nursed her through illnesses with "Christian friendship." Visiting Beth Elohim in Charleston during Passover, her first visit to a synagogue, Rachel complained that she would rather have spent an evening at the theater.[41] Her complaints about synagogue services focused not on gender segregation but on the lack of decorum where davening (praying) was individualistic, even chaotic.

The religious struggles of nineteen-year-old Gershon Lazarus are illustrative. Gershon complained that when his parents entertained Friday nights, they were lax with prayers and candle lighting, which he thought disrespectful to Judaism. He found Episcopal services at St. James to be more inspiring than Hebrew worship at the Charleston synagogue, where he felt a "want of decency." When he questioned his father and stepmother on the divinity of Jesus, neither answered to his satisfaction, nor did religious tracts from Jacob Mordecai convince him of Judaism's truth. One day, while his father lay on a sickbed, Gershon left a note explaining that he was going to St. James to be baptized. There Rev. Mr. Empie anointed him, prayed with him, and made the sign of the cross over him. Gershon drank the Communion wine. He returned home to find his father enraged. Aaron Lazarus wrote to the bishop of Virginia protesting Empie's role in urging his son to take "the awful step of abandoning his father's faith" without as much as study. He and Empie agreed that at twenty one Gershon would undertake a "thorough investigation" of Christianity and Judaism in Richmond under the joint tutelage of Bishop Richard Moore and Jacob Mordecai. After three weeks of hard study, Gershon later recalled, "the light of reason burst forth," and he re-embraced Judaism. He wrote to Mr. Empie renouncing his baptism. When Philah Lazarus married a Christian and converted, Aaron Lazarus not only ceased communicating with her but forbade his children to do so.[42] For Aaron Lazarus and Jacob Mordecai, each family intermarriage and conversion was felt as a stab in the heart.

In a free America, Jews soon realized all the religious possibilities open to them, and the Mordecai family itself expressed that diversity. After retiring to Virginia, Jacob and Rebecca Mordecai were pillars of Beth Shalome synagogue, where he served as parnas. Dutiful Emma lived with her parents and held "fast to the banner of the Lord of Hosts," writing on such subjects as "The Duty of Israel" for the national Jewish newspaper the *Occident*. Her sister Ellen was an evangelical Christian, author of the spiritual autobiography *The History of a Heart*, whose missionizing among the family was not always appreciated. George, married to an Episcopalian, was a communicant at Christ Church in Raleigh. Other brothers who intermarried attended their wives' churches with or without formal conversion. Alfred married a devout Jew but was religiously indifferent. Ellen Lazarus remained a Jew, even taught Sunday School, but joined the utopian, universalist "Church of Humanity." Rachel felt trapped between her devotion to her Jewish father and husband and to her own spiritual doubts and yearnings. She wrote her sister Ellen that the High Holidays bring her pain since they have "lost their solemnity," but she "cannot openly disregard them." She felt "guilty in re-peating prayers which I cannot admit the efficacy." While traveling to visit her dying father, Rachel fell fatally ill and, on her deathbed, "begged" for and received baptism.[43]

A CHRISTIAN REPUBLIC

In 1776, as delegates gathered in Halifax to write a state constitution, Samuel Johnston wrote his sister Hannah Iredell that "things here were drawing near a conclusion, and that I should get home in a few days, but unfortunately one of the members from the back country introduced a test." This thirty-second article was a religious test to forbid public office to anyone who denied "the truth of the Protestant religion." The debate on this article, Johnston continued, "has blown up such a flame, that everything is in danger of being thrown into confusion."[44]

North Carolina was hardly alone in writing a religious test into its state con-stitution. Whereas the federal constitution was neutral to religion, states, while granting religious freedom, restricted public office to Christians. Such provisions were colonial holdovers. They were often retained by popular will and the advo-cacy of clergy. At least ten states had, at some point and in some way, religious qualifications. In New York, Roman Catholics were denied public office, but not Jews; in Maryland the opposite was true. In Virginia, Thomas Jefferson proposed an Act for Religious Freedom in 1779, but it took seven years of vitriolic debate before it passed.[45]

From 1770 to 1820, North Carolina struggled to define the terms of its republi-canism. Debates raged over rights and privileges for slaves, free blacks, women, property holders, and religious dissenters. Yeomen farmers, who were most nu-merous, were Jeffersonian in their advocacy of limited government but not in their tolerance of religious liberty. The Jews' tenuous status was suggested in 1784 when Mr. Laney testified before the General Assembly as a character witness for his former business partner, Mr. Haryon, with whom he had "very great quarrel." Mr. Tisdale objected that "Mr. Laney is a Jew. I think Mr. Laney would be an im-proper witness here." However, "Mr. Laney, a Jew, was sworn."[46]

The 1776 North Carolina Constitution reflected a divided society. Wary of an established church, its framers granted freedom of worship and disallowed clergy from serving in the legislature or Council of State. Associating Roman Catholics with tyrannical European monarchies, they limited public office to Protestants. Quakers joined Roman Catholics in the fight for religious liberty. In other states, the question of rights allied Jews with minorities whose religious liberties were also threatened. Thus, Huguenots in South Carolina and Catholics in Maryland supported Jewish emancipation. Given Jewish numbers, the issue was largely a debating point, and Jewish rights were considered rhetorically with those of Hindoos and Mahometans. In France, England, and Germany, where Jewish emancipation was also being debated, there was a "disjunction between the attention to the Jews and their 'objective' importance."[47]

For North Carolinians, religious liberty meant freedom of Protestant worship. In Philadelphia in 1787, when the federal Constitutional Convention debated abolishing the religious test, North Carolina, according to James Madison, was the only state to vote against it. The state convention that met in Hillsborough in 1788 to ratify the federal Constitution turned raucous when religious questions arose. Federalist James Iredell, later a U.S. Supreme Court justice, argued that "under the colour of religious tests the utmost cruelties have been exercised." He endorsed "a generous religious liberty," noting that Jews customarily swore oaths on the Old Testament alone. Samuel Johnston, a Revolutionary War leader and later governor, added that if Jews, Mahometans, and pagans, "notwithstanding their religion, acquire the confidence and esteem of the people of America by their good conduct and practice of virtue, they may be chosen" for public office. Rev. David Caldwell, a Presbyterian divine, countered that "there was an invitation for Jews and pagans of every kind to come of us. At some future period . . . this might endanger the character of the United States." Although eleven states had already ratified the Constitution, effectively creating a United States of America, the North Carolina convention rejected it by a two-to-one margin. Not until a federal Bill of Rights was proposed did a second convention, meeting in Fayetteville, agree to ratify. North Carolina "defaulted its way into the Union in 1789," historian Milton Ready writes, "and then spent the first decades of the nineteenth century as if it did not exist."[48]

The state's 1776 constitutional religious test endured without being enforced. Roman Catholics served as speaker of the house and state supreme court justice. In 1808, when Jacob Henry of Beaufort, son of a German Jewish immigrant, was elected to the House of Commons from Carteret County, no member objected. Reelected in 1809, Henry was challenged. Hugh Mills of Rockingham County demanded that Henry not be seated because he "denies the divine authority of the New Testament and refused to take the Oath prescribed by Law." Mills argued that allowing Henry to take his seat "is contrary to the freedom and Independence of our happy and beloved Government."[49]

Politics lay behind the challenge. Henry represented Beaufort and, typical of the coastal gentry, was a Federalist. Mills, from the backcountry, was a Republican. Rivalries between east and west embittered state politics. The conservative east dominated state politics for a half century, pitting an educated, propertied elite against the greater numbers of less-educated, yeoman farmers. After the deaths of founding fathers like Iredell and Johnston, and the movement of population westward, Republicans dominated state government. North Carolina, where Federalists defended a Jew from Republican attack, contrasts to New York and Pennsylvania, where Federalists tarred Republicans as "the tribe of Shylock."[50] Proud Jews like Benjamin Nones of Philadelphia and Mordecai Noah of New York were ardent Republicans. American Jews did not subscribe to any single politics, and their loyalties owed to their local situations.

Henry's leading defender was William Gaston, an eloquent and learned man who was both Federalist and Roman Catholic. Gaston argued that Henry had every right to hold his seat as he was elected by the people. He cleverly argued that, according to the article's wording, "to deny" meant "an overt act" against the Protestant faith: "I may actually disbelieve the thing, and yet for reasons of courtesy refrain from denying it." Moreover, he held that Article 32 applied only to civil office, not to the legislature. Other members opposed Mills's resolution on constitutional grounds. At that point Thomas Love, a westerner, took the speaker's chair and called witnesses. Belcher Fuller from Carteret County reported that he had never seen Henry in a synagogue but had seen him attend Baptist and Methodist meetings. In fact, Henry later wrote, Beaufort contained only one church, which was used by all worshipers. Samuel M'Guire of Chowan County swore that Henry had taken his oath of office from a book in his pocket, but John Roberts, also from Carteret County, claimed it contained both Old and New Testaments. He was unsure if Henry ate pork. Two others swore that Henry had divided his book in two before taking the oath, one claiming that Henry had brought an Old Testament for that purpose. He had not actually seen the swearing in, however.[51]

Jacob Henry, after a night of preparation, rose in defense. He began with an apology: "I must confess that the resolution against me yesterday was quite unexpected." In a stirring speech, he argued that the state constitution's Declaration of Rights granting freedom of religion as a "natural and inalienable right" took precedence over any religious qualification. He asserted that his religion accords with American democracy. Belief was "a question between a man and his Maker." Nothing in his religion was "incompatible with the freedom and safety of the State." His religion inculcates virtue and detests vice. He did not question the beliefs of "those who made this objection against me," and the same "charity" should be extended to him. To his Protestant detractors, he ended ironically, citing the New Testament's admonition to do unto others as one would have done onto oneself.[52]

Henry not once mentioned Jews or Judaism. He expressed a universal "enlightenment theism," rooting republican values in "my religion." He defended a

The state capitol, 1818, in a painting by Jacob Marling. (North Carolina State Archives)

moral, civil religion rather than the traditional Judaism of revelation. His appeals to reason, ethical conduct, and religious liberty evoke Jefferson. Henry echoed an international rhetoric of Jewish emancipation in his appeal to the rights of man. Moses Mendelssohn had made similar arguments decades earlier: Jews were entitled to liberty of conscience. They should be judged by their conduct, not on their beliefs. The precepts of Judaism were moral and compatible with the interests of the state.[53]

Henry retained his seat on the technicality that the religious test applied only

Although Henry was reelected to the state House in 1809, his right to serve in the legislature as a Jew was challenged on the grounds that he denied the "truth of the Protestant religion" and the "divine authority of the New Testament." These are excerpts from his speech:

The religion I profess, inculcates every duty which men owes to his fellow men; it enjoins upon its votaries the practice of every virtue, and the detestation of every vice; it teaches them to hope for the favor of heaven exactly in proportion as their lives have been directed by just, honorable and beneficent maxims. This, then, gentlemen, is my creed, it was impressed upon my infant mind; it has been the director of my youth, the monitor of my manhood, and will, I trust, be the consolation of my old age. At any rate, Mr. Speaker, I am sure that you cannot see anything in this Religion, to deprive me of my seat in this house.

. . . I do not seek to make converts to my faith, whatever it may be esteemed in the eyes of my officious friend, nor do I exclude any one from my esteem or friendship, because he and I differ in that respect. The same charity, therefore, it is not unreasonable to expect, will be extended to myself, because in all things that relate to the State and to the duties of civil life, I am bound by the same obligations with my fellow-citizens, nor does any man subscribe more sincerely than myself to the maxim, "whatever ye would that men should do unto you do ye so even unto them, for such is the law and the prophets."

to the civil department, the executive branch, not to the legislature. Gaston prevailed.

Henry's speech was widely celebrated. The *American Orator* schoolbook reprinted it as a model for the next half century. The North Carolina debate resonated in Maryland. There, too, Jews allied with Roman Catholics and the new Jeffersonian party, the Democrat-Republicans, in opposing a religious test. In 1818 Catholic legislator Thomas Kennedy put forward a "Jew Bill." In support, H. M. Brackenridge cited "Mr. Henry, a Jew" from North Carolina who defended "republican truths." Holding a copy of the *American Orator*, Brackenridge added, "It is a part of our education as Americans to love and cherish the sentiments uttered by him on that occasion." The Maryland bill did not pass until 1826. Other states rescinded their religious tests, some after the Revolution, others by the 1820s, although New Hampshire not until 1968.[54]

The constitutional religious test festered in North Carolina for sixty years. At an abortive 1823 constitutional convention in Raleigh to redress geographic representation in the state legislature, a motion was made "to expunge the 32nd Article as hostile to the principles of religious freedom and unworthy of the lib-

PORTRAIT: JACOB HENRY

Jacob Henry played a celebrated role in North Carolina as a defender of religious liberty and first elected Jewish legislator, but the facts of his life are obscure. Jacob's parents were Joel Henry, a rabbi's son from Germany, and Amelia Henry, a native of Bermuda. The family came to Beaufort from Charleston, where Amelia returned after Joel's death. Amelia, at least, had once lived in New Bern. In 1801 Jacob married Esther Whitehurst, a Beaufort native born in 1787. The 1810 census lists Jacob Henry as the head of a Beaufort household of five white males, five white females, and twelve slaves. They had seven children.

Much in Jacob Henry's life identifies him with the gentrified, eastern elite that dominated the state's politics. The state constitution required property of 100 acres to serve in the House of Commons. In 1805 Jacob Henry possessed more than 300 acres and a town lot. His home, still standing near the Beaufort waterfront, was built in the West Indian style popular in the coastal Carolinas.

Henry's eloquence reveals him to be well read and educated. His politics were representative of his place and social class, allying him with men of enlightened principles like William Gaston, James Iredell, and Samuel Johnston, all of whom were Federalists of national reputation. After his term expired, Henry returned to Beaufort. In 1810 he wrote a description of the town for the newspaper, the *Star*. Although the Federalists opposed the War of 1812, muster rolls list Jacob Henry as a militia captain. About 1817 he moved to Charleston, and he appears on census records there in 1820 and 1830. In 1823 the Charleston *City Gazette* reported the death of his wife Esther Henry and two years later of his mother Amelia Henry. In 1836 he sold a Beaufort lot to his son Samuel Whitehurst Henry, a Charleston cabinetmaker. A newspaper article in 1847 refers to a Masonic funeral for Jacob Henry from his son's Charleston home.[1]

Henry's 1809 speech to the House of Commons proved his lasting legacy.

1. Malcolm Stern, *First American Jewish Families: 600 Genealogies, 1654–1977* (Cincinnati and Waltham: American Jewish Archives and American Jewish Historical Society, 1978), 115; Mary Hollis Barnes, "Jacob Henry's Role in the Fight for Religious Freedom in North Carolina" (19 Mar. 1984), typescript, NCSA; Ira Rosenwaike, "Further Light on Jacob Henry," in Leonard Dinnerstein and Mary Dale Palsson, eds., *Jews in the South* (Baton Rouge: Louisiana State University Press, 1973), 47–51.

erty of the age." Convention president Bartlett Yancy dismissed the motion as not relevant. In 1833 members of the General Assembly recommended again abolishing the clause: "Its spirit is in conflict with religious freedom; it has no practical use and it may be considered a mere bade of ancient prejudice." By a vote of 50 to 9 this proposal was forwarded to a proposed state constitutional convention.[55]

When the convention met in Raleigh in 1835, the religious-test debate lasted seven days and occupied a third of the convention report. Roman Catholics, Moravians, and Quakers supported its repeal. Governor John Branch argued passion-ately, "Why are the Jews to be excluded from office? They were the favorite people of the Almighty. Our Saviour and His disciples were Jews." If a Jew could serve as president of the United States, Branch asked, why not office in North Carolina? James Smith of Orange County answered that he was "not willing by expunging this article to let in Turks, hindoos, and Jews. . . . Must we swear the Turk on the Koran, must we separate the Holy Scriptures that we may swear the Jew on the Old Testament?" Speaking for its abolition, old Revolutionary War hero Nathaniel Macon, a friend of Madison and Jefferson and former Speaker of the United States House of Representatives, arose: "Who made man a judge, that he should pre-sume to interfere with the sacred rights of conscience." He had no objection to a "Hindoo" in public office. The learned William Gaston, quoting Jonathan Swift and Roger Williams, returned again to "Jacob Henry, a Jew." Moravian Gottlieb Shober countered, the religious test "tells the world we are a Christian people." Finally, the committee compromised by removing "Protestant" in favor of "Chris-tian." It passed 74 to 51, with Whigs in favor and Democrats opposed. Branch remained opposed; Gaston reluctantly endorsed the compromise. The *Newbern Spectator* denounced the vote as an "illiberal and disgraceful distinction which . . . has long been condemned by nearly every intelligent man in the State." Jews were not the only victims of illiberality. Free blacks, by a vote of 66–61, were dis-enfranchised. North Carolina was a white man's Protestant country.[56]

THE REPUBLICAN LEGACY

As the constitutional debate reveals, Jews loomed larger in the imaginations of North Carolinians than they did in numbers. Those who argued most vehe-mently in their defense, like James Iredell and Samuel Johnston, had personal acquaintance with Jews. Jacob Henry—erudite, a landowner—was a member of the state's eastern elite. The Mordecais in their educational achievement, cosmo-politan worldview, and upward mobility were married to the North Carolina gen-try personally and culturally. Church membership allowed Jews to affirm Prot-estant Christianity without having to deny it. As Jews, they sat in church pews. Gratz Mordecai, Jacob's grandson, wrote nearly a century later of his Warrenton ancestors: "The handicap of Judaism was surmounted by personal excellence." Rachel Lazarus insisted that Jews were "a respectable part of the people." Here she echoed Charleston writer Isaac Harby who referred to Jews famously as "a portion of the People." However much Jews argued for their rights as individu-als, they still bore a group identity. They were, as New Bern merchant Abraham Nathan was described, "of the Jewish nation."[57]

Jews were both gentrified North Carolinians and a global people. A "common cultural identity" bonded Jews across the English-speaking world. Like Jews elsewhere, they aspired to join an emerging bourgeois society and to be accepted by enlightened social elites. Jacob Henry's oratory on Jewish rights echoed political debates in Berlin and London. Rachel Lazarus's defense of Judaism, through the writings of Maria Edgeworth, traveled to Jewish libraries in England and Australia. Jewish newspapers like the *Occident*, including articles by Emma Mordecai, enjoyed worldwide circulation. Visits to and from family and friends in Newport, Charleston, and Richmond affirmed their membership in the Jewish people.

Living without synagogues or community, Jews remained conscious of their difference. The formal precepts of Orthodox Judaism were observed haphazardly, if at all. They invented a Judaism for their circumstances. Without synagogues, they maintained home ceremonials, which opened opportunity for women. Jews held to Judaism from a sense of filial duty. Aaron Lazarus felt his son's offense was "abandoning his father's faith," and Rachel Lazarus retained her Judaism, until her very end, less from spiritual conviction than from her obedience to father and husband.

North Carolina lacked an economy that could sustain a Jewish community. The state was rural and undeveloped, with few towns and cities. The decline of transatlantic trade closed doors to new migrations. In contrast to the polyglot colony, the state was increasingly insular and provincial. Cycles of the agricultural year regulated the economy and ordered society. The people, as the constitutional votes revealed, were uninterested in the world beyond their borders. Their lives centered on the rural church, the local mill, the country store, and the county seat. Few towns existed where a Jewish merchant could find customers for silk, crockery, and glassware. For a Jewish community to grow, more Jews would need to come to America, and North Carolina would need to awaken from its doldrums. That would happen in the coming decades.

3 SOUTHERN PATRIOTS

FROM GERMANY TO NORTH CAROLINA

1835-1880

In 1858 Herman Weil, just sixteen, left his native village of Oberdorf, Bavaria, for America. His father was an antiques merchant, relatively prosperous but still wanting his children to breathe the freer airs of America. He sailed to Baltimore to join his older sister Bertha. He soon left for Goldsboro, where another sister, Jeanette, was marrying an immigrant storekeeper, Henry Oettinger. The teenager clerked in his brother-in-law's store and peddled the countryside. Located at a railroad juncture, Goldsboro was a promising town for an enterprising young immigrant. Stores stretched along the tracks. Southbound trains brought credit and merchandise from importers, distributors, and manufacturers in Baltimore. Northbound went cotton, which storekeepers bartered or purchased from local farmers. Two years after Herman arrived, his younger brother Henry, only fourteen, joined him. A third brother, Solomon, came six years later. The H. Weil & Bros. store anchored downtown Goldsboro for a century.

Jews migrated in family chains. As historian Jacob Rader Marcus famously quipped, no Jew was ever the first to arrive in a community. He was always preceded by his uncle. Or a brother or an in-law. The Weils were typical of the 140,000 German Jewish immigrants who came to America from 1840 to 1870. Bavarian Jews were followed by Jews from Posen and West Prussia and from southern and western Germany. Alsatian Jews left France for homes along the Mississippi. The wave worked eastward to Austria, Bohemia, and Hungary. Jews immigrated at rates that quadrupled those of non-Jews. They were among some 5.5 million Germans who emigrated during the nineteenth and early twentieth centuries, peaking in 1854.[1]

By midcentury, half of German Jewry was estimated to live in poverty with perhaps 15 percent entering middle or upper classes. Jews were artisans, grain or cattle dealers, or, most commonly, peddlers. Village Jews were a segment of a "surplus population" displaced by the industrial revolution. Artisans left as manufactured goods came to the countryside. Periodic famines, the political turmoil of revolution, and the social disruptions of a growing urban and industrial economy pushed peoples from their homelands. In North Carolina, they came

Herman Weil
began as a peddler
in Goldsboro, 1858.
(North Carolina State
Archives)

to a place where Germans had long settled. For Louis Leon, it meant leaving Mecklenburg, Germany, for Mecklenburg County, North Carolina. Bavarian-born Solomon Bear found German compatriots in New Hanover County. From 1850 to 1860, Charlotte Jewry grew from nine to fifty-seven, nearly half of whom were German born.[2]

By 1877, 250,000 Jews were estimated to live in America. Although this "second wave" migration is labeled German, it drew from diverse regions and subcultures. Europeans Jews were migratory, and across the nineteenth century they flowed from east to west, from countryside to city. Berlin, Budapest, Vienna, Paris, and London witnessed exponential Jewish population growth. Migrations and shifting political borders obscured Jewish national identities. After 1795, when Poland was divided into three by its neighboring empires, a Polish Jew was reborn as Prussian, Russian, or Austro-Hungarian. In 1854 Lewis Lichtenstein of Tarboro was naturalized as a native of Poland, but his grave lists his birthplace as Prussia. Increasingly educated in secular schools, young Jews, conversant in German, were breaking from Yiddish-speaking communities and entering European society, which received them ambivalently.

Poverty, prejudice, and legal discriminations pushed Jews from Europe, and freedom and opportunity pulled them to a new land. Polish and German Jews confronted trade and residential restrictions. In 1813 Bavaria limited their marital rights, requiring all but the oldest son to leave if he wished to marry. State policy was to decrease Jewish population. German nationalists provoked anti-Semitic riots in 1819, 1830, and 1831. After the Revolution of 1848 failed, dashing hopes for a tolerant, democratic Germany, Prussian Jews migrated in growing numbers. German Jewish immigrants to America wrote letters home and published newspaper articles extolling America for its freedom and possibilities, a place where, as one Charlestonian beseeched his parents, "if only the Israelites knew how well you can live in this country, no one really would live in Germany any longer." Wilmington peddler Jacob Loeb sent a letter to his German cousin telling him to come. From 1840 to 1860, America's Jewish population grew at a rate fifteen times that of the nation.[3]

Jews arrived in North Carolina in stages, first residing in port cities. Ships carrying Virginia tobacco from Richmond to Bremen returned with German immigrants, among them Bavarian Jews. Richmond Jewry grew from 150 in 1830 to 1,200 in 1878. Baltimore's estimated 120 Jews in 1820 rose to 15,000 in 1874. With the extension of railroads, that city after midcentury increasingly served as a Jewish capital for North Carolina Jews, and the state's fledgling Jewish communities were its colonies. Steamship lines connected Wilmington and New Bern to Philadelphia. The Charlotte area, on the South Carolina border, retained ties to

Charleston although that city declined after 1820 when the cotton trade moved to Mobile and New Orleans.

North Carolina Jews created an ethnic niche economy in dry goods. The southern distribution network from Baltimore and Philadelphia—extending along rivers, roads, railroads, and sea-lanes—followed a national pattern. Cincinnati centered a web across the Mideast. New Orleans in the Deep South, St. Louis in the Midwest, and San Francisco in the Far West played similar roles. All were linked to New York financial markets. The endpoints were small-town stores that served as depots for peddlers, who traveled the countryside. Ties of credit and commerce, secured by family and landsleit (homeland folk) relationships, linked city and colony, wholesaler and retailer.

AWAKENING RIP VAN WINKLE

When the state constitutional convention debated the religious test in 1835, one delegate feared abolishing it would inspire more Jews to come to North Carolina. He need not have worried. Without economic opportunity Jews would not arrive in appreciable numbers. Although denying rights to Jews, the convention instituted reforms that enhanced the state's desirability. The rallying cry was "internal improvements." The ambitions to enhance commerce, finance public education, build transportation networks, and develop market towns were necessities for people whose livelihoods depended on commerce. To awaken from its doldrums, North Carolina had first to reform politically. Growing populations in western counties called for more democracy, challenging coastal planter elites. The west, without a coast or river transport, stood to benefit most from road and railroad building. North Carolinians were drawn to a new political party, the Whigs, under Henry Clay of Kentucky. A party of small farmers and merchants led by an educated elite, the Whigs' state spokesman was William Gaston, defender of Jewish rights. Joining the Whigs were Aaron Lazarus and Sam and George Mordecai. The 1835 constitutional convention affirmed the Whig agenda, and a year later the state's first popular election began a Whig domination that lasted into the 1850s.

Reform stirred Rip Van Winkle. The 1835 constitution revived a state bank; in 1849 George Mordecai served as its president. In 1839 the state devised a free public school system for white children, and the number of schools grew almost tenfold. By 1860 the University of North Carolina (UNC) had quadrupled its enrollment, and religious denominations had opened sixteen colleges, including Davidson and Wake Forest. In 1837 Marx Lazarus became the first Jew to enroll at UNC. Judah Benjamin, resettled in Louisiana, financed the educations of his brother Joseph and his nephew Lionel Levy at Chapel Hill, both graduating

Marx Lazarus, the first Jew to enter UNC, was an abolitionist, socialist, and Confederate. (Labadie Collection, Harlan Hatcher Graduate Library, University of Michigan)

in 1847. Two more nephews followed: Henry Sessions, class of 1856, and Coleman Sessions, class of 1857.[4] Beyond education, humanitarian institutions for the blind, deaf, dumb, poor, and insane were built. African Americans paid the price for progress. Fearing insurrections and reacting to northern abolitionism, North Carolina tightened its slave codes—slaves could not be taught to read and write—and disenfranchised free blacks.

North Carolina, too, felt faint stirrings of the Industrial Revolution that was remaking the global economy and transforming societies with new technologies in transportation, communications, and manufacturing. Steamships inspired the chartering of navigation companies. A plank road fever led to the building of eighty-four roadways totaling 500 miles. By 1848 the telegraph linked Raleigh to Richmond and Washington. With growing literacy and town settlement, the state claimed seventy-four newspapers by 1860.

A railroad craze struck North Carolina as it did the nation. The state stimulated growth by chartering companies and purchasing stock. In the 1830s, when a Wilmington & Raleigh Railroad was chartered, Aaron Lazarus and his brother-in-law Mordecai Cohen of Charleston served on its board. When the 161 miles of the Wilmington and Weldon Railroad were completed in 1840, the line was the world's longest. George Mordecai served as first president of the Raleigh & Gaston Railroad, which connected Raleigh to Virginia lines. In 1849 the state created the North Carolina Railroad Company. Slaves laid 223 miles of track from Goldsboro to Raleigh to Greensboro to Charlotte. Completed in 1856, the railroad linked the Piedmont to coastal ports, to the industrial north, and to southern market cities. Trains cut wagon freight rates in half.[5] The state's economic map was redrawn, and the outward flow of people stemmed.

With rail lines opening markets, industry and cash-crop agriculture dominated the state's economy. From 5 million pounds in 1830, tobacco production leaped to 33 million in 1860. North Carolina cotton fed the mills of England, both Old and New, and production quadrupled from 1840 to 1860. By 1860 North Carolina's thirty-nine textile mills ranked first in the South. The state was urbanizing. The railroad spawned new Piedmont mill and market towns like Burlington, Durham, Goldsboro, High Point, and Thomasville, while older settlements like Charlotte, Greensboro, and Salisbury grew into market and industrial centers.[6] A plank road and railroad enhanced Wilmington's importance as a seaport; with more than 5,000 residents, it grew into the state's largest city.

North Carolina's progress was relative. Its commerce and industry still lagged, and the state struggled to compete in national markets. Out-of-state capitalists and manufacturers exploited its produce and natural resources. In 1860 the state's leading industry remained turpentine production, followed by milling grain (corn

The Weil brothers store along the Goldsboro railroad tracks. (Wayne County Public Library)

and wheat), processing tobacco, and sawing lumber.[7] Cotton was shipped north to be milled and then returned south to be resold as finished goods. Jewish merchants purchased raw cotton from farmers and sold them ready-made clothes.

LOOKING NORTH, HEADING SOUTH

In 1857 Hinton Rowan Helper, a North Carolinian whose controversial book *The Impending Crisis of the South* challenged the economic benefits of slavery, neatly described the state's dependency on northern markets:

> The North is the mecca of our merchants, and to it they must and do make two pilgrimages per annum—one in the spring and one in the fall. All our commercial, mechanical, manufactural, and literary supplies come from there. We want Bibles, brooms, buckets, and books, and we go to the North . . . we want shoes, handkerchiefs, umbrellas, and pocket knives, and we go to the North. . . . Instead of keeping our money in circulation at home, by patronizing our own mechanics, manufacturers, and laborers, we send it all away to the North, and there it remains; it never falls into our hands again. In one way or another we are more or less subservient to the North every day of our lives.[8]

"Before the Civil War," historian Adam Mendelsohn observes, "the South was not only the largest market for clothing manufactured and sold in New York, but also a major destination for second hand garments sold by Jewish clothing dealers in London." Jewish peddlers hawked cheap garments to hardscrabble farmers and to plantation owners to clothe their slaves.[9]

In 1854 the *Raleigh Register* featured a front-page "New York City Business Directory" listing Jewish wholesalers. The clerks, peddlers, and storekeepers who came south as retailers or agents for firms in Baltimore, New York, and Philadelphia were emissaries of this commerce. Typical was Sam Archer, a "Dutch Jew" representing Einstein & Company of Baltimore, who came to Greensboro in 1858, soon after the railroad arrived. With westward expansion, Richmond merchants settled in Asheville, Morganton, and Salisbury. Charlotte and Wilmington, given their geography, retained ties to Charleston although this linkage declined after 1850 as Baltimore grew increasingly important. New Bern and Wilmington were connected by steamship to Philadelphia, Charleston, and New York as well as to Baltimore. In Wilmington, most Jewish merchants, up to 80 percent, were estimated to be "agents" of wholesaling firms in New York and Philadelphia. These agents took goods on consignment from the wholesaler, often a relative, and paid as the goods were sold. Partnerships often meant that one merchant continued to reside in the North. In New Bern in 1844, E. and F. Abraham advertised that their New Bern "Economy Store" is not "in any way connected with any other local persons in business excepting our two partners in Philadelphia." Lewis Sonnehill lived in Baltimore, but his agent Isaiah Pragg operated two clothing stores for him in eastern North Carolina.[10]

Of the forty-eight towns with a Jewish store from 1841 to 1861, more than half were in eastern North Carolina, and a third, including New Bern and Wilmington, were coastal or river port towns. In 1860 New Bern had some fifteen Jewish merchants while Wilmington had thirty-four. Almost three-quarters of the towns with Jewish stores were county seats, which served as market as well as government centers.[11] Jews from Richmond and Charleston opened stores along the state lines.

Jewish stores sprouted along the North Carolina Railroad in Kinston, Raleigh, Greensboro, Lexington, Mocksville, and Salisbury as the state's economic center gravitated from the coastal plain toward the Piedmont. At Charlotte, the western terminus, an early city historian observed, "The Israelites followed close on the coming of the railroad." Jewish merchants there increased from seven in 1850 to twenty-one in 1860. Moreover, fifteen Jewish clerks worked in these stores, virtually all of whom later opened stores of their own. Jewish stores clustered close by in Concord and Wadesboro. At the railroad's eastern terminus, Goldsboro, named for an engineer, developed a thriving Jewish community. Country stores opened in nearby Whitehall and Snow Hill. This pattern confirms Lee Shai Weissbach's study of 490 small-town Jewish communities nationally, which revealed that 76 percent had rail links by the late 1870s.[12]

From 1841 to 1861, R. G. Dun & Co. Credit Reports—written by local agents, who were lawyers, bankers, and merchants—list 129 Jewish merchants settling in North Carolina. These numbers were augmented by clerks and peddlers, some with out-of-state addresses. By 1841 L. H. Hornthal & Brother operated "one of the largest" stores in Plymouth, a river port that was the site of grain, paper, and lumber mills. When a gold rush struck the Cabarrus County area in the 1830s, drawing some 30,000 workers from sixteen countries, Jews were among the Cornish, Portuguese, Hungarian, and Turkish settlers. Several Jews, including J. M. Wolff and D. Elias, came from South Carolina to open stores in Gold Hill by the 1850s.[13]

Jews differed from other southerners not in their commerce but in the ethnic economy that relied on other Jews—very often family members—for credit, merchandise, and employment. The Kahnweiler brothers of Wilmington trace the geography of this network. In 1859 David and Daniel, with two Wilmington stores, were trading with contacts in Baltimore and New Orleans. They also partnered with Morris Katz, a former clerk, to open a Charlotte store. A third brother, Simon Kahnweiler, sailed to Europe and, upon returning, opened a business in New York. Jews formed partnerships among themselves and employed kinsmen and landsleit. Lewis Sterne, who began peddling around Rocky Mount before 1850, opened a dry goods store but sold out three years later to Odenheimer & Mensheimer, fellow "German Israelites." In 1855, when Samuel Wittkowsky needed clerks for his Charlotte store, he recruited six New York Jewish teenagers to fill the positions. D. Kahnweiler of Wilmington advertised in the *Jewish Chronicle* in Philadelphia for clerks.[14]

Of the merchants for whom their merchandising is specified, a quarter had general stores, a third sold dry goods, and a quarter proffered clothing. Other enterprises included a hotel, jewelry store, and auction house. In the 1850s several storekeepers, including the Myers brothers in Salisbury and Lazarus Fels in Yanceyville, expanded into distilleries. Few Jews were listed as farmers. R. W. Goldstein, identified as a Jew, settled in Moore County in 1847. He is reported to have married a "rich man's daughter" whose family owned slaves and real estate. Goldstein also operated a grocery and dry goods store.[15]

General stores sold whatever customers would buy from fertilizer to dry goods to groceries. Peddlers and storekeepers bartered fabric and novelties for eggs, chickens, or produce to be resold to town dwellers. In 1860 Oettinger's Dry Goods

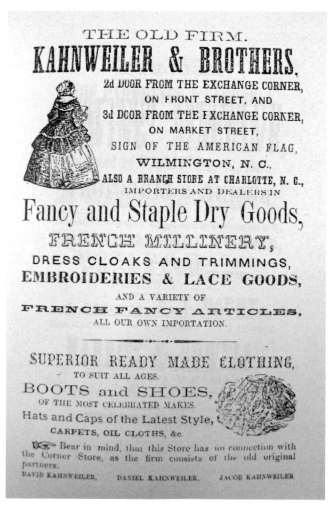

THE OLD FIRM.
KAHNWEILER & BROTHERS,
2d DOOR FROM THE EXCHANGE CORNER,
ON FRONT STREET, AND
3d DOOR FROM THE EXCHANGE CORNER,
ON MARKET STREET,
SIGN OF THE AMERICAN FLAG,
WILMINGTON, N. C.,
ALSO A BRANCH STORE AT CHARLOTTE, N. C.,
IMPORTERS AND DEALERS IN
Fancy and Staple Dry Goods,
FRENCH MILLINERY,
DRESS CLOAKS AND TRIMMINGS,
EMBROIDERIES & LACE GOODS,
AND A VARIETY OF
FRENCH FANCY ARTICLES,
ALL OUR OWN IMPORTATION.

SUPERIOR READY MADE CLOTHING,
TO SUIT ALL AGES.
BOOTS and SHOES,
OF THE MOST CELEBRATED MAKES.
Hats and Caps of the Latest Style,
CARPETS, OIL CLOTHS, &c.

Bear in mind, that this Store has no connection with the Corner Store, as the firm consists of the old original partners.
DAVID KAHNWEILER,   DANIEL KAHNWEILER,   JACOB KAHNWEILER

Advertisement for Kahnweilers', Wilmington merchants. (New Hanover County Public Library)

Store of Wilson advertised merchandise from "Ready-Made Clothing" to banjoes to "excellent cigars." As manufactured goods became available, the general store yielded to the urban specialty shop. In 1850 in Elizabeth City, M. Goldsmith advertised "The most Fashionable and Decidedly the Cheapest Gentlemens Clothing Depot ever Established in this Place!" In Charlotte, a historian noted, "Ready-made clothing first made its appearance with the advent of Levi Drucker." In Salisbury, Ezekiel Myers's inventory of glassware in 1854 included preserve dishes, celery stands, and champagne goblets. Town societies were growing sufficiently large, prosperous, and sophisticated to support such enterprises. A town store spawned branches in the countryside. In 1856 S. A. Lowenburg & Bro. of Beaufort, connected to a Philadelphia firm, had stores in Craven, Onslow, and New Hanover counties. The Myers family of Richmond owned a store in Salisbury, sold jewelry in Asheville to the summer trade, and opened a store in Morganton.[16]

TEXT: COHEN'S VARIETY STORE

This advertisement for Cohen's Variety Store appeared in the Hillsborough Recorder, 3 October 1866. Note the response to anti-Semitism in the last stanza.

COHEN'S VARIETY STORE

Run to COHEN'S very quick
For HIGH PRICES *is mighty sick,*
If you wish to keep him down
Buy the CHEAPEST GOODS IN TOWN.
Take your CASH and BARTER there,
He will be polite and fair.
BARGAINS there you can get
Ten per cent his profits net.
So rush along, be in the ring.
And do your trading while I sing.

FRESH ARRIVALS every day,
Cheap and Cheaper buyers say;
CALICOS of every Style,
HOOP SKIRTS there are pile on pile,
THE ENGLISH PRINCESS SKIRT or three,
And the DOLLAR SKIRT you'll see,
WORSTEDS, FLANNELS, HATS AND SHOES
CLOTHING ready made to use.
So don't delay, but push along,
While I sing this CHEAP STORE song.
M. COHEN has the SHAKER HOODS
And BALMORALS of finest GOODS
The latest Style of BONNETS there
You'll find untrimm'd or trim'd with care.
For GIRLS he has *the Hat for Fall*
Or Winter, and can suit them all.
For BOYS he's got the *Velvet Cap,*
The *Slick the Cloth* and PLUSH WITH Flap.
So hurry 'long in time to get

Your CROCKERY WARE by piece or set.
GOOD OLD RIO you can get
And SUGAR too, *that isn't wet.*
There you can get at lowest price
Your SALT & Dye Stuffs, & your SPICE.
In short of GROCERIES he will keep
A *Full Supply of Good and Cheap.*
OF HARDWARE he will keep on Hand
The best sold in this *Tar Heel* LAND.
So run along, and take a peep
At Goods that all agree are cheap.

In fifty lines I cannot tell
Of all he has, and how he'll sell,
But this I know, *he's selling cheap,*
And *profits large he doesn't reap.*
He'll take just what you bring to sell,
And *though called* 'Jew' *will* treat you well.
"No dead men wanted here," tis said,
But let them blow HIGH PRICE *is dead;*
So I'll advise you *call and try*
AT COHEN'S when you wish to buy.

Supposed to have been written by a gentleman who Suffered under *"High Price's"* reign from the year 1860 'till the opening on the 1st day of September, 1866, of
  M. COHEN'S Variety Store
    C. M. Latimer's Old Stand
      Hillsborough, N.C.

Peddling was nearly universal among Jews, historian Hasia Diner emphasizes. In America, Jews relived their European experience as middlemen between town and country, wholesaler and customer. Surveys in nineteenth-century France, Germany, and Poland revealed that 80 percent of employed Jews were peddlers, and as immigrants they resumed the profession whether in North Carolina, South Africa, Australia, or Argentina. Of the 125 Jews in Iowa in 1850, for example, 100 peddled. Short of capital and skills when they arrived in America, peddlers resumed their trade in city streets and the countryside. An American peddler might be an independent operator who owned his stock and sold from a wagon or a backpack. A storekeeper might load up a wagon as a "rolling store" to bring merchandise to the customer. Other peddlers were agents of national manufacturers who specialized in products like clocks or patent medicines.[17]

Peddling was both strenuous and dangerous, and newspapers reported murders and robberies. As foreign-born, traveling men, peddlers—and not just Jews—were suspect as hucksters, outsiders, and cheats. The stereotype of the "Jew pedlar" had its counterpart in the sharp "Yankee pedlar." Irish, Germans, and French peddlers also worked the state. Until fears of slave rebellions arose, blacks peddled by cart. Peddlers who trekked to farmhouses and plantations were commercializing the countryside, creating a market for consumer goods for people who lived distant from towns. Jewish peddlers carried news, both neighborhood gossip and, as immigrants, the cultures of foreign worlds. If the country store was the white man's preserve, the peddler crossed lines of gender and race by catering to women and African Americans. As outsiders and merchants in farm societies, peddlers were socially "disruptive." Peddlers broke the monopoly of the storekeepers, who often were planters or their sons. For women confined to the home and for slaves bound to the plantation, the peddler brought the cosmopolitan world to their door. When popular feelings arose against peddlers in 1819, male critics focused on the sale of shawls, casting peddlers as sexually suspect for allegedly seducing women with luxuries.[18]

Peddlers left little material or documentary trail. The credit reports mention fewer than twenty Jewish peddlers from 1841 to 1881, but the agents' familiarity with the "Jew pedlar" suggests a far wider presence. The 1850 federal census listed but ninety-seven peddlers in North Carolina, but that also understates. Highly mobile, peddlers were less likely to be counted. A clerk or storekeeper—or a son, brother, husband, or in-law—might throw a pack on his back or load a wagon and head into the countryside. Peddlers working North Carolina listed home addresses in Baltimore or Richmond. Herman Fulda, a Philadelphian, began peddling in Granville County in the 1830s. In 1855 Jacob Cohen lived in Philadelphia but peddled in North Carolina, where his father had a store. Peddlers had another

A country peddler, presumably Jewish, selling to women. (*Harper's Magazine*, 20 June 1868)

reason not to be enumerated. State tax laws discouraged northern peddlers. In 1847 North Carolina imposed a county tax of twenty dollars on peddlers.[19]

Jewish stores served as peddler way stations. Bernhard Weisel was among those appearing at "pedlar headquarters" in Greenville "once a week to replenish their waggons." Lazarus Fels of Yanceyville was a "very respectable Jew" who from his general store "has pedlars thro' the country." (After the Civil War, Fels left for Baltimore, where he entered the naphtha industry.) From Wilmington, a wholesale center, peddlers worked the backcountry. Peddlers aspired to storekeeping. Lewis Stern in 1850 had been peddling in Rocky Mount for a year and "has thereby made money" and "will soon open a store." By 1854 peddler Bernhard Weisel had married the daughter of storekeeper N. A. Cohen of Elizabeth City and opened a clothing store there.[20]

The Dun Credit Reports reflected popular attitudes about Jews and, given their confidentiality, revealed feelings not publicly expressed. Because Jews were mobile and obtained credit and merchandise through their own networks, agents had difficulties evaluating them. Elias & Cohen of Charlotte, who opened a dry goods store in 1851, "are Israelites and of course it is hard to know any-thing ab[ou]t them." One agent wrote of the general store of Hammersley & Co. [Hammerslough] of Asheville in 1860: "If they own any R[eal] E[state] I presume it is in the Holy Land. They have a nice stock but it is hard to find the means of a German Jew." Peddlers were especially difficult to assess. Bernhard Weisel ar-rived in Greenville in 1849 "w[ith] no prop[erty] but his horse & wagon." He was described as a "g[oo]d sort of fellow, rather most of these Jew pedlars, more of the Gentleman & making money." Yet, the Dun agent in Rocky Mount warned in 1858 of H. Mincherheimer, a "Jew [who] hawks or peddles goods with a waggon. . . . Such men are always regarded with distrust here."[21]

The reports demonstrate the persistence of a folklore that associates Jews with money. Of Drucker & Heilbrun, a general store in Catawba County in 1859, the agent reported, "Jews turn all things into money." In 1851 an agent paid N. A. Cohen of Elizabeth City a backhanded compliment: "Is a Jew and for a Jew stands quite high." Jews were also suspect because of their mobility. Thus, S. B. Benlinger of New Bern was a "German Jew, will move away." From 1848 to 1854 brothers H. and B. Bloomingdale opened and closed stores in Faison's Corner and Wil-son. "Jews transitory" the Dun Credit Reports noted. When they departed, the agent speculated, "I suspect they will be in bus[iness] at some other place."[22] (The Bloomingdales had better luck with a department store in New York.)

The Jews' mobility was driven as much by ambition as by failure. The boom years of the 1850s yielded to hard times. When Drucker & Heilbrun of Charlotte flirted with bankruptcy in 1861, the agent reported that "they are pressed by an overextension of business and tightness of the times." Moses Einstein had peddled around Kinston about 1844 before opening a store. In 1855, in debt, Ein-stein blew up his store after "unthoughtfuly placing a lighted cigar on a keg of powder." The Dun agent reported, "The explosions said to have caused every horse in the village to quake and totter like a drunken man. Shattering E.'s store into atoms and injuring him v[ery] much if not fatally."[23]

BECOMING SOUTHERN

Few and mobile, with northern ties and German roots, North Carolina's Jews lived in many worlds. The question of a southern identity did not yet impose itself. Loyalties focused on the state rather than on the South as a region. In 1831 came both Nat Turner's Rebellion and William Lloyd Garrison's abolitionist newspaper the *Liberator*. Starting in the 1830s and growing forcefully in the 1840s, a south-ern patriotism arose that asserted the superiority of the southern way of life to that of the North. As southerners defended themselves against abolitionists and dissented on national issues like tariffs and banking, historian John Hope Franklin observes, they "began to think of themselves as having a set of common values, common problems, common dangers, and common aspirations that set them apart from other Americans." Southerners grew fearful and embittered, conscious of themselves as a minority. For Jews, northern abolitionists also spoke in a strongly Christian evangelical tone that discomfited them. The nativist, anti-immigrant American Party, the Know-Nothings, made a strong showing in the state in the mid-1850s, but their target was Irish Catholics, not German Jews. In 1852 a Christian woman in rural Bethania described her Jewish neighbors, the Livingstons, as "very sociable, friendly" and coveted an invitation to their daughter's Jewish wedding.[24]

Southern folklore drew on European anti-Semitic stereotypes which represented the Jew as both Shylock and Christ-killer. In 1847 the *Greensboro Patriot* printed a poem on its front page that expressed such prejudices:

> Ye sons of people once chosen to God
> Ye daughters of Judah, how heavy the rod
> That chastises your crimes and awakens your fears
> How dark your exile—how bitter your tears.

Nine years later it explained, "How Jewish Girls Get Husbands: Buy Them." An old English blood-libel ballad, "The Jewish Lady," was sung in North Carolina. It tells of "a little boy" who knocked on the door of a Jew to retrieve a ball. The Lady, "all dressed in silk and lace," blindfolded the boy, took a carving knife, and "pierced his little heart through." An elderly Raleigh woman told a folklorist that she "has known it all her life." A dime novel, *The Life Confession and Execution of the Jew and Jewess*, set in Asheville in 1854, played to anti-Semitic stereotypes. The novel is a melodrama of a pawnbroker Gustavus Linderhoff—stooped, dark-eyed, and of "olive complexion"—and his gaudily dressed, greedy, and conniving mistress Fanny, who stab three orphan wards to steal their inheritance. A mob lynches them.[25] The depictions of Jews as dark, predatory, sensual, and avaricious, murdering Christian children, trace to medieval blood libels.

Intolerance turned violent in Goldsboro in 1857. Falk Odenheimer, a "Jew merchant," had a business quarrel with Dr. John Davis and the two landed in court. There Davis's nephew struck Odenheimer with a shovel, breaking his skull. In the ensuing fight, Charley Spaght, the merchant's stepson, shot Davis. "The cry soon started to hang Odenheimer," a local historian reported. Odenheimer was taken to jail, where a lynch mob gathered. One "Mr. Hollowell had to use considerable force to stop the mob, who were bent on vengeance," the historian continued.

"Nearly every Jew in town left, because it was not safe for them to remain." Both Davis and Odenheimer recovered. "The feeling against the Jews gradually died out and those who had run off returned," the story concluded. A year later Herman Weil arrived from Baltimore, and soon thereafter a community grew.[26]

Southerners identified Jews with northern commerce, to which they held a conflicted attitude, wanting its capital and technology but resenting its economic exploitation. Calls for homegrown industry echoed across the region. Laws doubled taxes on peddlers who sold out-of-state goods. In 1844 E. and M. Abrahams, whose "Economy Store" was a branch of a Philadelphia firm, posted in the *Newbernian* "An Appeal and Caution. To the citizens of Newbern and the public in general." It warned that "certain persons . . . have circulated things derogatory to our character and standing." German immigrant Isaac Long, who peddled and opened stores in Pittsboro and Chapel Hill in 1847, is described by the Dun Credit Reports as a "shrewd trader and has the reputation of having little principal [sic]. It may be owing in part to the fact as believed by many that he was a Jew who eschewed his religion to get a better run of trade." Reputedly, "his original name was not 'Long' but Levy." A later report states his name is "'Lang' that he was Jew, but he bitterly denies this." He is also the "best educated & the best informed merchant in the place." When he failed in 1860, his debts were owed to "Northern Creditors" in Baltimore and Philadelphia. Whether Long was in fact a Jew is less relevant than the negative assumptions about Jewish origins by all parties.[27]

Long also owned a "few negroes." Antebellum Jews, particularly German immigrants, were rarely slaveholders. Only 9 of the 129 Jews in the Dun Credit Reports are listed as owning slaves from 1841 to 1860. In 1845 a slave that cost $722 could be hired out for $143 a year, for a return of 18.5 percent, but that declined to 10 percent by 1860. Few saw it as a worthwhile investment, apart from whatever scruples they felt about slavery. Many merchants were listed as holding property worth between $5,000 and $10,000 so that slaves were affordable. Seventy percent of North Carolina's white families did not, in fact, own slaves. Of Wilmington's thirty-four Jews listed in an 1860 business directory, only two apparently owned slaves. The firm of Kahnweiler and Brother in Wilmington owned five slaves in 1860. When Warrenton merchant Jacob August advertised in 1859 "Negroes for sale . . . in consequence of my going to reside North," he printed a handbill attesting to the qualities of his "Eight Valuable Family Servants."[28]

One Jewish firm engaged in slave trading. In 1850 Ezekiel and Myer Myers opened a general store in Salisbury, financed by members of their Richmond family. The brothers "traffic in slaves," the Dun Credit Report noted. In 1853 Myer Myers advertised that they were "now in the market for the purchase of ONE

NEGROES
FOR SALE.

I will sell by Public Auction, on Tuesday of next Court, being the 29th of November, *Eight Valuable Family Servants*, consisting of one Negro Man, a first-rate field hand, one No. 1 Boy, 17 years o' age, a trusty house servant, one excellent Cook, one House-Maid, and one Seamstress. The balance are under 12 years of age. They are sold for no fault, but in consequence of my going to reside North. Also a quantity of Household and Kitchen Furniture, Stable Lot, &c. Terms accommodating, and made known on day of sale.

Jacob August.
P. J. TURNBULL, *Auctioneer.*
Warrenton, October 28, 1859.

Printed at the *News* office, Warrenton, North Carolina.

HUNDRED NEGROES." In 1858 they sold their store and opened a distillery but still "speculated in slaves a good deal" with $12,000 to $15,000 "invested in Negroes." At prevailing prices, they likely held fewer than ten slaves in their inventory.[29]

Frederick Law Olmsted, touring the South, observed that Jews conducted "an unlawful trade with the simple Negroes, which is found very profitable." North Carolina was one-third African American. Jews were disdained for selling to slaves. Peddlers were suspected of being secret abolitionists who encouraged slave rebellions. In 1819 the legislature made it illegal to "deal, trade, or traffic" with a slave without the master's consent or face indictment. In 1837 the fine was raised from $50 to $100, and forbidden products were listed. Nathan Kramer, a Raleigh clothier, was described in 1854 as a German Jew who had a "rather bad odor as to his trading with slaves." Three years later he was "accused of trading with Indians" and landed in "criminal court for trading with slaves" without a permit. Michael Grausman, a farmer and merchant in Warrenton and Raleigh, refused to own slaves on principle but employed free blacks. He built a home for the household nanny on his property and tutored her children.[30]

Marx Lazarus was a rare southern Jewish abolitionist. In 1860 he wrote an article for the radical journal, the *Dial*, published in Cincinnati, titled "The True Principles of Emancipation." He denounced "outrages sanctioned by prejudice against color" and condemned "this prolonged crucifixion of a martyr race." A socialist, he saw African bondage as but one example of the "manifold cruelties that labor elsewhere suffers" and warned against the "conversion of chattel slavery into that of labor for wages." Lazarus signed the article, "A Native of North Carolina and a Citizen of the World."[31]

THEY HAD WORSHIP

Jewish immigrants came to North Carolina in search of economic opportunity, not in quest of Jewish community. In Baltimore, Charleston, Philadelphia, or New York, where the immigrants first settled, they found synagogues and lived among family and landsleit who spoke their language, ate their foods, and observed their holidays. In coming to North Carolina, they were breaking from Jewish community.

The first break was immigration itself. "Until the middle of the nineteenth century, a fairly unified Jewish culture existed throughout much of Europe," historian Hasia Diner observes.[32] As the nineteenth century progressed, the haskalah (Jewish enlightenment) and religious reform were working eastward across Europe. This movement reflected the Jews' growing German acculturation. By midcentury, Reform-style congregations spread into Eastern Europe. Polish rabbinical students who wanted state certification were required to enroll in German universities where they studied secular subjects and examined Judaism critically from a historical perspective.

Jews brought their European Judaism with them. "Close ties," historian Avraham Barkai notes, "connected German Jewry with its American branch." Immigrant rabbis came to America versed in the religious debates of European Jewry and sought guidance from rabbinic mentors in Germany. Jews who immigrated to America tended to be poor, observant village Jews less influenced by urban, modernizing trends. When Herman Kahn, patriarch of the Greensboro Cone family, emigrated from Altenstadt, Bavaria, in 1846, he carried a letter from his brother-in-law reminding him to pray daily morning and evening, "to remember particularly the Sabbath day, to keep it holy," and "to learn your religion thoroughly." A Christian neighbor of the Livingstons in Bethania observed that "their cooking is altogether Jewish, abstaining from swine's flesh & lard & using goose grease & butter, also beef" and their daughters wedding was entirely in Hebrew with an English benediction.[33]

The arrival of new immigrants in the tens of thousands transformed American Judaism. Immigrants from Posen and Eastern Europe clung to their traditional Judaism, praying daily and observing kosher laws, whereas Jews from Bavaria and southwestern Germany had felt the emancipating effects of the Enlighten-

Herman Kahn emigrated from Altenstadt, Bavaria, in 1846. He joined his sister in Richmond, changed his name to Cone, and peddled. His sons Moses and Ceasar settled in Greensboro, where they built a textile empire. When Herman left Germany, his brother-in-law Joseph Rosengart gave the teenager an ethical letter, which to this day serves as a Cone family covenant.

Place your full trust and confidence in God who will send his angels to guard you. So, do not be discouraged, and do not be afraid of leaving or of the voyage, but consider your fate a good fortune, designed for you by God.

You may shed tears, because you are leaving your parents' house, your Father, Brothers and Sisters, relatives, friends and your native land, but dry your tears, because you have the sweet hope of finding a second home abroad and a new country where you will not be deprived of all political and civil rights and where the Jew is not excluded from the society of all other men and subject to the severest restriction, but you as a human being may claim all human rights and human dignity.

Be careful of your voyage and pay attention to your health as well as your belongings. Avoid the company of all but respectable and educated people. Be modest and polite to everybody. Thus you may surely expect good treatment for yourself.

Every evening and every morning turn to GOD with sincere prayers; do not be afraid of anybody and do not let anybody disturb your devotions. Even if some people should make fun of you at first, they will understand later and show their respect.

I recommend to you the faith of your fathers as the most sacred and the most noble. Try to follow all the Commandments most painstakingly and thereby attain actual happiness. Do not sacrifice your faith for worldly goods. They will disappear like dust and must be left behind in due time.

Remember particularly the Sabbath day, to keep it holy, for it is one of the most important pillars on which our Faith is established. Do not disregard this day and do not let gold or silver make you blind and do not let any business however tempting induce you to violate the Sabbath, but at least on this day think seriously about your existence and your work.

It is not man's destiny to accumulate worldly goods just to be wealthy, but to acquire them to be used as means for the attainment of eternal happiness. I am, therefore giving you as a keepsake an excellent religious book for your instruction. Make it your sacred duty to read one chapter each Sabbath and holy day with serious devotion and meditation. Do not lay it aside when you have read it through, but keep it and read it again from time to time.

You thereby learn your religion thoroughly, act accordingly and thus be honored by GOD and men. It will be your counsel in good times and bad, and will preserve you from all evil.

Honor your Father and your Mother, that your days may be prolonged. Even in that distant country you can show your respect and love towards your Father by always remembering his good advice and by frequently writing him loving letters, thus giving expression to your devotion to him and your Brothers and Sisters.

Although your sainted Mother is now in Heaven and although you never knew her, you can show her your greatest respect and love by following the

Faith as she did. You will thus be able to know her and be with her in Heaven.

Your Sister and Brother-in-law in America will surely receive you in their home with loving care. Consider their home as your Father's house and be respectful and modest toward them, show them your filial devotion and be attached and faithful to them, as you have always been toward us. Follow their advice and their suggestions and, whatever you may undertake, first ask them for their counsel. They will always give you the best advice and you will derive benefit therefrom, I am sure.

If you should be lucky enough to become wealthy in that distant land, do not let it make you proud and overbearing. Do not think that your energy and knowledge accumulated that wealth, but that GOD gave it to you to use it for the best purpose and for charity. Do not forget that you are also under obligation to assist your relatives and to help them to get ahead.

However, if you should not become wealthy, be satisfied with what you do have and try to be as comfortable and happy as if you had the greatest treasures.

Follow the middle way between avarice and waste. Do not be stingy, but live according to your position and your finances and be particularly liberal toward the poor, and charitable to the needy. Be glad to help and give part of your bread and give assistance to the distressed.

Do not let anybody call you a miser, but be known as a philanthropist. On the other hand, do not be extravagant or a spendthrift. Even if the necessity should occasionally rise to spend more than usual, never feel obliged to squander. It is of utmost importance that you keep your account of your expenditures and live with your income.

I am closing with the quotation:

"Do right, trust in God, and fear no man."
[signed] Joseph Rosengart
Buttenhausen, April 16th, 1846

---

ment and Napoleonic invasion. The unified synagogue-community, with its Sephardic Orthodox customs, yielded to new diversity as, historian Leon Jick notes, the immigrants "sought to recreate the traditional synagogues of their European villages." Richmond's Sephardic-rite Beth Shalome of 1789 was joined by Bavarian Beth Ahabah in 1841 and Prussian Keneseth Israel in 1856. In Charleston, Posen Jews founded Beth Sholom in 1852, which followed "the Polish *Miniek* [custom]."[34]

American Jews were inconsistent in their religious behavior. Charleston's Beth Elohim's new sanctuary in 1840 included an organ, which provoked a schism, but retained Hebrew services and gender-segregated seating. Immigrant rabbis felt shocked at what they found. Abraham Rice, America's first certifiably ordained rabbi, wrote after arriving in Baltimore, "The character of religious life in this country is on the lowest level."[35] As impoverished immigrants, the German Jews' first need was ensuring their security, not creating religious institutions. Their diverse national origins worked against cohesion. Besides the question of reform, tensions arose whether to be American or to hold to German culture. These problems were exacerbated by a Jewish population scattered across a vast landscape.

As Jews Americanized, they shed their European patronage. In America, Reform progressed rapidly and broadly, growing more extreme even as it backtracked in Europe. With their ties to Baltimore, North Carolina Jews by 1860 would have encountered all the possibilities open to American Jews from radical Reform to traditional Orthodoxy. Rabbi Henry Hochheimer of Baltimore's Fells Point Hebrew Friendship Congregation, whose marriage register records North Carolina weddings, was a moderate reformer with a Ph.D. from the University of Munich.

For those who wanted to affirm Jewish peoplehood outside religious bonds, a fraternal organization, B'nai B'rith (Sons of the Covenant), formed in 1843 to promote "Benevolence, Brotherly Love, and Harmony." Its mission statement called for "uniting Israelites" and for performing charity "on the broadest principles of humanity." B'nai B'rith connected communities in a national network and advocated for Jewish interests. It became a "secular synagogue." After abortive efforts in 1841 and 1855 to unite the nation's synagogues, in 1859 a Board of Delegates of American Israelites, borrowing its name from the British body, organized. Jews acted after President Buchanan responded indifferently to Jewish appeals after the kidnapping and baptizing of an Italian Jewish child, Edgardo Mortara. The board, dominated by easterners, fell victim to Jewish divisions and enrolled only a fifth of the nation's congregations.[36]

Jewish communities formed as an initial peddler or storekeeper drew the critical mass to form a congregation. Rabbi Max Lilienthal of Cincinnati, who emigrated to America in 1844, observed four factors needed to organize: ten adult males for the minyan (prayer quorum); stirrings of religious feeling, often inspired by approaching High Holidays; a committed leader; and support of an outside Jewish community. Typically, the first act was to form a benevolence or burial society according to the Talmudic injunction that first comes the cemetery, then the city. This society was a Chevra Kadisha (Holy Brotherhood), a traditional institution transplanted from Europe. It took responsibility for the ritual burial of the dead by cleaning, shrouding, and attending the body. The society also arranged for prayer services and oversaw care of the needy and transients.

As the economy prospered and Jews continued arriving, the number of synagogues in America more than doubled from thirty-seven to seventy-seven in the decade after 1850. By the Civil War, 160 communities in thirty-one states and the District of Columbia claimed a Jewish institution, and Jewish newspapers listed subscribers in more than 1,000 communities, including at least 11 in North Carolina. The state's Jews were scattered, yet they remained connected to urban centers religiously just as they were economically. Such linkages are documented in meticulous Yiddish in the Record Book of a Dutch immigrant peddler, Marcus S. Polack, who from his home in Baltimore traveled as a mohel (ritual circumciser). From 1855 to 1859 Polack performed seven circumcisions in four North Carolina towns. Although not always on the eighth day as Jewish law prescribed, Hillel Weisel of Plymouth, Abraham Asher of Elizabeth City, Jacob Pragg of New Bern, and Nathaniel Kramer of Raleigh all entered the covenant of Abraham with a brit milah (circumcision ritual). Rabbi Michelbacher of Richmond, Rabbi Zechariah of Charleston, or Rabbi Hochheimer of Baltimore presided at weddings. Without a Jewish cemetery, North Carolinians sent their dead to Norfolk, Richmond, Petersburg, or Charleston for consecrated burial.[37]

Unlike in Germany, where Jews registered as members of a community, in America Jews freely chose how and whether to affiliate. By midcentury, perhaps a half became synagogue members. Concerns were expressed for Jewish survival, and calls arose for Jewish unity. Christian missionaries, well financed and organized, targeted Jews. In response, rabbis advocated "regeneration." They disagreed whether to regenerate Judaism by strengthening traditional education and observance or to reform through accommodation to modern society. By 1870 virtually every synagogue in America was instituting reforms. Issues included the length of services, wearing hats, introducing English and German worship, sitting in mixed-gender pews, and playing an organ.[38]

Jewish religious ferment fit the times. If Wilmington Jews struggled to form a congregation, so did their fellow German Christian immigrants, who did not form a Lutheran Synod until 1858. Nationally, the first half of the nineteenth century marked an era of religious turmoil and spiritual experimentation. Established churches, too, were wracked by schisms between reformers and traditionalists, natives and immigrants. New groups like the Seventh-day Adventists and Church of Latter-day Saints arose. Mordecai descendants were drawn to spiritualist movements that espoused feminism and socialism, and Lazarus children joined utopian communes advocating socialism, hydropathy, and free love.

North Carolina's religious passions tended to be evangelical. By 1860 some 80 percent of the state's congregations were either Baptist or Methodist, which appealed especially to African Americans. Women were particularly drawn to revivals, camp meetings, and missionary societies. Protestant denominations, too, endured quarrels and schisms on issues of church doctrine, authority, and slavery, but religious life remained "rigid and orthodox." Clergymen, drawn to God's word, studied Hebrew. In 1851 the *Hillsborough Recorder* reported that Professor James Seixas would teach Hebrew to ministers at a local Methodist academy. Seixas was the son of the celebrated hazzan (cantor) of New York's Shearith Israel, Gershom Seixas. An itinerant teacher of Hebrew, who was apparently a Christian convert, he authored Semitic grammars and claimed to have taught at Harvard and Andover.[39]

The nation's two leading rabbinic lights, the traditionalist Isaac Leeser and the reformer Isaac Mayer Wise, encouraged the state's Jews to organize under their banners. The German-born Leeser had come to America in 1824 as a teenager, settling first in Richmond, where Jacob Mordecai served as his religious mentor. He advocated an American Jewish "regeneration."[40] Called as hazzan to Mikveh Israel in Philadelphia, he stood for tradition but introduced English sermons and supported a Sunday School. With the example of Christian evangelicals, he embarked on a prodigious program translating the Hebrew Bible into English, establishing a Jewish Publication Society, and founding a monthly journal, the *Occident*, which circulated internationally.

Hungarian-born Isaac Mayer Wise advocated moderate Reform. In 1857 he published his prayer book *Minhag Amerika* hoping that a distinctly American Judaism would unify the nation's Jews. Wise crafted a modern liturgy by abridging the service and including German and English translations. He intended to "reconcile Judaism with the age and its needs."[41] From Cincinnati Wise embarked on a busy travel schedule and published two weeklies, the *Israelite* in English and *Die Deborah* in German. In 1850 he visited Wilmington.

Touring the South in 1846, Leeser reported in the *Occident* that "many individuals are scattered in the towns of eastern North Carolina, Newbern, Elizabeth City, Edenton, &c." and encouraged them to create a synagogue in Norfolk. As midcentury approached and Jews streamed into American harbors, efforts began nationally to create institutions to serve religious needs and unify the community. "Synagogues," Leeser wrote in 1848, were "springing up as if by magic," and he questioned why North Carolina's Jews had not yet acted.[42]

In 1852 a Chevra Kadisha organized in Wilmington, later taking the name True Brothers Society. That year the *Wilmington Journal* called upon the city to establish a public cemetery and cited as models "the Jewish and other . . . races." When the city's Oakdale Cemetery opened, it included a Jewish section. On March 6, 1855, Isaac Leeser came from Philadelphia to dedicate it. The audience included "about twenty Israelites and at least two hundred of other persuasions." In the *Occident*, Leeser appealed to Wilmington's Jews to look beyond the cemetery:

> We have spoken with several gentlemen residents of this, the largest place in North Carolina, and they informed us that they had worship during the fall holy days, . . . it would afford us sincere pleasure could we announce to our readers that they had fully organized, and secured the services of a pious minister.[43]

On 2 August 1860 Wilmington Jews placed an ad in the *Hebrew Leader* of New York for a "Hazen, Schocket, Mohel" (cantor, ritual slaughterer, and a circumciser). Charlotte's Jews, too, began organizing even as a war raged. A notice in the 1863 *Western Democrat* reports on the Jewish New Year that "all business will be abstained from" and worship will be "properly conducted between the hours of 5 a.m. and 1 p.m."

One festering issue for North Carolina Jews was the constitutional religious test that limited public office to Christians. In 1845, writing in the *Occident*, Isaac Leeser observed the spread of "Jewish Emancipation" across the globe, hailing the removal of political disqualifications for public office but then noting "in North Carolina they are eligible to none whatever." He feared that North Carolina's example "may perhaps be used as an argument in other countries" to deny Jews political rights, particularly in Britain, which was debating a Jew Bill. At the cemetery dedication, Leeser had urged Jews and Christians to act to end this "disgrace to a state."[44]

In 1858 a legislative committee considered a bill to remove the article that "prohibited persons of the Jewish or Israelitish faith from holding offices." It called

Wilmington's Jewish cemetery, dedicated in 1855. (New Hanover County Public Library)

the test "a relic of bigotry and intolerance" but did not believe the legislature had the authority to alter or amend the constitution. The *Wilmington Journal* again objected: "This is not a matter which concerns simply the few persons of Jewish faith within our borders. It is a matter which concerns the reputation of the State of North Carolina." It added, "Jews pay taxes and are liable to perform all civil duties."[45]

Isaac Leeser beat the drum harder. "Several Israelites," as they signed themselves, sent petitions to each legislative candidate asking, "Will you, if elected, use your influence to remove the odious disability clause in the Constitution, which excludes the Jewish citizens of the State from holding offices of profit and trust?" Not one replied. S. A. Cohen of Charlotte wrote to the *Charlotte Bulletin* chastising the candidates for deferring to "the illiberal and biased few opposed to Judaism." The *Charlotte Bulletin* agreed and called on the governor to grant "full and equal rights to all good citizens, whether they be Protestants, Romanists, or Jews." In the legislature, Mr. Crumpler of Ashe County answered with an anti-Semitic tirade: Jews were cheats, unfair in their dealings, financial parasites who produce nothing. Cohen, "one of the Reviled," responded that Jews were obedient citizens. He noted, as civil war threatened, that "should she need the services of her sons in the present crisis, Jews will be found among those battling for her rights and institutions."[46]

In 1861, when a convention met in Raleigh to secede from the Union, a new constitution had to be ratified. A motion to preserve the Christian qualification passed 84 to 22. Asa Biggs, a former congressman and federal judge, countered with a motion to eliminate all religious tests. It failed 69 to 33.

SERVICE OF HER SONS IN THE CIVIL WAR

North Carolinians did not rush to secede from the Union or to fight a war. Unionist sentiment was strong, particularly in the mountains and among Piedmont Quakers. The public attitude, a Raleigh newspaper wrote, was "watch and wait." North Carolina with its yeoman farmers was not a slave society to the extent of its sister southern states. Its people rejected an initial call to secession in a referendum. Not until after Fort Sumter and Lincoln's call for troops to quell the rebellion did the state's secessionists prevail. Although the last of eleven states to secede, North Carolina contributed about a fifth of the Confederate forces and suffered more casualties than any other state. About 130,000 Tar Heels served— by one estimate, 97 percent of the state's eligible men—with some 20,000 dying in battle and another 20,000 falling to disease. Jews were as divided as other Americans on the war. An estimated 10,000 Jews fought in the war, about 2,000 for the Confederacy.[47]

Major Alfred Mordecai, commander of the Watervliet Arsenal in upstate New York, equivocated. Governor John Ellis urged him to resign and return to his native state. Confederate president Jefferson Davis offered him command of the Corps of Artillery. "How I wish he would join the Southern army," his sister Emma wrote nine days after Sumter. His nephews, including abolitionist Marx Lazarus, flocked to the Confederate standard, while his banker brother George financed the war effort. His son Alfred Jr., West Point class of 1823, was commissioned a Union officer. Pressed to defend the family honor, Alfred resigned from the United States Army in 1861, not wanting to "forge arms" against "his aged mother, brothers and sisters in the south."[48] With his northern-born wife, he sat out the war as a teacher of mathematics.

North Carolina Jews were swept in the war fever. Most were young German immigrants only a few years in the state. Louis Leon and his five New York friends, clerks at Wittkowsky's store, enrolled in the Charlotte Grays, whose first lieutenant was E. B. Cohen. Herman Weil, who spoke broken English after three years in America, was among the first to enlist in Goldsboro. Six days after Fort Sumter, Leopold Oettinger joined the Wilson Light Infantry. In Whiteville, Jacob Bamberger, a Bavarian-born storekeeper two years in North Carolina, was elected a first lieutenant in the Columbus Light Infantry. Wilmington Jews contributed some fifteen soldiers. In 1861 Charlotte's nine Jewish families sent eleven soldiers into the First North Carolina Regiment, and "the Jewish ladies" collected $150 to "assist Confederate volunteers." Town commissioners passed a resolution "testifying to the uniform kindness and liberality which has ever characterized the entire Jewish population of our town . . . for upbuilding the equal rights of the South," though still unfairly disqualified from office.[49]

Perhaps seventy-five Jewish North Carolinians served the Confederacy. Adjutant Isaac Hymans of the North Carolina 39th Regiment received the Confederate Roll of Honor, its highest award, for "courage and good conduct on the field of battle."[50] Dr. Simon Baruch directed a Confederate hospital at Thomasville. Judah Benjamin, raised in Wilmington and Fayetteville, was a confidant of Jefferson Davis and served the Confederacy as its first attorney general and later as secretaries of war and state.

The Civil War pitted Jew against Jew. The midwestern and northeastern Union regiments that occupied North Carolina contained hundreds of Jewish soldiers. In spring 1864, Major Louis Gratz, arriving with Sherman's army, was appointed acting assistant inspector general. A Bavarian immigrant, Dr. Nathan Mayer, a surgeon, had served at Antietam and Fredericksburg before his capture at Plymouth in 1864. He was paroled to Foster General Hospital in New Bern. Although

Jacob Bamberger, a
German immigrant and
Confederate officer.
(David Marblestone)

afflicted with yellow fever, he stemmed an epidemic through the use of calomel and castor oil. When the Union army occupied New Bern, Dr. Mayer was given charge of U.S. military stores in eastern North Carolina with the rank of brigadier general. In 1865 he left for Hartford, Connecticut, where his father served as rabbi.[51]

With Charleston, Savannah, Mobile, and New Orleans either occupied or blockaded, Wilmington was the Confederate "smuggler's den." The Wilmington & Weldon Railroad became the "lifeline of the Confederacy," as supplies traveled from the port to Lee's Army of Northern Virginia. From 1862 to 1863, some 585 sleek, high-powered steamships outran the Yankee fleet to Bermuda and Nassau, two or three departing daily. Blockade running was not a wholly patriotic activity, for southern cotton commanded high prices in France and England, and imported goods were sold at a premium. In 1864 a pound of tea went for $500. The number of Jewish merchants in Wilmington grew by one-half from 1860 to 1865. The Confederate War Department's local mercantile agent was J. M. Seixas of Charleston. He negotiated with the blockade-runners and kept the port supplied with coal and cotton. Another Charlestonian, Nathaniel Jacobi, served as the quartermaster's chief clerk. Governor Vance authorized Solomon Bear to purchase goods abroad as a state agent. Bear had fought with Wilmington's German volunteers but, discharged for ill health, embarked on blockade-running. E. Solomon and Company sent tobacco to Europe and returned with manufactured goods. The enterprise was risky. Kahnweiler and Company suffered grievous losses when its cargoes were lost.[52]

Harper's Weekly reported that Wilmington in the war years "swarmed with foreigners, Jew and Gentile. In fact, going down the main street or along the river you might well imagine you were journeying from Jerusalem to Jericho." Another resident recalled, "Jews swarmed there from far and near, like flies around the bung of a sugar cask . . . The worthies owned no allegiance, except to Moses, and consequently they were exempt from military service." As prices rose exorbitantly, Jews north and south were accused of profiteering. Such anti-Semitic allegations were belied by the Jews' war service. As wartime shortages and inflation exacerbated social tensions, Jews were available as scapegoats, most notably in U. S. Grant's notorious General Order No. 11, which expelled Jews from Mississippi, Tennessee, and Kentucky for allegedly "unprincipled" black-market cotton trading. Union major general Benjamin Butler complained about "five Jews were captured trying to run the blockade."[53]

Two Jewish soldiers in North Carolina units, Louis Leon and Albert Moses Luria, kept journals that express southern patriotism. Leon, from Charlotte, records the "life of the man behind the gun." Leon had first lived in New York City, where his parents still resided, before heading south with his brothers. His *Diary of a Tar Heel Confederate Soldier* records, with some humor, his early struggles to transform himself from clerk to soldier. A deadly shot, he served on the front lines as a sharpshooter. His diary details the drudgery of sloughing through mud, bivouacking under rain and snow, and marching bone-wearying miles. His battles included Gettysburg and the Wilderness, where he was captured. The last eleven months were spent in a federal stockade in Elmira, New York, where smallpox proved deadlier than bullets. On April 25, 1865, he took the "cursed" oath of allegiance to the United States, and after visiting his parents in New York, headed south.[54]

Jewish soldiers were a band of brothers. Leon's comrades included fellow Charlotteans Aaron and Jacob Katz, and he formed a two-man patrol to hunt deserters with Si Wolf. In camp he visited Donau, Langfried, Etlinger, and Oppenheim and went hunting in Kinston for bacon and cornbread with Wortheim. After each battle, he searched for his brother Morris, serving in a Georgia regiment. Leon confirmed that Robert E. Lee granted furloughs for Jewish soldiers during the High Holidays in 1863 and 1864.

Although German born and few years in the South, Leon wrote as a native son. "I care not how weary or hungry we were," he recalled as "our father" General Lee passed the marching troops, "when we saw him we gave that Rebel yell, and hunger and wounds would be forgotten." Not once did he mention "slavery," although he vented racist feelings toward the black soldiers who escorted him to prison. Unbothered by kosher laws, he enjoyed chasing a pig for slaughter. His comrades included Christians as well as Jews, and he regretted that 1862 was a "hard Christmas."[55]

Luria's diary, with its classical and literary allusions, speaks the voice of an acculturated southerner. His father Raphael Moses, a Georgia planter and lawyer, was a proud Jew and Confederate. Descended from early Savannah settlers, Luria had adopted his mother's maiden name in pride of her Sephardic heritage. He had enrolled in the Hillsboro Military Academy in 1858 and was appointed sergeant in a North Carolina regiment. At a Norfolk battle, Luria picked up a live Union shell and smothered the burning fuse. He declined promotion for heroism, wanting only to prove himself in battle. Luria shows little Jewish awareness although he was moved when his Orthodox family came to a Georgia train depot to see him depart: "I did not anticipate seeing them for as it was Saturday. I knew they could not ride." His parents visited him when he drilled troops in Weldon.[56]

Luria was an Old South Jew, but what could have motivated the more typical Jewish Confederates who were German immigrants but few years in the South? Indeed, many had fled their homelands to avoid conscription in the German

STORY: A CONFEDERATE DIARY

These excerpts are drawn from Louis Leon's Diary of a Tar Heel Confederate Soldier. *Leon enlisted in the Charlotte Grays even before North Carolina seceded from the Union. His regiment went first to Raleigh and then to Richmond before encamping in Yorktown, Virginia.*

April 25 [1861]—The day after we got here our company was sent out with spades and shovels to make breastworks—and to think of the indignity! We were expected to do the digging! Why, of course, I never thought that this was work for soldiers to do, but we had to do it. Gee! What hands I had after a few days' work. I know I never had a pick or a shovel in my hand to work with in my life.

A few days after that a squad of us were sent out to cut down trees, and, by George! they gave me an axe and told me to go to work. Well, I cut all over my tree until the lieutenant commanding, seeing how nice I was marking it, asked me what I had done before I became a soldier. I told him I was a clerk in a dry-goods store. He said he thought so from the way I was cutting timber. He relieved me—but what insults are put on us who came to fight the Yankees! Why, he gave me two buckets and told me to carry water to the men that could cut.

September 27 [1862]—Up to to-day nothing new, only to-day is my New Year (the Jewish New Year).

July 1 [1863]—. . . We got to Gettysburg at 1 P.M., 15 miles. We were drawn up in a line of battle about one mile south of town, and a little to the left of the Lutheran Seminary. We then advanced to the enemy's line of battle in double quick time. We had not gotten more than 50 paces when Nor-

man of our company fell dead by my side. Katz was going to pick him up. I stopped him, as it is strictly forbidden for anyone to help take the dead or wounded off the field except the ambulance corps. We then crossed over a rail fence, where our Lieutenant McMatthews and Lieutenant Alexander were both wounded. That left us with a captain and one lieutenant. After this we got into battle in earnest, and lost in our company very heavily, both killed and wounded. This fight lasted four hours and a half, when at last we drove them clear out of town, and took at least 3,000 prisoners. They also lost very heavily in killed and wounded, which all fell into our hands. After the fight our company was ordered to pick up all straggling Yankees in town, and bring them together to be brought to the rear as prisoners. One fellow I took up could not speak one word of English, and the first thing he asked me in German was "Will I get my pay in prison?" After we had them all put in a pen we went to our regiment and rested. Major Iredell, of our regiment, came to me and shook my hand, and also complimented me for action in the fight. At dusk I was about going to hunt up my brother Morris, when he came to me. Thank God, we are both safe as yet. We laid all night among the dead Yankees, but they did not disturb our peaceful slumbers.

September 2 [1863]—On a hunt to-day several of my comrades with myself came to a house, and the first thing we heard was, "Is there a Jew in your detachment that caught a deserter yesterday?" They would like to see him, etc. At last one of the boys told them that I was the Jew. After that I had a very good time there, and in fact wherever I went I was received very kindly, and was very sorry to see on the 4th that orders came for us to return to our brigade.

September 29 [1863]—All quiet to-day. Brother Morris returned from Richmond yesterday, where he has been for ten days on a furlough. Before our Jewish New Year there was an order read out from General Lee granting a furlough to each Israelite to go to Richmond for the holidays if he so desired. I did not care to go.

April 3 [1864]—I have not heard from my parents since the war, they living in New York, I thought I would send a personal advertisement to a New York paper to let them know that my brother and myself are well, and for them to send an answer through the Richmond paper. I gave this to a Yankee picket, who promised me he would send it to New York.

April [1865]—On the morning of the 12th we heard that Lee had surrendered on the 9th, and about 400, myself with them, took the cursed oath and were given transportation to wherever we wanted to go. I took mine to New York City to my parents, whom I have not seen since 1858. Our cause is lost; our comrades who have given their lives for the independence of the South have died in vain; that is, the cause for which they gave their lives is lost, but they positively did not give their lives in vain. They gave it for a most righteous cause, even if the Cause was lost. . . . When I commenced this diary of my life as a Confederate soldier I was full of hope for the speedy termination of the war, and our independence. I was not quite nineteen years old. I am now twenty-three. The four years that I have given to my country I do not regret, nor am I sorry for one day that I have given—my only regret is that we have lost that for which we fought.[1]

1. L. Leon, *Diary of a Tar Heel Confederate Soldier* (Charlotte: Stone Publishing, 1913). The complete text is also available online at http://docsouth.unc.edu/fpn/leon/summary.html.

army.[57] In contrast to Luria, who came from a plantation family, they had no reason to defend slavery.

Young Jewish men, like other southerners, were swept by fever for an adventure that promised to be short and glorious. For a store clerk, a sizable bounty sweetened the excitement. Leon enlisted at first for six months "full of hope for the speedy termination of the war." He noted, "We are all boys between the ages of eighteen and twenty-one." Traveling to Raleigh, he reported, "Our trip was full of joy and pleasure, for at every station where our train stopped the ladies showered us with flowers and Godspeed." Leon noted southern ladies "know how to treat their soldiers." Luria felt his duty to protect southern womanhood from violation by a "band of ruffians."[58] Their manly virtue was at stake. That sense of honor transcended Judaism.

The language of rebellion was couched in the rhetoric of republicanism. Two

Louis Leon, author of *Diary of a Tar Heel Confederate.*
(North Carolina Collection, University of North Carolina
Library at Chapel Hill)

persistent themes in both Luria's and Leon's writings are a defense of homeland and a resistance to tyranny. German Jewish immigrants recalled their own 1848 Revolution, when liberty's promise was crushed by a monarchial reaction. As southerners who had breathed "the free air of Dixie," they were defending their fatherland from, as Luria wrote, "the dominion of a military despot." Luria excoriated "that driveling, baubling fool, Abraham Lincoln." Like other southerners, Jews argued theirs was a morally justifiable war. Luria asserted, "My life, happiness, health and fortune, for a defensive war! Not a blow nor a cent for an *offensive* war!!"[59]

North Carolina expended its blood and treasure reluctantly but at great cost, bankrupting itself and sacrificing 40,000 of its youth. The federal army occupied the coast in 1861–62 and launched raids into the interior. Wilmington held out until 1865, when its bulwark Fort Fisher fell in a blood fest. In the mountains and Piedmont, where federalist sentiment was strong, hundreds died, and homes and farms were burned. Union soldiers raiding the home of David and Isaac Wallace in Statesville during Passover were disgruntled to find not bread

Albert Moses Luria,
"bravest of the brave,"
fell at Seven Pines.
(Raphael J. Moses)

but matzo, which they tossed away as just "more hard tack." General Sherman, battling through North Carolina, accepted the surrender of General Joe Johnston outside Durham in April 1865, shortly after Appomattox, thus ending the war. "Contraband," former slaves, crossed into Union lines by the thousands, creating encampments across eastern North Carolina.[60]

Facing defeat, Jews remained die-hard Confederates. On May 13, 1865, federal cavalry surrounded Governor Vance's home in Statesville. A Union guard was to escort Vance on muleback thirty-five miles to Salisbury to board a train for a federal prison in Washington. To save the corpulent governor from indignity, Samuel Wittkowsky, a local hatter, offered to drive Vance in his carriage. The Prussian-born Wittkowsky cheered the despondent governor and thus began a lifelong friendship.[61] When the Confederate government fled Richmond for Charlotte, Major Abram Weill, a Confederate agent, sheltered Varina Davis, the president's wife, and Judah Benjamin, after others had refused.

By one count, about thirty North Carolina Jews died for the Confederacy. The Soldier's Section of the Hebrew Cemetery in Richmond holds the bodies of North Carolina Confederates M. Aaron and G. Wolfe. Seven more lie buried in the prison camp cemetery in Elmira, New York. At Seven Pines in the Peninsula campaign, a year after enlisting, Leopold Oettinger, twenty-one, was killed. In that battle, Albert Luria grabbed the Confederate colors from a fallen soldier to rally his troops and was shot in the head. His father, Major Moses, found him dying in a field hospital. On his grave was placed the smothered shell on which his comrades engraved, "The pride of his Regiment and the bravest of the brave."[62]

"And the end of all is a desolated home to go to," Leon wrote in his final entry.[63] Captain Jacob Roessler of the 40th North Carolina Infantry, wounded in the arm during the Wilderness battle, left the service incapacitated. After three years of fighting, Jacob Bamberger, hospitalized after Fort Fisher, walked away from the Confederate army and kept traveling until he reached Kansas. Louis Leon returned to Charlotte to open a store. Active in both the B'nai B'rith Lodge and Confederate reunions, he died in 1919 at a United Daughters of the Confederacy soldiers' home in Wilmington and was buried in Charlotte's Hebrew Cemetery.

RECONSTRUCTING NORTH CAROLINA

At war's end, southern and northern Jews resumed relations as if a war had not been fought. Louis Leon's situation, with his parents in New York and his brothers in the South, was typical. Family and business ties remained unbroken. Nor did Jewish organizations break into southern and northern divisions as did the Baptist, Methodist, and Presbyterian bodies. The Board of Delegates of American Israelites remained apolitical. B'nai B'rith ignored the conflict. Eight years after the war, Isaac Mayer Wise inspired lay leaders to form a Union of American Hebrew Congregations that paid no heed to a Mason-Dixon line.[64]

North Carolinians acted after the war as if they had never left the Union. The new president Andrew Johnson, born in Raleigh, called upon the state to renounce secession, cancel the Confederate debt, and ratify the Thirteenth Amendment abolishing slavery. "With more than 350,000 newly freed slaves," historian Milton Ready writes, "North Carolina now had to adjust to an expanded concept of citizenship and civil rights that challenged older prejudicial beliefs and values that had been a part of a folk culture for centuries."[65] Among those prejudices was the constitutional requirement that only Christians qualified for public office.

Democrats, constituting a Confederate party, dominated North Carolina politics and wanted the state to hold to its prewar "first principles." In the 1865 election, they won handily. In conflict with their federally appointed governor, William Holden, and a U.S. Congress dominated by Radical Republicans, the legislature resisted efforts to require ex-Confederates to take loyalty oaths to the Union. In 1866, to regulate social relations with newly freed slaves, the state passed restrictive black codes.[66]

Even as Jews fought and sometimes died in defense of North Carolina, they were still constitutionally denied the right to public office. Compared to the racial challenge, the religious test paled. When a state constitutional convention met in Raleigh in 1865, Isaac Leeser assumed that North Carolina had conceded the issue, but the state held to its first principles. In July 1866 the executive committee of the Board of Delegates of American Israelites, meeting in New York, sent a letter "To the friends of Religious Liberty in the State of North Carolina." It warned, "Adopt this and North Carolina will be and continue as she is now the only State in the Union that denies religious liberty to her citizens." A second letter from board president Abraham Hart to the U.S. Congress protested an oath that required the state's constitutional convention delegates to "swear on the holy Evangelists of Almighty God."[67]

In September 1866 Leeser admitted failure: "[T]he only remedy is by agitation. . . . We have already spoken to resident Israelites on the subject and we are confident that it will not be allowed to lie dormant. Not that we care for Jews holding office, but for the principle." In fact, the people voted down the 1865 constitution although the religious test had no bearing. Finally, in 1868, under congressional mandate to create a new, racially egalitarian constitution, a state convention met. A Radical Republican majority of scalawags (white antisecessionists), carpetbaggers (northern settlers), and African American freedmen produced a progressive document that granted citizenship and civil rights to 350,000 former slaves, restored the vote to ex-Confederates, reformed county government, and mandated free public education. The religious test died without debate. Only those who "shall deny the Being of Almighty God" were disqualified."[68]

Leeser's claim that Jews did not aspire to public office was not wholly true. When a Democratic Club formed in Wilmington in 1863, at least six prominent Jews joined. In 1865 Abram Weill accepted the post of Charlotte alderman, helping to write the city's postwar charter. The Reconstructionist government in 1867 appointed to the Wilson town council Emil Rosenthal, a German-born peddler who had arrived two years earlier. In 1870 the storekeeper was elected to the seat. Jews who sought office mostly identified with the Democrats, the party of Vance. In 1878 Vance's friend Samuel Wittkowsky served as a Charlotte alderman. Solomon Fishblate, who had moved from Fayetteville to Wilmington in 1869, was an "unreliable" merchant whose store was closed by sheriff's order two years later. Yet in 1873 he was elected to a four-year term as alderman; then in 1878, he was elected to a three-year term as mayor as a Conservative. Wilmington's Germans and Jews, fearing Republicans and black rule, aligned with Conservative pro-business forces. When a rumor spread in 1868 that Maurice Bear had voted the Radical ticket, he denounced the "infamous" lie to the *Daily Journal* and swore that he had "voted the white man's ticket." His hostility to Republicans overrode his interest in Jewish rights. Henry Weil in Goldsboro was pleased to report in 1874 that "the whole democratic ticket was elected."[69]

The elections of 1868, the first under the new state constitution, saw blacks and white northerners win local posts, join juries, and even attend school together. Ex-Confederates, inspired by movements in Tennessee and Georgia, organized a Ku Klux Klan in opposition. From 1867 to 1869 the Klan engaged in a terror campaign of murder, beatings, and whippings—primarily against blacks but also against white Republicans—before fading. After several years of Radical Republican rule, Democrats were firmly in control by 1870 when the state rejoined the union. Slavery was replaced by tenancy and sharecropping, which left blacks—and poor whites, too—in virtual bondage to the planter who owned his home, implements, and farm plot. When Reconstruction ended in 1877, African Americans had made progress in politics, education, landownership, and entrepreneurship, but white racial social and economic dominance reasserted itself.

Jews were caught in the turmoil. In 1869 Solomon Fishblate, then a New York peddler traveling by train, quarreled with a man in Kinston who fired a gun at him, the bullet passing through his jacket. David Cohen, a storekeeper in Whitakers involved in cotton lawsuits, was murdered in 1874. Louis Weill served as town marshal of Monroe. The newspaper described him as a man of "good character," and the credit agent reported that he was "right popular." In 1877, "persistently set upon" by a robber who entered his store, he shot the man dead. Weill was taken to court, where "unacquainted with the laws [he] submitted his case with hardly a defense." Pleading guilty to manslaughter, he was sentenced to the penitentiary. Rockingham County citizens, including the judge and attorneys, petitioned for his pardon, which Governor Vance granted, claiming that he had never heard of a criminal Israelite.[70]

Although some Jews shared southern political fears of "darkeys," as one Goldsboro Jew wrote, others solicited black trade. Moses Pragg in New Bern "is very popular as a merchant with the colored people who trade extensively with him," while William Harris of Wilson is a "low jew" who "does a mongrel trade with negroes & the lowest characters." This Jew, an agent complained, "is no more than a 'carpet bag.'" Harris lived in Wilson County, a Klan stronghold. When northern white missionaries and philanthropists established St. Augustine's College and Shaw University in Raleigh for blacks, Michael and Regina Grausman sponsored the education of their employees' daughters, who were counted among the state's first African American nurses.[71]

After the war the foundations of the slaveholding plantation aristocracy crumbled, and African Americans held equal political rights. The racial, social, and political place of Jews was not yet fixed. While anti-Semites cast doubts on the Jews as a race—the leading southern anthropologist Josiah Nott suggested that Jews were "very mixed"—their defenders lavishly praised Jews as an ancient, pure white people who were flesh and blood of the Savior. About 1868 Zebulon Vance, governor and future U.S. senator, composed a philo-Semitic speech, "The Scattered Nation," which was delivered from lecterns and reprinted in newspapers across the nation into the twentieth century. Vance, a powerful orator, composed his speech to refute "objections to the Jew as a citizen." His motive is frequently ascribed to his gratitude to Samuel Wittkowsky's courtesies at war's end; but Vance, like southerners generally, was biblically learned, and the Old Testament shaped his rhetoric and worldview. In 1864 he had described war-weary North Carolinians as a "suffering and much oppressed Israel." "The Scattered Nation" was a notable example of a philo-Semitism commonplace in journalism and on the lecture circuit in the racially unsettled years between 1850 and 1915. Colonel A. M. Waddell of Wilmington in 1875 proclaimed of the Jews, "Prosperity has no height which that nation has not scaled . . . modern civilization owes it much."[72] A notable later example was Mark Twain's 1898 *Harper's* essay, "Concerning the Jews."

Vance considered the Jewish question from the perspectives of both scripture and an emerging racial science. In "The Scattered Nation," Vance lavishly praises the Jews as "remarkable." He admits that as a mercantilist the Jew has "serious" faults, which he attributes to Christian bigotry. He exalts Jews for their morality,

TEXT: "THE SCATTERED NATION"

Zebulon Vance, governor and U.S. senator, was a nationally prominent orator. His most popular speech was "The Scattered Nation," a soaring defense of the Jews, which he revised decades after its first delivery around 1868. It belongs to a genre of philo-Semitic writings that owes much to Victorian romantic nationalism. Benjamin Disraeli, Sir Walter Scott, George Eliot, and, later, Mark Twain wrote similarly of the Jews' ancient and modern glory.

The Jews are our spiritual fathers, the authors of our morals, the founders of our civilization with all the power and dominion arising therefrom. . . .

There are objections to the Jew as a citizen; many objections; some true and some false, some serious and some trivial. It is said that industrially he produces nothing, invents nothing, adds nothing to the public wealth . . . that he merely *sojourns* in the land but does not *dwell* in it . . . but I submit the fault is not his, even here. . . . These habits he learned by persecution.

The Christian is simply the successor of the Jew—the glory of the one is likewise the glory of the other. The Saviour of the world was, after the flesh, a Jew—born of a Jewish maiden; so likewise were all of the apostles and first propagators of Christianity. The Christian religion is equally Jewish with that of Moses and the prophets. . . . We owe to him, if not the conception, at least the preservation of pure monotheism. . . .

Many curious facts concerning them are worthy to be noted. . . . [T]he length of the trunk is much greater with the Jew, in proportion to height than with other races. In the Negro the trunk constitutes 32 per cent of the height of the whole body, in the European 34 per cent., in the Jew 36 per cent. What these physical peculiarities have had to do with their wonderful preservation and steady increase, I leave for the philosophers to explain. . . .

I think it may be truthfully said that there is more of average wealth, intelligence, and morality among the Jewish people than there is among any other nation of equal numbers in the world! If this be true—if it be half true—when we consider the circumstances under which it has all been brought about, it constitutes in the eyes of thinking men the most remarkable moral phenomenon ever exhibited by any portion of the human family. . . .

That the Jew—meaning the *class*—is dishonest, I believe to be an atrocious calumny; and, considering that we derive all of our notions of rectitude from the Jew, who first taught the world that command, "Thou shalt not steal," and "Thou shalt not bear false witness," we pay ourselves a shabby compliment by befouling our teachers. . . .

I have stood on the summit of the very monarch of our great Southern Alleghanies and have seen the night flee away before the chariot wheels of the God of day. . . . So may the real spirit of Christ yet be so triumphantly infused amongst those who profess to obey his teachings, that with one voice and one hand they will stay the persecutions and hush the sorrows of these their wondrous kinsmen, put them forward into the places of honor and the homes of love where all the lands in which they dwell, shall be to them as was Jerusalem to their fathers.[1]

1. Maurice Weinstein, ed., *Zebulon B. Vance and "The Scattered Nation"* (Charlotte: Wildacres Press, 1995), 68, 81–82, 88, 89, 92–93.

charity, and perseverance. Politically, he roots the origins of democratic, representative government in Israelite society. Racially, Vance speaks of Hebrews as white persons, his "wondrous kinsmen." Citing authorities, he argues that Jews are a Semitic race, closer in height and width to Europeans than to Africans. He is outraged that civilized Jews, flesh of the Lord, should suffer prejudice as if they were uncivilized, barbaric Africans. Vance describes a hierarchy of Jews from the "lowest," least intelligent Arab Asians, to the "Talmudical" North African East Europeans, to the most "intelligent and civilized" Central and West Europeans, who "have become simply Unitarians or Deists." In short, the Eurocentric Vance places German Reform Jews, whom he would have known best, atop the Jewish race (although Wittkowsky was Polish born).

Vance's anthropology, by modern standards, is nonsensical, but for the state's Jews "The Scattered Nation" was much beloved. Wilmington's Jewish youth presented the governor with a silver-headed cane; Asheville's B'nai B'rith helped dedicate a Vance monument; and Wittkowsky delivered an emotional tribute at Vance's funeral in 1894. "The Scattered Nation," and the Jewish enthusiasm for it, points to a popular anti-Semitism that needed refutation.

NEW MIGRATIONS

After a lull in the 1870s, German immigration again swelled. Between the Civil War and World War I, some 70,000 more German Jews arrived, joined by other Central and Eastern European Jews. By 1880 an estimated 230,000 to 300,000 Jews lived in America. This wave differed markedly from the earlier German migration. In 1861 Bavaria had rescinded its anti-Jewish restrictions. With the founding of the German Empire in 1871, Jews were granted equal rights. Economically, the market and Industrial Revolution improved the Jews' position, and they moved from villages into cities, entering the middle class. Peddlers opened stores, and storekeepers became merchants and industrialists. Educated in the public schools, and increasingly in the universities, younger Jews acculturated as Germans.[73] In contrast to the earlier migration of single young men, more young women arrived. The pushing factors of poverty and state-sponsored discrimination abated, although forced military conscription—three years in the oppressive Prussian army—continued to motivate young Jews to leave Germany, as it did Christians. Nor did Jews, despite their civil rights and economic prosperity, find social acceptance. Political anti-Semitism struck Germany in the 1870s, provoking riots. Pulling Jews to America was the family chain.

As immigration worked its way into Eastern Europe in the 1870s, Jewish migrants from Posen and West Prussia were so "massive" that their Jewish populations declined by a half. In American communities, tensions rose between "Polishers," poorer artisans and peddlers, and the earlier arriving Bavarians, who were acculturated Americans. Most immigrants settled in the East Coast ports of Baltimore, Boston, New York, and Philadelphia, while Chicago and San Francisco also gained. In 1867 the North German Lloyd Steamship Line forged a link to the B&O Railroad. Ships carrying lumber and tobacco to Bremen returned to Baltimore with immigrants. Other steamship lines followed, and the city became a debarkation point for German Jews. By 1880 Baltimore's Jewish population grew to 10,000, and the city's importance rose as an import, manufacturing, and distribution center for Jewish merchants across the mid-Atlantic and southeastern states.[74]

According to the 1870 census, of 300 identified Jews in North Carolina, 210 were born in Germany, Bavaria, or Prussia; 18 were born in Poland; and 26 were American born, of whom only 4 were native North Carolinians.[75] Even a small town typically contained a multinational mix. In 1877 Tarboro's 24 Jews listed birthplaces in Prussia, Poland, Bavaria, Alsace, Germany, and England. In the late 1870s, Durham included Polish, Bavarian, Prussian, Dutch, and American-born Jews.

In his inaugural address on July 4, 1868, Governor William Holden declared, "Let us welcome capital and immigration, furnishing as they will the indispensable means to our progress and prosperity . . . Let us receive with courtesy and kindness every citizen of the Northern or Eastern States who may cast his lot among us." The *Durham Herald* declared, "Strangers locating here every day. Come On, we have room for all who come." Such sentiments recur in the southern press. The *Goldsboro Argus* editor reflected, "In the bleak aftermath of a ruinous war, it is understandable that a community welcomed newcomers like the Weils who would put their shoulders to the wheel and help get the economy moving again." North Carolina looked north for labor, capital, machinery, and technical expertise. Immigration societies and land agencies formed across the state, advertising in newspapers and sending agents to New York. Meeting in Goldsboro in 1868, the Eastern North Carolina Immigration Association, representing eighteen counties, sent two agents to Germany. In 1874 a newly established state board of immigration declared that "kindness, sympathy and protection will be extended to all such as desire to become citizens or to invest capital among us." The underlying intent was to replace black labor with white immigrants. The effort met little success: from 1870 to 1880 the state's foreign-born rose from 3,029 to 3,742.[76]

The state remained cash poor even as production of money crops, cotton and tobacco, increased. Landowners, lacking capital to pay wages, had a labor supply in poor landless blacks and whites. Planters divided their properties for sharecropping or tenant farms. The landowner might take three-quarters of the crop if he provided seeds, stock, tools, a house, and firewood, or one-half if the tenant furnished his own provisions. The planter often operated the store where share-croppers purchased their provisions, indebting them further. By 1880 more than one-third of the state's farms were worked by tenants, although farm owner-ship also increased.[77] Sharecropping, enforced by state law, allowed planters to maintain their racial and economic dominance; for African Americans it meant poverty and white control.

The 1868 constitution, like its 1835 predecessor, spurred industrial growth, most notably railroads; but in 1870, when North Carolina rejoined the Union, the state was massively in debt from the expense of rebuilding. Daniel Tompkins, a Charlotte mill owner and publisher, preached a "gospel of salvation through manufacturing." As the *Raleigh Sentinel* put it, "The *manufacturing system*, we are convinced, is the policy now to be depended upon to relieve our State of the evils that press upon her."[78] Mill fever struck the flour, timber, and textile industries.

When Zebulon Vance hailed the Jew as a "money king," he spoke admiringly of a commercial people. As a Richmond newspaper wrote in 1866, "Where there are no Jews, there is no money to be made. . . . We hail their presence in the Southern states as an auspicious sign." Thus, the credit agent writes of Solomon Goodman of Williamston, "[B]eing a Jew he understands the handling & count-ing of money & unless he is an exception to his brother Israelites is apt to keep and turn it to good account." After the war, reports note the increasing arrival of "new men," "newcomers," and "northern men." In 1866 thirty-one new Jew-ish merchants came to the state, twenty-three of whom located in four large towns. By the late 1870s twenty-five to thirty new Jewish merchants were added annually. Jewish stores in Wilmington doubled from 1865 to 1875. Downtown re-sembled a "grand bazaar" with groceries, liquor shops, and wholesale merchants. In 1880 Jews owned seventeen of the city's dry goods establishments. By 1878 Charlotte, Goldsboro, and Wilmington all counted more than one hundred Jews. In the 1880s Jews followed westward railroad expansion to Greensboro, Hickory, and Morganton. Statesville and Asheville had nascent communities.[79]

North Carolina Jews depended on their own internal credit system through their families in Philadelphia and Baltimore, which distinguished them from other southerners. Zebulon Vance had noted, "If a Jew is broken down in business, the others set him up again." When Jonas Rosenbaum's store failed in Raleigh in 1879, with "offers of assistance from friends, he intends continuing." Jackson & Elson of Fayetteville started their Cheap John Store in 1873 with "small capital" but "were helped by their Jewish friends & seem to be d[oin]g well." Jewish sources of capi-tal were not known and thus aroused distrust. Of S. Aronson who opened a store in Warrenton in 1867, the agent noted, "You can learn more of him in Baltimore than any where else." So-called, Cheap John Stores, where a merchant rented a house or store to sell bulk goods, were often fly-by-night operations. Jews were "the doubtful floating kind." H. Friedman & Company of Gatesville "came here from New York [in 1880], sold goods for a short time, and returned again." Jacob Levy appears in Greenville, Plymouth, Lexington, and Durham.[80] The opening of a new market or factory, the extension of a rail line, or their own failure and ambition pulled Jews to new territories.

In the fifteen years after the Civil War, some twenty-three women were listed as merchants. Several were widows who continued to trade after their husbands' deaths. When Nathan Kramer died in 1861, Fanny Kramer continued doing a "pretty large business" at their Raleigh clothing store for another six years. Mrs. Isaac Oettinger was Raleigh's largest milliner. Typically, a husband put his business in his wife's name to protect his assets from creditors. In 1876 Sarah Joseph was listed as a Raleigh saloonkeeper after her husband Theodore "compromised with his creditor"; he "now does bus[iness] as ag[en]t for his wife." The Dun agents often, but not always, spoke of the practice of changing titles from husband to wife as a "swindle." Thus, Henrietta Cohen's country store in Edgecombe County was a "farce," the agent observing that "this is her race." The postwar years were hard times. Some forty-five Jewish merchants went bankrupt between 1867 and 1873, and another twenty-four in the five years following the Panic of 1873. Within one five-year period, nearly a quarter of Wilmington's Jewish merchants failed.[81]

With success, Jews broke from the ethnic credit system and integrated into the southern economy. S. A. Cohen, who owned a general store, became an investor and director of the National Bank of Charlotte as early as 1868. Herman Weil incorporated a building and loan association in 1873. By 1868 former peddler Emil Rosenthal owned $10,000 in real estate, and he "has been advancing on mortgages to farmers." Jonas Cohen of Enfield also carried "a great many old balances for farmers with the hope of collecting this Fall." Samuel Bear's three-masted schooner, the *Mary Bear*, hauled lumber and merchandise from Wilmington to Norfolk, Baltimore, and New York.[82]

Like the South itself, Jews were making the transition from the agrarian to the industrial economy. Of the 1870 investors in the North Carolina Railroad, William Myers was the fourth-largest shareholder, while Myer Myers ranked eighteenth. Wholesaler Oscar Marks manufactured mattresses in New Bern. Gustavus Rosenthal, who had started as a clerk in Wilmington and then owned a store in Raleigh, invested in the Alamance cotton mills. The Schiff brothers, who moved to Charlotte in the late 1860s, were tobacco traders, farmers, tanners, and saddlers. They partnered with non-Jews to invest in a Thomasville sawmill. Some Jews acquired genuine wealth. The Weil brothers of Goldsboro, Wittkowsky and Rintels of Charlotte, and Wallace brothers of Statesville had businesses estimated to be worth more than $100,000 before 1880. Credit agents always identified them as Jews but invariably as men of "strict integrity" and "high toned." The Dun agent reported that "no Gentile is this County c[oul]d do the bus[iness]" of the Wallace brothers.[83]

That a North Carolina newspaper in 1875 referred to "our Jewish fellow-citizens" suggests that they were accepted yet different. A credit agent described Emil Rosenthal of Tarboro in 1871 as "a Southern Jew" even as the immigrant merchant inscribed his business ledger in German, "Mit Gott!" (with God). Their social place was not fixed. A New Bern Christian expressed delight at attending a party where she "danced with all the Jews in town," including "Emanuel's longest nosed clerk." The "Germans" felt complimented by her presence.[84]

For Jews, fitting in, as it had in colonial days, meant aspiring to the middle class. Their correspondence reveals them to be cultured, informed, and well traveled. Bon mots in French dot the Weil correspondence. Mina Rosenthal attended the Wilson Collegiate Seminary for Young Ladies, where she studied mathematics and classical history. Her fiancé Henry Weil complimented her on her Hebrew and German and speculated on her French. Rebecca Cohen Drucker's autograph album includes finely penned belles lettres on "religion, virtue, and truth." Jews were a respectable people. During a Goldsboro revival in 1873, Henry Weil joined those who "went to the Methodist Church, expecting to hear some grand and eloquent speaking, it being announced the Bishop would lecture." When Kinston churches found themselves impoverished by the war, Jews helped pay for a monthly preacher.[85]

Jews aspired to a cosmopolitan high culture based on German traditions of *Bildung* and *Kultur*—education and civilization—that transcended their regionalism. At a temple benefit at the Wilmington Opera House in 1873, the Concordia Society featured Mrs. Kahnweiler and Mrs. S. R. Weil singing arias from Verdi's *Ernani* and Meyerbeer's *Robert le Diable* as well as a Professor Rueckert playing a violin obbligato. Parlor music was a popular entertainment. In 1873 Wilmington's "young men of German birth" organized the Irving Literary and Debating Association, while Tarboro hosted a debating society named for Grace Aguilar, the Anglo-Jewish novelist.[86] Subjects included the comforts of rail versus steamship travel or whether labor was more valuable than capital.

North Carolina's German Jews formed a social circle among themselves. Although Wilmington Jews never had their own neighborhood, their homes clustered in well-to-do neighborhoods, interspersed with those of elite families.

On 19 March 1878, "Danciger" reported on Jewish life in Tarboro for the newspaper Jewish South, *which was published in Atlanta.*

Tarboro is considered the prettiest town in the eastern "Old North State," and is the most prosperous of its size in the state, it is the County seat of Edgecombe and has communication by the Tar River (on which fly two steamers making regular trips between here and Washington N.C. every other day) and by the branch of the W. & W. R. R. which has its terminus here, thereby giving us all the facilities for shipping and travel that could be desired. Our main produce is cotton of which staple there is 20,000 bales on an average made every year. The population of the town is estimated to be about 2,000 of which number there are 90 yehudim [Jews], 35 adults and 25 children. There are 11 yidisha stores, three of which do the *leading* clothing business, but all are doing well, and I am glad to say are on good terms, without that *business rishes* [ill will] that is such a discredit to our co-religionists in larger places. The greatest harmony and good feelings prevail among the families and many pleasant and agreeable evenings are spent at different houses, at which our musical star Mrs. A. Whitlock delights us with her superb soprano voice, by singing for us some of her delightful songs. Only one thing we (that is your correspondent and the rest of the young men) are sadly in need of, are a few charming beautiful, and accomplished young ladies, and if there are any such among your readers who wish to make us boys happy they would confer an everlasting favor by choosing this place as their summer resort. 'For what is home without a'—sweetheart.

Henry Weil's letters describe social life with the "whole Jewish crowd" with whom they enjoyed river excursions, theatrical performances, and home card parties. The B'nai B'rith Lodge outfitted a library for reading and debates. Social columns reported "our Jewish crowd" visiting each other in Durham, Tarboro, Goldsboro, Statesville, and Wilmington. Communities organized Purim Balls, a fundraising masquerade popularized in New York in 1860. Though without a congregation, Charlotte Jews in 1873 "turned out *en masse*" for a "grand masked ball at the Central Hotel." Wilmington hosted such a ball in 1877, followed by Charlotte and Tarboro in 1878, Durham in 1887, Goldsboro in 1889, and Statesville in 1895. These ostensibly philanthropic events grew so ostentatious nationally that rabbis and others protested against their "extravagance and impropriety."[87]

Family relations survived immigration. Solomon Bear had arrived in Wilmington from Bavaria in the 1840s and was joined in 1851 by his brother Samuel. "The two kept house together until they married," a memoir recalled, and they part-

We have a Y.M.H.A. which numbers among its members all the young men, in all about 15; its object is to promote literary and social enjoyments, and to prevent us from participating in a game of *swigger* or something worse, and although started not long ago, has made splendid progress. . . . We shall in a few days have a good library for the benefit of its members, and with debates, essays, reading, etc., we spend quite a pleasant and instructive Sunday afternoon.

Zenobia Lodge, No. 235, I.O.B. B.[B'nai B'rith] gave their annual masquerade ball on the 4th, and quite a number of Yehudim from the neighboring towns participated in the unbounded enjoyment the unique masks and their actions afforded. Altogether it was a pleasant and enjoyable affair, owing to the untiring efforts of the committee of arrangements . . .

In the matrimonial line we have on the list: First, our popular friend, Mr. Sol Lipinsky to Miss Eva Whitlock, whose wedding will come off on the 11th of April . . . Next comes Mr. D. Lichtenstein to Miss Hanna Zanders, whose engagement was announced but a short time ago, and as the lady is but 15 they have concluded to wait about a year, and in the meantime enjoy the pleasures of an engagement while my friend L. can sing, "Thou art so near, etc." While I am not of an envious nature, I cannot help feeling that in a matter like the above it is better to be born lucky than—good looking.

Last night we had a very interesting service at our little *shule*, at which the reading of the *Maggilla* by our venerable co-religionist, Mr. G. Zanders, was the main feature.

We have an organized congregation and own a good *Sefer Thora*, and services are held in the rooms of the B.B. Lodge. A Sunday-school is supported by it and is doing good work, instilling in the young minds the laws of Moses. . . .

"Danciger."

nered in business. Samuel sent for his brothers and sisters, creating a clan that through marriage linked them to German Jews across the state. Letters went to the groszaltern (grandparents) in Germany. When Henry Weil and Mina Rosenthal announced their engagement, he "spread the intelligence all over the land, both in the New and Old World." In 1868 thirty-one-year-old Samuel Bear returned to his native Bavaria to marry his cousin Babette Forcheimer, whom he brought back to Wilmington.[88]

RELIGIOUS REGENERATION

At Civil War's end, Isaac Leeser returned to the South reminding Jews that "the work of regeneration ought to be commenced at once." He lamented, "It is curious that in all North Carolina there is not a Jewish congregation." He noted that Wilmington has "more than one hundred and twenty souls . . . many in Newbern, others in Fayetteville, others again in Charlotte." The situation was not only

Samuel Bear of
Wilmington found
his bride, Babette
Forcheimer, in
Germany. (New
Hanover County
Public Library)

"hurtful to Israelites" but also harmful "to their respectable standing in the community." Leeser complained that "Wilmington is perhaps the only place in the
whole world where so many Jews live without a union." In Charlotte, Leeser observed that Jews "have the means as far as standing and wealth are concerned"
to form a congregation. They "listened patiently, and confessed that they were
delinquent, and that it ought to be different."[89]

Nationally, the postwar years were marked by Jewish institutional growth,
which could not have escaped the attention of the state's Jews. Synagogue building swept the nation, doubling congregational seating capacity from 1860 to 1870.
Inspired by Wise, who wanted to unify all the nation's synagogues, lay leaders
in 1873 organized a Union of American Hebrew Congregations (UAHC). Nearly
half the delegates were southerners. Two years later, Wise's Cincinnati temple
became home of a Hebrew Union College (HUC). Concerned with the unity of a

scattered people, the UAHC and Board of Delegates of American Israelites from 1876 to 1880 surveyed American Jewry. In 1877 they reported 277 congregations in 174 cities.[90]

The 1870s were birthright years for institutional Judaism in North Carolina. Charlotte's Jews founded a cemetery society in 1867, chartered a Hebrew Benevolent Society in 1870, and organized a Ladies Benevolent Society in 1874, although these groups did not evolve into a congregation. The Hebrew Cemetery Company of Wake County organized in Raleigh in 1870, and four years later tailor Michael Grausman, who had rabbinic training, donated a room of his house for a synagogue. His daughter Helen "sought out all the Jewish people she could find in Raleigh" and with her husband David Elias organized the Hebrew Benevolent Association. On Yom Kippur in 1874 Goldsboro's Jews met at the Weil home and then broke the fast at the hotel (complaining that "they are used to a better table"). In 1875 they purchased burial ground in the city's Willow Dale Cemetery, and two years later began "an effort to build a Synagogue." That same year, Tarboro Jews organized Chevra B'nai Israel. Durham's handful of Jews in 1878 closed their stores, and "all faithfully observed the festival of 'Rosh Hashana.'"[91]

As they organized their communities, Jews also institutionalized their global and national Jewish affiliations. In 1860 Isaac Leeser reported that in Wilmington, "A collection was also taken up for the Morocco refugees." B'nai B'rith Lodges organized in Wilmington in 1874, Tarboro in 1875, Charlotte by 1879, and Goldsboro in 1886. North Carolina Jews headed to district and national conventions in Savannah, Charleston, and Baltimore. In its first year, Goldsboro's Zunz Lodge sent funds to victims of the Charleston earthquake and to the Atlanta orphanage. Through B'nai B'rith's global Jewish advocacy, North Carolinians, too, were agents of Jewish destiny. These developments traveled family and commercial routes from urban centers.[92]

As Max Lilienthal had noted, a committed if not charismatic leader was a necessary catalyst to create a congregation. In most communities, one or two names occur repeatedly as heads of societies and congregations. In Charlotte, Henry Baumgarten, a professional photographer, provided leadership. David Wallace was recalled as the "Hebrew of Hebrews" of Statesville. In Durham, Myer Summerfield, a Prussian-born Orthodox clothier, led the cemetery society, which met at his store. Henry Morris was the leader of Tarboro, and Michael Grausman, of Raleigh. In Wilmington, Nathaniel Jacobi, Solomon Bear, and Abram Weill headed efforts.[93]

Soon after Leeser visited in 1867, a Wilmington newspaper noted, "ARRIVED.— The Jewish Rabbi, Mr. Myers . . . He comes highly recommended as a scholar and gentleman." The *Occident* headlined, "EVERYTHING HAS BEEN ORGANIZED ON

ORTHODOX PRINCIPLES." The congregation included twenty-three paid members, thirty-three contributors, and "one widow lady." For a synagogue and schoolhouse, the congregation rented the former session room of the First Presbyterian Church. When the "Jewish Synagogue" was consecrated, the *Journal* boasted that the state's first synagogue was in Wilmington. Governor Jonathan Worth sent warm regards.[94]

Jewish regeneration lasted but one year as dissensions splintered the congregation. Unable to sustain orthodoxy, membership declined, and services moved to Jacobi's home. Rabbi Myers left on a steamer for New York. The congregation passed resolutions of thanks but could not afford to pay him. His furniture was sold at public auction. Even without a congregation, so many "Israelitish" stores closed on the High Holidays in 1871 that downtown "presented the appearance of Sunday."[95]

Women's philanthropy sustained religious efforts. Wilmington's women were no doubt acquainted with benevolence society and Sunday School efforts in Philadelphia, Savannah, and Charleston. A Harmony Circle organized in 1870 and two years later took the title Ladies Concordia Society to "promote the cause of Judaism and to aid by its funds the maintenance of a temple of worship." Rosalie Jacobi, the synagogue leader's wife, was president. These societies' secular titles emphasize community peace—likely among Jews as well as with Christians. The Jewish women created counterparts to church-affiliated societies, and their festivals at Concordia Hall drew Christians. They raised funds for an organ, the Torah, and the parsonage and financed the Temple's maintenance. For more than a century, Concordia supported the religious school.[96]

In November 1872 Isaac Wise reported in the *American Israelite* that "our co-religionists of Wilmington, N.C., have resolved to establish a 'MINHAG AMERICA' congregation in that city, and to erect a synagogue," to be called Mishkan Israel (Tabernacle of Israel). Forty men gathered at the home of Abram Weill. Solomon Bear was elected president, serving until he died in 1904. Within weeks, fifty-seven donors, including Christians, contributed $2,100.

Once again, Wilmington's Jews turned to Philadelphia. In 1872 Dr. Marcus Jastrow, a celebrated rabbi and Talmudic scholar who had overseen the "gradual modification of the old Orthodox ritual" at Rodeph Sholom, addressed a large crowd at City Hall. The newspaper noted that "the majority of the Hebrew population belong to the Reformed portion." As rabbi, they hired in 1876 Jastrow's student, Samuel Mendelsohn, who left a Norfolk pulpit. Born in Kovno, Mendelsohn was a Lithuanian serving a German congregation. He had attended rabbinic school in Berlin and graduated in 1873 from Maimonides College in Philadelphia, where Jastrow was his teacher and uncle by marriage. Networks of family and

Rabbi Samuel Mendelsohn at the Temple of Israel, Wilmington. (New Hanover County Public Library)

commerce extended to the pulpit. Mendelsohn was a scholar of ancient rabbinic jurisprudence who contributed to the *Jewish Encyclopedia* and Jastrow's dictionary of rabbinic Hebrew, still regarded as authoritative. "He was always studying," a congregant recalled.[97]

In building their Temple, Jews blended their hybrid identities. For the groundbreaking, they chose the centenary of the Mecklenburg Declarations when North Carolina proclaimed its independence. President Sol Bear expressed his "earnest . . . affection for the State of their adoption." Abram Weill offered a Hebrew prayer. M. Katz gave the priestly blessing. The cornerstone laying featured a parade from the Masonic Hall with the Cornet Concert band, two Masonic lodges, President Bear in a white silk sash, temple members, Jewish youth, the mayor, and the architect. Stores closed on the route. The Honorable A. M. Waddell praised Jews "as a class" for being "orderly, industrious, and intelligent members of society." Rabbi Jastrow gave a race-proud speech, declaring, "Every sanctuary in Israel is a monument of religious liberty." By emphasizing "ethical values" and "brotherly love" rather than "religious dogma," Jews connected not just to their traditions but to their Christian neighbors. Three hundred attended a City Hall banquet.[98]

For his dedicatory address, Mendelsohn sketched the "condition of his race in North Carolina." He "spoke feelingly of the Christians who had assisted his people in building their temple," which was for the "welfare" of Christians and Jews alike. Church building in the South—synagogues included—was a civic duty. The original title K. K. Mishcan Israel yielded to the modern American name, Temple of Israel. The "handsome and imposing edifice," the newspaper reported, was in the "Moorish order of architecture." This Oriental style, popularized in Germany, found elaborate expression in Wise's Plum Street Temple in Cincinnati. The architecture romantically evoked the Jews' eastern origins, distinguishing the synagogue from nearby churches built in neo-Gothic and neo-Romanesque styles. Its rich materials and detailing—including an ark in the "Renaissance style . . . of decoration revived by Raphael"—attested to wealth and refinement.[99]

Typical of American congregations, Temple of Israel's commitment to Reform was inconsistent and wavering. The Temple included an organ and family pews. There were no daily services nor were skullcaps required. Rather than Wise's *Minhag Amerika*, the prayer book first chosen was Rabbi Benjamin Szold's *Abodat Yisrael*, amended by Rabbi Jastrow, which mediated between reform and tradition. In 1878 the Temple joined the UAHC, which became the governing body of Reform congregations. In 1876 Wilmington Jews hired a schochet (ritual slaughterer) to ensure kosher meat. "All who hold the Israelitish faith" follow these "sanitary regulations" minutely, the *Star* explained. The *Star* recommended the "purity and healthiness" of kosher meat to all regardless of religion.[100] Ironically,

this advice came as American Jews were loosening their dietary strictures. With
their resplendent Temple and progressive values, Jews rationalized their differences with their Christian fellow citizens.

ISRAELITISH CITIZENS

The story of North Carolina's German Jewish immigrants was being replayed
across America. Through family and commerce, they maintained ties to larger
communities in Philadelphia, Charleston, and Baltimore. Although scattered,
their social circle was "our Jewish crowd," and they were mindful of religious
duties: burying their dead in consecrated cemeteries, circumcising children, and
closing stores on holidays. Given their mobility and few numbers, they were late,
relative to Jews nationally, in organizing. When they did so, their practices followed the conventional practice of forming cemetery or benevolence societies
before instituting congregations.

Like their German cousins, the immigrants served as economic middlemen
aspiring to the urban, middle class. Indeed, North Carolina and German Jews

Wilmington's Temple of Israel, 1876, the state's first synagogue. (New Hanover County Public Library)

achieved full political rights nearly at the same time, 1868 and 1871 respectively. Their wrestling with tradition also had European parallels although in North Carolina, distant from rabbinic and communal authority, reform accelerated. Certainly, North Carolina Jews in their religious devotions were acting as respectable American citizens. In the South especially, churchgoing was expected. Their religious efforts were endorsed by civic leaders, newspaper editors, and Christian ministers. Yet, as citizens and neighbors, Jews still found themselves received ambivalently. German immigrants were elected Confederate officers but also scorned as war profiteers. Newspapers editorialized to remove the constitutional religious test while legislators voted to keep it. Credit agents rated Jews doubtful and high toned.

Fighting for the Confederacy was an extreme example of the Jews' accommodation. After the war, with the African Americans freed, the South sought to reestablish its social order. A footnote of the Reconstructionist struggle to expand democracy was to enfranchise Jews by removing office-holding disabilities. Zebulon Vance's "The Scattered Nation" secured the Jew's racial and civic place as Americans. Having North Carolina's most venerated statesman as their champion was a benediction. Jews, Vance proclaimed, were white folk, God's own, who like southerners are a glorious and enterprising people whose history exemplifies triumph after defeat. Such people were needed to rebuild the South. As the economy expanded, growing numbers of Jews established themselves in the budding cities and mill and market towns. The South looked North, even to Germany, for white people to redress its racial imbalance. Skilled in commerce with new sources of capital, Jews were welcomed to a defeated, impoverished state seeking its redemption.

1880-1920

As Ben D'Lugin of Wilmington tells the story, his father Jacob and uncle Abe, young immigrants from Lithuania, walked into the Baltimore Bargain House seeking credit to buy merchandise. They had saved a few hundred dollars peddling and now wanted a store. The brothers were ushered into the office of Jacob Epstein, the proprietor. Epstein himself was a Lithuanian immigrant who personified the American Dream. He had begun as a peddler, opened a store and then a wholesale house, and became a man of vast wealth and philanthropies. The Bargain House rose six stories on a city block and spawned Epstein factories and warehouses.

Epstein asked the boys how old they were. They answered, sixteen and twenty.

"Well," Epstein responded, "you know you are both under age legally for me to collect from you if you don't want to pay me, but you boys look like you've been working hard." He then told them to pick out merchandise and come back to his office. He looked the boys in the eyes and shook their hands, telling them they seemed honest fellows.

"Go to Wilmington and I'll ship the merchandise to you, and I want you to pay me back a little bit every week, whatever you can afford, and I'll sell you more merchandise." He was giving them "the opportunity to be successful."

So that is how the D'Lugin family in 1904 got its start in Wilmington.

Much of the history of North Carolina Jews is written in the ledgers of the Baltimore Bargain House. The D'Lugins were part of a larger immigration of more than 2 million mostly East European Jews who came to America from the 1880s to 1920s. Epstein was one of them. He had begun wholesaling to peddlers in 1881, the year this great migration commenced. He sent Yiddish-speaking agents to Baltimore's Locust Point docks, where immigrants debarked. Epstein gave credit liberally and pointed them to promising locales, even advising them on their diets. "Eat prunes," he told them. Having peddled the countryside, he understood the rural economy and saw how a new rail line or factory created opportunity for a store. He ran coastal steamers and offered free train tickets to bring

his customers to Baltimore on semiannual buying trips. In the 1890s a Raleigh storekeeper could board a train before breakfast and be in Baltimore for dinner. Epstein made them feel at home. There, the storekeeper could have his photograph taken free, bank his money, and send funds to relatives overseas. A receipt for Morris Goodman of Raleigh in 1892 is written in Yiddish. By 1920 the enterprise comprised twenty-seven acres of floor space, and its catalog was sent to 160,000 retailers (of whom Jews were a small proportion). The catalog listed everything from baseball gloves to picture frames, corsets to commodes. Shopkeepers purchased stock for their stores and furniture for their homes. The catalog offered advice on fashion trends, merchandising, and salesmanship. "We read the cata-

The Baltimore Bargain
House sponsored
Jewish peddlers and
storekeepers. (Jewish
Heritage Foundation
of North Carolina)

logue of the Baltimore Bargain House with wonder that there can be so many marvelous things in the world," recalled Min Munich, a storekeeper's daughter in Oxford.[1]

Epstein's largesse cannily blended generosity and profit. He rewarded bar mitzvah boys with gold coins and played matchmaker for the lonely peddler and the storekeeper's daughter.[2] When Jacob D'Lugin married Eva Kaminsky in 1915, Epstein sent silverware. Epstein "was a great man," recalled Harry Freid, whose father came to Weldon in 1906, "everybody looked up to Epstein. He helped so many Jews."

THE THIRD WAVE

With the East European immigration, North Carolina's Jewish numbers grew nearly tenfold from an estimated 820 in 1878 to 8,252 in 1927. (Both figures are significant undercounts.) Poverty, persecution, and high birthrates pushed Jews from Russian lands to America. In 1910 Eastern Europe was home to nearly 6 million Jews pressed in the Pale of Settlement, an area of Latvia, Poland, Lithuania, Belorussia, and Ukraine that the czar prescribed for Jewish residence. In 1881 the

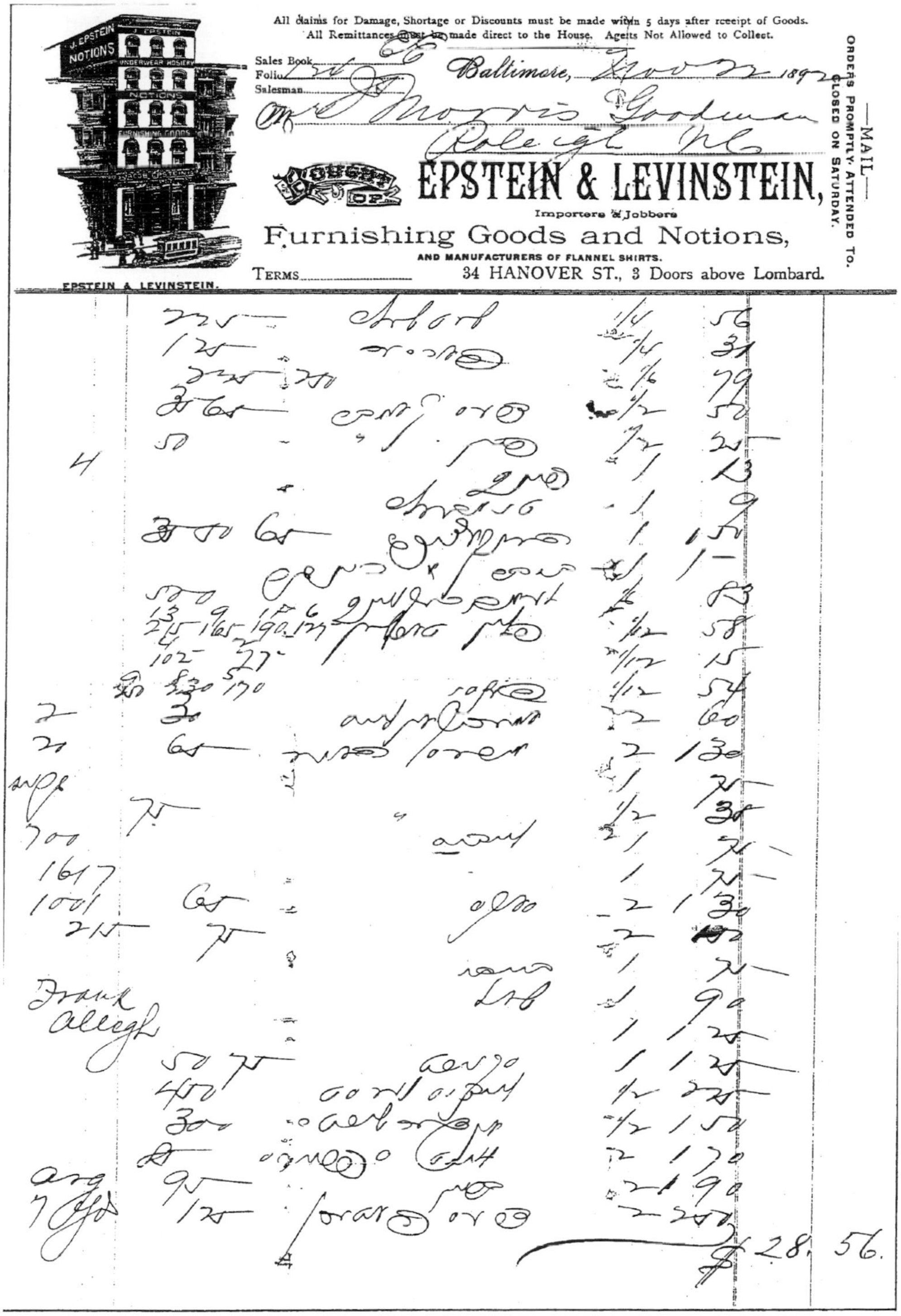

All claims for Damage, Shortage or Discounts must be made within 5 days after receipt of Goods.
All Remittances must be made direct to the House. Agents Not Allowed to Collect.

Sales Book
Folio
Salesman

Baltimore, Nov 22 1892

M. Morris Goodman
Raleigh NC

BOUGHT OF
EPSTEIN & LEVINSTEIN,
Importers & Jobbers
Furnishing Goods and Notions,
AND MANUFACTURERS OF FLANNEL SHIRTS.

TERMS
34 HANOVER ST., 3 Doors above Lombard.

—MAIL—
ORDERS PROMPTLY ATTENDED TO.
CLOSED ON SATURDAY.

$128.56

Receipt for Morris Goodman of Raleigh, written in 1892 in Yiddish. (Jewish Museum of Maryland)

liberal Czar Alexander II was assassinated, unleashing bloody pogroms and anti-Semitic legislation. Rioting mobs, supported by police, rampaged through more than 100 cities. Jewish boys as young as eight were pressed into the army for twenty-five years. The May Laws of 1882 restricted Jewish trades and residence. Quotas limited higher education to very few. Czarist policy confronted Jews with the choice of baptism, poverty, death, or emigration.

Immigrant Jews carried to North Carolina anxious memories. When Russian soldiers rode through Min Munich's village, her grandfather locked doors and hid the children fearing they would be kidnapped. An aunt, a revolutionary, was murdered along with two of her children, and her grandfather's house was burned. Harold Bloom of Roanoke Rapids recalled how Jewish girls were buried under hay and furniture to hide them from rapacious Cossacks. Arriving by the night train to rejoin her husband in Troy, Belah Polakavetz clutched her children when she looked out the window and saw a crowd holding torches. She feared Cossacks only to find her husband Jake with his American friends.[3]

Like the Germans before them, the East Europeans came in family chains. Most were young. Departure for America meant saying farewell to relatives who may never be seen again. Munich recalled her Uncle Grishin pressing a gold locket into her hand as a parting gift. When Jacob Stein left Seduva, Lithuania, he put a stone in his pocket as a keepsake. A father or older sibling traveled first as a pioneer, and those left behind knew that years might pass before enough was earned for family to follow. The Blooms of Linkerva, Lithuania, sent their eldest daughter Etta and their brother-in-law Adolph Guyes, whose task it was to earn enough to pay transport for seven relatives. It took two years.[4]

The migration was harrowing. When Jacob Polakavetz left Novy Bug, Ukraine, he traveled to the Bulgarian coast, where drunken sailors tried to steal his rubles, his life savings. He hid behind crates, avoiding people until he reached Constantinople, where a Jewish family sheltered him until he shipped out. Isra Eisenberg, thirteen, fled Rowna, Russia, in 1904 when Russian officers came to his school pulling out "recruits" to fight the Japanese. His brother Morris, who worked at a pants factory in Durham, sent him money to come to America. Isra fled with some army deserters for Germany, evading robbers and czarist police. Border guards arrested him, but he escaped. The teenager made his way to Rotterdam and then to Liverpool. In New York, immigration authorities held him four days until his brother sent a train ticket to Durham. Jeanne Goldberg Rauch of Gastonia recalled her "mother telling how she and her friends walked for several days across much of Latvia" to get to the boat. As they slept in barns, rats ran across their faces. "They were determined to get to this country," she emphasized.[5]

Immigration routes to North Carolina were circuitous, and America was a desired but not the only possible refuge. Samuel Munich had tried Argentina before returning to Lithuania and deciding America looked better. Others joined the Lithuanian Jewish migration to Rhodesia and South Africa. Jacob Stein left at fifteen for Johannesburg, where his father had a tailor shop. He opened a supply store at a Rhodesian mining camp. After the Boer War erupted in 1899, he headed to London, working in a pub until he obtained an American visa. Frank Goldberg had left Latvia for a South African sheep ranch. His childhood sweetheart, Ida Sadie Paradies, had immigrated to Atlanta, and love pulled him there. In 1917 they settled in Gastonia.[6]

Crossing the Atlantic itself was an ordeal. Jake Polakavetz wrote his wife Belah to bring a basket of dried fish and fruit for the month-long journey because food cost too much. The seven Blooms subsisted for weeks on buns and black bread. Poorer families booked space in steerage, a five-foot high compartment in the ship's mechanical room. They slept in two-tiered bunks that stretched in rows along the ship's length. In rough weather, the hold was closed, Belah Polakavetz recalled, and the entrapped passengers tossed and turned in the hot, fetid chamber made worse by crying children and seasick passengers, some suffering from typhus or dysentery. Steerage smelled of disease and excrement. For six-year-old Min Munich the voyage was an adventure although her mother arrived "limp and anxious." The "vision" of the Statue of Liberty remained with Min forever. Six-year-old Jennie Bloom's memorable American moment was her first banana. Wives and children reunited with fathers and husbands after years of separation. The Goldberg children had not seen their father for ten years. "When we got to Wilmington, my father didn't know his children, and we didn't know him," Anna Goldberg recalled. "When I first saw him, it felt strange. He didn't know how to do." When little Bennie Schwartz arrived in Wilmington with his mother, he mistakenly embraced his uncle Joe rather than his father.[7]

Emigration rose in 1891 and 1892 after Jews were expelled from Moscow and peaked at record levels from 1903 to 1909 after pogroms resumed. Immigrants crowded into ghettos in New York, Philadelphia, Baltimore, and Chicago. By 1920 New York's Jewish population exploded to more than 1,500,000 while Baltimore's swelled to 65,000. Nearly a quarter of these immigrants abandoned the ghettos for small-town America. Harry and Rachel Meisels left Brooklyn for "a smaller and less crowded" Fayetteville. Morris Katz wanted to "get away from the ghetto of the East Side, come down here where you can see trees and breathe free air." The Weinsteins left New York for Raleigh when a sister wrote, "Come south. The streets are paved with gold." In Chicago, Lithuanian immigrants Annie and Morris Pearson received a letter from North Carolina in 1894 advising them, "opportunities to be found here." They loaded their wares and children in a wagon

and headed to Richlands, paying their way by peddling paint, sundries, and razor blades.[8]

Those who left ghettos were fueled with ambition to be self-employed, not wage earners in a factory. In 1910, when more than 70 percent of New York's Jews were factory workers, 77 percent of Durham's Jews were independent tradesmen. Generally, the larger the city, the more likely Jewish immigrants were employed in factories; conversely, the smaller the city, the more likely they were mercantilists. In a small town, an immigrant could realize the American dream to become self-made.[9]

Jews of German origin, now middle-class Americans, felt uneasy as impoverished, Yiddish-speaking, religiously Orthodox East European immigrants arrived in their communities. Miriam Weil of Goldsboro advised her niece about dating an East European Durham boy because "all of the Jewish people in Durham that I have ever heard of are of the very ordinary sort." (This ordinary boy, Louis Jaffé, later won a Pulitzer Prize.) But the Germans also felt a family and spiritual kinship, honoring the mitzvah (religious commandment) that each Jew is responsible for the other. Germans and East Europeans may have differed by class, language, acculturation, and religious orientation, but there was much "continuity and convergence" in their pattern of settlement and in the mobility that took them from peddling to storekeeping. Responding to appeals from B'nai B'rith "to get positions for Roumainian Jews in New York," Statesville's Jews in 1900 voted to "place an order for three (3) of these men." Emma Schiff Simmonds of Charlotte wrote to New York philanthropist Jacob Schiff that Charlotte's "small benevolent society" has been "stirred to do something for the unfortunate Russians of our faith." Jacob Schiff created a coalition of Jewish societies that formed an Industrial Removal Office (IRO) to resettle Jewish immigrants across the country. B'nai B'rith Lodges served as local conduits, and traveling agents organized communities to find employment and lodging.[10]

From 1901 to 1917 the IRO resettled 73,960 immigrants, but only 113 found homes in North Carolina. In 1913 IRO agent Abraham Solomon toured North Carolina, organizing committees in Charlotte, Greensboro, Raleigh, and Wilmington "to cooperate with us in the work . . . of the biggest problem confronting American Jewry, namely the distribution of Jewish immigration." Each town agreed to accept two "removals" monthly. One immigrant, Hyman Dubrow, asked to join his brother in Raleigh. B. Aronson reported that the brother "just does make a living"

Jake Polakavetz came to Troy as an immigrant peddler. (Richard I. Levin) selling secondhand shoes, but "he is willing to gladly share what little he has with him." Bernard Nevelson in Kinston asked the agency to send his cousins Louis Kaplan and Ephraim Rappaport. "I will help them with whatever I can," he wrote. "I can not give them best to eat all the time but they will get plenty of goods to peddle." The work was not easy. Michael Kirschbaum of Charlotte wrote in broken English of an "American gentile . . . cobler" seeking a shoemaker for fifteen dollars a week to work eight to ten hours daily and twelve hours on Saturdays.[11] The IRO screened applicants for Sabbath or kosher observance before sending them to the small-town South.

As East European Jews were arriving in America, the South was industrializing and urbanizing. By 1881 the state had a Bureau of Immigration. Like other southerners, North Carolinians hoped that European labor could revive its farms, serve its industry, and preserve white racial dominance. "What North Carolina wants is people; people to develop her immense resources and make her what she ought to be," the *Greensboro Patriot* wrote. From the 1880s to early 1900s plans were proposed for German Polander, Waldensian, Italian, Scotch, Dutch, Polish, and Hungarian colonies, but such efforts yielded little. The state's Bureau of Immigration was abolished in 1905.[12]

North Carolina Jewish colonization schemes responded to a global effort to solve the "Jewish problem" of a poor and persecuted people in need of a homeland. Colonies appeared in several states, and a Galveston Plan redirected thousands to Texas. In 1882 Calvin Cowles, assayer of the Charlotte mint, advertised in Baltimore, New York, and Philadelphia, offering forty acres in Wilkes and Alexander counties to each Russian Jewish family willing to cultivate cereal or tobacco. In 1891 the Reverend Dr. Wessler of Russia visited the state "in regard to the Russian Jew question." He claimed to have purchased 80,000 acres in the foothills near Lenoir. Next fall, Jewish settlers would arrive, each family receiving eight acres. That year Roanoke River planters reportedly had an agent in Odessa to bring "500 families of the best agricultural classes of the Jews" to work farmlands. A later notice stated the "effort to procure Hebrew families for Warren County" was abandoned, and the syndicate now sought English families.[13]

In the 1880s popular opinion turned against immigration. In 1887 the State Department of Agriculture reported that "the people of North Carolina are almost a unit opposed to foreign and promiscuous immigration." Farmers and factory workers alike feared immigrants would depress wages, and manufacturers were wary of labor unionists. Racially, Jews were suspect. Democratic boss Furnifold Simmons warned about the "degenerate progeny of the Asiatic hoards [sic]," and in 1910 state immigration advocates requested only "Teutonic, Celtic, or Saxon." While 10 million immigrants arrived in America, the percentage of foreign born in the state declined from .27 in 1880 to .23 in 1890, while that of the nation rose from 13.3 to 14.6. In 1900 the state's percentage was the nation's lowest. With the economy struggling, whites and blacks alike were leaving by the tens of thousands, particularly from the rural east. Agrarian North Carolina, without a major city, offered little opportunity. Yet immigrant Jews trickled southward in small but growing numbers. Jews constituted a disproportionate 15 percent of the South's immigrants. The number of Jews in the state listing Yiddish as their mother tongue rose from 603 in 1910 to 935 in 1912. While Jews had an economic niche as merchandisers of dry goods or scrap collectors, Italians opened restaurants or labored as stoneworkers, Chinese ran laundries, and Greeks owned cafes, candy stores, and soda fountains. Lebanese and Syrians peddled.[14]

The paucity of immigrants was another sign that the South was lagging behind other regions. Southerners looked at an America entering a Gilded Age. In the Plains states, agriculture, supported by German and Scandinavian labor and the Homestead Act, was expanding. Railroads were opening the West. In the Northeast, new immigrants provided labor for urban and industrial growth. Capitalists like Carnegie, Morgan, Frick, Vanderbilt, and Rockefeller amassed fortunes that endowed hospitals, libraries, museums, and colleges. Innovators like Bell, Edison, and Westinghouse created new industries.

A NEW SOUTH

In 1886 an Atlanta journalist, Henry Grady, spoke to the New England Society in New York City, where he espoused the creed of "The New South." The South's cities, Grady proclaimed, were buzzing as "vast hives of industry." The economy was diversifying beyond one-crop agriculture, and race relations, with slavery overthrown, were enjoying a new harmony. He welcomed the northern investor who came to build its factories. Southerners would "out Yankee the Yankee," Grady promised. "The words 'New South,'" historian Paul Gaston observes, symbolized the "passage from one kind of civilization to another."[15]

Calls for industrial progress dated to antebellum days, but North Carolina's manufactures ranked next to last among South Atlantic states. By 1900 only 187,000 people were urban, while 1,707,000 were rural. The state had economic advantages: plentiful cheap labor, hydroelectric power, forests for timber and furniture industries, cotton fields for textile mills, tobacco markets to supply cigarette factories. From 1880 to 1900, the state's railroads grew from 1,600 to 3,380 miles, stretching westward to Asheville. Rails connected mill towns to national and international markets. By 1900 a society dominated by yeomen now found 40 percent of its farms under tenancy.[16] Unemployed townspeople and impoverished country folk, black and white, flocked to the new mill towns, driven by the

1893 depression when cotton dropped to a nickel a pound. Men worked in the furniture factories, while the cotton mills drew women and children. A racial division of labor reserved higher-paying, skilled positions for whites and unskilled jobs for blacks.

New South capitalists preached a "gospel of manufacturing." Benjamin Cone, a textile magnate, recalled that his firm's Salisbury Cotton Mill began in 1887 when a Presbyterian minister, Rev. Pearson, gathered the town's civic, business, and religious leaders at a tobacco warehouse. The pastor sermonized, "Next to religion Salisbury needed a cotton factory." The town would prosper, poor whites could make an "honest living," and investors would make "handsome interest." Citizens pledged $66,400.[17] The New South creed blended civic uplift, Christian charity, and personal profit.

The rallying cry was to "bring the cotton mills to the cotton fields." To encourage southern industry, a federal law removed taxes from cotton manufactured where it was grown. From 1880 to 1900, historian Hugh Lefler notes, "The number of mills increased four-fold; the capitalization twelve-fold; the value of products eleven-fold, and the number of workers, nine-fold." In 1900 30,273 men, women, and children worked in 177 cotton mills. J. W. Cannon, a Concord merchant, underwrote a new factory town, Kannapolis.[18] After the 1890s, northern capitalists came South to invest, some relocating their mills.

Old South planters became New South capitalists. R. J. Reynolds in Winston-Salem and Washington Duke were planters who after the war opened tobacco factories on rail lines. The cigarette craze of the 1880s ignited a fire, and the Bull Durham logo was plastered around the globe. Duke's American Tobacco Company controlled three quarters of the nation's tobacco production until the Supreme Court busted the trust in 1911. The state also became a national leader in furniture. From 1 factory in 1881, the state claimed 6 in 1890 and 106 in 1902. High Point's first furniture factory opened in 1888; fourteen years later it had 24.[19]

Inspired by the Social Gospel, industrialists erected mill villages, anchored by company built schools and churches, that redrew southern maps. Workers rented cottages with the mill providing utilities. Social services from nurses to baseball teams encompassed the workers' lives. A sober, dependent work force served the industrialists' self-interest, but the social and economic control was expressed as Christian duty. Whole families, parents and children, were locked in the mills often over generations. Manufacturers, as well as the workers themselves, resisted efforts to organize labor. Textile strikes in 1900 failed utterly, and union activity was dormant for the next two decades.[20]

With industrialization, the state's population center shifted from the east to the Piedmont. In 1900 90 percent of the state's cotton mills concentrated there.

Charlotte, N.C. — South Tryon Street.

Tobacco factories spawned the towns of Durham, Winston, Rockingham, Oxford, Hickory, Roxboro, and Mount Airy. "The growth of these cigarette cities is a wonder," a Methodist minister noted of Henderson in 1887. After a factory opened, it grew from 1,421 to 4,191. Market towns became urban industrial centers while hamlets grew into municipalities. In 1900 less than 10 percent of the state's population was urban; by 1920 nearly 20 percent was.[21] Greensboro's population grew from 497 in 1870 to 10,035 in 1900, Gastonia's from 236 to 4,610. In 1870 only Wilmington had over 10,000 people, but in 1900 Charlotte, Asheville, Winston-Salem, Raleigh, and Greensboro also did. Charlotte, at the hub of highways and four rail lines, emerged as a regional distribution and manufacturing center, powered by Duke hydroelectricity. Its population grew from 7,094 in 1880 to 18,091 in 1900 to 46,338 in 1920. In 1909 a trust company erected a fourteen-story skyscraper. These trends reflected an urbanizing New South.

PORTRAIT: SAMUEL WITTKOWSKY

"If the question was asked 'who is the most useful citizen of Charlotte?'" the *Charlotte News and Times* inquired in 1902, "The answer would hang for a long time on the name of Samuel Wittkowsky, Esq., who is not only an adopted citizen of his present home, but a native of a foreign land." Wittkowsky was born impoverished in eastern Prussia in 1835. With $50 sent by an American relative, he bought a steerage ticket to New York in 1853. Not knowing English, he worked his way to Charleston, where he clerked for a relative. In 1855 he moved to Charlotte to clerk at the store of Levi Drucker. There he joined another clerk, Jacob Rintels, and with $450 the two formed their own firm. They opened stores in Alexander, Caldwell, and Watauga counties. During the war Wittkowsky manufactured hats, one of which he presented to Governor Zeb Vance. At war's end Wittkowsky saved the captured governor from humiliation by giving him a ride in his carriage after the Union army offered him a mule. Wittkowsky & Rintels reestablished themselves in Charlotte, and ten years later their retail and wholesale house occupied a three-story building with assets worth $800,000. In a town of 6,000, they had 100 employees. Wittkowsky traced his success to "three P's": "'Push, Pluck and Perseverance.'"

Sam Wittkowsky's wholesale house in Charlotte. (Charlotte Jewish Historical Society)

The Charlotte newspaper crowned Wittkowsky "the Building and Loan King of North Carolina" for originating the concept in the city and state. In 1883 he served as president of Charlotte's Mechanics Perpetual Building & Loan (later Home Federal Savings and Loan). He led state and national building and loan leagues. His enterprise spread home ownership across the city, creating new suburbs. When he died in 1911, he was a millionaire.

Wittkowsky was remembered for his generosity and public service. With Vance, a Charlotte lawyer, he founded a Masonic Lodge and became its master. As alderman in 1878, he helped draft the city charter. A year later he was elected first president of Charlotte's Chamber of Commerce and helped found Charlotte Country Club. "He identified himself with the progressive element of Charlotte," a writer observed in 1888.

A newspaper described Wittkowsky as the "wonderful Hebrew builder of Charlotte," but his Judaism was problematic. His business partners were Jews, and he hired Jewish immigrants as clerks. When East European Jews arrived, he enjoyed conversing with Fannie Silverstein in Polish. Yet, when asked to contribute to the synagogue, he replied that he would rather give money not to build one. He joined Vance at the First Presbyterian Church to hear sermons. A local Jew observed that Wittkowsky "does not believe in perpetuating Judaism or any religion." Yet, in his eulogy to Vance, Wittkowsky spoke as an "Israelite . . . for my race in North Carolina." Wittkowsky was an ethnic Jew who retained his Jewish identity and associations but without belief or affiliation. Christian North Carolinians saw him as a Jew.[1]

1. See *Charlotte Observer*, 11 Jan. 1931; Jerome Dowd, *Sketches of Prominent Living North Carolinians* (Raleigh: Edwards & Broughton, 1888), 238; *Durham Morning Herald*, 13 June 1909; Letter from Mrs. N Simmonds to David M. Bressler, 25 Nov. 1905, IRO, AJHS; *Carolina Israelite*, 1951; Charlotte Nearprint, AJA.

JEWISH NEW SOUTHERNERS

These trends brought Jews southward. When James B. "Buck" Duke decided to make cigarettes in 1881, he, like other southern capitalists, sought cheap immigrant labor. On a New York dock, Buck Duke met Moses Gladstein, a nineteen-year-old Ukrainian, who was leading a strike of Jewish workers at the Goodwin Tobacco Factory. Duke contracted with Gladstein to bring more than 100 workers to Durham, and he hired Joseph Siegel, the Lithuanian-born factory manager, to supervise them. Not to be outdone, Duke's Durham rival, W. T. Blackwell, hired Joseph's brother David, a supervisor at Kinney Brothers, to bring workers to his Bull Durham factory. The rollers' workday extended six days a week from early morning until ten at night. They were paid seventy cents for rolling one thousand cigarettes, about eight to ten dollars a week. In Duke's two-story wooden factory, six rollers sat at a long table. Black workers hauled tobacco from a nearby log house. A worker took a paper, rolled the tobacco on a marble slab, pasted it into a

Moses Gladstein, labor contractor hired by Buck Duke, and his family. (Special Collections, Perkins Library, Duke University)

tube, and cut it with a blade. A worker could roll twenty-five hundred cigarettes a day, and Brodie Duke remarked that he wished that he could make money so fast.[22]

The New York Jews could not produce cigarettes to meet demand, and two years later Duke installed the Bonsack cigarette rolling machine, which manufactured 250,000 cigarettes a day. The New Yorkers threatened to destroy the machine and its mechanic. The Jews allied themselves with native workers, country folk new to the factory, and threatened a revolution. Roller Bernhard Goldgar, a socialist, asked, "Were not the masses, like myself suffering from the same causes, was not their cry for freedom my own?" The Jews organized Local Chapter 27 of the Cigarmaker's Progressive Union (CMPU). Roller, William Blumberg, wrote in the union journal, *Progress*, that it was "the first of its kind in the State of North Carolina."[23]

Over the next fourteen months mechanics improved the Bonsack machine's efficiency, and a second one was installed. Buck Duke, after meeting with the CMPU in New York, reduced the rollers' quota and cut wages to three dollars weekly. He hoped that "many may leave." North Carolina, reported roller Morris Bernstein, regarded labor as "chattel." A worker wrote, "We would soon be compelled through starvation to submit to any terms he offered no matter how enslaving." Duke advertised for five hundred boys and girls to replace them. With "the leading New York hands" gone, local workers were "unable to support a Union themselves." Southern workers, as former farm tenants, were accustomed to defer to their bosses. A worker reported that Duke "knows that Durham or native hands would never rebel or attempt to belong to a union." The Jewish workers, a roller wrote, were sucked into "the great whirlpool of destruction which the capitalists have prepared for us."[24]

The CMPU folded, to be replaced by a local assembly of the Knights of Labor, a biracial international labor brotherhood. Its local Inside Squire in 1887 was David Kaufman, a storekeeper. In 1888 a letter to a Knights newspaper spoke of the "New Yorkers" who had resisted Duke's tyranny but succumbed to machines and unorganized labor. The Knights failed: racists scorned it as a "Nigger" organization, and conflicts flared between farm and industrial laborers. Gradually, all but a few Jewish workers left town. One "distressingly poor" former roller committed suicide in New Jersey by throwing himself before a train. Labor contractor Moses Gladstein, fortified by a $1,000 settlement with Duke, opened a Durham dry goods store.[25]

In 1883, as Duke released his Jewish workers, David and Joseph Siegel opened a tobacco factory in a house on Poplar Street. Three years later they employed some ten rollers to produce 570,000 cigarettes monthly of Cablegram, named for the transatlantic telegraph. They hired Duke's former rollers. A year later their factory burned, and the brothers left town. Jews suspected arson, but fires were frequent in the dust-filled, wood-framed factories.

An 1884 Durham history exulted, "Durham today is an asylum for the poor, a place where the 'wandering Jew' . . . finds a peaceful and profitable retreat." New South boosters boasted of the harmony of labor and capital. Yet, Washington Duke wrote candidly in 1896:

> We never had any trouble in the help except when 125 Polish Jews were hired to come down to Durham to work in the factory. They gave us no end of trouble. We worked out of that, and we now employ our own people. . . . People want emigration. If good citizens come, well and good, but there are plenty of North Carolinians here who are glad to work.[26]

"Polish Jews," Duke implied, were not "our own people." Duke expressed the growing disillusion southerners felt toward immigration. In 1913 the IRO agent, seeking to locate Jewish immigrants, reported from Raleigh that "the South is non-union in its sentiments and psychology and there is a pervasive fear of getting men from the North who are potential labor agitators." In Wilmington, which had but three Jewish factory workers, he reported, "the few Jewish workingmen here find it hard to get along because of anti-Semitism." Ceasar Cone, a member of the American Jewish Committee, could not support bringing Jewish laborers to Greensboro without risking resentment from his 7,000 native white workers, although his "cotton king" partner Emanuel Sternberger chaired the IRO's Greensboro committee. Thus ended a Jewish labor movement in North Carolina.[27]

Jewish new southerners would be capitalists, not proletarians. Upwardly mobile German Jews rose with the New South as they climbed from peddlers to storekeepers to industrialists. By 1897 Gustave Rosenthal had progressed from Wilmington clerk to Raleigh merchant to secretary of the Alamance Cotton Factory to president of Durham's Commonwealth Cotton Mills. Max Hoffman, owner of a general store, founded Scotland Neck Cotton Mills. Jay Hirshinger in Charlotte and Meyer Summerfield in Durham operated garment factories. Moses Long, owner of a shoe company, became an officer of the Asheville Cotton Mill. In 1906 former clerks and storekeepers Eli and Jacob Oettinger left Kinston for Greensboro, where their manufacturing plant for the Guilford Buggy, soon displaced by the newfangled automobile, was quickly converted into a lumberyard. The Weils' dry goods enterprise in Goldsboro spawned a rice mill, brickyard, icehouse, plywood corporation, lumber company, and fertilizer factory.

Out-of-state Jews also invested. In the 1890s Charles Cohen of Petersburg, Virginia, and Gustavus and Clarence Milhiser of Richmond founded textile mills that led to a new industrial town, Roanoke Rapids. In 1911 Abraham and Charles Erlanger bought 250 acres outside Lexington to build Erlanger Cotton Mills to supply cloth for their BVD underwear factory in Baltimore. Within a year the plant employed 1,400 people. In 1904 the mountain hamlet of Toxaway changed its name to "Rosman" to honor Joseph Rosenthal and Morris Omansky, business partners of Joseph Silversteen, owner of a local tannery and timber company. Jews also invested in mills in Gastonia, Oxford, Roxboro, and Burlington. No other Jewish industrialists, however, achieved the magnitude of brothers Moses and Ceasar Cone and their partners Herman and Emanuel Sternberger.

In 1887 the Cone brothers, drummers for their father's Baltimore wholesale house, invested $50,000 in an Asheville mill. A year later they expanded to Salisbury and Gibsonville. Cheap, coarse cotton plaids had a limited market, so they diversified into fine fabrics and gave their products brand names like Cotton Club and Golden Chain. In 1890 Moses Cone formed Cone Export and Commission Company, with offices in New York, that became the marketing agency for 90 percent of the South's mills. Recovering from the Panics of 1893 and 1896, Ceasar Cone built the massive Proximity Cotton Mills in Greensboro to produce denim. With partners Herman and Emanuel Sternberger, they built Revolution Mill to manufacture flannel. Next came the White Oak plant, the world's largest denim mill, which by 1910 supplied a third of the world's denim, including fabric for Levi Strauss. Typical of Jews, Moses and Ceasar brought their brothers Julius, Clarence, and Bernard into their enterprises.

Near their factories, the Cones and Erlangers built mill villages with dairies, schools, and churches. The *New York Herald* described Cone villages as "spotless towns," and the international YMCA selected one as a global training center. For both blacks and whites, Cone schools were open nine months although state law mandated four. Employee illiteracy dropped from 40 to 1 percent. The Jewish brothers donated four dollars for every dollar that Christians contributed to build a church or parsonage. The Cone Memorial Band offered summer concerts. A federal inspector saluted the Erlanger Mill Village as "beautiful . . . free from the crowding, and noise and dust and dissipations and vices of the city." Hogs were raised scientifically the "Erlanger way." The Erlanger Fair awarded prizes for jams and jellies, and a Miss Erlanger beauty pageant continued even after the village incorporated into Lexington.[28]

Jews helped create the New South economy. "Merchants, peddlers, and mail-order catalogues disseminated modern products, styles, and sensibilities, spreading a 'consumer ethic' through the countryside," historian Deborah Weiner observes. Nowhere is this more evident than the enterprise of David and Isaac Wallace, German-born brothers who had arrived in Statesville in the early 1850s

PORTRAIT: MOSES AND CEASAR CONE

For twelve years Moses and Ceasar Cone had worked the South by train, foot, or horse and wagon, selling staples to mill, city, and country stores for their father's Baltimore wholesale house. In the cash-poor economy, mill stores paid them in cloth, which they resold. The brothers became agents for these mills, creating Cone Export and Commission Company, the "plaid trust." In 1894 they scraped together money from family and grocer friends to form the Proximity Manufacturing Company in Greensboro, so named because it was near the cotton fields. Ceasar soon brought brothers Julius, Clarence, and Bernard into the business. From their days as drummers, they had befriended Herman and Emanuel Sternberger, German immigrant brothers, who sold merchandise and brokered cotton in Clio, South Carolina. They, too, had been investing in mills, railroads, and real estate. In 1898 Moses Cone invited the Sternbergers to become partners in Revolution Mills, so named because it radically transformed flannel manufacture. The Cone brothers created a textile empire that grew to eighteen mills and two finishing plants in three states, employing 16,500 workers. Twelve North Carolina communities claimed Cone mills. White Oak, opened in 1902, was the South's largest cotton mill.

Moses (left) and Ceasar Cone, traveling salesmen who became textile magnates. (North Carolina Collection, University of North Carolina Library at Chapel Hill)

A touring reporter for the New York Yiddish newspaper *Forward* abandoned his socialist principles in expressing awe for the "Jewish baronial family, or great-estate owners (Pritzim)" in Greensboro. The Cones were outsized in their philanthropies as well in their industries. Cone sisters Etta and Claribel, intimates of Henri Matisse and Pablo Picasso in Paris, donated art to the Weatherspoon Gallery in Greensboro. Ceasar Cone was a board member of the American Jewish Committee as well as a benefactor to the YMCA, a sanitarium, and a training school. Moses Cone lived on 3,500 acres in the Blue Ridge Mountains near Blowing Rock where his wife Bertha opened a school for Appalachian youth. The Cones helped transform a local academy into Appalachian Training School, forerunner of Appalachian State University. After Moses's death in 1908, Bertha endowed Greensboro's Moses Cone Memorial Hospital, and their mountain estate was donated as a federal park. The Cones lie buried on a nearby slope.[1]

1. *Forward*, 14 Sept. 1929.

as dry goods merchants. During harvest season, wagons by the hundreds trekked from the mountains to Statesville, where produce was shipped by rail to Charleston. Since the 1840s mountaineers had collected ginseng for the China market, and the state ranked among the nation's largest producers of medicinal herbs. The Wallaces, expanding into a wholesale house, hired a botanical manager, Mordecai Hyams, a Charleston Jew who had purchased herbs for the Confederate Army in Charlotte. Hyams traveled with David Wallace's son Isidore to educate mountaineers on "unusual and unlikely" herbs. Storekeepers who bought from the Wallaces collected and prepared the herbs. Overcoming the Panic of 1873, the Wallaces' herb trade grew to 2,000 specimens worth $100,000. Their drug catalog expanded from 30 to 700 items. Another Jew, Louis Pinkus, opened a second herbarium.[29]

The Wallaces linked Appalachian storekeepers and mountain pickers to northern markets. In 1874 David Goldberg, a Wallace clerk, sailed to Europe to find buyers in Germany, Holland, and England. In 1876 Hyams sent some "300 medicinal plants, 125 varieties of mosses, and 400 boxes of roots to the Centennial Exposition in Philadelphia," where, as the centerpiece of the North Carolina exhibit, it won a medal. At the State Department's request, the exhibit went to the Paris Exposition of 1878, where it won another medal. Hyams's discovery of one, long-lost plant still bears the name "Hyams sparking shortia."[30]

The mountain gatherers, a New York newspaper reported, were "usually women, children, and maimed or broken down men." Living far from villages,

White Oak Cotton Mills, Greensboro, N. C.

White Oak Mills in Greensboro with a Cone mill village in the foreground. (North Carolina Collection, University of North Carolina Library at Chapel Hill)

they walked barefoot for miles to trade herbs, roots, and barks for salt or kerosene. "But for this," the editor added, "many country merchants during the recent depression in financial affairs would have gone into bankruptcy." Hyams's son John, a Marion storekeeper, once shipped "feathers, Wool, Wax, Seneca, and Ginseng" to the Wallaces and asked in return, "Send us a banjo." By the 1880s, railroad cars lined the Wallace depot laden with peaches, blackberries, and wheat. The brothers sold ginseng by the ton and shipped more than a million pounds of herbs annually. After the Panic of 1893, though, the firm crashed. The company emerged from bankruptcy, but competition and a poor economy reduced its trade. The family busied itself with textile mills and real estate.[31]

Herbs were used for medicines and to flavor liquors. The Statesville area supported some forty-two distilleries, including those of Julius Lowenstein, who by 1884 was shipping corn liquor, rye whiskey, and brandy across the South. Lowen-

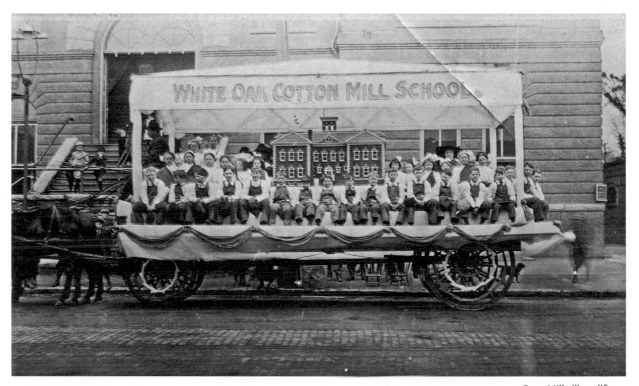

Cone Mill village life. (Southern Historical Collection, University of North Carolina Library at Chapel Hill)

stein's in-law M. W. Meyer and Henry Clarke were "Distillers of North Carolina Mountain Liquors." Jews, with their European history as tavernkeepers—and unbothered by temperance—were entrepreneurs in the national liquor industry, especially the southern trade. In Louisville, a quarter of the distillers and wholesalers were Jews. Prior to prohibition, North Carolina was the nation's leading wine-producing state. The major vintner was Sol Bear & Co. of Wilmington. In 1882 Bear purchased a shipwreck at auction that contained 500 casks of spirits. The firm produced scuppernong, blackberry wines, ports, clarets, and champagne. Bear shipped 200,000 gallons annually, and by 1895 he was president of the North Carolina Liquor Dealers, Distillers, and Grape Growers' Association. In 1905 his son Irving went to the Rhineland, where he studied to be "an expert wine chemist."[32]

SMALL-TOWN JEWS

As they stepped from trains, Jewish immigrants saw opportunity in the new industrial towns. Mill workers needed shoes and uniforms, and managers and capitalists could afford fancy clothes from specialty shops. Farmers drove their wagons to town on Thursdays and left on Saturdays, shopping at stores and staying for a show at the opera house. On market days, tobacco warehouses bustled

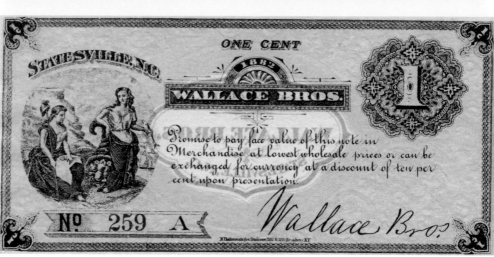

with customers. As town dwellers engaged in commerce, Jews were typical New
Southerners.

Historian Lee Shai Weissbach describes the half century that began in the
late 1800s as the "'classic' era of small-town Jewish life" when immigrant families established themselves in the nation's heartland. Small-town life occupies
a mythic place in the American imagination, Weissbach observes, as the country's "heart and soul," its most representative experience. North Carolina fit that
profile with its mill and market towns and budding cities, but the state lacked

Sol Bear, a Confederate veteran, served as Temple president. (Cape Fear Museum, Wilmington)

fragrant, fruity
scuppernong wine

Bear's Scuppernong Wine has, in its way, made North Carolina famous. No other native or foreign wine compares with this home product.

—in its rich, fruity, delicious flavor,
—in its lightness in alcohol,
—in its great medicinal properties,
—In its purity, or in the care used in its manufacture.

It is indeed the virgin juice of the luscious North Carolina Grape!

Your guests will appreciate Bear's Scuppernong at your afternoon or evening social functions.

Scuppernong.   Belle of Carolina.
   Port   Blackberry.   Sherry.

SOL. BEAR & CO.,
'Phone No. 994.   Wilmington, N. C.
Cor. Front and Marstellar Streets.

Advertisement for Sol Bear & Co., makers of Belle of Carolina wine. (New Hanover County Public Library) an Atlanta or Baltimore that might serve as a Jewish capital. North Carolina Jews were exceptional. Jews remained an urban people who preferred to live among their own. In 1878 71 percent of American Jews lived in cities with more than 1,000 Jews; fifty years later that figure rose to 92 percent.[33] Even in rural southern states Jews concentrated in Atlanta, Memphis, or New Orleans.

For a small-town Jewish community to survive, it needed to draw East European immigrants, Weissbach has shown. Towns that did not saw their Jewish communities wither. The German Jews were too few and too mobile to sustain community; low birthrates and intermarriage also diminished numbers. East European immigration transformed Jewish communities. From 1878 to 1927 Charlotte's Jewish population grew from 104 to 400; Fayetteville's from 52 to 116; Raleigh's from 78 to 150; and Wilson's from 16 to 140. By 1913 a majority of Charlotte's Jews were East European. In each case, the rate of Jewish growth exceeded that of the town's. From 1905 to 1925 Asheville Jewry grew sevenfold while the city grew threefold. Every hamlet seemed to have at least one "Jew Store," as they were often called. Places like Sylva, Hamlet, Norwood, Spindale, or Zebulon had a Jewish family or two. Jews owned stores in Manteo and Murphy, the two towns that proverbially defined the state's axis from coast to mountains. In Weldon, Whiteville, Hickory, Hendersonville, Oxford, Rocky Mount, and Salisbury, small communities grew. Charlotte, Durham, Greensboro, Kinston, Raleigh, Tarboro, Wilson, and Winston-Salem—where German Jews had lived, some since antebellum days—were now sufficiently large to form congregations.

Jews felt welcomed, but their experiences varied whether they were isolated in small agrarian towns or lived communally in larger industrial cities, whether they resided on the coast, piedmont, or mountains. North Carolina towns had distinct cultures and economies. Class lines were also significant. In Charlotte, an observer reported in 1913 that "most of our Jews here are engaged in tailoring, shoemaking, and the pool and cigar business." By contrast Raleigh was "unique" in having no Jewish tailors or shoemakers, and the town's forty Jewish families were described as "moderately successful."[34] Greensboro's German Jews included lawyers and industrialists, whose wealth and prominence eased the civic acceptance of newcomers. In Durham and High Point, by contrast, the communities were almost entirely immigrant East European, and Jewish artisans and shopkeepers remained on the civic and social margin. In Wilmington, Jews had arrived at the city's beginnings. The presence of Jews since a town's creation eased the integration of later arrivals. Thus, Durham's Jews created a folklore that traced community origins to Duke's cigarette rollers, although virtually all the Jewish residents had come later to sell merchandise.

SOUTHERN HOSPITALITY

Arriving in North Carolina, the East Europeans tell a common story that attests to Jewish solidarity. First sheltered by family in New York or Baltimore, they traveled by rail to a North Carolina relative who long awaited them. The Munichs, fresh off the boat, stayed with Baltimore relatives until they boarded an all-night train to Oxford. Unable to sleep on wooden seats in a smoky car that halted at every whistle-stop, they were welcomed at the Oxford depot by a husband and father, whom they had not seen for three years. Harry Kaplan, a young Lithuanian immigrant who knew no English, was shipped by train to his uncle with a sign around his neck, "Kaplan, Raleigh." Jake Polakavetz arrived in High Point as a "perfect stranger," but the Doctor and London families welcomed him with "southern hospitality," he recalled. Celia Doctor taught him some English: "good morning, how are you, what size do you wear . . . may I use your outhouse, and thank you very much." She also taught him to count and make change.[35]

Stories also attest to the kindness of Christian strangers who appreciated both the Jews' religion and enterprise. Stopping in Troy, Polakavetz met Reese Blair, the town's leading businessman and a devout Christian. "He had never met a foreigner or a Jew," Polakavetz recalled. "He was convinced that my coming to Troy was the advent of the coming of Christ." Blair offered him a deal. If Polakavetz would settle in town, which lacked a clothing store, Blair would lend him a shop, a horse and wagon, and money to buy stock. Blair found him a place at Miss Emmie's boardinghouse and sealed the deal with a handshake. Isaac Evans left his job as a cutter in a New York garment factory to join his sister Jennie in Rocky Mount. Not liking the town, he headed to Fayetteville, where he roomed at a boardinghouse. That night a mule livery went up in flames. Evans joined the fire brigade. The next morning a Mr. Van Story expressed thanks and offered to rent a store to him on Market Square for ten dollars a month. Wanting commerce for their towns, New South businessmen encouraged Jewish settlement.[36]

PEDDLING AND SCAVENGING

Jewish immigrants, with few skills and little capital, shared the southerners' "collective history" as a "People of Poverty" in a land of prosperity, but the ambition of North Carolina Jews was to rise out of the working class, not with it. In that regard, Jews differed from southern workers whose families were locked into mills for generations. Bernhard Goldgar, the Durham roller, turned rapidly from proletarian to capitalist; in 1887 he advertised that he had "started with hardly anything in this city three years ago," but now had three stores and a thousand dollars in real estate. North Carolina Jews felt little proletarian solidarity or nos-

Harry Stein recalled the day when his father Jacob and uncle Kalman opened The Brothers Store in Fayetteville. They advertised, "Our Motto: Honest Dealings to All."

Opening day brought lookers, well-wishers, loafers, and more than one curiosity seeker who walked up to Jacob and said, "Reckon I ain't never seen no Jew before. Ya don't look no different from most folks, but ya sure talks different."

Jacob assured him he had neither horns nor a forked tail, and pursued the strange conversation by introducing himself. "My name's Jacob," he said. "Vat's yours?"

"Evans," the man answered, extending his hand and smiling. "Jim Evans, from out here 'cross the river, Flea Hill."

"Farmer?" Jacob asked.

"Yep," Then he added kinda proudly. "I does a little preaching on the side, too."

They shook hands and Jacob said, "Vell, preacher, pleased to meet you. Make yourself at home." He paused, then inquired, "Say, Preacher, I vant to esk you somethin'."

"What's at?"

"Vy is it everybody vants to go to Heaven, but nobody vants to die?"

The Reverend farmer broke into a smile as he turned the question over in his mind, then laughed and said, "Dat's a good one, Jacob. Yes, suh, dat's a good one. I'll have to give it a little thought. Ha! Ha! Yes, suh." Leaving, he slapped Jacob on the shoulder, still laughing, and added, "It'd take Solomon to answer that'n."

Starting to walk away, Jim said, "You're O.K., Jake. See ya' 'round." He didn't buy anything, but he had seen his first Jew and wasn't scared at all.[1]

1. Harry Stein, *Pathway to a Future* (New York: Carlton Press, 1980), 68–69.

talgia. No Workmen's Circle (*Arbeiter Ring*) formed in North Carolina although Georgia, Tennessee, and Virginia had chapters.[37]

Immigrants came to North Carolina broke and with few choices. Polish-born Louis Kittner had arrived in New York with three cents. Sheltered by Virginia relatives, he shined shoes at railway depots. His son Joe recalled, "Our father went to the train station and reached into his pocket and pulled out the change he had and said, 'I want a ticket. How far will this take me?' And the ticket agent said, "It will take you to Weldon." Arriving there, he saw the town needed a cobbler. Lithuanian immigrant Michael Barker was peddling pottery around Wilson in 1905. "He got down in this area and his mule died," his grandson Dennis recalled. "So he just stayed." Newly arrived Harry Richter was set up as a peddler by his brother-in-law Jake Polakavetz. "I was sixteen years old and I didn't speak English," Richter recalled, "Jake said peddling was the best way to learn the language

In Baltimore, peddler Henry Farber found merchandise and his wife Molly. (Jim Farber)

and meet people." Tired of walking, he bought a horse and wagon, but quit after the horse wandered off.[38]

Peddling required no skills and little capital. As Jake Polakavetz put it, "All I had ever done was study Torah and sell wheat." On Sundays, Aaron Dietz loaded "hardware, pots, pans, bedding" from the Baltimore Bargain House on his mule and headed on foot into the countryside. "About Thursday, there would be enough goods sold, so he could ride." Another Bargain House peddler, Morris Freid, suffered sore feet. "When he would get to the top of the hill, he would roll down to the bottom so that he didn't have to walk," granddaughter Susan Bloom Farber recalled. A peddler found customers as they sat on porches or worked in barns. Short, stocky Morris Eisenberg had an eighty-mile route extending from Hillsborough to Burlington to Chapel Hill. Morris Witcowsky, who peddled northeastern North Carolina from Richmond, carried a 120-pound pack on his back with a 40-pound balancer on the front. Some twenty peddlers worked his territory, earning about $8.40 a week.[39]

Peddling was so pervasive that native merchants felt threatened. Starting in 1879, the state legislature passed ever more stringent rules to govern peddling.

The children of
A. M. Shrago, an
Edenton peddler in
the 1890s, on his
horse and wagon.
(William Shrago)

In 1885 peddlers had to obtain an annual ten-dollar permit which rose to fifteen with a horse or mule. "Cheap John merchants" selling in temporary quarters were taxed fifty dollars. Failure to display a license subjected the peddler to arrest. To obtain a peddler's license, an applicant had to be "a native born or naturalized citizen of the United States," although the law allowed county commissioners to exempt "any poor and infirm person who has no other means of support."[40]

Lewis Harris arrived in High Point in 1888. His brother in Richmond had given him needles, thread, and novelties to peddle and bought him a train ticket as far as he could go. Arriving in High Point, he threw a blanket on the ground to sell his goods, only to have a policeman arrest him for peddling without a license. The teenager, who knew no English, broke into tears. Two women, wives of manufacturers, took pity, bought him a license, and took him to a boardinghouse owned by "German John" Rommel, who deciphered his Yiddish. The ladies paid for his room and set him up in business. When "Hebrew" peddlers were arrested, judges typically suspended sentence with payment of court costs—as in the case of Isaac Shellom in Wilmington in 1909, "on condition that the peddler depart from the city."[41]

A. M. Shrago (far right) at his store in Goldsboro. (William Shrago)

Peddlers suffered the dangers of the road. Samuel Tucker, an "immigrant Jew" peddler from Richmond, sought shelter one night in 1892 in Franklin County with two brothers, Calvin and Thomas Coley. They murdered him with an axe, stealing $169, and tossed his body in a ravine, where eighteen months later it was discovered under some vines. Richmond Jews saw to Tucker's burial and monitored the Coley brothers' trial. Fellow peddler Aaron Dietz testified. Convicted, the brothers were publicly hanged in front of a crowd of ten thousand. The immigrant's ambition was to leave such a perilous, backbreaking occupation and settle down with a store. The number of peddlers in Durham declined from twelve in 1902 to two in 1911.[42]

Jews created an ethnic economy in dry goods. Jews loaned each other money, rented properties, and bought each other's stock. Living at the margins, they relied less on the corporate economy than on themselves. In their stores, second-generation sons and daughters worked as salespeople. Accumulating some capital, perhaps with a loan from a relative, the clerk set off for a store of his or her own. When Emil Rosenthal moved to Goldsboro in 1882, he sold his Wilson store to his nephews, Jonas and David Oettinger, for payments of $200 monthly. "We understood perfectly that the written terms were for our benefit," Jonas recalled.[43] This pattern was typical of small towns nationally and was not exclusively Jewish. The New South businessman was a newly arrived young man who had climbed from clerk to merchant. Charlotte's William Belk began with a New York Racket Store, brought his family into the enterprise, and built a regional department store chain.

The motto of Siegfried Sternberg's Asheville business was "We buy anything, and we sell everything." Sternberg once purchased a dying circus elephant for $80, intending to sell its hide, but when the pachyderm unexpectedly recovered, he sold it back to the circus for $500. A 1904 Durham newspaper described Adolph Max as a man "who buys anything from a goose to a church." Junk peddlers brought commerce to the countryside not by selling but by acquiring. The peddler picked up scrap as he emptied his wagon of goods. J. I. Lessem, who peddled around Fayetteville, collected "scrap iron, copper, bones, hides and furs," which he brought to Louis Levin's Fayetteville Junk Shop. When Lessem came to a stream, he swam across, pulling the horse and wagon behind him. At his Statesville store Louis Gordon sold secondhand furniture in the front and collected scrap in the back. Like other peddlers, scrap collectors aspired to be dealers, not just agents. They played the traditional Jewish role of middlemen, linking the rural economy to national markets. The scrap was sold to larger yards in Richmond or Baltimore, recalled Seymour Levin, whose father began collecting by horse and buggy in Burlington in 1909. Nearly every North Carolina city had a Jewish-owned scrapyard.[44]

Jews hustled to make something of very little. Max Samet turned an old saloon into a secondhand store. "Once a woman walked into his shop asking for an elegant chest of drawers," his grandson Leonard Samet recalled. "He assured her that if she would return in an hour, he would have exactly what she wanted." Rushing home, he emptied his bedroom dresser, threw it on his wagon, and returned to the store to make the sale. Prices were rarely fixed, and, as Harry Stein recalled, a storekeeper might write his actual cost in Hebrew so only he, and not the customer, knew the bottom price as they haggled. Jews often sold on credit, which accounted for more profit than the mark up. Raleigh's Willie Pizer peddled goods by wagon as a credit merchant. If a storekeeper bought pants from a wholesaler for five dollars and sold them for ten, Pizer would pay seven fifty and sell them on credit, collecting weekly until he might make fifteen.[45]

Poorer immigrants began as grocers with the family living in rooms behind or above the store. These stores sprouted on downtown side streets and near fac-

Louis Gordon's scrap-
yard in Statesville.
(Saul and Kalman
Gordon)

tories, in both black and white neighborhoods. Israel Gordon had a small wood-
framed shop in Durham's African American Hayti neighborhood. His family lived
in two rooms behind the store. In Youngsville, Aaron Dietz could not afford a
boardinghouse so he slept on a cot in the store.[46]

Businesses were family enterprises. Wives were "the breadwinners," recalled
Hazel Gladstein Wishnov, while their husbands played cards, speculated in real
estate, or went door to door collecting payments.[47] Because African American
housekeepers cost but several dollars a week, women were not homebound for
cooking and childcare. Several wives recall husbands who were poor businessmen, and women were more attuned to the customers' needs and fashions.
Jennie Nachamson took buying trips to Baltimore to stock their Kinston store,

Max Samet and his family at his secondhand furniture store, a former saloon, in High Point. (Leonard Samet)

and Carrie and Birdie Kronheimer served as buyers at their brother's Durham emporium.

Jewish stores lined downtowns selling dry goods, ready-to-wear clothing, shoes, groceries, and jewelry. Artisans tailored clothes and mended shoes. Pawnshops helped out the mill worker until the next day. Dry goods stores outfitted workers. Racket stores sold a variety of merchandise—shoes, washtubs, groceries, ready-to-wear clothes—at cheap prices. Frequently the stores were titled Boston, Baltimore, or New York either as outlets of out-of-town companies or to emphasize their big city prices and fashions. "The Pattersons and Lewises, they brought style here," Morris Kaplan recalled of Hendersonville's first Jewish merchants. Jewish stores clustered in downtowns. In Asheville, Jewish stores lined Main Street and Patton Avenue. Tarboro's Main Street was nicknamed Little Jerusalem. In Charlotte, Jewish stores centered around the Square at Trade and Tryon Streets. In

HORSES AND MULES BOUGHT DIRECT
FROM THE WEST.

WE SAVE YOU THE OTHER FELLOW'S
PROFIT.

FEEDSTUFFS GROWN
ON
OUR OWN FARMS.

FARM IMPLEMENTS AND MACHINERY
OF BEST MAKES.
WAGONS AND HARNESS,
BUGGIES AND SURREYS.

Ben Susman stands before the door of his livery in Washington. (Brown Library, Washington)

1908 Kinston's Queen Street sported two Jewish-owned jewelers, a grocer, three clothing stores, five dry goods stores, a shoemaker, and a junk dealer. All but two were established by East European Jews who had arrived after 1890. In 1909 eight of Raleigh's clothing stores were owned by Jews. By 1919 in Wilmington, six of the sixteen clothiers were Jewish owned, and eleven of the nineteen dry goods stores.[48]

Anchoring downtowns were Jewish-owned department stores. North Carolina Jews, too, were merchant princes in the mold of Straus or Gimbel in New York or Rich in Atlanta, upwardly mobile peddlers who turned from rags to riches. In 1890 Prussian immigrant Solomon Lipinsky gave his store the Gilded Age name of Bon Marché to "bring the world of fashion" to Asheville. Novelist Thomas Wolfe wrote Lipinsky's son Louis, "When I first saw Paris, as a kid of twenty-four, I could not quite get used to the fact that *they* had a Bon Marché, as well; I kept wondering what the hell they were doing with *our* name." Another Ashevillean, Prussian immigrant Morris Meyers, opened the Palais Royal. In 1895 Russian-born peddler Solomon Coplon had opened his first store in New Bern, which by 1900 had grown to be "the largest department store south of Richmond." During fall and spring market seasons, customers arrived by horse and carriage from three states. In

Malever & Co. pawnshop in Charlotte. (Charlotte Jewish Historical Society)

The Lindy family at their store in Charlotte. (Al Rogat)

1911, as the depression receded, Benjamin Kronheimer opened a 25,000-square-foot department store in Durham, replete with an elevator, that drew downtown westward. The place to shop in Raleigh was Kline & Lazarus.[49]

The Jews' mobility, both geographic and occupational, was typical of New South entrepreneurs. With the rise of the tobacco, furniture, textile, and timber industries, people were on the move. The opening of a mill or factory pushed and pulled Jews from one town to another. Jewish clerks, salesmen, and merchants seeking new opportunities shared railway cars with farm workers heading for jobs in textile towns, planters raising capital for mills or banks, or northern mechanics installing machinery in new factories. Wholesalers and manufacturers sent salesmen and drummers on the road. Tailors and shoemakers arrived in greater numbers as artisans left Eastern Europe in increasing numbers, displaced by manufactured goods.

Small-town Jewish communities, historian Lee Shai Weissbach observes, were marked by "fluidity and motion," constant "population turnover." Failure and ambition, cycles of boom and bust, pushed and pulled Jews to and from towns. Of the thirty-five Jews in Durham in 1887, only five remained by 1902. A bank failure

A row of Jewish stores in downtown Asheville. (Ball Collection, Ramsey Library, University of North Carolina at Asheville)

in 1888 and the Panic of 1893 drove merchants from town even as new immigrants arrived. The national depression of 1907, which lasted three years, led to failures and departures. It "broke me," recalled Hendersonville's Harry Patterson. He lost his general store and became a clothes presser. Hard times brought pawnbrokers and loan agents to town. In Durham, several stores tottering near bankruptcy burned, and their owners were charged with arson. "There was one irresistible fact of a Jew and a fire, but that was all" the evidence, a newspaper reported of a 1911 case.[50] Although nationally the insurance industry remained wary of Jews, none was convicted locally. Other reports mention Jews victimized by crime or charged with possessing stolen goods.

Poorer Jewish peddlers and storekeepers were bound only by their stock and

OETTINGER'S—THE DEPENDABLE STORE
WILSON, N. C.

118468

Every city has its leading store. In Wilson it's Oettinger's. To many residents of Eastern North Carolina the slogan *"It Pays To Deal At Oettinger's, The Dependable Store"* is a household synonym, verified by business relations extending for more than forty-six years.

Oettinger's store in Wilson. (J. Robert Boykin III)

leases and were free to move on. Starting from Baltimore, Michael Marks moved to Kinston, to Thomasville, back to Baltimore, and finally to Greensboro about 1904. Aaron Weinstein, who had peddled in Louisiana and Mississippi, moved from Gastonia to Gibsonville before settling in Lumberton in 1907. Jacob Dietz tried a store in Youngsville, Louisburg, Zebulon, and Hope Mills before finally settling down in Wendell. "Each move that he made was an improvement," Geri Dietz felt.[51]

The Jews' relentless upward mobility paralleled the progress of the New South. The grocer's ambition was to open a Main Street dry goods store. In 1899 Abraham Kaplan operated a Raleigh grocery, four years later a furniture store, and seven years after that a women's specialty shop. Lewis Blomberg arrived in Asheville in 1887 as a peddler, and three years later opened a cigar and news shop. By 1907 he owned New York Junk and Hide Company and then Blomberg Sporting Goods and Toys. In 1920 he acquired his brother's Racket Store, and a year later he was a dealer of army-navy surplus clothing.[52] One store spawned a second or a third, usually operated by a sibling or in-law. Lithuanian immigrants William Heilig and Max Meyers opened a furniture store in Goldsboro in 1913, beginning the nation's largest furniture chain.

The first Heilig &
Meyers furniture
store of Goldsboro,
forerunner of a national
chain. (Amy Meyers
Krumbein)

As agents of change, Jews nationally helped create a "mass entertainment" industry, bringing cosmopolitan culture to the provinces. New media created new opportunities without an entrenched hierarchy to block a Jew's progress. The Blomberg Amusement Company ran Asheville's Strand movie theater. In Dover, the Nachamsons opened a "moving picture parlor," next to their store. (The cinema closed because the town's lights went out whenever the projector turned on.)[53]

Younger Jews climbed into the professions. In 1913 E. J. Stern of Charlotte was described as "an efficient architect, rapidly rising." Sidney Stern, born in Wilson in 1879, had quit school at fifteen to work as a clerk in a Scotland Neck dry goods store. Dissatisfied with the pay, he became first a fishmonger, then a butcher, and finally a grocer. In 1908 he followed his brother David to UNC, where he studied law. The brothers relocated to Greensboro, where they became leading attor-

PORTRAIT: SIMEON ARCHIBALD SCHLOSS

"Every town with even a smidgen of civic pride had an opera house," historian Paul Wilson observes, where local folks enjoyed touring minstrel shows, solo performers, and theatrical troupes. From Reconstruction to World War I, some eighty-two North Carolina hamlets and towns held 159 theaters. North Carolina's foremost entrepreneur was Wilmington's Simeon Archibald Schloss, whose ties to the New York Theatrical Syndicate brought the cosmopolitan world down home.

S. A. Schloss was the son of Marx Schloss, a Bavarian immigrant who had served as a Confederate quartermaster. A hotelkeeper, Marx Schloss had operated inns in Salisbury, Charlotte, Raleigh, and Wilmington. Like many opera house managers, S. A. Schloss rose from mercantile ranks. After stints as a clerk, auctioneer, and merchant, he toured as a cornetist with a minstrel troupe before managing the Wilmington Opera House, Thalian Hall, in 1895. Forging a link to the syndicate, he leased Raleigh's Academy of Music (1898) and then Greensboro's new Grand Opera House (1901). Soon followed theaters in Charlotte (1903); Winston-Salem (1905); Asheville (1906, 1910); Monroe (1907); Tarboro, Goldsboro, Wilson (1908); and Concord (1909). At its peak Schloss Theatres Circuit operated fourteen houses in three states.

"Schloss appears to know just what the people want," a New York theater paper commented. The Polish pianist Paderewski and the New York Philharmonic toured, and there was an occasional Shakespeare play. More typical, Wilson notes, was a steady run of farces, musical comedies, minstrel shows, and melodramas like *Ten Nights in a Bar Room*. Minstrel shows flourished in the 1870s and still played into the 1920s. The term Opera House dignified entertainments that did not always aspire to high culture. Schloss expanded into a music store and, because theaters required posters, a billboard company that gave rise to Charlotte's Outdoor Advertising. After Schloss died in 1913, his widow Mary Bear Schloss ran the company, but the syndicate soon expired, done in by competition with the Schubert Brothers and a new popular entertainment, the movies.[1]

1. Paul Wilson, "That's Entertainment!," *Our State*, Oct. 1996, 31.

neys. Even more rapidly than the Germans, the East Europeans pursued professional careers. After their Durham dry goods stores failed, David Gladstone and Benjamin Lovenstein took law courses at Chapel Hill and passed the bar. Dr. Sam Rapport and Dr. Nathan Rosenstein held positions in the state's optometry society, with Rosenstein serving as president. When Ike Zuckerman entered pharmacy school in 1910, the newspaper noted that "he is one of the number here going from soda fountain clerk to higher position."[54]

Jews were moving tentatively from the ethnic into the corporate economy. Several Jews found positions in the insurance industry, a trade widely regarded as anti-Semitic. In Greensboro, Charles Weill and M. E. Block ran agencies with Christian partners. Increasingly, Jews found employment as salary earners in corporate firms. Since the early Republic, Jews had sat on boards as founders and directors of banks and loan companies. In Wilmington alone, eleven Jews served from 1885 to 1915. Prominent merchants held such posts in Asheville, Charlotte, Durham, Greensboro, Statesville, and Wilson. Those relationships demonstrated trust. When Ben Duke's bank found itself short of cash during the 1907 depression, he borrowed $10,000, on a handshake, from clothier Abe Wilson's shoebox stash. In Greensboro, junk dealer Max Temko loaned money to the Richardson family for its nascent drug company.[55]

The passion for real estate struck the immigrant Russian storekeeper as well as the native-born Jewish capitalist. Land speculation was rife as the state grew urban. Growing populations and expanding suburbs sent land prices soaring. The Wallace brothers created the Statesville Land Development Company, which sold 700 town lots in 1891, and they bought rural acreage. The Schloss and Nathan families were among the developers of Wrightsville Beach, a barrier island resort. In Eastern Europe, Jews were rarely permitted to own land, but the immigrants did so passionately in America. "Real estate, they all did that," recalled Durham's Abe Stadiem. By 1910 more than half of Durham's Jews owned land. "He'd buy a couple of houses and rent them," Lou Silver recalled of his grocer father. "Then he'd start building houses." When Russian-immigrant Max Shevel, a furniture dealer, died in 1917, his widow Sarah was left with three houses, two buildings, sixty lots, and some $30,000 in real estate. The Kaplan family, nominally Raleigh storekeepers, purchased ten properties from 1900 to 1910 and twenty-eight the following decade.[56]

Jewish merchants purchased farmland as investments or, under the crop lien system, through foreclosures, a practice some Jewish merchants pointedly disapproved of. Nathan Ballenberger gave up his Goldsboro store and, shortening his name to Berger, became a farmer near Pikeville. German Jewish merchants like the Weils, Hahns, Oettingers, Rosenthals, and Katzensteins all had farmland holdings in eastern North Carolina in the hundreds of acres. Lionel Weil applied himself to scientific agriculture and operated a fertilizer factory. East European immigrants who came to America as country Jews also had ambitions to farm. Morris Pearson owned a store in Richlands but loved the country life. "Looks as if papa wants to farm a little, plant a crop of corn, cotton, and tobacco," his son Harry wrote his brother. "Oh the fruit, . . . the people say he has the best crop in the neighborhood." A. I. Kaplan's Raleigh dairy farm provided kosher milk every Passover, and an outing to the farm was a popular community pastime. Aaron and Israel Weinstein, Lumberton merchants, became "gentleman farmers" with perhaps a thousand acres of tenant farms. "They had a feel for the land," recalled Aaron's grandson David. Commonly, in both town and country, Jews kept home gardens and backyard hen houses, and maybe a dairy cow. Jews also served as butchers, though not always kosher. In 1911 Isaac Cohn had a slaughterhouse in New Bern, as did Julius Schwartz in Durham and Raleigh.[57]

BECOMING SOUTHERN

The challenge for native and immigrant Jews alike was to become southerners while remaining Jews. They built friendly relations with Christians, both personally and institutionally, but they also maintained distinctly Jewish affiliations. They organized for Jews in Europe and Palestine while joining local school boards and town councils. Their southern and Jewish worlds were hardly separate, for each was blending. A Durham Hebrew baseball team preserved Jewish solidarity but in a distinctly American way. Jews embraced diverse and contradictory identities. During the Columbus celebration of 1892, a Wilmington Jewish ball featured Jews captaining the *Niña*, *Pinta*, and *Santa María* while a regimental band played "Dixie."[58] That Jews had their own observances speaks to both their Americanism and their exclusion.

The store was where immigrant Jew met Christian America. Selling meant learning English and creating the goodwill necessary for success. However strange Jews' accents and appearance, southerners found them friendly and hardworking. The immigrants willingly Americanized. A first step was to anglicize their names. Lipe and Yetta Tevio were reborn as Philip and Ethel Dave. Hyman Isakovitz was known in Raleigh as Herman Glass. The Girards and Gurneys of Gastonia were originally Goldbergs. German and Russian Jews bore such family names as Brady, Clarke, Jackson, Pearson, Scott, Smith, Taylor, Wallace, White, Whitlock, Williams, and Wilson. Henry Clay Greenberg, Pinckney Bernstein, and Vance Weil were named for southern patriots.

Native-born Jews participated in memorializing the Confederacy. Southerners held nostalgically to the Lost Cause, mythologizing a bygone day of courage and gentility even as plantation life yielded to urban, factory living. When a monument arose on the Bentonville battlefield in 1895, teenaged Gertrude Weil was enlisted in the "Hampton Guards" to escort an aged Confederate general. Louis Leon attended Confederate reunions in Charlotte, and Pauline Goldsmith served as president of the United Daughters of the Confederacy in Mount Airy. At Sol Bear's funeral in 1904, the Daughters laid laurel upon his bier, and uniformed Confederate veterans stood guard. After Zebulon Vance's death in 1894, an obelisk arose in Asheville's Pack Square. Annually, B'nai B'rith and the United Daughters of the Confederacy jointly sponsored a wreathe laying ceremony at the monument underwritten by New York philanthropist Nathan Straus. Rabbis and ministers both spoke, including Rabbi Stephen Wise who expressed gratitude for Vance's tolerance.[59]

German Jews and Lutherans celebrated their shared culture. Jews were leaders of Wilmington's German American Alliance, Schultze Club, and Germania Cornet Band. When the kaiser died in 1888, Daniel Kahnweiler organized the memorial at St. Paul's Evangelical Lutheran Church, and Rabbi Mendelsohn presided in both English and German. Goldsboro Jews included German in their religious school. Jews returned to their ancestral homeland. During a 1903 trip to his birthplace in Württemberg, Sol Weil met a "female cousin who started crying and got him all worked up." Families in America and Germany corresponded in Judeo-German. After a half century in America, the Sternglanz family of Tarboro, suffering a bankruptcy, returned to Germany in 1889.[60]

In Gilded Age North Carolina, no less than in the nation, hundreds of elite social clubs and societies had formed for the newly rich. As immigrants flocked to emerging towns and cities, the Progressive Era inspired a new organizational frenzy dedicated to public betterment. Societies, both black and white, local and national, arose in support of temperance, public health, arts and music, and women's suffrage and against child labor. Jews joined, and sometimes led, campaigns to build hospitals, YMCAs, and orphanages. They served on school boards. B'nai B'rith Lodges raised funds for yellow fever sufferers and the Red Cross. Raleigh's Hebrew Benevolent Association cared for the poor regardless of creed. Jews were founders and leaders of merchants associations and chambers of commerce. In Durham, the chamber founders in 1902 included not just German Jews but also increasingly prosperous Russian storekeepers. Since colonial days, the Masons had strong Jewish contingents. Nathaniel Jacobi led the state's Odd Fellows, and in 1895 Rabbi Mendelsohn was chosen Provisional Grand Councilor of the Order of Chosen Friends, a fraternal order with 4,000 members statewide.[61]

The New South spawned a class of educated "new women." Denied the vote, they acted in philanthropic spheres. In Wilson, Miriam Rosenthal along with Kate Connor and Mary Daniels were a progressive "Catholic, Hebrew, and Methodist trinity" who took charge of welfare in a community that lacked nurses, hospitals, or a community chest, recalled Daniels's son Josephus. Recognizing that social needs were systemic, beyond charity, the new women turned political. In 1898 Mina Rosenthal Weil invited feminist and social activist Charlotte Gilman Perkins to Goldsboro. Sarah Weil, a Bostonian never at home in Goldsboro, lobbied the state legislature on progressive issues, one of which spread public libraries across the state. Mina Weil helped create the North Carolina Federation of Women's Clubs in 1902. Her daughter Gertrude led the North Carolina Equal

Suffrage League in Charlotte. Gertrude Weil, with Laura Weill Stern, traveled the state raising funds, organizing clubs, and confronting the Democratic machine on behalf of women's rights. They removed barriers to women's service on school boards, creating opportunities for women like Bertha Sternberger and then Flora Stern to become the first women on the Greensboro School Board.

The Progressive Era extolled competition as manly, healthy, and virtuous. Asheville optometrist Michael Robinson was a rugged outdoorsman, a founder of the Carolina Mountain Club, who still rarely missed a Friday-night service. Advocates of muscle Jews took inspiration from German Zionist Max Nordau, who sought to overcome stereotypes of Jews as physically small and weak, a timid, victimized people who prized books, not brawn. For immigrants and their children, sports was an agency of Americanizing, and Jews joined the sporting fraternities. Durham's best boxer was Max Summerfield, son of the synagogue president, until he got knocked out in the eighth round during a 1901 match against Charley Clark. The fight was held at a gambling den, and when a fan yelled, "Police!" Summerfield turned his head only to catch Clark's uppercut. Wilmington's Arthur Bluethenthal was an all-American on Princeton's undefeated football team in 1911 and later coached at Princeton and the University of North Carolina. Jews competed as "Hebrew" teams in sandlot baseball. Jews were regarded as especially adept at basketball, a city game. When a "Hebrew Quintet" beat the Durham Boy Scouts 35–7, the newspaper reported, "The Scouts played a good game, but they were simply outclassed by the Jews."[62] Jews were members of the earliest basketball teams at both Trinity College and the University of North Carolina. Whatever their sport, the athletes were always distinguished as Jews.

Social lives reveal a cultural blending, the recognition that acceptance meant "conformity to southern values." Wedding ceremonies were led by a local or visiting rabbi, but the affairs themselves show Jews aspiring to middle-class respectability. Augusta Cohen and William Sultan's 1888 New Bern marriage was a "Hebrew Wedding in High Life." "A large and select company of our Hebrew friends . . . and a number of our leading Gentile citizens" attended. After Rabbi Max Moses of Goldsboro performed the ceremony, a repast of "splendid collation" was served, gifts of silver and crystal were presented, and telegraphs were read from across the country and "the big water." The men, smoking a "fragrant Havanna, . . . walked home mellow with old wine and filled with good cheer." In 1885 the Richmond rabbi presided at the "epicurean" Winston-Salem wedding of Sigmund Rosenbacher, who wore "English worsted," and Carrie Rose, draped in silk, velvet, and diamonds. Jewish children accommodated to Easter and Christmas. Mattie Rosenthal of Wilson wrote Christmas exercises in her school notebook, and Sarah Pearson of Kinston wrote her brother in 1911 about "What Santa Claus brought

Wilmington Hebrew
basketball team.
(Cape Fear Museum,
Wilmington)

me." In 1900 Wilmington's young Jewish smart set formed a Mistletoe Club that met in homes on Christmas night for parties and dances.[63]

Jewish residential patterns illustrated class differences between Germans and East Europeans. Wilmington's German Jews lived among the town's Christian elite, which encouraged some social relations. Lillian Sternberger recalled, "While we were not intimate, we were invited to weddings, big parties, and attended funerals." East European immigrants often located in neighborhoods between black and white, reflecting their in-between social, racial, and economic status. Jews who operated groceries in black areas might be the only whites living in the neighborhood. Often they lived in rooms behind their stores. In the 1890s Wilmington's immigrant Jews settled around Fourth and Walnut Streets in a racially mixed neighborhood near their groceries and dry goods stores. They catered to farmers and workers, both white and black. By 1915 as many as eighteen Jewish-owned stores lined Fourth Street. A similar pattern existed in Durham. Jews settled on Pine Street in The Bottoms, near the railroad tracks, the tobacco factories, and a red-light district. The town's first Jewish residents, Abe and Fannie Goldstein, purchased cottages to rent to new immigrants. Jewish peddlers and salesmen found room and board there. As Jews became more prosperous,

they moved up hill to a white neighborhood, drawn by a synagogue and a new public school. Two-thirds of the community, some thirty-five families, lived in this "ghetto without walls." North Carolina's Jewish residential pattern paralleled national trends that saw, for example, New York Jews settle first in the Lower East Side ghetto and then move to middle-class apartments in the Bronx and Brooklyn.[64]

Protestant Christians saw Jews as both unsaved and blood of Jesus. On their rounds, peddlers built friendships with customers, both black and white. Farmhouse doors opened. Often the peddler was welcomed to the family table or given

Immigrants Joseph
Lipman and Celia
Passman under the
wedding canopy in
1911. (Elbert Lipman)

a warm bed. Peddler Morris Fried "would trade a thimble to a couple if they would let him sleep in the barn," his granddaughter recalled. In Candor, Harry Richter, a gold miner, boarded with William and Malissia Haywood, who in their nightly Bible study read only the Old Testament in deference to their guest. Malissia taught the immigrant English, reminded him to send money to his parents in Europe, and baked his biscuits without lard. "The orthodox Protestants granted us dignity; they were the first to make us feel that we really belonged," Richter reflected. Christians brought newborns to Jewish stores for Hebrew blessings. Isolated Jews in country towns formed intimate friendships with Christian customers and neighbors. In Kinston, Harry Pearson's days were filled at card tables and baseball games. "Visiting was the Carolinian's customary way to relax," historian Sydney Nathans observes. Customers invited Jewish storekeepers to their farms for Sunday socializing.[65]

In 1886, when Wilmington's Front Street Methodist Church burned, the Temple of Israel invited the Methodists to worship Sundays at the synagogue, which they did for two years. When the new church was completed, Alfred Hankins composed a poem of "Farewell," blessing "Israel's seed" who "welcomed us with open door." The Reverend Dr. Yates, a Methodist preacher, spoke at Jewish services. The newspaper noted that the Hebrews "are not bound by any narrow-minded denominational differences, but are anxious for the advancement and comfort of all." But Christians also prayed for the conversion of the Jews. Converted Jewish missionaries were well received in churches. Mark Levy, an Englishman based in Richmond, who was general secretary of the Society for the Propagation of the Gospel among Jews, toured North Carolina in 1901 and 1904. He lectured at churches on such topics as "Israel's Love for the Gentiles and Christian Love for the Jews." In Winston, he spoke at a YMCA prayer meeting as a missionary of the "Hope of Israel Movement." In Durham, a newspaper reported, "All are welcome, but Levy especially invites Jews." In Wilmington, he caused a "mild sensation during services at Temple of Israel." Rabbi Mendelsohn denounced him as "untrue to the principles of the Jewish faith and the traditions of his people." Levy rose from a seat and "made bold enough to attempt to reply," but a congregational officer "promptly silenced" him. Other Jewish converts—A. Lichtenstein of the

Jewish Christian Mission of St. Louis and Rev. J. H. Rosenberg from the Southwestern Presbyterian University—also toured. Rev. Abraham Cohen of South Carolina ministered for ten years at New Bern's First Baptist Church and directed the Oxford Orphanage. Churches that welcomed self-declared Hebrew Christians often enjoyed warm relations with synagogues, but testimonies on "My Conversion to Christianity" fell on deaf Jewish ears. Also visiting were Christian sectarians, whose religious fundamentalism led them to adopt Jewish practices. In 1911 a fourteen-foot boat motored into Wilmington harbor with five "Israelites from the House of David." They came from a Michigan colony called "Jerusalem," and the unshaven men "preach the doctrines of the Bible from the Israelite standpoint."[66]

Jews remained a curiosity. When Jennie Nachamson gave birth, she recalled that "all our country friends came to town just to see what a 'Jew baby' looked like." In Youngsville, Jacob Dietz had "nobody to talk to," Charlotte Horwitz recalled. "He didn't understand them. They didn't understand him." According to family legend, Louis Schwartz intended to settle in Winston, but his garbled English got him a ticket to Wilmington. Newspapers mangled Jewish names so that Rabinowitz became Robin Novitz and Siegel was christened Seagull. Rabbi Mayerberg was addressed as "Rev. Father." To pawn a watch, one went to "A Jew." Thomas Wolfe was gleefully curious about a local "bearded orthodox old Jew, clothing in rusty greasy black, and wearing a scarred derby," who received news of his son's suicide with "Oi yoi yoi yoi yoi." The throaty, accented "rich excited voices" of the women and the "hysterical quarrels" of the families were objects of amusement.[67]

The Leo Frank lynching, which allegedly traumatized southern Jews, was little felt except perhaps among Asheville's Jews, who were linked to Atlanta by geography, commerce, and family. Ashevillean Wolfe noted a "fetich" of Jewish persecution but "no interest in a pogrom." Yet, a violent anti-Semitism lurked beneath the civility. In 1909, shortly after German immigrant Aaron Kahn arrived in Charlotte, he and his brother Max were standing on a street corner when a burly white man asked him for a match. "You are a Jew, aren't you?" the man asked. "Yes," Aaron replied. The stranger then knocked him to the ground and stomped him until his rib cage broke. He died a week later and was buried in the Hebrew Cemetery.[68]

REMAINING JEWS
Old country customs did not always translate well in the American South. The High Point newspaper front-paged "Alright for a Gentile" in 1909, describing the "Jewish Rabbi['s]" attempt to pick up a registered letter at the post office one

Saturday. He refused to violate the Sabbath by signing for it, so he went into the street and returned with a "small boy who was of the gentile species" to sign in his stead. The newspaper was perplexed at this "rather amusing thing." Jews struggled to negotiate between religious law and American civil law on marriage and divorce. Couples took civil vows before a justice of the peace before solemnizing their marriage before a rabbi with a religious ceremony. In 1905, when Fannie Goldstein sued her husband Abe for divorce, she went to a Durham court with her ketubah (wedding contract), naively believing the civil law would enforce its provisions. Her excitable Yiddish amused and perplexed onlookers as she waved it in her hand. The couple traveled to Norfolk to a beth din (rabbinic court), which issued a divorce.[69]

Food daily challenged Jewish tradition. The Jewish world was allegedly shocked in 1883 when a "trefa (unkosher) banquet"—featuring seafood and milk mixed with meat—was held in Cincinnati to celebrate Hebrew Union College's first rabbinic ordination. Among America's Reform Jews, such menus were common in the 1880s. The line was drawn at pork. Wilmington's Concordia Society's 1889 Purim Ball featured an "elegant supper" of mayonnaise lobsters, beef tongue, and Neapolitan ice cream. Most East Europeans, certainly not all, held to kosher laws. Morris Pearson in Richlands wrote his son in New York, "I'd ask you to send out at once so it may reach us in time before Friday 1 tongue and about 3lb of corned beef."[70] Storekeepers Henry Farber and Max Perman, isolated in Weldon and Warrenton respectively, traveled to Baltimore to learn to kill chickens ritually. The trains that brought dry goods from Baltimore, Atlanta, or Richmond also delivered kosher provisions. Barrels of herring, cheap and nutritious, came down. Once a conductor, smelling the pungent fish, tossed a barrel off a train, thinking it contained rot. Next to the backyard chicken house might be a grapevine to make Passover wine, and communities much honored local kosher pickle makers.

Distance from family and community both here and abroad meant constant correspondence. Morris Pearson in 1913 made a classic Jewish parental lament to his son Louis in New York: "I didn't receive not even a postal from you & for one while I have thought that you have forgotten all about your folks at home." Betrothed men sent heartrending letters to sweethearts in Baltimore and New York. With their family and business ties to Baltimore, Philadelphia, and New York, fiancés, siblings, cousins, and mothers-in-law were constantly arriving and departing for holidays and vacations. Youths especially were sent to friends and relatives in cities to meet potential spouses. These visits, which might last ten days, featured introductory parties. Wilmington Jews found spouses in Atlanta, Charlotte, Raleigh, and Richmond. From 1885 to 1910, about 80 percent of Wilmington's German Jewish youth married out-of-town Jews while 10 percent found

Max Bloom, a peddler, with his wife Lula Peele, a Halifax County farmer's daughter. (Hannah Grant)

local partners. The intermarriage rate was less than 10 percent.[71] As a youth in rural Enfield, Sigmund Meyer never set foot in a synagogue, and his father was too busy at the store to educate him Jewishly, but he and his brothers always understood that they were to marry Jews.

Assimilation was also inevitable. Of the four Oettinger children in Kinston to survive into adulthood, only one married a Jew. Fishblate women suffering from various ailments turned to Christian Science although their families remained in the Jewish fold. Lila Waters Durham, wife of a Durham Baptist minister, claimed to be of Jewish origin. Wilmington's St. James Church included Jews who had intermarried and assimilated. Intermarriage was uncommon and undesired. Several reports describe out-of-state Jews who ran away to North Carolina to be married furtively, and the Israelites were "very much exercised over the matter." Christian women also converted to marry Jewish men. Such reports began in 1883. In 1891 Miss Addie Jenkins "was received into the full fellowship" of the Jewish faith at the home of Rabbi Mayerberg in Goldsboro, and "immediately afterwards she was married to Mr. Julius Rosenbaum of Tarboro." Louis Weill married the daughter of a Methodist minister who raised their children as Jews. In 1904 when Lithuanian-born Max Bloom fell ill while peddling in Halifax County, a farmer named Peele sheltered him. His daughter Lula nursed Max back to health, and the two fell in love. Max took Lula to Wilmington, where she lived with the rabbi for thirty days to study Judaism. After her conversion, they married. Lula Peele Bloom became so frustrated maintaining a kosher home that one day she gave up and fried pork chops. When Max came home, he tossed out the window not just the pork chops but also the pan and dishes.[72]

The Progressive Era's passion for uplift inspired Jewish organizations, too. The state's Jews remained connected to global Jewry through an expanding Jewish media. Scholarly and popular books, journals, and newspapers proliferated, including in 1877 the *Jewish South*. In 1912 the *Tageblatt*, a religiously Orthodox Yiddish newspaper in New York, sent its chief correspondent, Louis Tinsburg, to North Carolina, where he was to report on Jewish life. In 1888 a Jewish Publication Society, founded to Americanize immigrants, offered biographies for children, classics of Jewish literature, and an English translation of the Bible. In 1900 Mrs. K. H. Scherman came from Philadelphia to solicit new members for the society. By 1918 it listed 123 North Carolina subscribers in seventeen communities, ranging from deli owner B. May of Wilmington to Sir Philip Henry of the Zealandia estate in Asheville. Children and grandchildren of immigrants recall grocers and storekeepers who were avid readers. Letters between the Pearson brothers in Kinston and New York were full of book talk.[73]

An 1893 meeting of World Parliament of Religions in Chicago inspired Reform women to form a National Council of Jewish Women. It reinforced Jewish home values, provided for immigrants, and advocated for social justice. In 1912 came Hadassah, the women's Zionist society, and a year later the National Federation of Temple Sisterhoods. Jewish defense organizations arose in response to persecution here and abroad. German Jews founded the American Jewish Committee in 1906 to combat czarist persecutions, and East Europeans organized the American Jewish Congress in 1915 with a Zionist agenda. In response to the Leo Frank trial, B'nai B'rith created an Anti-Defamation League in 1913.

If Jews were acculturating as southerners, they affirmed their Jewish identity, their difference, by establishing local societies as well as chapters of global Jewish organizations. Their activity was a Jewish response to the Progressive Era's passion for uplift, emphasizing cultivation of the mind through music and literature and the body through sports. Mostly, Jews wanted to associate with other Jews. The Young Men's Hebrew Association (YMHA), modeled on the YMCA, had organized in New York in 1874, and branches formed in Raleigh, Tarboro, and Wilmington. Local social clubs for youth waxed and waned. Despite its aspiring title, a Hebrew Social and Literary Society in Durham in 1913, "composed of nearly all the younger members of the race in the city," was more engaged in basketball than in poetry. B'nai Brith Lodges in Charlotte, Goldsboro, Tarboro, and Wilmington were joined by Durham (1910) and Kinston (1915) as East Europeans joined a society with a German legacy. In 1883 Wilmington hosted a B'nai B'rith district convention that drew one hundred delegates from thirty-four lodges in five states. Local Jews rose to regional and national office.[74]

JEWISH AMERICAN YOUTH

For a people who prized education, North Carolina was not inviting. Its citizens resisted public schools—the poor distrusted book learning, and the wealthy had private academies. In 1885 the state supreme court overthrew a school tax. North Carolina, a historian noted, "in 1900 had perhaps the poorest school system in the United States." Nearly 20 percent of whites and 48 percent of blacks were illiterate. For immigrant children, school marked their first encounter with America. Yiddish-speaking children—lost in English, not knowing Washington from a washtub—were thrown into classrooms with native-born. Lithuanian-born Joe Dave found Durham educators who were "very liberal in their thinking . . . very courteous and helpful to all students who came from Europe." Typically, immigrant children were assigned to lower grades than others their age but advanced quickly. Fourteen-year-old Rebecca Moscovitz of Troy felt embarrassed to sit at an undersized desk in a class of six-year-olds to learn English. In six months, she rose six grades, praised daily by her teacher.[75] Placed with young children, Harold Bloom, who had his bar mitzvah, felt humiliated and dropped out. Jewish students were routinely listed on honor rolls, and children of Yiddish-speaking immigrants won awards in state oratory and debate competitions.

"Everyone at school has been very kind and I have made a lot of friends who come home with me," Rebecca Moscovitz recalled, speaking for many immigrant children. Yet Jewish children in larger towns also remembered taunts and fights. Benjamin Schwartz in Wilmington recalled, "My first three years in school were tough." Big kids threatened to hit his "head against this wall if you don't talk Jew talk." A bully cornered Roy Levy on a schoolyard to ask why he killed Christ. "I didn't do it," Roy answered. "My brother Dave did it." Taunts of "Jew babies" or "Christ-killers" point to anti-Semitism learned at home or church. In his autobiographical novel *Look Homeward, Angel*, Thomas Wolfe recalled how neighborhood kids "made war upon the negroes and the Jews." They chased home an Isaac Lipinski or Edward Michalove—the names were real Asheville Jews—shouting "Goose Grease" for their "Semitic diet" or mocking their Yiddish with a nonsensical "Veeshamadye." Persecuting Michalove made Wolfe "glad at heart because of the existence of some one weaker than himself." Public schools were thoroughly Christian with daily Bible readings and hymn singing. In 1913 Goldsboro's B'nai B'rith boldly asked the school superintendent to halt classroom Bible readings. Six years later Rabbi Mayerberg was still being assured that such lessons would end.[76]

Wealthier Jews, like other elites, sent their children to private schools or military academies. Oettingers and Rosenthals attended Wilson's Collegiate Seminary for Young Ladies. Arthur Bluethenthal of Wilmington went to Phillips Academy in

STORY: MIN MUNICH GOES TO SCHOOL

Min Munich was a small child when her family left Lithuania for Oxford. After only days in America, Min was taken to elementary school.

I was too frightened to go into the class and refused to let go of my father's sturdy and supporting hand. . . . I was put into the only first grade that existed at the time, where my younger cousins near my age, had already been placed. . . . I sat frozen to my desk, my hands primly folded, as was the custom with the students in those years, afraid to move a muscle, but watching all that was happening around me, until my cousin Dora, a bit older than me and already a veteran of two months in the American educational world, trying to make me more comfortable, spoke to me in Yiddish. Since we had not yet learned that there were rules to follow, we got up from our desks when we wanted to. . . . Dora achieved great stature in my eyes when she escorted me around the building. One of the great wonders which we did not know in Russia was the first objective of the tour . . . the gleaming white bathroom with water toilets which flushed water when we pulled a handle. We must have used up gallons of Oxford's water supply with this novelty. This was America!

Miss May's patience with us was indescribable. She somehow led us through the mystery of the English word through pictures, songs and various motions. Gradually we learned enough words to communicate, and when we began to read THE SUNBONNET BABIES, we were off and going. Dora

Min Munich, a Russian immigrant child in Oxford in the early 1900s. (Joan Samet)

learned more quickly so she was promoted to the second grade. Nathan and I remained, going the regular route to eventual graduation. The two older cousins, Sarah and Mose, had already reached the fourth grade, all within that one year![1]

1. Min Klein, *This I Remember* (May 1983), 9–10, JHFNC.

Louis Jaffé, son of a Durham immigrant storekeeper, as a student at Trinity College. (Louis I. Jaffé Jr.)

Exeter, New Hampshire, before enrolling at Princeton. As southerners, boys were packed to Oak Ridge Military Academy with some moving on to Virginia Military Institute (VMI) or the Citadel. Gaston Lichtenstein of Tarboro and Samuel Mayerberg of Goldsboro were sent to Hebrew Union College in Cincinnati.

The University of North Carolina, Davidson, and Wake Forest recovered from wartime deprivations, and Christian denominations founded new colleges in the 1880s and 1890s. In 1896 Washington Duke underwrote the move of rural Trinity College to Durham, requiring that women be admitted on equal status with men. The legislature in 1887 chartered the State Agricultural and Mechanical College in Raleigh and four years later "a normal and industrial school for white girls" in Greensboro. By 1907 Women's College in Greensboro enrolled six Jews, with Laura Weill of Wilmington as its valedictorian in 1910. A local college allowed Jewish students to study and live at home, even help in the family store. Chapel Hill was the school of choice for Jewish men—at the time, women were not admitted until their junior years. In 1912 16 of its 1,158 students were Jews. Staunchly Presbyterian Davidson's student body included George Sternberger in 1915. In Raleigh, Helen Grausman was the first Jewish student at St. Mary's College, and Gertie Rosenthal was the first at Peace College; both recalled finding "love" and lifelong friendships at college.[77]

Immigrants valued a college diploma as a passport to America. For the children of Yiddish-speaking immigrants, the university—with its training in languages, science, and the arts—brought them into modern, secular society. Russian-born Max Temko, a Greensboro junk dealer, and Michael Margolis, a Durham grocer, sent sons to Yale, Duke, and UNC. Widowed grocers Lena Katz and Sara Zuckerman in Durham saved pennies and nickels from their groceries to send children to college. Leslie and Lionel Weil, UNC classes of 1895 and 1897 respectively, joined the prestigious Phi Society, a literary and debating club. Gaston Lichtenstein earned a bachelor of Hebrew Letters from Hebrew Union College in 1899. Fluent in seven languages, he became a prolific author on local history as well as a Hebrew tutor. Wilmington Jews attended elite colleges like Smith, Vassar, Princeton, Williams, and Penn, as well as Trinity and UNC. Gertrude Weil was the first North Carolinian to attend Smith College.[78]

Those who graduated as doctors, attorneys, and engineers almost invariably left North Carolina. Miguel Grausman Elias of Raleigh remained in New York after graduating from Columbia Medical School. Arthur Morris of Tarboro, an alumnus of the University of Virginia Law School, settled first in Norfolk and then New York. His Morris Plan revolutionized the banking industry by basing loans on character and earnings. Charles Mendelsohn, a rabbi's son, earned a Ph.D. from the University of Pennsylvania and became a classics professor. College-educated youth felt family obligation pulling them back to the store, and generational gaps opened between mercantile fathers and college-educated sons. Louis Pearson, a high-school valedictorian, held an engineering degree from Penn, but after working on the New York subway system he returned to the Kinston store. Lionel Weil had ambitions for graduate study in chemistry. On a buying trip to a shoe wholesaler in Boston, Weil took his father to a laboratory at MIT. A broken decanter of carbon bi-sulfide perfumed the air with a rotten stench. His father advised, "Son, I think the shoe business ought to be good enough for you." He returned to Goldsboro.[79]

Campuses were citadels of the progressive South. In 1883 the University of North Carolina awarded an honorary doctor of laws to Rabbi Samuel Mendelsohn of Wilmington, a rabbinic scholar. Three years later, graduation featured Zebulon Vance delivering "The Scattered Nation." In 1912 UNC student Samuel Newman founded a Hebrew Culture Society, the first such organization on a southern campus. A year later, it joined some eighty campuses in the Intercollegiate Menorah Association after a visit by its founder, Harry Hurwitz of Harvard. Frank Graham, campus YMCA secretary, offered the Menorah Society an office, but national headquarters ordered him not to host a Jewish group. Graham conceded it was "quite unorthodox," but his invitation stood. The Menorah Society was dedicated to "the study and advancement of Jewish culture and ideals." Its liberal Judaism, rather than immigrant orthodoxy, appealed to an Americanizing youth. Newman found at UNC "the refreshing influence of the famous exponents of liberalism and the New South." The "prevailing religious atmosphere" was the Social Gospel, which to Newman resembled "prophetic Judaism in its noblest expression." At Trinity, Joe Dave, class of 1916, enjoyed compulsory daily chapel and Bible study as an "opportunity to learn" about his Christian friends. Yet, however much Jews blended into campus life, they still felt marked. Abe Rosenstein, the Trinity yearbook noted, "is a true Israelite, and has a great share of his race's talent for music."[80]

Faculty ranks were still largely the preserve of Anglo-Saxon gentlemen. Solomon Cohen Weill of Wilmington became the first Jew to teach at Chapel Hill in 1884 when, as a law student, he served as acting professor of Latin and Greek. He was a university trustee from 1887 to 1895. From 1902 to 1917, Russian-born Abraham Rudy taught German, Spanish, and French at North Carolina State. A pioneer of language immersion and an advocate of Esperanto, the international language, Rudy was remembered as brilliant and peculiar. He invented a flying machine that his students mischievously hung from the college smokestack in 1911. He lived on a farm financed by a Jewish agricultural society and led a youth group at the Orthodox synagogue. Etta Spier, an 1895 graduate of Women's College, joined the faculty there after obtaining a master's from Columbia. From 1907 until her death in 1938, Spier taught rural and public education. The first dean of Trinity College Law School was Samuel Fox Mordecai, descendant of Jacob Mordecai, who—raised as a Christian—playfully called himself "Mordecai The Jew" or a "Methodist, Episcopal, Baptist Jew" after his various religious and collegiate affiliations. When considered for the university presidency, the witty, eccentric dean wrote a satirical poem, "Trinity's Jewish President." It ended,

> And I'm sure that my election
> > Shows great powers of selection
> In those who chose for President
> > Mr. Mordecai, the Jew.

At his death in 1927, a colleague eulogized, "In religion he was Christian, but how he did love the sound of his Hebraic name and the tingle of his portion of Patriarchal blood." Mordecai—like Benjamin Disraeli, another Christian of Jewish origin—expressed a pride of race and heritage that was the legacy of Victorians raised on the Bible and Sir Walter Scott.[81]

RACE AND SEGREGATION

Native-born Jews were acculturated southerners and their racial attitudes and practices did not differ markedly from other whites. East European immigrants did not have a racial history with black people, but they benefited from white privilege. Immigrants employed black housekeepers and store workers at minimal wages. An immigrant family who arrived in Durham in the 1890s, hired a house worker, known to the children as "Uncle," who slept under the porch with the cow. The Nachamsons in Dover hired a cook for $1.50 a week and a nurse for $1.25, which they felt was "very expensive," to care for their three children. When they opened a "moving picture parlor," they reserved five nights a week for whites and two for blacks.[82]

Black and Jewish relations were primarily those of employer to employee, landlord to tenant, or storekeeper to customer. Some 90 percent of the customers at Louis Schwartz's Wilmington furniture store were black. Friendships grew between Jews and their African American nannies, housekeepers, and store workers within the limits of the paternalism that governed racial relations generally. Jennie Nachamson warmly recalled the kindnesses of "Brady, a big Negro, who was a friend of ours." Peddler Morris Witcowsky felt that Jews "were probably the first white people in the South who paid the Negro people any respect at all." He addressed blacks not with the slave terms "aunt" and "uncle" but as "Mr." and "Mrs." Peddlers kept "a book on the *shvartzers* [blacks]" to whom they sold on credit, Witcowsky explained, which implied no insult, and his black customers were reliable. Civil rights and feminist advocate, Pauli Murray, raised in Durham around World War I, shopped with her aunt and uncle at Dora and Moses Greenberg's grocery. They were "very friendly," and she felt their "humanity" surmounted the "walls of segregation." Her uncle, Reverend Small, knew Hebrew, forging a bond. The Greenberg's son-in-law, attorney Benjamin Lovenstein, achieved notoriety in Durham as counsel to black defendants. "Mr. Holstein," as he was called, campaigned statewide to commute the sentence of a client, Major Guthrie, after he was convicted of murder. Lovenstein was not an egalitarian—he "drew a color line" when asked to work with a black lawyer—but he was committed to equal justice.[83] Jewish grocery store owners were among the very few, if not the only, whites to live in black neighborhoods. Lena Gordon, a grocer's daughter who lived in Durham's Hayti, grew up with black playmates. Their physician Dr. Merritt, an African American, arose from his bed at night to tend to her ill father. Yet newspapers also reported fights and scraps between blacks and Jewish storekeepers over prices or stolen goods. Several accounts mention Jews who kept guns, suggesting tensions.

Nationally, the early 1900s were formative years of a black-Jewish alliance that saw Jews like Joel and Arthur Spingarn help create a National Association of Colored People. The Union of American Hebrew Congregations held to a social-justice agenda. As early as 1886, Rabbi Mendelsohn of Wilmington delivered a sermon at the black First Baptist Church. When African American pharmacist James Shepard of Durham created the National Religious School and Chautauqua for the Colored Race—forerunner of North Carolina Central University—he invited Rabbi Abram Simon of the Washington Hebrew Congregation to join its board. Visiting Durham from 1909 to 1911, Rabbi Simon spoke at both the synagogue and White Rock Baptist Church. Jews crowded into the black church's front rows, reserved for whites, to hear Rabbi Simon call on blacks to emulate both Booker T. Washington and W. E. B. Du Bois in aspiring to both industrial education and the genius of Plato, Darwin, and Shakespeare.[84]

That Jews were not wholly prejudicial to skin color was suggested in 1900 when Ethiopian seaman Samuel Valskovitz, a "Negro of Hebrew Faith," jumped ship in Newport News and came to North Carolina. A Wilmington newspaper noted, "He did not fail to have the attention of all Israelites," who were "surprised" to discover him circumcised and conversant in Hebrew. Although his English was poor, he spoke ten languages including Hebrew and, it was claimed, Yiddish. "Valskovitz is quite an attraction," the *Durham Herald* noted, "and especially so among the Hebrews." Indeed, a local legend of a black man entering the synagogue to read Torah persisted for the next century. He later became a celebrity in New York.[85] Speculation about black Jews in Cochin and Abyssinia was rife in the national media as race scientists speculated on Hebrew origins.

In the late nineteenth and early twentieth centuries, Jewish identity was racial, not only religious. As millions flocked to America, opponents of open immigration doubted whether allegedly swarthy newcomers could be assimilated. Antiblack racism shaped these attitudes. The Jews' racial status was openly questioned. Racial extremism swept the South from 1889 to 1915, leading to Jim Crow segregation. Social customs were enacted into law. Social Darwinists spoke of race war and survival of the fittest. Eugenicists launched public health campaigns to quarantine and sterilize supposed inferiors. Southerners exalted their own white, Anglo-Saxon blood. Recognizing Jesus' Jewish origins, some also admired Jews for their antiquity and racial purity. In 1888 North Carolina's *Tobacco Plant* newspaper trumpeted, "What a wonderful race of people is this Jewish race . . . well may they be proud of their race." The Cone brothers were admired for "the clear vision which characterizes men of their race."[86] In applauding Jews for their reluctance to intermarry, southerners were also praising them for segregating themselves.

In 1910 Rev. Arthur Abernethy, A.M., Ph.D., a rustic journalist, Klansman, and backwoods preacher from Rutherford College, published *The Jew a Negro, Being A Study of the Jewish Ancestry from an Impartial Standpoint*. Abernethy offered "proofs" from ethnology and Scripture that "the Jew of to-day, as well as his ancestors in other times, is the kinsman and descendant of the Negro." He claimed that Jesus was "exalted into the Godhead" as a blue-eyed, blond with "clear complexion." The Jews' hidden blackness, he argued, could be seen not in skin color but on the "tell-tale finger nail formation." He blamed Jews for every modern vice from Wall Street finance to Tin Pan Alley music to the Higher Criticism of the Bible. After "the Negro is eliminated from the citizenship of the United States," Abernethy predicted, "the American government will turn its attention to the alien Hebrew."[87] Abernethy, an Appalachian, spoke for poor, southern whites. Similar anti-Semitic appeals depicting Jews as parasites and sexually libertine inflamed Georgia mobs that lynched Leo Frank in 1915.

Abernethy was not a marginal figure. Although his degrees were dubious, he became a nationally syndicated columnist, author of fifty books, and North Carolina's first poet laureate. His racial views and religious fundamentalism were rooted in southern folk culture. No Jews were known to have lived near his Rutherford College. Curiously, in 1899 the school had given an honorary LL.D. to a prominent Jew, Judge M. Warley Platzek, later a New York State Supreme Court justice, who was born in Fayetteville in 1854 (and would be buried in Wilmington).

Abernethy's book did not sell. Jews remained white people although they were increasingly socially segregated. Clubs and societies that Jews had joined, if not helped found, began closing their doors. In 1877 banker Joseph Seligman was famously denied a hotel room in Saratoga, New York, because of his race, not his religion. Social prejudices felt in Boston and New York worked their way to Atlanta and Richmond as the region integrated into the national cultural mainstream. Wilmington's Cape Fear Country Club excluded Jews, although the Cape Fear Club and the Carolina Yacht Club did not.[88] In small towns, these prejudices were less felt, and Jews were welcomed. Sol Lipinsky, a temple president and B'nai B'rith activist, joined the Asheville Country Club.

Southerners felt no contradiction in being both philo-Semitic and antiblack. A North Carolina legislator and Baptist minister, Thomas Dixon, author of *The Clansman*, praised the "Jewish race" as "the most persistent, powerful, commercially successful race that the world has ever produced" while also asserting "the negro is the menace."[89] Jews could be assimilated without changing the complexion of America; black people could not.

POLITICAL RACES

In 1876 Zebulon Vance's election as governor began two decades of Democratic reign, and a year later President Hayes ended federal occupation. The election of President Grover Cleveland in 1884 to the presidency as a Democrat aligned the South with the nation. State Democratic control was narrow as blacks and Republicans contended, and each party factionalized. Democratic courthouse rings ruled local politics. The revived Democrats came from business and professional classes. State-financed railroads were sold or leased to private companies to the advantage of party leaders. Democratic conservatives resisted not just "Republican-Negro control," but progressives in their own party who wanted to regulate railroads and to protect labor rights. In reaction, the state's numerous small farmers—suffering from crop liens, depressed prices, and high freight rates—organized Farmers' Alliances as part of a national movement that began in Texas in 1876. By 1890 North Carolina had 2,147 chapters with 90,000 members. Politically, they organized as a People's or Populist Party. Nationally, Populists stood with labor against the capitalists. The Panic of 1893, which depressed farm prices, intensified populist passions. In the Deep South, Jewish merchants who held crop liens found their stores set afire.

Populist disdain for financial markets sometimes employed a coded anti-Semitic language. Governor Elias Carr, who served from 1893–97, hoped to wean blacks to the Democrats by charging that "our negro brethren, too, are being held in bondage by Rothschild." Presidential candidate William Jennings Bryan in 1896 repeated canards about Jewish financial manipulators. Even Senator Zebulon Vance warned that "money changers were polluting the temples of their liberties." In 1904, after a state bond scandal, the *Raleigh News & Observer* accused New York Shylocks, and a year later the paper denounced an investor as a "gentleman with a Jew name."[90]

In 1894 outraged North Carolina Populists formed a Fusion ticket with the Republicans under the reform banner. African American voters held the political balance, and both parties sought their support. In the 1894 elections, the Fusionists swept the state, promising "to restore to the people of North Carolina local self-government." Democrats suspected reforms were intended to establish "Negro rule." In 1897 Fusionist Daniel Russell, a Republican, was elected governor, and African Americans won seats in the legislature, posts in county government, and appointments to state boards. Four African Americans were elected to Congress. Democrats were outraged. Democratic boss Furnifold Simmons of New Bern, supported by Josephus Daniels of the *Raleigh News & Observer*, organized a white supremacy campaign.

Political tensions were felt most violently in eastern Carolina. Both New Bern and Wilmington had black majorities. White fears arose of "Negro domination." In Wilmington, nearly half the aldermen were African American as were most policemen, some forty magistrates, and the port custom's collector. Whites alleged crime and corruption. A newspaper warned that people would never accept "the remotest possibility of conditions which shall give the negro a place upon the same plane as the Anglo Saxon's."[91]

In this unsettled era, not only the African American's race was an issue, as Abernethy's later book reflected. Historian Eric Goldstein argues that southern Jews generally supported black disenfranchisement but "shied away from high profile engagement with racial issues." Jews aspired to whiteness, he argues. Their southern accommodation demanded it. Wilmington's Jews identified with the Democratic cause. In 1873 S. H. Fishblate served his first term as a Conservative alderman, a post he held altogether for sixteen years. Fishblate was a New Yorker, who had moved to Wilmington about 1868. In 1878 the city's aldermen selected him mayor. In the 1880s Solomon Bear joined Fishblate on the board. In 1893 the board again voted Fishblate mayor through an electoral system, the newspaper noted, intended "to keep the colored population from getting control of the city government." Yet, as mayor, Fishblate promised to end "rowdyism" in the streets, whether "white or black." Elected from a racially mixed ward, he rejected white demands to end the African American Jonkonnu festivities.[92]

Wilmington's racial tensions climaxed before the 1898 election. Alex Manly, editor of the African American *Daily Record*, refuted a Democratic claim that under Fusion government black men "would increase their 'advances' to women." Manly wrote that "poor white men were careless in the matter of protecting their

Clothing store
of Sol Fishblate,
Wilmington merchant
and politician. (New
Hanover County Public
Library)

women." Many a "'Big Burly Black Brute'" who had been lynched for such liaisons had white blood himself or was "sufficiently attractive" to draw the love interest of "white girls of culture and refinement," Manly argued.[93]

Furnifold Simmons reacted by issuing an "Appeal to the Voters of North Carolina," declaring "North Carolina is a WHITE MAN'S STATE, and WHITE MEN will rule it." The *News & Observer* printed daily on its front pages inflammatory headlines and racist cartoons of rapacious black beasts. It warned that Wilmington blacks were securing arms. The business community passed a resolution opposing "Negro Domination," and white labor unions sought to eliminate blacks from the workforce. Nathaniel Jacobi, a Jewish community leader, apparently helped draft a resolution calling upon businessmen to notify their "male Negro employees" that they would be fired if Republicans won the election. Jacobi, who owned a hardware store, acted to stop blacks from ordering guns. "Business interests" asked the Republican government to resign and submitted a slate of moderate white "gentlemen," including Samuel Bear Jr., as candidates. Meeting at the Opera House, attorney A. M. Waddell declared that he would end black-Republican rule, even "if we have to choke the current of the Cape Fear River with carcasses."

Democrats and white-vigilante Red Shirts paraded by the thousands in Fayette-ville, Goldsboro, and Wilmington, intimidating blacks. An appeal to President McKinley to send U.S. Marshals to preserve order was denounced as a new federal occupation.[94]

On election day, frightened blacks stayed home while Democrats stuffed ballot boxes. After voting in Wilmington, Governor Russell hid in a mail car to escape a lynch mob. The next night whites held a mass meeting, attended by Fishblate and Jacobi, that issued a "White Declaration of Independence." The U.S. Constitution, it argued, did not anticipate African American enfranchisement or white "subjection to an inferior race." They asserted that the "action of unscrupulous white men in affiliating with the negroes" was "causing business to stagnate." The declaration demanded that Manly close his press and leave town in twenty-four hours, or he "will be expelled by force." Fishblate, playing to the crowd, proposed that the mayor, police chief, and aldermen resign immediately. Fishblate declared, "The choice in this election is between white rule and Negro rule. And I am with the white man, every time!" The amendment was adopted "forthwith." The Declaration was signed by 455 white citizens, among them nine Jews including Jacobi and Fishblate.[95]

The next morning, 600 armed whites led by Waddell and joined by Fishblate marched to the Love and Charity Hall that housed Manly's press and set it aflame. Although some white leaders counseled peace, and some personally protected blacks, the redeemers let loose a monster. All day, armed white mobs, including gun-toting ministers, rampaged, meeting feeble black resistance. The Wilming-ton Light Infantry imposed martial law by arresting blacks and pointing cannons at black churches. African Americans fled for forests and swamps. Estimates of black dead, some mowed down by Gatling gun, vary from eleven to sixty. A Committee of Twenty-five marched on City Hall and forced the mayor, aldermen, and police to resign. White Republicans and black elites were jailed, placed on trains under armed escort, and banished from the city. In the North, protest rallies demanded federal intervention, but President McKinley refused. The *Jewish Exponent* of Philadelphia compared the riot to a "pogrom."[96]

In New Bern, sixty miles up the coast, Jews also found themselves ensnared in racial politics. In 1880 Meyer Hahn of New Bern was elected Craven County sheriff on the black-Republican ticket. The all-black township of James City, founded by former slaves, supported him 387 to 13. He was reelected in 1882, 1884, and 1888, defeating a wealthy white Democrat. Meyer and his brother Adolph had arrived in New Bern from New York as "newcomers" in 1866. Adolph had likely first come as a soldier in the Union occupation army. The German-born brothers operated a bakery, livery, and dry goods store. The Dun Credit Agent described them

Sheriff Hahn (Rep.) :—" I brought a batch of convicts to the penitentiary yesterday. I brought the on[e] [D]emocratic-Populist in Craven county among the number and when I got ready to leave I picked out t[he] [bl]ackest negro in the bunch to chain him to."

as "sober enterprising men" of "excellent habits and good standing."[97] Adolph left town, but his son Joseph ran the bakery. The Hahns served on Jewish cemetery boards, and Meyer was first congregational president.

The newspaper noted disapprovingly that the Hahns attended black-Republican meetings. Joe Hahn was elected register of deeds in 1892 and sheriff in 1894. He won James City by 311 to 5 as the Republican-Populist Fusion ticket swept the state. That year Meyer was also elected county treasurer, and two years later they ran against each other for sheriff with the nephew winning. The Hahns' divisions reflected the uneasy alliances among Populists, Republicans, and African Americans. Speaking at a black political rally in 1896, Joe Hahn confessed that Fusion was not to his liking but advised the crowd to "all vote the straight ticket."[98]

As racial tensions flared during the 1898 election, white supremacists targeted Joe Hahn after he chained a black and white prisoner together for their transport from the New Bern jail to Raleigh's Central Prison. The outraged *Raleigh News & Observer* headlined, "CHAINED TO A NEGRO, Sheriff Hahn's Negro Deputies and His Idea of a Joke." It noted that Hahn was "more or less famous and infamous as the man who has nothing but negro deputies." The next day the newspaper front-paged a racist cartoon depicting a strutting Hahn holding a rope at the end of which is a forlorn white farmer and a cartoonish African American.[99]

On 27 October the Hahns were two of four whites among four hundred blacks at a rally for voters who "intended to cast their ballots for negroes." Joe Hahn presided and "advised the negroes to be quiet on election day, but if white men 'insulted' them 'to beat them like the devil.'" Newspapers were outraged. The Raleigh newspaper asked, "Has he any right as Sheriff of Craven county to imperil lives and property by giving such advice to a crowd of ignorant negroes?" The *New Berne Daily Journal* echoed, "Joe Hahn defied public decency." A letter signed SUPREMACY asked, "What I want to know is, whether a man in Craven county can give such advice to negroes without being in danger. I do not believe that he can." Four days later, at a counter-rally of "resolute men of the Anglo-Saxon race," a speaker counseled, "When the day of reckoning comes, don't vent yourselves on the poor dupes but on the miserable scoundrels who led them." Among the names shouted was "Hahn." In Wilmington, rioters had placed nooses around the necks of such "white niggers."[100]

Yet New Bern did not explode. The "revolutionary proceedings at Wilmington" have "stirred the people of New Berne," the newspaper noted, but "while negro domination has been and is our portion, it is not so rank as to necessitate rash or precipitate action." It called for "cool deliberation." In 1899 county commissioners as "an active and visible expression of the wish of the white people" removed Joe Hahn from office. The *New Bern Journal* observed, "Personally, Sheriff Hahn has made an efficient, honest and thorough going official, but it was the system which he represented that was obnoxious." It objected that "a white man" had appointed "negro deputies." In his resignation letter, Hahn thanked the county board "for your uniform courtesy extended me during my official term, but feeling party affiliations render the course I am now pursuing to be the best interest of all concerned."[101]

In all the accusations against the Hahns as race traitors, not once was their Jewishness mentioned nor their whiteness questioned. Hahn was admonished to heed his "white intelligence." Nor did anti-Semitism play a role in Wilmington, although modern historians, most notably Fishblate's descendant Laurie Gunst, argue that a Jewish anxiety to "fit in" motivated his racist politics. A local memoirist reflected, "Mayor Fishblate was a Jew, and he had many enemies among the people, but only for that reason." Charles Chesnutt, a black North Carolinian, was disappointed that Wilmington Jews did not ally with African Americans. In his novel about the riot, *The Marrow of Tradition*, he cites a "well-known Jewish merchant" who manned an anti-black checkpoint: "A Jew—God of Moses!—had

so forgotten twenty centuries of history as to join the persecution of another oppressed race!"[102]

Fishblate, Jacobi, and the Hahns very much fit a national profile of Jewish political involvement. Despite sporadic anti-immigrant outbursts, American politics became more inclusive over the nineteenth century, historian Hasia Diner notes. Mercantile interests dominated politics. Jews "saw public service as befitting a merchant—custodian of public order." In small towns, Jews were "mainstays." Often they were newcomers active in synagogues or Jewish societies. Newspapers welcomed their elections as proofs of democracy. Jews did not ally with any one party—two Jews opposed each other for mayor of Mobile—and not until the 1920s would a "Jewish vote" be regarded as safely Democratic.[103]

Jacobi's and Fishblate's Democratic politics were consistent with those of white merchants of their class. The Chamber of Commerce endorsed white redemption, and the *Charlotte Observer* noted, "The business men of the State are largely responsible for the victory." Fishblate was a political opportunist in constant financial straits. Jacobi was not only a merchant, but also a Confederate veteran, as were many Democrats. Of Wilmington's several hundred Jews, only nine signed the White Man's Declaration, and all were merchants or manufacturers. Yet, given the numbers of Jews in Wilmington, most were uninvolved. Nationally, rabbis and Jewish journalists advised against a Jewish partisanship that might provoke anti-Semitism. Yet, the politics of Fishblate, Jacobi, and the Hahns challenge the notion of an accommodating Jewry that avoided racial controversy.[104]

The Wilmington riot remains a unique instance of the violent overthrow of an elected civil government in the United States. It led to one-party Democratic government and opened the door to Jim Crow. The *Raleigh News & Observer* reported, "Negro rule is at an end in North Carolina forever." Within two years the state imposed literacy tests, a poll tax, and a grandfather clause to disenfranchise African Americans—and poor whites as well. In 1904 less than half of the state's electorate voted.[105]

Reconstruction had extended democracy, and Jews, often recent immigrants, were politically involved, especially in small towns. Democratic machines ran city and county politics, and business interests dominated. In the mountains, an assimilated Jew, Kope Elias, led the Democratic machine. A state senator in 1887, Elias nominated his friend Grover Cleveland for the presidency and fought patronage battles with Vance. Though a member of his wife's Methodist church, Elias was denounced by the *Raleigh Caucasian*, a populist paper, as "an anti-Christian lawyer." In Enfield, Prussian immigrant Simon Meyer—identified by the newspaper as a "whole-souled, genial descendant of God's chosen people"— chaired the Democratic executive committee in the racially tumultuous election of 1898. He was also the town's fire chief, magistrate, mayor pro tem, town commissioner, and director of the bank and tobacco warehouse. In 1896 Joseph Stern was a town councilman in Scotland Neck, and he was succeeded by his son Sidney, a fishmonger, who was also town treasurer. William Cohen, a druggist, served as Weldon alderman and treasurer from 1902 to 1904. In Tarboro, dry goods merchants Jacob Feldenheimer served as a commissioner in the 1870s, and in 1885 Henry Morris was selected Tarboro mayor.[106]

In the Progressive Era, Jews joined campaigns for civic betterment, which included both Republicans and progressive Democrats. Battles erupted over public schools, city charters, health services, street improvements, and women's suffrage. In many towns, Jews, women as well as men, served on school boards. Jay Hirshinger served on the Charlotte school board and obtained funds from Andrew

Carnegie in 1891 to build the city's first public library. A temperance movement turned the state dry in 1909, ten years before the nation. Jews, often involved in the liquor trade, tended to support the wets, who were regarded as pro-business. Political progressives across the South focused on city government reform. In 1904 Lionel Weil began an eighteen-year term as a Goldsboro alderman during which he oversaw civic improvements and a new charter that created the state's first city-manager government. In Asheville, Sol Lipinsky, founder and president of the Merchants Association, played a similar role on his city council.[107]

REFORM AND ORTHODOX

Reform Jews created a progressive American Judaism. Inspired by Protestant movements, they voiced a modern, prophetic Judaism that emphasized social justice rather than traditional rabbinic law. In 1885 radical Reform Jews, meeting in Pittsburgh, issued a platform that proclaimed an ethical, rational, universal religion that befit a Progressive Era. This Classical Reform Judaism dismissed Orthodoxy as "primitive" and rejected Zionism and messianic hope. Americans of the Jewish persuasion were a religious community, not a nation. In their temples, men, hatless and without prayer shawls, sat with their wives in family pews. They listened to a largely English service accompanied by organ and mixed-gender choir. Their "minister" led prayers from the *Union Prayer-Book*. Reform Judaism is often described as the normative religion of German Jews, and it flowered in the South. Although the South held 14 percent of the nation's congregations, it had 41 percent of the members of the Union of American Hebrew Congregations (UAHC), which evolved into the Reform governing body.[108]

To be respectable in the South meant attending church. Sociologist John Shelton Reed observes, "By being more Southern—that is, by participating in organized religious activities—Southern Jews are at the same time more Jewish." High rates of local affiliation contrast with national estimates that only a minority of Jews joined synagogues. Temple Emanuel in Statesville reported in 1883 that "every Jewish citizen in town was a member," and by 1890 its fifteen families supported weekly Friday night and Saturday services. In Durham, thirty-one of the town's thirty-seven families affiliated. For southerners, the synagogue was the "Jewish church." Jewish organizing occurred as Christian revivalism was sweeping the state. Synagogues rose alongside new churches as the New South experienced an urban construction boom. In Charlotte, the number of churches grew from sixteen in 1887 to sixty in 1911. With new peoples arriving daily, religious choices grew diverse. The synagogue joined new Christian Scientist, Seventh-day Adventist, Congregational, and Roman Catholic churches. From the 1880s to the late 1910s, some twenty-three Jewish congregations formed in seventeen towns.[109]

When Goldsboro dedicated its synagogue in 1886, the newspaper reported "a gala day" for the "large audience" of Hebrews and Gentiles. Ten-year-old Edna Weil presented the key to congregational president A. Lehman, with a prepared speech:

> While our beautiful city, Goldsboro, increases in wealth and refinement and makes religion and education the object of her culture, may this edifice stand among its sister churches, which point their spires to heaven, as an evidence of the devotion of the Hebrew community of Goldsboro to the truth of their faith, and of their regard for the reputation of their city for moral and intellectual elevation.

Civic and religious leaders stood on the podiums of synagogue dedications. When the cornerstone was laid for Orthodox B'nai Israel in Wilmington in 1914, the mayor and a Presbyterian pastor as well as the Reform rabbi all addressed the crowd.[110]

Synagogue architecture followed national fashions. Although the Temple of Israel in Wilmington was built in the distinctly Jewish Moorish style, other early Reform-oriented synagogues resembled churches. Goldsboro's Oheb Sholom (1886) and Statesville's Temple Emanuel (1892) were Romanesque revival, a popular church style. The Queen Anne architecture of Tarboro's B'nai Israel (ca. 1908) and neoclassical design of New Bern's Chester B'nai Scholem (1908) blended into their neighborhoods. Early synagogues in Durham, Greensboro, Kinston, Asheville, and Winston-Salem were converted churches. East European Orthodox Jews constructed utilitarian brick edifices in Charlotte (1915) and Wilmington (1915) ornamented with Jewish motifs. In small communities like Weldon or Winston-Salem, rooms above a store sufficed. In 1908 Lumberton's handful of Jews gathered in a wooden building that was little more than a shack. Such names as the Raleigh Hebrew Congregation or the Hebrew Community Center of Weldon and Roanoke Rapids affirm a local civic identity.

The Jewish church was an agency of Americanization as well as of Jewish solidarity and tradition. Jews contributed to church building, and Christians donated to synagogue funds. In the late 1870s, Christians attended Wilmington's annual Hebrew Fair at City Hall to buy cakes and handicrafts homemade by Jewish women. Kinston's Jews, a Christian recalled, "sent clothing to the missionary and patronized the church fairs." After the Episcopal church burned in 1900, Abe Oettinger, who sang in its choir, was the first to donate to its rebuilding although not a congregant. When Reform Jews built a Temple in Raleigh in 1912, Governor Max Gardner and Episcopal bishop Joseph Cheshire contributed. Tobacco magnates J. S. Carr and Benjamin Duke donated $500 each to build a Durham syna-

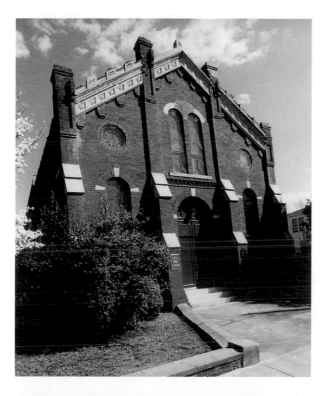

(Top left) Oheb Sholom, Goldsboro (1886); *(bottom left)* Chester B'nai Scholem, New Bern (1908); and *(top right)* Temple Emanuel, Statesville (1892). (Photographs by Tom Rankin [top left] and Julian Preisler [bottom left, top right], Jewish Heritage Foundation of North Carolina)

Dedication of Ortho-
dox B'nai Israel in
Wilmington. (New
Hanover County
Public Library)

gogue, and smaller donations came from African American bankers and insurance executives. When Duke had trouble climbing the synagogue steps, he told
the congregational president to install a handrail and send him the bill. In Charlotte, Russian-born M. B. Smith approached the chief of a work crew demolishing
a post office to ask about purchasing wood paneling for the unfinished synagogue. The crew agreed to finish the synagogue's interior, including the ark and
bimah. When Smith went to pay, the "Christian gentleman" informed him that
"my co-workers, myself, and the company we represent are glad to have done
all of this work free of any charges whatsoever as our contribution to your new
House of Worship."[111]

In building a Romanesque revival edifice, Goldsboro's Jews not only fit in with
local churches but they replicated the architecture of their "mother synagogue"
in Baltimore. Congregational developments traveled family and commercial
routes between urban centers and country towns. During a fundraising drive
for a local synagogue in 1883, "every member going north to buy his spring stock
was requested to obtain a letter with the congregational seal from the president
to solicit subscriptions." The cantor of Baltimore's Oheb Sholom, Alois Kaiser, ad-

dressed Jews at Goldsboro's Odd Fellows Hall. The thirty-three members voted to adopt Oheb Sholom's name, bylaws, and minhag (religious custom), including its prayer book. Similarly, Tarboro Jews described themselves as a "'colony' of Richmond." When they organized Chevra B'nai Israel, they followed the Polish-rites of that city's Keneseth Israel.[112]

North Carolina Jews saw themselves as a national people. Simon Wolf, a lawyer and diplomat who was the nation's leading public Jew, dedicated Goldsboro's Temple, while Rabbi Benjamin Szold performed the honor in Statesville. A Committee on Revising Services in Tarboro sent queries to Rabbi Isaac Mayer Wise in Cincinnati. Solomon Schechter, president of the Jewish Theological Seminary (JTS), visited Asheville in 1904 to heal a congregational breach. Philadelphia's Rabbi Marcus Jastrow, a religious moderate, spent weeks in Wilmington, speaking often at the Temple.[113]

In 1900 Rabbi Edward Calisch of Richmond's Beth Ahabah observed that "the country Jew has been much discussed . . . and has loomed large . . . for his urban brother in faith." Rabbi Calisch chaired the UAHC's Circuit Preaching Committee, founded in 1895. His national plan was to connect every small community to a nearby city with a rabbi. In March 1896 Calisch, a proponent of Classical Reform, traveled to Raleigh, Henderson, Tarboro, and Rocky Mount. From 1896 to 1910, he performed dozens of weddings across the state. After 1896, Hebrew Union College rabbinic students engaged in circuit riding, visiting Asheville, New Bern, and Statesville. The success of Reform Judaism in the South can be attributed in part to the UAHC's work as the "only organized body that has attempted systematically" to serve small-town Jews. At the time, Orthodoxy was chaotic and Conservatism was not yet a movement. The rabbinic challenge of bringing Judaism to country Jews was demonstrated at a New Year service in Greensboro. The rabbi blew the shofar (ram's horn), only to be answered by the mooing of a cow. "He didn't think it was funny a bit," recalled Beatrice Weill. "We all got the giggles."[114]

Although early congregations were Reform, that label masks diverse and inconsistent practices that reflected constant negotiation. Classical Reform arrived late. North Carolinians preferred Rabbi Szold's moderate *Abodat Yisrael* prayer book, amended in English by Rabbi Jastrow, which anticipated Conservative Judaism, rather than the Reform movement's *Union Prayer-Book* (1892). Goldsboro's Oheb Sholom included an organ and a mixed-gender choir and seating, but its bylaws stated that worship was bound by "Biblical injunction, rather than expediency" and in Hebrew rather than in English. Unlike Baltimore, men were required to cover their heads. In 1913 Oheb Sholom ordered six copies of both *Union* and Szold-Jastrow prayer books and asked the rabbi to recite the haftarah (prophetic reading) in English as well as in Hebrew. Tarboro's constitution of 1884 also stated that "the form of worship shall be according to the Prayer Book of Dr. Szold." Statesville's bylaws suggest the decorum of Classical Reform, but in 1892 Rabbi Szold was invited to dedicate the synagogue. In 1900 Statesville's Jews rejected motions to remove hats and adopt the *Union Prayer-Book*. In 1908 Statesville reversed this decision, as did Goldsboro in 1920. Asheville's Beth Ha-Tephilia also had a "see-saw history . . . in one generation a 'Reform' group dominated; in another an 'Orthodox.'" Over time, congregations affiliated with the Reform movement's Union of American Hebrew Congregations: Wilmington in 1878, Goldsboro in 1890, Tarboro in 1898, Asheville in 1908, New Bern in 1911, and Greensboro in 1916.[115]

The mass migration of millions of Jews threw American Orthodox Judaism into disorder. In 1900 the *American Jewish Yearbook* estimated that 80 percent of America's Jews were "unchurched," not affiliated. Immigrant Jews coming to North Carolina knew that in Hickory or Hendersonville kosher food or a prayer quorum of ten men would be less available than in Baltimore or New York. The immigrants tended to be traditional rather than scrupulously Orthodox. Historian Jonathan Sarna recognizes three types of immigrants: the "learned and pious"; the hustler wanting "to make a fortune"; and "the freethinking radical." Most Jews, Sarna noted, blended all three types. Durham immigrant Bernhard Goldgar was by turns a socialist and a capitalist. He did not keep kosher but served as an Orthodox shul (synagogue) president. Jews recall fathers who were freethinkers but became congregational pillars. They were "Jews by nature" who went through the motions of prayer."[116]

American Orthodox Jews divided. East Europeans and Americans of German and Sephardic origin contended. The move to create American Orthodox rabbis began in 1886 with the founding of Etz Chaim yeshiva in New York and in 1897 of the Rabbi Isaac Elchanan Theological Seminary. In 1915 they merged into Yeshiva College, which blended secular and Judaic studies. In 1887 an Association of American Orthodox Hebrew Congregations sought to install a chief rabbi, but American Jewry was too chaotic and democratic to defer to his authority. To counter Reform, the Jewish Theological Seminary (JTS) opened in 1887 as a "bridge" between tradition and assimilation, between natives and immigrants. Its president, Solomon Schechter, who came from a Hasidic, Yiddish-speaking family, was a renowned scholar of historical Judaism at Cambridge. JTS's American Orthodoxy evolved into a Conservative Judaism that remained loyal to hala-cha (Jewish law) while engaging with modernity. In 1898 Americans and East Europeans created the Orthodox Jewish Congregation Union of America—the Orthodox Union. Its Modern Orthodoxy accommodated secular society and learn-

ing. Four years later, immigrant rabbis, resisting modernism, formed Agudath
ha-Rabbanim (United Orthodox Rabbis).[117] These developments trickled to North
Carolina as self-ordained immigrant reverends yielded to yeshiva-educated rabbis and then to university-trained rabbinic professionals.

From 1880 to 1920 East European Jews established some seventeen Orthodox
congregations in North Carolina. These immigrant shuls rose in nascent cities
like Asheville, Charlotte, Durham, Fayetteville, Gastonia, High Point, Raleigh, and
Winston-Salem and in the country towns of Hendersonville, Kinston, Lumberton,
Weldon, Wilson, and Rocky Mount. Asheville, Raleigh, and Wilmington supported

both an Orthodox synagogue and a Reform temple, a typically southern pattern. In Tarboro and New Bern, East Europeans grew so numerous and Germans so declined that congregations turned from Reform toward traditional Judaism.

North Carolina congregations, whether German or East European, followed a familiar pattern. A religiously committed settler was the catalyst. An immigrant, with background in a cheder (Hebrew school) or a yeshiva, led services, which were held in a home or in rooms behind or above a store. In Gastonia, David Lebovitz, son of a Lithuanian cantor, maintained an ark and Torah in his home. In Hendersonville, Abraham Lewis, the town's first Jewish settler, summoned his brother-in-law Beryl Cohen from a Jerusalem yeshiva to serve as hazzan and schochet. For holidays, Jews rented a public hall—Elks, Masonic, Odd Fellows, Academy of Music. A reverend, often a landsman, was hired. High Holiday services in Gastonia around 1910 were led by Herman Boaz, a peddler of eyeglasses, while Joe Mann, a Whiteville clothier, served communities down east.[118] Traveling schochets made monthly or semimonthly rounds to slaughter a cow. Led by a prosperous merchant, the congregation drew bylaws, purchased a burial ground, acquired a state charter, and raised funds for a building.

The East European shul, in contrast to the German Reform temple, was an Old World transplant, a haven of Yiddishkeit (traditional Jewish way of life) in a Christian landscape. In the small-town South, the shul served as a chevra (fellowship) and landsmanschaft (homeland society) where Jews gathered not just to pray but to gossip in Yiddish or to seal a deal on renting a store or buying goods. Here was the comfort of familiar faces, accents, and attitudes. "Their whole life was really the synagogue," Ed Pizer of Raleigh reflected, "being a Jew was 99 percent of your life.[119]

The chevra was intense and intimate, impassioned by personal feuds, business conflicts, and family jealousies. In Durham and Asheville, Orthodox shuls splintered although dissenting congregations never lasted more than a few years. As Melvin Gladstein of Durham recalled, "Every time somebody got mad, they started their own synagogue." The American rabbi was an employee of a board. Wealthier merchants as the largest contributors held power, provoking resentment from poorer storekeepers. Public bidding for synagogue honors resembled a tobacco auction, recalled Winston-Salem's Gertrude Sosnik Solomon. Even a small community might contain an ethnic mix of Poles, Litvaks (Lithuanian-Latvians), Galicianers (Austro-Hungarians), Ukrainians, and Romanians. Their Yiddish accents and worship differed in small ways, which loomed large at services or board meetings. Synagogue constitutions contained a provision like that of Durham, which fined members not "less than twenty five cents nor more than one dollar" for "disturbing the meeting and for not coming to order when in-

STORY: MAMA NEEDS A SHUL

Elsie Samet describes the religious fervor that led High Point's Jews to organize a shul, an immigrant synagogue.

Mama was a verbal and volatile woman with a penchant for drama. . . . Papa was a quiet man and a strict observer of the Sabbath. When Mama and Papa came to America from Lithuania they both worked hard, and now they had a modest home, a cow and chickens and a nice back yard where Mama grew fresh vegetables. It was a good life in America. Papa liked to sit in his favorite chair and read the Siddur when he came home from the morning minyan. Mama came into the living room and sat down on the sofa.

"Mendelebah?"

Papa looked up from his book.

"Vous? (What?)"

"Mendelebah it's a shonda! (shame)"

"Chesna vous is a shonda? (Celia, what is a shame?)"

"Mendelabah, it's a shonda we have no shul. It's a shonda you should have to go to a room in back of Cohens' Feed and Grains store for a minyon. It's a shonda the boys have to study their Hebrew lessons in the Goodkowitz's kitchen while Mrs. Goodkovitz is selling pickles and herring, and everyone is coming in and out and out and in."

With one last outburst Mama said: "We have to have a shul for Bessie's wedding!"

. . . "Chesna, it takes money to build a shul."

Mama acted as if she had not heard the remark.

"First we have to find a piece of land. It should be close enough by so no one should have too far to walk. We will talk to everyone. Tomorrow I will call Mrs. Sirull, Mrs. Bernard, Mrs. Cohen, Mrs. Goodkovitz and all the other ladies. We will invite everyone to come in the afternoon."

In the morning Mama was on the phone making the calls. "We have something very important to discuss. Bring the children. They can play in the yard."

That afternoon everyone gathered in the living room. The older children were told to watch the younger children. Mama served tea and cake and Bessie and Dora took cookies and milk out to the porch for the children. In the living room Mama wasted no time and came straight to the point.

"Here in America everything is good for us. We have nice American children. What we don't have is a shul. We need a shul for minyans. We need a place for the children to study. We need a place for Bar Mitzvahs and weddings. We need a place to pray!" And taking a big, deep breath Mama shot off the big guns: "If we don't build a shul it will be a shonda for the Goyem! (It will be a shame for the Gentiles.)"

Mama's determined tone of voice left her audience momentarily speechless. When what she said began to sink in everyone started to speak at once.

"We'll buy a piece of land!"

"Maybe we can get a loan from the bank!" From Mrs. Goodkovitz, "We should have a meeting room and a study room for the boys!" From Mrs. Rabinowitz, "We have to have a mikvah (ritual bath)!" The more they talked the more enthusiastic they became. The men gathered on one side of the room and the women on the other excitedly making plans for their future synagogue. These first families raised enough money to buy a piece of land. They borrowed money from the bank. Their shul was built.[1]

1. Elsie Samet, "Mama Needs a Shul," typescript, JHFNC.

structed to do so." Goldsboro's bylaws warned against "personal remarks and indecorous or sarcastic language." Durham shul president Morris Haskell resigned in "disgust" after two days in office. Hyman Fleishman, first president of Fayetteville's congregation, became so incensed at one meeting that he suffered a fatal heart attack.[120]

Immigrant shuls were served by "reverends" without semicha (rabbinic ordination) who were, as Charlotte's Agudath Achim advertised, a "combination Rabbi Schochet and Teacher." Gibby Katz of Durham recalled, "He circumcised you, married you, buried you, and killed your chickens." The reverends were paid poorly and moved frequently. In 1909, according to Wilmington's B'nai Israel's minutes, "Rabbi Rubin was engaged at a salary of $9.00 a week plus .05c for each chicken which he killed, but he only remained here a few weeks." Unwilling to compromise, reverends found themselves in conflict. In one rural community, a reverend once suffered a fatal heart attack while in the arms of a female congregant. Another left town in the middle of the night after being duped by counterfeiters posing as pious Jews.[121]

More than worship, which members could lead, the reverend was needed to ensure kosher food. In 1888 nine families in Winston-Salem hired Max Shapiro as a teacher and schochet. High Point had but five families in 1905, but still hired a schochet. Charlotte, according to a 1913 report, had "no synagogue . . . or a Jewish organization of any kind," but "there is a schochet." Two years later, when they wrote congregational bylaws, seven of the nine articles on religious practice concerned the sale of meat and poultry. Many reverends, like Rabbi Stein of Gastonia, operated kosher delicatessens in their homes. In Raleigh the shul was upstairs above Rabbi Prinz's deli. Rev. Max Shapiro, who served Durham and Winston-Salem, drove his wagon through Jewish neighborhoods shouting for housewives to bring him their chickens. Passions were aroused over the pricing and allocating of meat, which was a primary source of the reverend's income. Conflicts between rabbis and schochets, customers and butchers, embroiled American Jewish communities—in 1902 New York City suffered a violent kosher meat boycott. Orthodox synagogues in Raleigh and Durham splintered when the rabbi and the schochet disputed. When a new schochet, Mr. Somers, arrived in Durham in 1901, he started a congregation of his own. Once a reverend killed a chicken for a poor congregant, but the headless fowl ran away. The reverend declared it treyf (unkosher), only to have the poor congregant assault him.[122]

What happened religiously when East European immigrants arrived in a German Jewish community? In Baltimore or New York, Jews divided between uptown Germans and downtown Russians, those who worshiped in cathedral-style sanctuaries and those who davened (prayed) in shtibels (storefronts) or rented rooms. North Carolina communities were too small to factionalize, and synagogue finances were too precarious to let any Jew remain an outsider. The small-town South also had an ethos of hospitality and neighborliness that was welcoming. Many "Germans" were Prussian immigrants whose Orthodoxy and Polish roots did not differ markedly from those of newly arrived East Europeans. In Asheville in 1892, twenty-seven German and Russian Jews met at the Lyceum Hall to charter Beth Ha-Tephila, which, their constitution declared, "shall be Conservative." A New York observer visiting Wilmington in 1913 found Germans and East Europeans on "relatively good terms." When Russian Jews met to organize a shul, Nathaniel Jacobi, a Temple leader, chaired the meeting. In Durham Meyer Summerfield, a Prussian immigrant, served as first president of the East European Orthodox congregation.[123]

The state's two leading Reform rabbis—Samuel Mendelsohn of Wilmington and Julius Mayerberg of Statesville and Goldsboro—bridged divides. Both were Lithuanians educated in the "historical school" of Judaism at European universities. Both served Reform temples for some forty years. In 1895 when East European Jews organized B'nai Israel, Rabbi Mendelsohn led the Orthodox service in Hebrew and sermonized in Yiddish. An observer described Mendelsohn as "at bottom more Orthodox than reform." Rabbi Mayerberg, after Sabbath, went to the immigrants' stores to help wait on customers. Upon finishing Rosh Hashana services at the Temple, he led Orthodox worship at a rented hall. Orthodox Jews in Durham and Charlotte, wanting an American rabbi to represent them to the public, invited Reform rabbis from Washington and Savannah to dedicate their synagogues.[124]

With numbers and resources lacking, compromise was necessary. Goldsboro's board noted in 1895 that "certain Israelites were holding services outside the Temple" and invited them to join. In 1907 nine men organized the Greensboro Reform Congregation, but a year later changed "Reform" to "Hebrew" to welcome newly arriving East Europeans. President Emanuel Sternberger asked both Reform and Orthodox Jews to build one synagogue. In respect to Orthodox practice, Reform Jews tied up their horse-and-buggies a block from the synagogue and walked to services. A congregational history boasted, "The community has ever escaped the pitfalls of sectarian strife." The Raleigh Hebrew Congregation, which endured from 1885 to 1912, was also an ethnic and religious mix: "Much of the early business was directed toward reconciling their religious viewpoints in an effort to remain a single congregation," a member recalled. The hesitancy to embrace Classical Reform owes in measure to sensitivity to Orthodox members. When communities grew to a critical mass, Reform and Orthodox parted. In Asheville, "newly arriving families found the congregation insufficiently orthodox" and in 1898 formed Orthodox Bikur Cholim (now Beth Israel). The Raleigh Hebrew Congregation divided in 1912 into Reform Beth Or and Orthodox Beth Jacob (now Beth Meyer).[125]

Given a choice, some East European immigrants in Raleigh, Asheville, and Greensboro chose Reform. Women, not always educated in Hebrew, preferred English worship and enjoyed egalitarian seating. An American-born generation, wanting to escape the immigrant legacy, was religiously liberal. That was a national trend. Of the students enrolled in Hebrew Union College from 1904 to 1929, some 70 percent claimed East European descent. Moreover, Orthodox worship was becoming more decorous. A "hazzan craze," which started in the 1880s, replaced the cacophony of voices typical of Orthodox worship with the performance of an operatic cantor. Among the Asheville congregation's first acts was to order both an organ and a cap and gown for the Torah reader.[126]

Orthodox synagogues were male preserves. Unlike in churches, where women constituted a majority, men dominated synagogues. Orthodox synagogues had separate women's sections. In Durham, women sat in a balcony; in Raleigh, they divided side by side; in High Point, front and back. Abe Stadiem recalled that in Durham the older women "would sit up there in their chairs and never move, even in the summer when it was so hot you could die." American Judaism evolved as women achieved greater roles in congregational life. Women historically took responsibility for philanthropy but not for ritual or governance. To raise funds to build Raleigh's Temple Beth Or, every morning six women gathered in a kitchen to make chicken salad sandwiches, which were sold to businessmen at a downtown drugstore. In 1902, when Asheville's Jews purchased a former church, the Jewish Ladies' Aid Society organized "at the request of the Jewish men of our community" to "help pay for the edifice." One of High Point's Torah scrolls was donated by Mrs. J. Silver and the other by the Ladies Aid Society.[127]

Jewish Ladies Aid Societies blended traditional roles in American ways. European Jewish communities held societies for visiting the sick (Bikur Cholim), welcoming strangers (Hachnoses Orchim), and burying the dead (Chevra Kadisha). Jewish women borrowed the Ladies Aid name from church groups, and their charity work was a Jewish response to the Christian Social Gospel. Jewish women who collected for the immigrant needy, the Hebrew school, or European or Palestinian Jewish relief were the counterparts of church ladies raising funds for Sunday Schools, missionaries, or their own poor. A respectable, middle-class southern woman was expected to engage in church work. Here again, Jews were accommodating to the South while remaining Jews.

North Carolina Jews provided for the new immigrants' social welfare and their Americanization just as their urban cousins organized orphanages and settle-

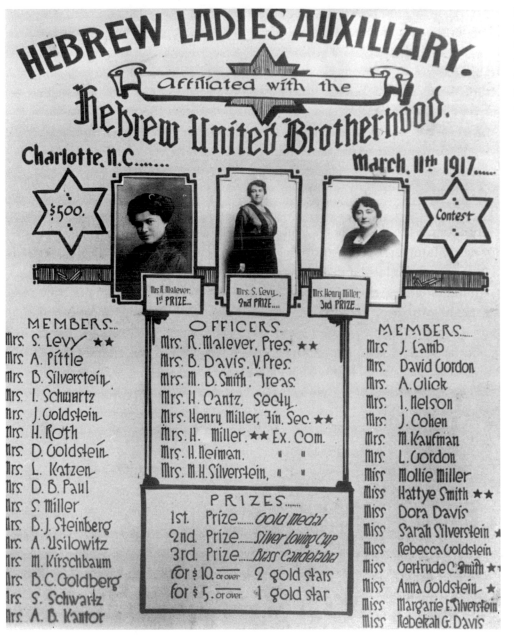

ment houses. In 1895 Wilmington Jewry created a Hebrew Relief Association. The newspaper noted, "The Jewish poor never applies to the Associated Charities of this city for assistance." In Asheville, "'The Aid' . . . brought forth new purposes: the care of the cemetery, the making of shrouds, and visiting the sick." In Asheville, consumptive "supplicants" arrived from northern ghettos. "They seem to feel that if they can get here to breath [sic] Asheville air they will be cured," a society report of 1916 noted. Over a two-year period, thirty-five women, who paid thirty-five cents monthly dues, received forty-five appeals and aided thirty-six indigents. They included a woman from New York whose husband had abandoned her and their four children, and "a poor shoemaker, too sick to work." Ada Pollock led a "Sunshine Committee" that visited the sick. Some died far from home. With fabric donated by Lipinsky's Bon Marché department store, the women sewed shrouds, and the community saw to ritual burial. So many single Jewish immigrant men arrived in Raleigh that merchant David Elias rented a hall on Fayetteville Street and enlisted his daughter Clarice to teach English and give dance lessons. With a donated sewing machine, women made layettes for new families. In Charlotte, Emma Schiff Simmonds sustained a ladies benevolence society of ten to fifteen members, collecting three dollars annually, to provide relief for needy families. Greensboro's Hebrew Aid Society, organized in 1914, served as a loan agency for local indigent Jews and fed and sheltered itinerants.[128]

Immigrant Jews, needing a meal, shelter, or a ticket to Baltimore or New York, streamed into towns. Newspapers reported of a "Jewish tramp" or "object of pity," who arrived destitute and knocked on Jewish doors. In Charlotte, Simmonds noted that fellow immigrants "are liberal to the call of the passing jewish [sic] beggar." The poor tailor Harris Miller always gave. IRO agent A. Solomon observed, "The less successful our Orthodox friends are, the more humane and sympathetic are they." When he called a meeting in Wilmington, three Reform and twenty-two Orthodox Jews attended. When R. Group, a New York baker, was injured in a train wreck in Henderson in 1911, he asked to be taken to the nearest town with a Jewish community. Durham Jews cared for him and his family and when he died saw to his ritual burial.[129]

In most towns, one merchant was delegated as a community payroll officer for needy itinerants. In Goldsboro, Rabbi Mayerberg tramped store to store collecting "for the roving scholar or the dowry-seeking father who wanted to find a husband for his daughter in faraway Russia or Poland." As a child, Mose Samet recalled coming downstairs for breakfast only to see "strange people sitting at the breakfast table," his mother always ready to "take care of any homeless people coming through." Local Jews boarded peddlers and salesmen wanting kosher meals. Bearded, black-hatted shiliachim (messengers) collected funds for an orphanage in Brooklyn or a yeshiva in Jerusalem. Rabbi L. A. Peres came to High Point from Jaffa, Palestine, in 1911 with endorsements from the renowned Rav A. I. Kook. Wilson's Michael Barker, although financially strapped, kept a ledger with receipts from the Zion War Orphanage in Jerusalem, the Hebrew Orphan's Home in Atlanta, and the Hebrew kindergarten in New York.[130]

Not every Jewish itinerant inspired sympathy; more than a few were regarded as schnorrers (professional beggars). These panhandlers were considered a community nuisance, especially in towns on major roads. Leo Finkelstein of Asheville recalled pseudo-rabbis and con artists who made southern circuits in winter. He called them "Jewish Jitter Bugs," masters of "artistic chiseling." In 1913 Raleigh Jews created a "Protective League against Schnorrers."[131]

Jewish settlers tended to be young families, and concern for their children's Jewish futures was a motive to organize. New Bern's congregation traces to 1893 when little Chester Reizenstein asked his mother why they did not have a church. A dozen families responded by forming a congregation naming it Chester B'nai Sholem in his honor. Often religious schools met before congregations formed. Greensboro held its first holiday services in 1907 to provide for the six Jewish students at Women's College. Jewish Sunday Schools were an American institution based on Protestant models. More traditional was the cheder, a private tutorial conducted by an Old World reverend—or rebbe, as he was called—to prepare boys for the bar mitzvah. What these reluctant scholars mostly remember was rote drilling, a pinched cheek, or a ruler's thwack for mispronouncing a "v" for a "b."

Congregations small and large held after-school religious schools, often meeting daily. They waxed and waned depending on leadership and community support. In Kinston, Sarah and David Pearson, "when they come from school, they go to the Rabi to learn jewish [sic]," their brother Sam wrote. Often a rebbe, a storekeeper, held cheder in the back of the store, tutoring boys for the bar mitzvah. The Talmud Torah, with European roots, had graded classes and a curriculum that extended beyond worship skills to Jewish history, culture, and literature. Taught by older siblings, frequently college students, they also tended to be Zionist.[132]

The Sunday School was a meeting ground for Reform and Orthodox. Asheville with two synagogues maintained a single school for nearly half a century. In Durham, Lily Kronheimer, from a Reform family with antebellum southern roots, served as principal at the East European Orthodox synagogue. Children recalled her angelic manner in contrast to the graybeard taskmasters. Another German doyenne, Gertrude Weil, was a much beloved teacher at Goldsboro's Oheb Sholom. "She couldn't have cared less" about differences between German and Russian children, former student Amy Meyers Krumbein felt. In Greensboro, David Stern and Bernard Cone led Sunday School at Ceasar Cone's house. Jacob Sussman, an Orthodox immigrant, felt misgivings about sending his three children to a school taught by American Reform Jews until one day they came running home reciting the Shema. Overcome, he proclaimed it the happiest day of his life.[133]

In towns without congregations, Judaism was not entirely absent. Among German Jews, customs of parlor Bible reading persisted. Abe Oettinger's diary from

1886 to 1900 records visits to Kinston's churches to hear preachers, but on High Holidays he kept his children from school, closed his store, and stayed home to read the Bible. He and his wife fasted on Yom Kippur. In Mount Airy, Albert Goldsmith, a German immigrant with rabbinical training, gathered the few local families, mostly East European, at his Sabbath table. "Judaism flourished" in Oxford, Min Munich recalled, although only five families lived there. Her home had an almer (cabinet) where her father kept a Torah. The Mazurs, wealthy mill owners, opened their house for the holidays, saving the family from a horse and buggy ride to the Durham synagogue. Her father, a former yeshiva bucher (seminary student), led services. Scattered Jews headed to the nearest synagogue for holidays. In the early 1900s country Jews gathered in Monroe and Carthage for the High Holiday services although neither town ever had a congregation. These visits were affectionately recalled by both hosts and guests for the social bonding. The Durham Hebrew Congregation drew Jews from Graham, Oxford, Henderson, and Chapel Hill. Asheville was a magnet for mountain towns. Charlotte Jews, Minnie Sutker recalled, traveled to small towns "to try to induce people to move to Charlotte so they could have a minyan." Benjamin Silverstein rode his bicycle 203 miles to Wilmington on one such recruiting trip.

Assimilation was also inevitable. Of the four Oettinger children, only one married a Jew. Fishblate women, suffering from various ailments, turned toward Christian Science. Charlotte's Emma Simmonds, writing in 1905 of "100 to 150 souls," noted, "The most prominent of jewish [sic] birth here have lost interest in the perpetuation of Judaism." She noted, "The german element has intermarried with the gentile & comingled [sic] until they lost desire for a demonstrative Judaism." German Jewish "society is somewhat of a social affair," she noted. Services were "sporadic . . . except a private kind amongst the strictly polish or Russian orthodox class" with whom she is "unacquainted." She explained, "Our family has not intermarried—but I am more a part of a gentile population having grown up with them—but have never lost my Judaistic instincts." Her desire was to "convert the non-jewish jew."[134]

AMERICAN PATRIOTS

World War I demonstrated the Jews' Americanism as the national mood turned anti-German. Their position was ambivalent. Jews of German origin had held onto their native culture, and East European Jews had no love for Russia as an ally. In 1914 Polish immigrant, Bennie Shapiro, "an energetic young Kinstonian" and "a well educated Hebrew," told the newspaper that he was not so much pro-German as anti-Russian, recalling how his parents had hid him in a Warsaw cellar when czarist police rampaged. Nonetheless, American patriotism led him to the National Guard. Harry Stein had a brother in the German army fighting the Russians on the Prussian front. In Wilmington, where German culture persisted, the B'nai B'rith in October 1917 featured a speaker on "Patriotism" who explained that "the order is distinctly American in origin and ideals." Jews who thirty years earlier had draped stores in black at a kaiser's death now held a Masquerade Ball at the YMHA where an "Airplane man" wore a banner, "We'll Kill the Kaiser Yet."[135]

For new immigrants, who had fled the czar's army, enlisting expressed gratitude. "When the war broke out, I had just become an American citizen," recalled Russian immigrant Edward Leyton of High Point, "I wanted to serve my new country, so I signed up and was sent to France." Asheville claimed twenty boys in the service. Durham's Jews, listing twenty-four men in uniform, boasted, "Every Jewish youth between the ages of twenty-one and thirty who was eligible for service was either in the army or navy." Raleigh's first draftee was Max Pizer, who fought in the Wildcat Division at Marne and Chateau Thierry. Ike Schwartz, son of a Raleigh butcher, signed up after graduating from UNC in 1918 and rose to the rank of major. Professor Charles Mendelsohn, the Wilmington rabbi's son, earned fame as the cryptologist who broke the German diplomatic code. War service gave immigrants and their sons American cachet. After Harry Levine returned to Rockingham in 1919, he placed an ad for his New York Bargain House, "'Home Again.' Yes I, Harry Levine, is [sic] back once more. Last year I was fighting the Germans, and this year I will fight the High Prices of Clothing, Shoes, Dry Goods, Ladies' and Children's Ready-to-Wear."[136]

Wartime propaganda heralded national unity, and North Carolinians expressed pride in their Jewish neighbors' Americanism. Arthur Bluethenthal joined the American Field Service in 1916. At Verdun, he won a Croix de Guerre for "conspicuous bravery" and volunteered for the Lafayette Flying Corps. During a German attack, he was shot down and killed. Wilmington mourned. Businesses closed, flags were lowered, and citizens gathered at the Opera House. "Let us pause a moment," the mayor proclaimed, "and do honor to one of us who has died for us." Wilmington's airport would be named Bluethenthal Field. When Statesville's John Whitlock Wallace, a graduate of Trinity College and the Columbia School of Journalism, was wounded by machine gun fire, the newspaper reminded readers that "this young soldier belongs to the distinguished race which gave the world its two friends—Abraham, 'friend of God' and Jesus Christ, 'friend of sinners.'"[137]

While Jewish boys enlisted, their sisters and mothers volunteered for Red Cross and War Bonds campaigns and opened homes for soldiers at nearby camps. Helen Elias served as Raleigh's first Red Cross nurse. During the influenza epidemic of 1918, she tended stricken men at a makeshift hospital, the drained State College

Raleigh's first draftee, Max Pizer, on right, fought in the Wildcat Division in World War I. (Francis Penslar)

pool, until she was afflicted herself. Charlotte's Minna Weill, supported by the Jewish Welfare Board and National Council of Jewish Women, turned the temple basement into a rec room for soldiers at Camp Greene. She brought "substantial" checks to Jewish veterans at Oteen Hospital.[138]

The Jewish War Sufferers campaign of 1918 demonstrated that their fitting in did not require loss of Jewish difference. When philanthropists organized in New York to assist imperiled Jews in Europe, North Africa, and Palestine, Jews had responded in North Carolina. In 1882 Tarboro's congregation sent twenty dollars to Baltimore and Cincinnati "for the benefit of russian [sic] refugees." In 1905 Statesville forwarded fifty dollars to philanthropist Jacob Schiff in New York for victims of Russian pogroms. To protest czarist discrimination against Jews with American passports, B'nai B'rith lodges organized statewide in 1910 in response to a national campaign to abrogate a Russian trade treaty. During World War I, millions of East European Jews, trapped between German and Russian lines, suffered massacre, starvation, and expulsion. Jewish organizations, led by the Joint Distribution Committee, enlisted Christian leaders to launch a nonsectarian fundraising campaign. Quotas were assigned every city and state.[139]

North Carolina was asked to raise $100,000. Lionel Weil of Goldsboro contacted Ellis Goldstein and H. Fleishman of Dunn, and the three convened a state meeting in Raleigh on 1 August 1918. They asked Governor Thomas Bickett to proclaim a Jewish Relief Day. The meeting drew fifty Germans and East Europeans. They would begin soliciting "Jewish citizens" and then invite "our Gentile friends." Weil argued, as did national campaign leaders, that the "suffering Jews in the war zone are not only our wards but those of humanity at large." Jewish Relief Day would be a Sunday, the Christian Sabbath, and ministers were asked to hold a "union service" followed by an "intensive campaign."[140]

North Carolinians raised $143,148.00 from 326 towns, including places where no Jews lived and no quota had been set. Donations ranged from $1 in Saxapahaw to $13,492 in Goldsboro. Asheville, Greensboro, and Wilmington all raised more than $10,000. Oxford, with a handful of Jews, sent $1,175. The North Carolina Plan became a national model. Weil's campaign scrapbook attests to public attitudes. Invariably, mayors and ministers responded favorably. Hickory had "only one or two Jew families in this entire community, and they are people of very limited means," the mayor wrote, but he pledged that "our gentile population" would give generously. In Hillsborough, without Jews, the mayor chaired a union prayer service at a Baptist Church, and the mills and four churches met the quota of $350. Although no quota was set for the mill village of Erlanger, a total of $1,474.68 was donated by "practically every man, woman and child at work in the plant here," general manager J. M. Gamell wrote. The mill was Jewish owned, but nowhere was that fact raised. The Everette mayor proposed that farmers be approached at tobacco markets in Greenville and Robersonville, and young ladies volunteered to solicit. Mrs. A. Arenson of Rockingham reported, "The co-operation of the non-Jews is wonderful in this town. Every man, woman and child has offered his help to me."[141]

Personal acquaintance with Jews motivated Christians. "I was raised near Statesville and have known the Wallaces and Hoffmans and others for years, and I am very fond of them," wrote Newton mayor Walter Feimster. Numerous correspondents, including Charlotte's mayor, cited Jewish generosity to civic and Christian causes. Judge W. R. Allen asserted, Jews "have been foremost in giving of their time and money for the upbuilding and improvement of our city and county. They gave more than a third of the cost of our public hospital" and contributed liberally to Liberty Bonds, War Savings Stamps, Red Cross, and Y.M.C.A." He asked, "Shall we be less generous and liberal than they?" The *Raleigh News & Observer* editorialized, "They ask little for themselves, and they give much for all purposes . . . [the Jew] proves in this country a useful and valued citizen."[142]

Southerners expressed a philo-Semitism that sprung from a romantic religiosity and even a Lost Cause nostalgia. Several cited Vance's "The Scattered Nation." Confederate veterans recalled how Abram Weill had sheltered Jefferson Davis. Lillie Archbell of Kinston felt gratitude for Judah Benjamin, "mothered" in North Carolina, and she recalled local "families of the Hebrew race" who died for the Confederacy. Christians, she felt, were obligated to the authors of the "Book of Books." As Archbell wrote, "Jesus Christ was a Jew. . . . When Israel cries for help, God measures and weighs the nations."[143]

The North Carolina campaign calls into question stereotypes of southern Jews as people for whom "fitting in" meant not calling attention to themselves. Indeed, the campaign was launched only three years after the Leo Frank lynching had allegedly cowed southern Jews and when nativist, anti-immigrant sentiment was rising nationally. Jews asserted their difference even as they universalized their cause. North Carolina's Jews saw no incompatibility between their American patriotism and Jewish loyalty, nor apparently did their Christian neighbors.

SOUTHERN ZIONISM

Of all the solutions to "The Jewish Problem"—colonial, political, religious—none so stirred Jewry as Zionism. With their American, Reform heritage, German Jews, who had been dominant in the South, were often regarded as non- or anti-Zionist in contrast to East Europeans, who were enthusiastic. The nation's two leading Zionists, Louis Brandeis of Louisville and Henrietta Szold of Baltimore, claimed both Central European and southern roots. With Szold's founding of Hadassah

TREE FUND   תרומת עצים

JNF

THE OBJECT
OF THE
TREE-FUND
IS THE REAF-
FORESTATION
OF EREZ ISRAEL

JEWISH
NATIONAL FUND

תעודת
התרומה היא
לטעת
בארץ ישראל
יערות
עצ״ים

קרן קימת
לישראל

No
T25489

In Honor of
Chamisha Osar B'Shvatt
5708- 1947-'48

עצים
33
TREES

Planted by the
Bnai Israel Sunday School
and Faculty of Wilmington, N.C.

Jewish National Fund
certificate for planting
trees in Palestine.
(B'nai Israel,
Wilmington)

in 1912 and Brandeis's Zionist leadership in 1914, the movement grew in legiti-
macy.[144] The Balfour Declaration of 1917 gave it international authority. With the
East European migration, Zionists societies rose in the early 1900s across the
South. In 1901 Durham Jews purchased shares in the Jewish Colonial Bank in
Palestine, and in 1904 a Zionist Society organized in Asheville.

The Weils reflected the ambivalence of German Jews. Mina Weil was Szold's
personal friend and a dedicated Zionist. She and her husband Henry visited Palestine in 1909. In the *Goldsboro Argus*, he gave a tourist's view of Jewish and Christian holy sites, admitting that "my heart beats a little faster" as he approaches
Jerusalem. He heard of "Jewish colonies . . . which are getting along fairly well,"
yet he disdained Zionism "since it has for its purpose the settling of poor Jews

. . . on barren soil" where they will starve or be dependent. His Zionist daughter Gertrude felt her father "lacked foresight."[145]

Brandeis's leadership, the Balfour Declaration of 1917, and the founding of Hadassah and the Zionist Organization of America transformed an inchoate movement. Zionist memberships nationally grew from 12,000 in 1914 to more than 176,000 in 1919. North Carolina homes held blue and white pushkes (charity boxes) collecting coins for Palestine and certificates for trees planted there. Emissaries of Zion recruited North Carolinians. Henrietta Szold traveled to Wilmington. When a Mrs. Pavlov visited Kinston in 1916, Jennie Nachamson enlisted fifteen of the town's eighteen Jewish women into "The Daughters of Zion." The ZOA sprouted at least two state chapters by 1917, and the Kinston district counted fifty members. Brandeis insisted that "multiple loyalties" were unobjectionable.[146]

NEW SOUTH LEGACY

That some North Carolinians bore the label of "Israelitish citizens" or "our Hebrew friends" points to both their acceptance and difference. In building congregations and organizations to preserve their ethnic and religious bonds, Jews were also acting in consort with other North Carolinians who were creating the institutions of a New South. Jews were dedicated to Americanizing themselves even as the region itself was culturally and economically reentering the national mainstream. Jewish immigrants were signs of a changing South.

Synagogue histories reflect conflicts on where to draw boundaries between Judaism and Americanism. Cultural pluralism allowed Jews to affirm a dual identity. In some respects their hyphenated "Jewish-American" identity coalesced, and in others it compartmentalized. Synagogues were Jewish churches, blessed by the civic leadership. Worship and home ceremonials, however, evoked ancient and foreign practices. German Jews held onto "our crowd," while the East Europeans clung to Yiddishkeit. Family, religion, and nationality tied them to distant lands. In the Jewish War Sufferers Campaign Jews portrayed such solidarity as the highest expression of American patriotism. Christian southerners paid deference to biblical Israel, seeing in Jews the roots of their own religion and nationality. They recognized in Jews a shared experience as a marginal, defeated, impoverished people. "For good or ill," wrote Raleigh editor Josephus Daniels, "being a Southerner is like being a Jew." The South made multiple their hyphenated dual identity.[147]

North Carolina Jews were immigrants and natives, peddlers and industrialists, schnorrers and magnates, Confederate veterans and Russian army deserters. Few and diverse, they bonded religiously. As a people, the Jews felt a shared heritage and destiny despite the discontinuities of their histories and their differences of class, acculturation, and religious ideology. The emerging mill and market towns of the New South welcomed new people, especially entrepreneurs who could remake their economy. The Orthodox, Yiddish-speaking East European Jews who began arriving in the 1880s, as the Duke tobacco workers learned, were not at first regarded as "our people." However, they did not arrive in sufficient numbers to present a social or political threat. In contrast to the urban North, where Jewish proletarians were marked as aliens and radicals, in the South peddlers or storekeepers were respected as exemplars of God's own people and welcomed as neighbors. North Carolinians appreciated these honest, hardworking people, who, like themselves, were rising from poverty to prosperity, from old to new, from defeat to success.

1920-1968

When Julienne Marder moved from Brooklyn to Brevard in 1939, she left a community where she was "an almost majority" to a town where she was "a small minority." American-born and college-educated, the twenty-year-old felt comfortable in the small mountain town, but her mother Ida, born in Lithuania, found the move "traumatic." Julienne's father Frank, a lawyer, had accepted a post at the new Ecusta Paper plant.

As they unpacked, a mover assured them that they would fit right in once they joined the country club. But back then, Jews were rarely welcomed at such places. Nor would they join a church. After a visit by Rabbi Moses Jacobson of Temple Beth Ha-Tephila, they settled in Asheville, where they found an established Jewish community. A realtor suggested Biltmore Forest was convenient to the Brevard factory, but that upscale development excluded Jews.

In Asheville, they lived once again a largely Jewish life. Although descended from Orthodox immigrants, they affiliated with the Reform temple, impressed by the Rabbi's warmth. They found a circle of Jewish friends. Ida joined Sisterhood and resumed her Hadassah membership. Julienne was popular with the Jewish boys. At a Thanksgiving dance held by the Council of Jewish Women, she met Harry Winner, a storekeeper from Canton. A year later Julienne and the personable merchant married, and the former Brooklynite found herself living in the mountain town of Canton, overlooked by the Champion Paper Mill.

Harry was also the son of immigrants but a Savannah-born southerner, a member of an extended family of small-town storekeepers scattered across the Southeast. Harry had wanted a Jewish spouse even if it meant waiting for an out-of-towner and a northerner. "When I moved to Canton I couldn't have been more different," Julienne reflected, citing her accent, religion, dress, and education. Yet, folks in Canton "opened their arms, and they received me, and it changed my life." Living among Christians "was a wonderful experience." Her new husband had endeared himself to the community, "and the people were so happy that Harry had found himself a Jewish girl." Julienne joined the North Carolina Association of Jewish Women as Canton delegate—the town had two other Jewish

Julienne and Harry Winner stand behind Ida and Frank Marder and their son Dennis. (Leslie Winner)

families, the Raiffs and Schulmans, both storekeepers. For holidays they drove forty miles on mountain roads to the Asheville temple.

When their children grew to school age, the Winners moved to Asheville, residing like most Jews in the northern suburbs. The postwar years were prosperous. Harry's shop expanded into a multistory department store. He opened stores in Canton and Salisbury. Harry became temple president, and Julienne held similar posts at Sisterhood and Hadassah. After the war, doors opened. Their friendship circle grew to include Christians, among them a young Episcopal priest and his wife. Julienne served on college and hospital boards. Their three children earned two law degrees and a doctorate, and served as state legislators, a judge, and professor.

Julienne Winner's story was representative of Jews generally and of southern Jews particularly. As immigrants yielded to a native-born generation, orthodoxy gave way to a more liberal Judaism. College-educated, younger Jews were abandoning the store for the professions. Communities sustained themselves through constant migrations from the north until newcomers outnumbered natives in most communities. Jews created networks to ensure that their children remained in the Jewish fold. Yet, even more than their northern cousins in urban Jewish enclaves, southern Jews had a broader perspective on Christian America.

SMALL-TOWN JEWS

The 1920s marked an era of community building. East European immigrants were climbing the economic ladder into the middle class. Their synagogues were no longer rented rooms above dry goods stores but architecturally impressive edifices that attested to prosperity and permanence and stood equally with churches. The number of congregations in the state rose from one in 1876 to twenty-two in 1927, and sixteen had synagogues.

Jews had fought in America's war, played on its sports fields, been educated in its schools, and served its government. "People didn't talk about where they were from back then, they wanted to be Americans," Leah Tannenbaum of Greensboro reflected. By 1937 two-thirds of the state's Jews were native born. The philosopher Horace Kallen spoke of a cultural pluralism that expanded Americanism beyond the norm of white, Anglo-Saxon Protestantism to embrace multiple identities. Even as Jews assimilated politically and economically, they remained Jewish religiously and culturally. Jews could preserve their group identity while enjoying rights as individual citizens. They were hyphenated Jewish-Americans.

The 1920s were critical years in American Jewry, historian Lee Shai Weissbach notes. The nation's Jewish population had grown from 229,087 in 1877 to 4,228,029 in 1927, rising from .52 percent of the American population to 3.58 percent. By

1927, Weissbach observes, "the era of mass migration was coming to an end, and the development of individual Jewish settlements was reaching a sort of crescendo." Of the 2,790 cities in America with more than 2,500 people, nearly 90 percent had Jewish population. East European immigrants formed the "vast majority" of America's small Jewish communities. Typically, these towns were found on commercial routes—overwhelmingly, on rail lines. National surveys revealed that the larger the city, the larger the percentage of Jews. In urban New York State, almost 17 percent of the population was Jewish; in rural North Carolina the figure was .2 percent.[1]

North Carolina remained a place of small towns, and its largest city Charlotte paled compared to Atlanta or Baltimore, which were magnets for Jews. In 1927 the state had thirteen towns with more than 100 Jews, but none with more than 1,000. Other rural states had similar profiles, but none so extreme. A 1929 survey noted the "exceptional fact" that 53 percent of the state's Jews resided in rural communities. They were scattered in 188 towns, mostly in the Piedmont. In 1927 Asheville reported 700 Jews, and Charlotte and Greensboro, 400. However, Brevard claimed 12; Fairmont, 19; Lenoir, 11; and Wallace, 18. Jews were found in Ahoskie, Bessemer City, and St. Pauls.[2] Jewish numbers were small and widely dispersed.

North Carolina Jewry reflected global developments. World War I and the Soviet revolution stemmed the immigrant flow. Moreover, American public opinion turned against unrestricted immigration. Congress passed quota laws in 1921 and 1924 that capped immigration by nationality. In 1921 119,036 Jews entered America; in 1925 only 10,292 did so. The flow of new immigrants to North Carolina slowed. The state's Jewish population rose from 4,915 in 1917 to 8,252 in 1927, but declined to 7,337 in 1937.

NEW SOUTH RENEWED

Jewish settlement reflected a changing economy. After a brief downturn, the 1920s were boom years. The state embarked on the nation's largest road-building program. National parks and forests spawned mountain tourism. Farm tenancy and sharecropping began yielding to agribusiness. By the 1920s North Carolina was the southeast's leading industrial state; its plants were national—and even world—leaders in cotton, tobacco, and furniture. The state produced half the nation's cigarettes and half its cotton yarn. Educational reform led to universities of national rather than just regional repute. Even as it honored its Confederate dead, enforced racial segregation, and denied suffrage to women, North Carolina gained a reputation as progressive. When New Yorker Harry Golden, a labor journalist, relocated to Charlotte, he explained, "I sense that the next big story of

America would develop there, the shifting of a whole social order from agrarian-ism to urbanization."[3]

The changing economy pushed and pulled Jews. With prohibition, Statesville, a distillery center, saw its Jewish community decline, and the synagogue built in 1892 was rented to a church in 1923. Stable numbers in some towns masked comings and goings. Of the seventy families in Durham in 1937, only five claimed roots dating before 1900.[4] Typically, both poorer and wealthier Jews were more likely to move: the poor pushed away by failure, and the wealthy pulled to new opportunities. The impulse to move was not only economic. Orthodox Jews and families concerned about their children finding Jewish spouses headed to places with larger, more resourceful Jewish communities. Educated youth departed for big-city opportunities. Baltimore remained a magnet.

The 1920s was a generally prosperous, economically expansive era. Nation-ally, Jews were rising from immigrant poverty to the middle class "Their enter-prising spirit and their intense striving for place were in consonance with the business ethos of the place," historian Henry Feingold notes. By 1929, nearly half of Jews were involved in trade and perhaps a fifth were occupied with "small-scale manufacturing and sales." That trend was especially so in North Carolina, where, in contrast to the urban north, Jews had never developed a proletarian class. Former Bargain House peddler David Lebovitz of Gastonia now owned five retail stores. He gathered a group of investors to put up a mill and drew the Gold-berg family into town to run it. Opportunity drew Jews to an urbanizing state. In 1925 Polish-born Herman Leder arrived in Whiteville, followed brother by brother until they built a chain of twenty-one, small-town stores. "Jewish by birth but all American," the newspaper front-paged. "We are one of you," the brothers adver-tised.[5] In 1928 Leo Brody, son of an immigrant who had wandered from Poland to South Africa to America, came to Kinston to open a branch of his father's South Carolina store. He, too, brought brothers until they had stores in Greenville, Goldsboro, New Bern, and Rocky Mount. Stadiem stores were located in Greens-boro, Durham, Kinston, and Wilmington, and five Finkelstein brothers operated pawnshops from Wilmington to Asheville. Seven Fleishman brothers from Balti-more spread out down east.

Drawn by cheap labor, Jewish industrialists joined other garment manufactur-ers relocating factories to the South. Starting on a small scale, they built major industries. In 1923 Nathan Block brought twenty-five sewing machines from his Baltimore factory to Wilmington. By the 1930s Block was producing 100,000 dozen shirts annually. Sam Fuchs opened his Kinston Shirt Factory in 1939, which ex-panded into Hampton Industries. Morris Speizman, who arrived in Charlotte in

1936, received a bank loan to purchase secondhand textile machinery, and soon Speizman Industries began exporting to Latin and South America.

Jews also had a passion for real estate. In 1910 52.7 percent of Durham's Jews owned real estate; that figure rose to 63.5 by 1925. Florida developers launched a mountain land boom in the Hendersonville area in the 1920s, drawing Jewish families. Louis Williams, a Texas junk dealer, opened a real-estate office there. Attorney Sidney Stern created a Greensboro development company that built middle-class housing for blacks near the North Carolina A&T campus.[6]

Farming marked Jews as normative North Carolinians, but most Jews pursued agriculture as commercial investments rather than as workers of the soil. Some merchants obtained land through foreclosures, a practice that other Jewish merchants pointedly disavowed. Herbert Bluethenthal had a "tremendous farm with many cattle" in eastern North Carolina, and Henry Schafer of Mount Airy owned some three buildings, fourteen houses, and a 900-acre farm with 2,475 peach trees in Surry County. The Oettingers owned 200 acres of tobacco farms. Agriculture rooted Jews culturally as well as materially in North Carolina.[7]

The store integrated Jews into town society, and Jews added to the local color. Leo Finkelstein was eight when he started working at the Asheville pawnshop opened by his father in 1903. In 1906 a posse pursuing a notorious desperado turned to Finkelstein for guns. During the Depression one preacher pawned his Bible on Mondays and redeemed it on Fridays. Winter coats were pawned during summer months. When the sheriff needed to break up a labor strike, the pawnshop rented shotguns. Durham's Louis Stadiem's clientele included ladies of the night, who pawned jewelry, as well as the infamously prodigal Brodie Duke, who enjoyed smashing straw hats over his customers' heads. At Joe Lipman's store in New Bern, customers short on cash paid with eggs or chickens or occasionally some moonshine, which he sweetened with peaches and apples.[8]

As the twenties roared, Jews as outsiders tested the boundaries of a conservative society. Jews had long histories as distillers and saloonkeepers, which Prohibition did not wholly inhibit. In 1926 the Durham constabulary visited Mose Levy's grocery in the black neighborhood of Hayti. To his surprise, the police found in an upstairs closet 192 jars of corn liquor. The defense claimed that Levy needed the forty-eight gallons for a "Hebrew Celebration," the approaching High Holidays. Spirits for "sacramental purposes or like religious rites" were legally exempt from prohibition. Lawyers also cited the undeniable benefits of a drink after a day's work. The newspaper reported the verdict: "Twelve of his peers, and all of them Gentiles, said Mose was not guilty of the charge of illegally possessing no less than eight full cases of copper-distilled, corn beverage which the 18th amendment

PORTRAIT: SELMA KATZENSTEIN

"Miss Selma Katzenstein," noted John Tarwater, a Warrenton local historian, "she's one of the best farmers in this section of the state and unless I'm mistaken she operates on a larger scale than any other woman-farmer in all of North Carolina." Miss Selma had under cultivation some 552 acres of grain, cotton, and tobacco crops land.

Farmer Selma Katzenstein with niece and nephews. (Alex and Charles J. Katzenstein)

German-immigrant brothers Emil and Alex Katzenstein had come to Warren County in the 1870s. Emil had first opened a country store, where he bartered for hides and sold "Chrismast whiskey." Alex, a gold panhandler, acquired farmland. He converted a stagecoach depot into a house and opened a seed store, cotton gin, and tobacco warehouse. His son Charles went to Chapel Hill and then Columbia Law School. His daughter Selma had ambitions to be a doctor but was too frail. Her father bought her a five-foot shelf of Harvard Classics. He died during the Depression when tobacco had dropped to a few cents a pound. Selma took over the farm. Obtaining books on scientific agriculture from state and federal agencies, she planted cotton and tobacco. "Tobacco was the prima donna of all crops," she told her nephew Alex. "She loved the whole thing from the plant bed to the warehouse floor," he recalled. Buyers praised her tobacco as "some of the finest that is brought to the Warrenton market." Miss Selma increased her landholdings to some 2,000 acres and managed twenty-two tenant farms. "Farming was in her blood," her nephew recalled.[1] In 1934 she brought to Warrenton her young German cousin Herbert Katzenstein and rescued his parents in 1939 as war erupted. The family matriarch, Miss Selma was surrounded by her niece and nephews who visited often to help with farm chores. She was buried next to her parents in a consecrated Jewish family cemetery on a county road.

1. Carl Goerch, "Discovering Warren County," *State* 8, no. 10 (3 Aug. 1940): 3; Letter from Alex Katzenstein to Leonard Rogoff, 24 June 2001, JHFNC.

Dunn merchant and gentleman farmer Louis Baer at tobacco market. (Marcia W. Simon)

Louis Gordon settled in Statesville in 1917. He peddled scrap and sold furniture from his store. His son Saul recalls one transaction.

We lived out at the edge of town, we had a big piece of property, and we had a barn behind the house, we had goats, horses, chickens, it was a regular old farm. A guy came in and said Mr. Gordon, I have a cow I don't need, I need a new suite of furniture for my living room. I would like to trade you my milk cow for the furniture. He said we can work that out, we have a place to put another milk cow. Dad traded with the man, and he called me over—I must have been fifteen years old at the most. He said I want you to put this piece of furniture on the pickup truck and the man will lead you to his house, I want you to unload the truck and take the cow home. We got all that straight. We got there and unloaded the furniture, but the cow didn't want to get on the truck. We were about two and a half miles from the house. I wasn't old enough to drive the pickup so I had to lead the cow, walk that cow all the way to the house. We got to be real good friends. I milked that cow twice a day for years. . . . I took the milk inside the house and our mother and a maid and I would give her the milk and next thing we knew we had buttermilk, and they made cottage cheese and all this good stuff.

sometimes humorously prohibits." Levy wanted his ritual corn liquor returned, but the judge ruled against an "unofficial Jewish holiday" and ordered the sheriff to "pour it out." Nationally, Jewish hucksters, often self-declared rabbis, turned to bootlegging under the sacramental exemption, and Prohibition inspired among Jews "a remarkable increase in the thirst for religion." Jews were hardly alone, and poor farmers augmented their incomes with homebrew. When prohibition ended, Rev. Goodkowitz supplemented his salary by hauling beer from Baltimore to the Asheville Elks Club.[9]

ETERNAL ALIENS

World War I had raised suspicions of enemy aliens, and a murderous 1920 Wall Street bombing gripped the nation in a red scare. Rumors spread that Jewish Bolsheviks, having fomented revolution in Russia, were plotting against America. Attorney General Mitchell Palmer launched raids against supposed radicals, arresting thousands. In the *Dearborn Independent*, Henry Ford spoke small-town resentments against "The International Jew: The World's Foremost Problem" and disseminated the anti-Semitic czarist forgery *The Protocols of the Elders of Zion*. Jews were accused of polluting American culture through Hollywood and Tin Pan Alley. A revived Ku Klux Klan marched under the banner of "100 percent

Americanism," clamoring first against Catholics and African Americans but also against Jews.

Banks, hospitals, and law firms either did not hire Jews or limited their employment. Led by Columbia and Harvard, northern colleges saw burgeoning Jewish enrollments as a threat to Anglo-Saxon civilization and imposed quotas. Hotels posted signs excluding Jews. North Carolina was largely removed from such passions—its Jews were too few and too familiar—but popular prejudices were felt. The Klan, with 3 million members nationally, was relatively weak in North Carolina but held rallies. A 1927 Durham event featured the mayor introducing a Georgia Klansman before a fiery cross at the civic auditorium. The theme was "true" Americanism. The local newspaper observed, "Members of the Negro race and the Hebrews who were present heard nothing which could offend them." Leonard Rapport of Asheville recalled the Klan as "sort of bourgeois" and "socially acceptable." He called them "below-the-belt Kiwanians." Jews were invited to join. Among them were Yiddish-accented, immigrants like Raleigh pawnbroker S. H. Dworsky and Weldon cobbler Louis Kittner. "They didn't know they weren't supposed to like Jews," his son Harry Kittner speculated. Other Jews remained anxious. In 1921 storekeeper Philip Leinwand of rural Rowland received a letter warning him that the "Ku Klux Klan is close on your trail and you had better watch your step."[10]

Southern folklore passed down anti-Semitic prejudices. "Jew down" meant to bargain for a lower price and to be "jewed" meant to be cheated. Greensboro journalist Chester Brown noted that it was "not uncommon for many of us to hear, 'You are the first Jew I have ever met . . . But where is your beard, or where are your horns?'" Abram Lewis, Hendersonville's first Jewish merchant, found a man standing outside his store not to buy anything but to see the Jew's horns. Mercantile competition pitted Jew against Christian. A prominent Hendersonville merchant told customers not to shop at a Jew's store. According to one version of the story, Harry Patterson challenged the anti-Semite to a duel, which ended in fisticuffs that got both men arrested. Another version describes the diminutive Mrs. Patterson beating the merchant with her umbrella. (The Christian merchant eventually apologized.)[11]

Schools still promulgated Christianity with prayer and Bible readings. Jewish children learned to sing "Onward Christian Soldiers" although some mouthed the words or kept their eyes open as if they were not really praying. Leonard Kaplan's mother drew the line when he was asked to play baby Jesus in a second-grade Christmas pageant. In towns with few Jews, children joined their friends at vacation Bible camps or Methodist youth groups not from religious conviction but for companionship. An Asheville teacher, Ma Bryson, finding four Jewish students in class, called it "Little Jerusalem," Michael Robinson recalled, and cancelled classes on Jewish holidays.

Durham's Gibby Katz remembered, "I got beaten up three times a day just because I was a little waif of a Jewboy." His friend Joe Hockfield was jumped by three kids and got revenge by ambushing them one at a time. Kaplan recalled rock fights with neighborhood kids who called them "dirty Jews." "I had several fights at school just over 'my being there,'" recalled Monroe Evans of Fayetteville. An older student taught self-defense at Hebrew School, and "the first time that I hurt the other kid in a tussle, it seemed to clear the air." David Citron, who moved from Atlanta to Charlotte in 1932, encountered a "lot of prejudice" as the lone Jewish student at his school, but helped by "a gentile friend and a very nice teacher," he was elected student body president. "Everybody was friendly," recalled Joan Samet, but "I never got invited to parties."[12]

The national anti-Semitic mood was felt in the state. Evangelist Mordecai F. Ham castigated Jews in revivals across North Carolina during the 1920s and 1930s. At a crowded Charlotte tabernacle, he railed, "Modernism and Bolshevism are ruling the world. Publicity, commerce, money are all in the hands of the Jew." Inspired by Henry Ford, Ham targeted Julius Rosenwald of Chicago, chairman of Sears Roebuck, as an exemplar of vice. Rosenwald had endowed schools for African American children across the South. According to Ham, Rosenwald planned to mongrelize the white race by breeding black men with white women.[13] Stores closed during Ham rallies, and newspapers front-paged his sermons. In Elizabeth City, 4,000 attended. The mayor introduced him in Charlotte. In his thirty-year career, Ham claimed to have saved 300,000 souls, including Charlotte teenager Billy Graham.

Ham's anti-Semitism did not go unanswered. An iconoclastic editor in Elizabeth City, W. O. Saunders, in his newspaper the *Independent* refuted the "false and defamatory charges made . . . by a mendicant mouth-artist." Saunders wrote leading citizens of Chicago inquiring about Rosenwald's character and then reprinted their sterling endorsements in *The Book of Ham*. The evangelist accused Saunders of calling Christ "a liar" and sharpened his attacks on Jews. Saunders pursued Ham at his North Carolina revivals, where he passed out free copies of his book. Saunders found himself sued, threatened, shot at, and tailed by an assassin. He was joined by the Anti-Defamation League, which distributed *The Book of Ham*. While Saunders was damned as an "infamous infidel," the ADL was denounced for "out and out spiritual apostasy which is underhandedly working, not only to wreck the Christian foundations, but also the free government of the United States."[14]

The freethinking Saunders aligned himself with southern progressives, and his defense of Jews occurred at the very moment the state legislature was embroiled in debate on teaching evolution. The theological question of whether Jews, without Christ, were outside salvation was another battle between religious liberals and fundamentalists. Mainstream Protestant churches did not welcome Ham revivals. Ham conflated Jews with all the supposed sins of modernism, including "evilution," socialism, alcohol, labor unions, women's rights, and racial equality.[15] In Charlotte, evangelist Vernon Patterson, who had invited Ham to the city, approached the rabbi in search of understanding. When the city council opposed giving civic space to Ham revivals, its lone Jewish member, Max Kahn, dissented.

Ham's rantings were both a catalyst and an expression of an anti-Semitism embedded in folk culture. In 1925 a Lorillard tobacco salesman from Philadelphia was arrested and imprisoned in Martin County for allegedly kidnapping at gun point and assaulting Effie Griffin, an "American girl." The newspaper described the salesman, Joseph Needleman, as "a clean-cut young man." He declared his innocence and expressed fears for his safety. That night a Klan mob, including a Primitive Baptist preacher, gathered from two counties to fix the "damn Jew." They drove to the jail and broke into Needleman's cell. He was told, "We have come to give you what you deserve" and that his "father's money will do no good." The mob, some masked, drove him to a country road, took him from the car, and gave him a choice: "Now, Needleman, which do you prefer, to have your head cut off or be mutilated?" He told them "to do as they pleased." A knife-wielder castrated him. Bleeding profusely, he walked to town, where a doctor was called. He lay near death for weeks.[16]

In contrast to Leo Frank, victimized by anti-Semitic public opinion, Joseph Needleman "heard expressions of sympathy." State newspapers headlined the story, and the national press followed. The Kinston newspaper noted, "Feeling here is running high against the perpetrators." Governor A. W. McLean offered a $400 reward for the arrest of each mob member, and county commissioners doubled the bounty. The *Williamston Enterprise* boasted that in Martin County "black and white, Jew and Gentile, Greek and Barbarian, yellow and brown, high and low have dwelt together . . . in perfect peace and unity." In truth, eastern North Carolina had a long history of lynchings and jail abductions, and the Williamston sheriff likely was complicit. In Needleman's case, twenty-three persons were arrested. The trial exonerated Needleman—Griffin's accusations were quickly discredited—while the knife-wielder received a maximum sentence of thirty years. Others were fined or sentenced to years of hard labor. Two years later, Jews, locally and nationally, collected funds to help Needleman sue for damages.[17]

Williamston was a mill and market town where Jews had resided since ante-bellum days. Jews generally prospered and felt welcomed, and the story was not passed down. Jews knew the perpetrators' families well. As was true of black victims of mob violence, both Leo Frank and Joseph Needleman learned that white outrage was aroused most violently by offenses against women.[18]

The Needleman case demonstrated the Jew's place as a focal point between southern diehards and progressives. The trial judge castigated the "old senti-ment" that mob violence was the public guardian of woman's honor. The trial marked the first successful prosecution of an "entire lynch mob" in state history, historian Vann Newkirk notes. Progressives had long supported anti-lynching campaigns. Industrial and political leaders—the governor was a former federal banker—were mindful, too, of northern Jewish capitalists, financiers, and textile magnates who helped fuel the state's growth. Jews found friends among cosmo-politan elites—editors, educators, and public officials—who gave the state its pro-gressive reputation. In 1921, when Durham immigrant grocer Harry Murnick paid his water bill, he was punched and choked by a manager who called him a "God-damned Jew." Murnick took the manager to court, where he was convicted and fined. Murnick sued for damages. State supreme court chief justice Walter Clark, deciding for Murnick, argued, "The World has long outlived this treatment of an historic race, except perhaps in 'darkest Russia.'" He cited Shakespeare, Sir Wal-ter Scott, and Benjamin Disraeli on the Jew's humanity. Novelist Thomas Wolfe, enamored of a Jewish woman, felt "shame" and "piercing pain" when he recalled his childhood "persecution" of Jews.[19]

COMMUNAL LIFE

Jewish communities remained tightly knit, and, as social outsiders, they main-tained their own circles. Sundays meant trips, often on dirt roads, to join friends and family in neighboring towns. A sociologist studying the state's Jews in the 1930s observed, "Almost any Jewish merchant in the larger towns can speak familiarly of ten or twenty Jewish merchants in small towns throughout the state." They employed each other. Country families enjoyed home hospitality in large towns for holidays. On Sukkot in 1936 families gathered from sixty miles to celebrate in Enfield. Durham's Nachamsons, with eight marital daughters, hosted open houses for Jewish college boys, while Gastonia's Lebovitzes, with six, invited Jewish salesmen for weekends. When matriarch Belah Polakavetz, from Troy's lone Jewish family, died in 1934, Celia London, her best friend, rushed from High Point to bathe the body and sit with it all night, according to Jewish custom.[20] Landsmen networks across communities made the state's scattered Jews feel as if they were an extended family.

Greensboro pajama party, 1927. (Charlot Marks Karesh)

"We lived in a small town, but we weren't isolated," recalled Susan Bloom Farber, whose Jewish family was the only one in rural Jackson. "It wasn't as if we were small-town people that never knew what city life was like." Buying trips to Baltimore or New York, as Abe Brenner of Winston-Salem recalled, "combined business with pleasure," an opportunity not only to purchase seasonal merchandise but to see a show, eat at a deli, and renew family ties. Always a "distant relative somewhere . . . knew someone to date."[21] Mothers-in-law came for the births of grandchildren, and a wedding or a bar mitzvah was a family reunion. Cousins from Baltimore might spend a summer holiday with country kin. These links extended abroad as letters and packages flowed to parents and grandparents in the old country. Families packed bundles of secondhand clothing. Shoes were scuffed and clothes were slightly torn to avoid the tariff that applied to new merchandise.

The 1930s marked the advent of the ethnic Jew whose allegiances were more social and cultural than religious. "Belonging to a Jewish community took precedence over belief in Judaism," historian Deborah Dash Moore observes. Only a minority of American Jews affiliated with synagogues. National surveys in the

1920s and 1930s found low rates of synagogue affiliation and attendance, especially relative to church attendance by Catholics and Protestants, who were also undergoing a "'religious depression.'"[22] What prevailed among Jews, if not ritual observance, was Yiddishkeit, a Jewish way of life imbued with the tastes, accents, and flavors of the old country. Jewish nostalgia focused on food and family life. Children attached to their *zeydes* and *bubbies* (grandfathers and grandmothers), who might still live in their households. "They would talk Yiddish to keep us from hearing what they were talking about," Raleigh's Burton Horwitz recalled. The children usually understood if they did not speak it. Into the Jewish lexicon came phrases like "kosher-style" for traditional foods without rabbinic certification and "once-a-year Jew" for those who attended on the High Holidays but not otherwise. B'nai B'rith clubrooms were places to gather for cards and lunch. "Jews were more comfortable being around other Jews," recalled Kinston's Jerry Kanter. In the 1920s Charlotte Jews, excluded from the powerbrokers' City Club, opened the Progressive Club with downtown social rooms. Larger towns had Jewish-style delis where merchants gathered for pastrami and rye and a schmooze (conversation): Tenner's in Charlotte, Lee's or Fine's in Greensboro, Rose's in Fayetteville, or the Marcus Famous Delicatessen in Raleigh.

Traditions were loosening. One sign was diminishing kosher standards. In cities that no longer hired a schochet, kosher meat was available from a non-Jewish butcher. A few families taught their African American cooks the art, although

without the ritual blessing. Rev. Rubinstein of Raleigh had a circuit across eastern North Carolina. Jews arranged for a local farm to keep a cow, and the schochet traveled there to dispatch it. In Hendersonville, the rabbi killed chickens at his home Tuesday, Thursday, and Friday mornings and cows every Monday, Wednesday, and Friday. A common refrain was that a kosher cow was one that had stopped giving milk, and its meat was tough and unappetizing. In Asheville, women went to Chicken Alley, where Jake Rosen slaughtered birds, kosher and nonkosher alike. Morris Apter, a kosher butcher in Durham, complained that the community no longer supported him. Rev. L. M. Wallace of Charlotte suffered "a very tough time" when he opened a kosher food mart.[23]

American-born Jews recognized the inconsistencies of their parents' religious behavior. They did not share Old World habits and nostalgia. Often, Jews kept kosher out of respect for an elderly parent or grandparent who lived with them.

Jerry Kanter's father insisted that they keep their Kinston home kosher, but his sisters wanted bacon. "You belong to the Elks Club and you go over there and eat fish stew," Kanter told his father, "and what the hell do you think is in the bottom of the pot?" The father relented. The Stadiems kept a kosher home but ate oysters. Hanging in Dr. LeBauer's Greensboro basement were country hams poor patients bartered for medical services.[24]

Intermarriage, once rare, became more common. Strictures against boys interdating were less severe than those for girls. "You just didn't go out with non-Jews," recalled Miriam Miller Warschauer of her own youth. "You could be friendly with them, but you just didn't date them." When Ruth Perman, from Warrenton's lone Jewish family, reached her teenage years, she was sent to relatives in Baltimore to keep her in the Jewish fold. Young Jews from immigrant Orthodox families who intermarried might be denied congregational memberships or even kicked out of the house. Intermarriages typically involved Jewish men marrying Christian women. Christian women who converted to Judaism were accepted into the community. Reform Jews grudgingly accepted intermarriage. When Benjamin Cone married an Episcopalian in 1937, the "community was shocked." Ben himself reflected, "Happens every day. My mother didn't exactly like it, but she came to be fond of my wife."[25] His brother Ceasar II soon followed.

For youth, another agency of American-Jewish blending was the summer camp movement. Jewish camping, tracing to the 1890s, at first shared national camping's obsession with Native American culture. Camp Osceola, owned and directed by Rabbi George Solomon of Savannah, opened about 1926 near Hendersonville.

The Rabbi wrote that the camp was a "place where the Jewish boy can not only feel thoroughly at home with Jewish influences, but at the same time be developed in the manly sports and activities." In the same year, Rabbi Samuel Wrubel, director of Camp French Broad for boys in Brevard and Camp Dellwood for girls in Waynesville, imbued young Jews with "courage" and "sportsmanship" to "demonstrate to the world at large that distinctive only in his religion the Jew is not different from his fellows." Jewish camping in the South, the Rabbi wrote, focused on "fellowship," Jewish social bonding. At a time when the Jewish race was disparaged, attending Friday night services or enjoying sports camaraderie "restores them to a superior feeling."[26]

SHULS TO SYNAGOGUES

New synagogues attested to the Jews' rise into the urban middle class. A postwar revival saw 1,000 synagogues built nationally in the 1920s. In the postwar decades, congregations organized in Asheville, Charlotte, Wilson, Hendersonville, Winston-Salem, and Salisbury. Rented rooms or converted churches were replaced with new, downtown cathedral-like temples in Durham, Fayetteville, Gastonia, Greensboro, High Point, Raleigh, and Winston-Salem. Greensboro's Temple Emanuel, endowed by Cones and Sternbergers, was an imposing neoclassical structure erected in fashionable Fisher Park, where it formed a trinity with Episcopal and Presbyterian churches. High Point featured Romanesque arches and ornamental brickwork, a Star of David serving as a rose window. Gastonia built a neoclassical temple. In contrast to the prevailing American church styles, Fayetteville Jews replicated a European baroque synagogue. Downtowns were undergoing building booms, and Jews staked their space.

Inspired by progressives like Mordecai Kaplan of the Jewish Theological Seminary, these buildings accommodated not just immigrant male daveners (worshipers) but an assimilating youth and women who were demanding places in community life. The synagogue-center was an American innovation that brought under one roof a sanctuary, school, and social hall. As Durham's Building Committee wrote in 1921: "A synagogue, particularly in the South, is not only a House of Worship but equally as important a community center. Here convenes the women organizations, the various clubs, the Sunday school, the Hebrew school and the general community religious and social activities." It was a place for Jews to meet other Jews. The High Point temple included not only a sanctuary and mikva (ritual bath) but an "all purpose meeting room."[27] To raise funds, synagogues offered naming opportunities, and families achieved community status by bidding to engrave their names on a pew, ark, or Torah mantle.

Although synagogues presented a modern, united front, their facades hid

inner turmoil. The meeting called to build a Durham synagogue was raucous, loudly argued in Yiddish, with much arm waving. In Fayetteville, a lot was purchased in 1922 on Cool Spring Street "after many discussions and a number of arguments." In towns with East European enclaves, immigrant elders clung to their Orthodoxy. They held financial power and were often the only ones attending services. Younger, American-born Jews had little interest in sitting through lengthy, Hebrew-language services while a Polish-born rabbi intoned his d'var Torah (Bible lesson) in Yiddish. Congregational conflicts reflected divisions between young and old, liberals and traditionalists. The question was whether to be inclusionary or exclusionary in setting boundaries of Judaism. Battles raged on whether to accept memberships from intermarried Jews, permit mixed-gender seating, or bury those of uncertain Jewish ancestry in consecrated cemeteries. After a "hot and heavy" board meeting in Winston-Salem, congregational president Sosnik returned home with a black eye. Often disputes focused on musical instruments in worship, traditionally banned since the fall of the Second Temple in 70 CE. Around 1930, after bitter debate, Charlotte's Hebrew United Brotherhood voted to install an organ. One night it disappeared, never seen again. Hendersonville's Agudas Israel, founded in 1922, voted "unanimously" to place a piano in the front but also to have all seats face the "Sofer Torah." Rabbi Israel Mowshowitz observed that Durham's Jews were "Orthodox, Southern style." They drove and kept their stores open on the Sabbath. Kosher laws were often disregarded, and the mikva was rarely used. Women came down from the balcony and sat with men. Such "hybrid" orthodoxy was commonplace in the South and Midwest.[28]

Observant elders fought to maintain traditional East European Orthodoxy. Storekeepers rose early to wrap themselves in tallis and tefillin (phylacteries). Before school, children knocked on doors to awaken men for the daily morning minyan in Durham and High Point. At closing time in Charlotte, Jerry Levin went store to store summoning merchants to his father's shoe shop, where the men held a daily minyan. Others recall immigrant women who did not sway from Orthodoxy. In Fayetteville the Fleishmans kept a mikva (ritual bath) on their back porch. Anna Goldberg Shain was once caught sewing on the Sabbath by her mother-in-law who reprimanded her, "Animals don't have religion, but people do."[29]

Stalwart Jews like Louis Schwartz at Wilmington's B'nai Israel or S. H. Dworsky at Durham's Beth El held long tenures as shul presidents, resisting compromise. Charlotte's Elazar Katzen was recalled as "a nice, sweet old man," but he was "troublesome." Wrapped in a big tallis, the short, rotund immigrant shouted in his gravelly voice when the davening did not suit him. Struggling to gather a minyan on Shabbat mornings, Wilmington's Orthodox Jews violated Jewish law

Monroe Evans records the problems of preserving traditional Jewish prayer and community.

The usual problem was that Saturday was the one day in the week when the farmers came to town to shop and therefore was the only profitable day in many stores. So Shabbat services were started at six thirty in the morning (in the dark winter) and they were over by eight o'clock or just a little thereafter. The biggest obstacle here was that Mr. Morris Goldberg was the Torah reader with a beautiful voice and a love to sing and he set the pace. If someone pushed he added a few trills and the services lasted longer. I was told there were many arguments about what psalms to read and where in the service to read them. Each member had his own prayer book and each had a slightly different pronunciation of the Hebrew because each country from which they had immigrated had their own customs. Most had been born in Lithuania and they prevailed. It was several years before it was agreed to buy prayer books so all would have the same sequence of the services. Many times there was a Yahrzeit (a service on the anniversary of the death of a family member) the wife of the mourner would send chopped herring and kichel (a very crispy thick cracker) or a bottle of sweet wine and even a little "schnapps" once in a while. The men would only take a swallow, but it sort of proved that they were a "mensch" (manly).[1]

1. Monroe Evans, *A History of Beth Israel Congregation and the Jewish Community in Cumberland County, North Carolina* (Fayetteville, 2002), 63.

by telephoning members or by praying with less than then ten males. With Saturday a shopping day, Fayetteville began services at six thirty and ended by eight so men could work.[30] The mikva drew giggles from younger girls. Boys had no interest in the kaporos rite, swinging chickens around their heads to expiate sins on Yom Kippur as their grandfathers did. Baseball was abundantly more available. At Greensboro's High Holiday services, Mush Fine stepped outside to check World Series scores on his car radio and report back to worshipers. "It was very important," Adelaide Israel recalled.

While the synagogue struggled to draw members, Jews flocked to social, philanthropic, and Zionist organizations. These groups blended American forms with Jewish content. Hadassah, Council, and Sisterhood raised funds at linen showers, card tables, or theater parties. B'nai B'rith lodges were card-playing societies. Jews were realigning their religious allegiances, as children of East European immigrants acculturated and loosened their Orthodoxy. By 1931 the Reform movement was equally divided between Jews of German and East European origins. In its 1937 platform, Reform Judaism called for a renewed liturgy, reaffirmed Jewish peoplehood, and spoke favorably of Palestine as land of Jewish "memories and hopes."[31] Conservative Judaism was by the 1940s the nation's largest Jewish movement, adhering to Jewish law but compromising with modernity by employing bilingual prayer books, seating men and women together, and accompanying worship services with an organ.

When Asheville's reform and orthodox Jews contended in 1919, some urged a "conservative" compromise. In an open meeting that was "stirring" in its "appeals for a vital Judaism," Old World authoritarians yielded ground. President Sol Lipinsky called for "recognition of the necessity of the new day. This was an American generation." A temple history proclaimed, "Democracy was at work." In 1926 forward-looking rabbis of the Central Conference of American Rabbis held their national conference in Asheville.[32] Bearded, frock-coated, Yiddish-speaking, immigrant reverends no longer sufficed. The transition from Orthodoxy was marked by conflict that broke the unity of a congregation-community. In Winston-Salem in 1932, Jews interested in a "more liberal type of Judaism" splintered from Orthodox Beth Jacob. They intended to create a Conservative congregation, but impressed by an interview with Rabbi Simon, a Hebrew Union College (HUC) graduate, they aligned with Reform. The Orthodox Jews agreed to share their synagogue, but after the rabbi placed flowers on the bimah for confirmation, the group was asked to leave. Calling itself Temple Emanuel, the group rented rooms above a store. With new arrivals, Greensboro's Temple spawned in 1942 a Conservative congregation, which first met downstairs. Charlotte employed a common formula: Reform on Friday nights when younger families came; conservative on Saturday mornings when traditional Jews attended the Torah service. "We tried to accommodate everybody to keep one synagogue," recalled a rabbi. By 1942 newcomers and descendants of early German settlers organized Reform Temple Beth El. Often Asheville and Greensboro Jews kept memberships in both congregations.

Rather than a mohel, schochet, and hazzan, Jews now wanted "a teacher, a counselor, an administrator." A modern, English-speaking rabbi could relate to their children and serve as a Jewish ambassador to the gentile community. Products of Polish yeshivot (seminaries) yielded to university-educated rabbinic professionals from Yeshiva College, Hebrew Union College, or the Jewish Theological Seminary (JTS). In 1921 North Carolina had two ordained rabbis; in 1938 it claimed fifteen.[33] In 1931 Greensboro's Temple Emanuel hired Rabbi Fred Rypins, an HUC graduate who had served in Wilmington. Two years later it hired Naphtali Kagan to serve as schochet and bar mitzvah tutor. The rabbi and the schochet were poles of a changing Judaism. The tall, handsome, silver-haired Rypins was at home on the golf course as well as the pulpit. Rev. Kagan, a kohen (priest), was

an immigrant traditionalist, who draped a large prayer shawl over his head as he gave the priestly blessing. Rabbi Rypins led Confirmation for boys and girls alike who could recite the Ten Commandments, even if they never learned Hebrew. Rev. Kagan taught boys Torah trope in his small apartment. In Charlotte, William Greenburg, a JTS graduate, arrived in 1932 as Charlotte's "first modern English-speaking rabbi," while Rev. L. M. Wallace came as mohel and hazzan.

Many Jewish communities contained a learned immigrant Jewish elder who preserved the community's kosher standards and educated its youth, mostly boys for the bar mitzvah. Rev. Louis Ershler in High Point or Beryl Cohen in Hendersonville drilled generations. Cohen was graduate of the Diskin Orphanage and Yeshiva in Jerusalem. In Williamston, Sam Zemon tutored the boys. A salesman from Baltimore, he and his family lived in the backrooms of their ladies' ready-to-wear store. "My dad conned him into giving me some brush up Hebrew lessons," Richard Levin recalled.[34] Some boys were sent north to spend their bar mitzvah years with relatives in Baltimore or Richmond. High Point's Leonard Kaplan recalled a ten-dollar bar mitzvah: "Everybody would go downstairs in the

House of Jacob Sunday School with Rabbi Prinz, Raleigh, 1928. (Francis Penslar)

little social hall, and they had one bottle of schnapps and some schnitzel and maybe a little bit of herring if it was a more affluent family."

Old World taskmasters struggled to impose cheder discipline on a recalcitrant, All-American youth who had other interests than attending daily Hebrew lessons after school. Joseph Reznick, bar mitzvahed in 1932, recalled his experience in Winston-Salem's Orthodox synagogue: "The rabbi and the children were at war." Wilmington's Rabbi Minsky felt no inhibitions about slapping the hands of girls in his class. In Fayetteville, a very large Rabbi Rutberg sat in front of the class reading the "yiddisher paper," but unleashing his wrath at any student who looked up from his siddur (prayer book). Raleigh's Rabbi Prinz awarded pickles to students who translated from the Chumash, Jesse Margulies recalled, but "if you made a mistake, he could sit ten feet away from you and he'd flip a match stick and he'd hit you right between the eyes." Margulies added, "He never missed."[35] Louis and Charlotte Gordon brought to Statesville a retired rabbi to tutor their five sons. Installed in a small house between baseball and football fields, he opened a window shouting for the reluctant scholars in Yiddish, "Kum, Sauleh, it's your turn for the Hebrew lessons." The brothers yelled back, "No way," and continued their ball games.

By contrast, the American rabbi accommodated to the kids. Charlotte's Rabbi Greenburg played baseball with the boys behind the Temple, retrieving the ball when sometimes it broke a neighbor's window. Leonard Kaplan recalled an improvement when a young JTS rabbi arrived in High Point who made misbehaving students do push-ups rather than "clop" them. At Reform congregations, an hour and a half weekly in religious school could not inspire much commitment or learning. Greensboro's Rabbi Milton Ellis did not have any takers for his Saturday Hebrew classes until he offered a reward. "If you come to Hebrew class, I'll take you horseback riding," Carolyn Weill LeBauer recalled, "That's how I learned Hebrew," adding "what little I learned, which I've since forgotten."[36]

Younger women, no longer content with a separate, subordinate role, led congregational changes. Fayetteville laid its synagogue cornerstone in the name of the Hebrew Ladies Aid Society, but women worshipers were confined to seats in a small, hot balcony. After sweltering for one year, women moved downstairs despite grumbling from the very Orthodox. The balcony became the domain of noisy, disruptive children who were exiled there. At Wilmington's B'nai Israel, women crowded into the balcony on holidays and Friday nights, dressed in their very best. Conversation flowed, quieting for the sermon but otherwise so noisy that the rabbi thumped his book. In Greensboro, where Reform services were held in the sanctuary and Orthodox in a basement chapel, women abandoned their husbands for English worship upstairs. "Every major transformation of the American synagogue," historian Karla Goldman notes, "was integrally associated with the major redefinitions of the place that women were to take within and beyond its walls."[37]

In Greensboro, Etta Spier, a college professor, and Miriam Lindau asked the board in 1922 to grant them equal membership. Spier, a Temple founder and religious school director, led the state's League of Women's Voters and American Association of University Women. Having just won the electoral right to vote, women now demanded equal rights in synagogue governance. Both women were also active in the North Carolina Association of Jewish Women, which had just held its first convention in Greensboro. The male trustees deliberated a year before granting their request. In 1926 Goldsboro's Oheb Sholom granted women "full privileges of membership . . . with voting rights."[38] Salisbury's Temple Israel emerged from the local Council of Jewish Women chapter. When the community grew to thirty families by 1939, the women organized a Conservative congregation.

PORTRAIT: GERTRUDE WEIL

"Straight-backed, straightforward, but never strait-laced" a biographer wrote of Gertrude Weil, the most remarkable Jewish North Carolinian.[1] Born in Goldsboro in 1879, Gertrude Weil attended public schools and the progressive Horace Mann School at Columbia Teacher's College in New York. In 1901 she became the first North Carolinian to graduate from Smith College. Broadly educated, Weil studied radical socialism, dined with the southern progressive George W. Cable, and attended racially integrated classes with the children of writer Charles Chesnutt, a black North Carolinian. After she toured Europe, her family called her home.

While Weil men built businesses and oversaw philanthropies, the women founded drama clubs, music societies, and social service agencies. The family endowed parks, schools, and libraries and paid the town's first public-health nurse. It donated land for Cliffs of the Neuse State Park and sponsored lectures, scholarships, and buildings at Chapel Hill and Women's College. Brothers Leslie and Lionel served as trustees of the University of North Carolina, their alma mater, and were awarded honorary degrees.

Gertrude's mother Mina Rosenthal Weil wrote, "My greatest desire for my children is to feel . . .

Gertrude Weil, far left, as a suffragist. (North Carolina State Archives)

that the world will be better for their having lived, not great but good is what I wish them to do." Among Mina's personal friends was Henrietta Szold, founder of the woman's Zionist organization Hadassah. Mina and her sister-in-law Sarah Einstein Weil brought to Goldsboro Charlotte Perkins Gilman, the well-known feminist and socialist, who inspired them to create a local Women's Club. At Mina Weil's death, the newspaper noted, "The public knew little of her good deeds." Barefoot schoolchildren received free shoes at the Weil store. Coal was sent to the needy. Prizes were given at both black and white high schools.[2]

Rabbi Solomon Herbst wrote of Gertrude, "Frequently I come across young men and women who tell me that they have gone through college with the financial help of Miss W. Negro preachers have informed me that their churches receive substantial contributions from her. She visits sick people at the hospital *every day* carrying flowers . . . Whatever the Temple needs—she provides. . . . Her whole life is a Kiddush Hashem (holy to God)."[3]

"Federation Gertie" was one of the Progressive Era "new women" remaking society. In 1912 she led a state effort to give women the right to serve on school boards. As an officer of the North Carolina Federation of Women's Clubs, Weil recognized that philanthropy could not bring social reform unless women secured the vote. In 1914 she helped found the North Carolina Equal Suffrage League, serving as its president in 1919 and 1920. The state legislature rejected suffrage, but it succeeded nationally. In 1920 Weil helped found the state's League of Women Voters and became its first president, focusing on child and women's labor. In 1927, as president of the Goldsboro Bureau of Social Service, she stated, "It is not enough to eliminate

one case of poverty after another, but to eliminate poverty itself." A self-declared socialist, Weil was politically out of step with conservative North Carolina, but state leaders respected her, and she worked closely with her friend UNC president Frank Graham. After she attended an Anti-Lynching Conference of Southern White Women, Governor Max Gardner appointed her in 1932 to the North Carolina Commission on Interracial Cooperation. In the 1940s when the commission endorsed integration, some prominent whites quit but Weil stayed.[4]

Gertrude Weil was no less active in Jewish causes. She attended Sabbath services loyally, knocking on doors to bring others. At Temple Oheb Sholom, she was Sisterhood president and a religious school teacher. She twice served as president of the North Carolina Association of Jewish Women, founded by her aunt Sarah, and advised its youth group. Her family's efforts to save German relatives from Nazi persecutions strengthened her Zionism. In 1951 she visited the Jewish state, declaring there could be "no Judaism without Israel" and was active in Hadassah locally and regionally.[5]

Modest and mirthful, idealistic and pragmatic, Weil was widely read, a persuasive speaker, and a wise and witty conversationalist. The civil rights movement arrived when she was in her eighties, but she fearlessly crossed racial lines. Weil remained in her downtown home as the neighborhood turned black and opened her door to African Americans for meetings of the Goldsboro Bi-Racial Council, which she helped found. She painted a white face on a black jockey hitching post in front of her home. When the city denied blacks use of the municipal swimming pool, the Weils donated one in a black neighborhood. Elderly Miss Gertrude was the first to jump in.

Among her awards were an honorary doctorate from North Carolina Women's College, a B'nai B'rith distinguished service award, and her alma mater's Smith Medal. "I grow more radical every year," Weil quipped in her eighties, "Who knows? I may live long enough to become a communist!"[6] In 1971 she died in Goldsboro in the house where she was born.

1. Ellen-Fairbanks Diggs Bodman, "Weil, Gertrude," in William S. Powell, ed., *Dictionary of North Carolina Biography*, vol. 4 (Chapel Hill: University of North Carolina Press, 1996), 153–54.

2. Anne Firor Scott, "Gertrude Weil and Her Times," *Southern Cultures* 13, no. 1 (Spring 2007): 90; Moses Rountree, *Strangers in the Land: The Story of Jacob Weil's Tribe* (Philadelphia: Dorrance, 1969), 115.

3. Solomon Herbst to Dear Colleagues, 1 Mar. 1953, AJA.

4. Steven Niven, "Gertrude Weil," in Howard Covington and Marion Ellis, eds., *The North Carolina Century: Tar Heels Who Made a Difference, 1900–2000* (Charlotte: Levine Museum of the New South, 2002), 525.

5. Ibid., 526; Scott, "Gertrude Weil and Her Times," 99, 101.

6. Scott, "Gertrude Weil and Her Times," 99, 101.

BECOMING SOUTHERN

The extent of Jewish-Christian social integration varied by community, owing in some cases to structural factors and in others to personalities. Though black-balled from the downtown Durham club, Jews served as president of Greensboro's Rotary. As Greensboro's leading industrialists, Jews could not be denied or excluded, and the city's Quaker heritage encouraged tolerance. Intermarriages between Jewish and Christian elites enhanced their familiarity. Christians asked Rabbi Rypins to perform weddings, and his wife Ruth ran a preschool from her home that drew the city's elites. First Presbyterian Church, across the street from the Temple, placed a stained-glass Star of David on a window in gratitude for help in retiring its debt. The rabbi, the Presbyterian pastor, a Catholic monsignor, and Guilford College's Quaker president formed a Friar's Club that met monthly to discuss racial and social issues. Rabbi Rypins in 1938 was perhaps the first Jew in America to head a Ministerial Association. Yet, in nearby High Point and Winston-Salem, Jews found doors closed to them at country or downtown business clubs. Durham and High Point were East European enclaves with a legacy of immigrant Yiddishkeit. Jews there were less well assimilated than the German Jews in places like Asheville or Statesville. Exceptions could always be found to the general bias. Jacob Stein, with a Yiddish accent, was a Fayetteville delegate to Rotary International conferences. High society was closed to Jews, but Cathryn Ginsburg of Greensboro was presented at the 1935 North Carolina Debutante Ball. Louis Lipinsky, a third-generation southerner who twice served as Merchant's

In 1921, Sarah Einstein Weil called thirty-five Jewish women from across the state to her hometown of Goldsboro. Her ambition was to bridge the state's ethnic, religious, and geographic divides. From this meeting came the North Carolina Association of Jewish Women, the country's first and only such organization. Its leaders—Sarah Weil, Gertrude Weil, Flora Stern, Ruth Rypins, Edna Lichtenfels—were active in woman's clubs and state federations. Its founding came one year after women's suffrage.

The NCAJW embarked on a progressive agenda. It undertook censuses of the state's Jewish communities. By 1927 it counted 781 women from sixty-six towns. By 1937 two-thirds of its more than 500 members came from the state's eleven largest towns with the remainder settled in ninety-eight communities. The state was divided into eight districts, and it held regional meetings culminating in an annual state conference which featured national speakers.

The NCAJW focused on education. In 1930 it held a ten-day camp for Sunday School teachers at Camp Osceola in Hendersonville and organized teacher-training institutes for women whose "zeal" was often greater than their "preparation." A Jewish library was established. The organization led the

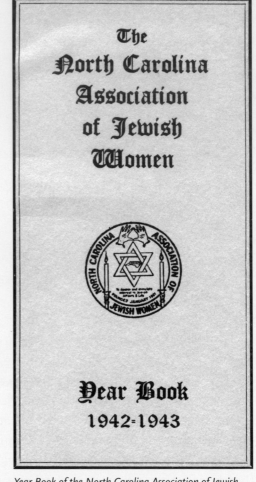

Year Book of the North Carolina Association of Jewish Women, founded in 1921. (Jewish Heritage Foundation of North Carolina)

Association president, joined the Charlotte Country Club and Myers Park Club in the 1920s although both were regarded as restrictive.[39]

In contrast to racial and religious prejudice was an appreciation of immigrant gifts. In rural Troy, local lawyers and officials sought out Jake Polakavetz for his Talmudic advice. Ministers talked Bible as they prepared Sunday sermons. Polakavetz was invited to churches, but as an Orthodox Jew he would not attend, except for funerals and weddings, although he happily donated to their building funds.

effort to establish a Hillel Foundation at Chapel Hill to serve the state's campuses. By 1937 its Sophia Einstein Student Loan was assisting more than three dozen college students. It also created a youth auxiliary, the North Carolina Association of Jewish Youth, which sponsored picnics, dances, and conferences. In 1956 the NCAJW led the campaign to create an assisted-living home for the Jewish elderly. In 1960 a twenty-four room mansion on 117 acres was purchased in Clemmons, outside Winston-Salem, and two wings were added to create the Blumenthal Home for the Jewish Aged.

"The social part of the Association is to bring Jewish people together whenever and wherever it is possible," wrote president Hinda Honigman in 1938.[1] Its meetings were bonding experiences, especially for small-towners. Immigrant families were assisted and helped with their naturalization. The NCAJW spawned a men's auxiliary, the NCAJM. The associations flourished in the postwar years, but their leadership aged and demography changed. The two groups merged. Federations and Community Relation Councils now served similar purposes. Newcomers flooding into the state did not share the sense of roots or community that had made the NCAJW such a vital and vibrant organization. Only its student loan fund survived.

1. *American Jewish Times*, Apr. 1938, 41.

Cities, college towns especially, contained a cosmopolitan elite. Durham's Rabbi Chaim Williamofsky, ordained in a Polish yeshiva, enjoyed scholarly conversations at Duke's Religion Department. Well-traveled college faculty frequented Louis Jaffe's bakery for his rye and black breads. Every city contained a Jewish-style deli, which, like the Greek or Italian café, was appreciated by natives as well as the Jewish salesman on the road. "If you wanted a lawyer at lunchtime" in Greensboro, Adelaide Israel recalled, "you would go to Mush Fine's" behind the courthouse.

Typically, communities held an "ethnic broker . . . a communicator who is respected by his group and acts as a spokesperson in intergroup relations."[40] Men like industrialist Morris Speizman in Charlotte and optometrist Nathan Rosenstein in Durham were European born, but they were recognized as both civic and Jewish leaders. Min Munich Klein represented Jews before Greensboro's women's groups. They interceded personally with the minister who delivered a sermon thought anti-Semitic, the civic club president whose group did not admit Jews, or the newspaper editor who identified a lawbreaker as a Jew. They were Jewish ambassadors at faith gatherings.

The tentative civic position of Jews was reflected in politics. With Franklin Roosevelt's ascendance, a "Jewish vote" began coalescing around the Democratic Party, and the New Deal brought Jews into the federal government. North

Carolina remained a one-party, Democratic state. Julius Cone was a Greensboro councilman from 1923 to 1940. Harriss Newman was elected to the North Carolina legislature from New Hanover County in 1931 and 1933, chairing the powerful Appropriations Committee. Benjamin Cone represented Guilford County in 1935. Max Kahn won election to the Charlotte City Council in 1933. Abe Shapiro, an immigrant reverend's son, was a Winston-Salem judge. Sigmund Meyer and Henry Bane of Durham held party offices and were appointed judges, but then lost elections.[41] Jews civically involved in Community Chests, merchants groups, and hospital drives in the 1930s would find the public more willing to support their political aspirations in the postwar years. For the most part, Jews remained political outsiders.

The twenties and thirties were eras of sports mania. Whether as fans or athletes, Jews bonded to their communities and achieved status. Harry Schwartz starred on Charlotte's Central High School football team. As captain of UNC's 1928 team, he received all-American mentions. His brother Benny was a collegiate wrestler. Lou Silver went to Duke on a wrestling scholarship. In 1937 UNC boxer Max Novich won the conference championship, and a year later Joe Murnick was undefeated team captain. Fayetteville's E. J. "Mutt" Evans and Charlotte's David Neiman were record-setting track stars. Abe Neiman played on the conference champion UNC basketball team. "Tramp athletes" were lured from the north with scholarship offers. Archie Israel, nicknamed "Yom" after he missed practice on Yom Kippur, was drawn from Connecticut to Chapel Hill but followed a coach to play football for Elon College's Fighting Christians. In an era of ethnic heroes the Tenner brothers boxing entourage arrived in Charlotte from Savannah, led by boxer Lukie, trainer Al, and manager Sol. Lukie was Southern Featherweight Champion, and he earned his credentials by defeating local hero Crayton Rowe and taking him again in a rematch. He challenged World Champion Joe Dundee at Madison Square Garden. The brothers opened "Tenners," a Jewish-style deli and restaurant that centered gustatory life for both Charlotte's Jews and the downtown business lunch crowd into the 1940s.[42] Baseball was America's game. Felix Hayman, born in Statesville in 1877, operated a meat market but neglected beef for baseball. He owned Wearn Field, and in 1919 he purchased the insolvent Charlotte Hornets Baseball Club. He introduced night baseball to Charlotte. The shrewd owner once traded a shortstop to Chattanooga for a turkey. "Felix came out ahead on that deal," a fan observed, "that turkey was tough." Hayman was a father figure to his players ready with a handout for those down on their luck. He managed the club until he died in 1932.[43]

Even as Jews found social acceptance, they were conscious of anti-Semitic undertones. In the 1930s the national spotlight shone on Winston-Salem's Jews.

Z. Smith Reynolds, heir to a $20 million tobacco fortune, was a married eighteen year old when he became enamored of Libby Holman, "a sultry torch singer" born Elizabeth Holzman in Cincinnati to Jewish parents. Reynolds, piloting his plane, pursued the older woman. In 1931, six days after his Reno divorce, Reynolds secretly married Holman. The *New York Times* broke the story.[44] Libby traveled with a fast theater crowd, and her parties at the family's Reynolda House in Winston-Salem discomfited conservative southerners. The newlyweds quarreled, allegedly over his discovery of his wife's Jewishness, although she insisted that it was over sex. One drunken party night, Holman went to Reynolds's room with a friend, reputedly her lover. There was a gunshot, and Reynolds lay dead with a bullet in his head. Holman and her friend claimed suicide. Holman also announced that she was pregnant.

Libby's father, Alfred Holzman, an attorney, arrived to oversee her defense. Concerned that a "small-town jury" would not trust outsiders, they hired Benet Polikoff, a local Jewish attorney. As the trial began, Holman, knitting baby clothes, insisted on her innocence. "I loved Smith as I never loved anyone before or ever will again," she told a reporter. Holman suspected anti-Semitism lay behind her indictment even as she disparaged her Jewish origins. Smith's uncle, Will Reynolds, to avoid scandal, asked that charges be dropped. The judge dismissed the case for lack of evidence. The *Winston-Salem Journal*, noting the "sensational stories," regretted that the "officers handling the investigation have been laid open to the charge of persecution, the community of racial prejudice." Will Reynolds denied any such bias: "Of course the family knew Libby was a Jewess. Smith told me himself. He remarked that maybe it would do the Reynolds blood a lot of good to have Jewish mixture in it. I agreed with him." And, he added, "Some of the dearest friends I have are Jewish. I have a keen admiration for them. As a race, they don't make any finer people."[45]

Holman left the "hick town that tried to lynch me." Failing at comebacks, she faded from the limelight and committed suicide in 1971. Two movies, *Reckless* with Jean Harlow and *Written in the Wind* with Lauren Bacall, retold her story. Her husband's inheritance endowed the Z. Smith Reynolds Foundation, a trust that funds progressive causes.[46] The Holman and Needleman cases point to anti-Semitic stereotypes that associated Jews with city vices, representing Jews as libertines, lustful sexual predators.

Relations with African Americans reflected the prejudice and paternalism that governed black-white relations generally. Blackface minstrel shows were popular entertainments at temple functions well into the 1940s. Jewish stores catered to black trade, and the two peoples often lived in close proximity. Jews primarily knew blacks as customers, employees, or tenants. Like other southerners, both white and black, they invested in housing in black neighborhoods. Yet, Jews and blacks also had common interests. Durham with its black-owned bank and insurance company was known nationally as the "Negro Wall Street." Immigrant Jews patronized the Mechanics and Farmers Bank there, which loaned Jews money to build their synagogue. Other cities had thriving black business districts like Raleigh's East Hargett Street. Church and state supported black colleges and normal schools spawned a black middle class.

Cooks and housekeepers in Jewish homes became "family." Carolyn Weill LeBauer of Greensboro recalled her nanny: "I adored Elsie, and if I got scared during the night—Elsie had a room on the second floor right across from mine—I didn't go jump in bed with mother and daddy. I went and jumped in bed with Elsie. Elsie was the one who was gonna take care of me." Housekeepers might bring their own children into homes, and children played together. Elsie Doget named her own daughter after Carolyn. Elderly, black housekeepers or store employees were kept on payrolls beyond their working years. Cooks picked up Yiddish and were practiced in koshering a chicken or setting a Passover table. For Weldon's Freid family, Dale made challah and gefilte fish as well as fried chicken and salmon cakes. When college graduates returned home, they paid obligatory and mutually affectionate visits to a "Mary" or "Aunt Lola." In Raleigh, a nanny named Sally raised two generations of Horwitz children. When she died at ninety-one, the family so loved her that Burton Horwitz "thought my kids were going into the box with her."[47]

Few Jews crossed the color line. Bill Levitt and Sidney Rittenberg were UNC student radicals who joined the labor movement. Levitt, a leader of the campus Young Communist League, helped form a two-man picket line to force stores in black neighborhoods to end discrimination. A personalism alleviated the effects of segregation without leading to social equality or systemic change. Meyer Levin was "boss" at a Williamston factory, but on Saturday nights he answered his door when an employee or his girlfriend knocked needing a loan for bail or a word with a sheriff. The Russian-born Jew's nickname was "black man's Jesus." Drs. Sidney and Maurice LeBauer maintained an integrated waiting room at their Greensboro medical practice, s did optometrist Samuel Robinson in Asheville. Robinson addressed his black patients as Mr. and Mrs. to the disgust of his receptionist. "Patients were seen first come first served," his son Michael recalled, and "whites sometimes walked out if blacks were served before them." Active in the Boy Scout movement, Robinson worked to bring black groups into the council. His ten-year-old son Michael insisted on sitting in the back of the bus with his nanny. Laura Weill Stern Cone served on the Bennett College board in the 1930s

Josephine and Isabel Freid with their nanny, Mary Davis.
(Jewish Heritage Foundation of North Carolina)

and was an officer of the state Commission on Inter-Racial Cooperation in the 1940s. In 1935 Herbert Falk Sr. joined Greensboro's first interracial committee.[48]

If North Carolinians identified Jews with blacks, the 813 Rosenwald Schools in 93 counties were reminders. Julius Rosenwald asserted that as a member himself of a persecuted people, he "always felt keenly for the colored race." He committed his Sears Roebuck fortune to black higher education, including Elizabeth City Normal and Industrial School. Booker T. Washington convinced him to support primary education. From 1912 to 1932 Rosenwald helped underwrite 5,300 schools in fifteen southern states with North Carolina having more than any. Rosenwald gave matching grants that required communities to raise funds "in cooperation between citizens and officials, white and colored." Sharecroppers gave so that their children could attend modern, well-lit classrooms. Rosenwald Schools—

following Washington's philosophy of black uplift—emphasized industrial and agricultural education. The fund also supported the University of North Carolina Press's efforts to address "southern problems."[49]

THE PROBLEMATIC SOUTH

The Depression derailed North Carolina's progress. By 1933 more than a quarter of its people were on relief with the mountains and coastal plain hit hardest. The cigarette industry endured as economic tensions led people to smoke more, but farmers got less for their tobacco. From 1928 to 1932, farm income plunged nearly two-thirds. Agrarian North Carolina had to import food. Banks failed weekly, wages dropped a third, and manufactures declined 40 percent. A third of the furniture plants closed. The state ranked near the bottom in per capita income. In 1938 Franklin Roosevelt proclaimed the South "the Nation's No. 1 economic problem."[50]

Depression memories ran deeply. When a bank failed, Nathan Rosenstein of Durham sat on a step crying that he had lost everything but his friends. The Kaplan brothers, whose Raleigh department store employed forty clerks, "went totally under." "There were no bankruptcy laws in those days," Leonard Kaplan recalled, "and so they took you down to your underwear." When the mountain land boom crashed, Louis Williams gave up real estate and returned to collecting junk. Sam Margolis, an immigrant grocer's son, dropped out of Duke to work in his father's store. He recalled, "Everything fell apart." Michael Barker of Wilson "lost all my life insurance lost the store I was in and lost my stock of merchandise."[51]

Jewish communities created free loan societies to help cash-strapped storekeepers meet a payroll or pay a wholesaler. Merchants staggered their paydays, loaning money back and forth. Rosa Schafer in Mount Airy opened a soup kitchen for destitute children. Harry Freid's mother gave him two lunch bags to take to school, one to be given to a hungry classmate. At a 1935 Winston-Salem Sisterhood meeting, the women passed a "fast motion" to buy a destitute family a ton of coal. Tarboro could no longer sustain a congregation. Gastonia, unable to pay its rabbi, closed its temple from 1930 to 1933, although two Orthodox Jews, Jack Witten and Maurice Weinstein, held home services. Wilson's Jews numbered 140 in 1927, but ten years later counted only 70. The state's Jewish population declined.[52]

Business and political leaders, traditionally distrustful of federal government, welcomed tobacco support while railing against supposedly socialistic programs that helped the rural poor. Yet, the New Deal brought substantial benefits. From 1932 to 1940, the federal government pumped some $480 million into the state.

Among the 813 Rosenwald Schools for African Americans in North Carolina was Elmwood in Iredell County. (North Carolina State Archives)

The Civilian Conservation Corps, with more than sixty camps, restored forests and built parks, roads, and flood control projects. The Blue Ridge Parkway and Great Smoky Mountains National Park brought tourism to the mountains. The Works Project Administration hired not just construction workers but also actors, artists, writers, and musicians. Although per capita net income was but 55 percent of the national average by 1940, North Carolina had the highest increase of any state. By 1937 the *Greensboro Daily News* reported "grinning storekeepers."[53]

Economic crisis provoked labor unrest. From 1928 and 1932 the state had suffered from strikes, some turning violent. In 1932 the American Federation of Labor sent truckloads of workers and organizers to rally mill workers. Mill villagers did not always take kindly to union organizers who were suspect as outsiders and communists. After Gastonia's bloody Loray Mill strike in 1929, a labor leader fled to the Soviet Union. In 1934 the United Textile Workers called a national general strike that saw 400,000 workers close virtually every mill in the state.

Jews were found on all sides of the labor crisis—except as workers. Jews were both industrialists and labor organizers. Most were storekeepers who depended on the workers' patronage. Charlotte merchants advertised in labor journals that their merchandise carried union labels. In Durham, Jewish stores signed a newspaper advertisement: "Labor unions are America's greatest safeguard for economic progress." Other merchants donated food and tents to the strikers and extended credit to see them through hard times. State senator Harriss Newman of New Hanover County campaigned in 1938 on his "enviable record as the friend of labor" and listed railroad unions endorsing him. Yet, Jewish trade unionists were marginalized. In Charlotte, a Jewish organizer recalled a congregation stopped soliciting his membership when they learned that "he works for the CIO."[54]

Corporate paternalism still governed relations between industrialists and workers. Mill worker Lacy Wright recalled, "Cone Mills was always a little bit better to their help, and paid a little better wages. . . . If you got into bad circumstances they would see that you had something to eat." Moses Cone conceded that philanthropy was not their sole motive: "We regard as a good business investment such amounts as we can spend in securing the comfort and good will of our people." Yet, at Cone Mills, Wright recalled that "the company go on them people so bad about trying to organize . . . that they fired I don't know how many of them." Union leaders were removed from their homes, furniture and all. By 1939 North Carolina was the least unionized state in the country.[55]

Folklorist Arthur Miller discovered the Jews' difficult position when the Library of Congress sent him to North Carolina to record regional dialects in 1941. He found black workers striking a Jewish-owned shirt factory in Wilmington. The women picketed chanting, "Oh Mr. Block, hallelujah, You know you can't do as you please. Oh, Mr. Block, hallelujah, Jesus is watching you." Miller continued to a rock quarry only to be confronted by a shotgun-toting overseer who chased him away, cursing Jews. Miller was perplexed since his truck carried only a federal seal. (Miller later found more cordial audiences as a playwright.)[56]

By Harry Golden's count, 22 percent of the South's textile mills were Jewish owned. Of the unionized plants, nearly two-thirds had Jewish owners. In Gastonia, the nation's largest textile mill city, only two of seventy-eight plants unionized; both were Jewish owned. Jews felt vulnerable, Golden observed, and avoided labor strife. When strikes spread to Frank Goldberg's mills in Bessemer City, the strikers' children called his school-aged daughter Jeanne a "dirty Jew" and pelted her with stones. "During the strike was the only time that happened to me," she recalled.[57]

SOUTHERN BUSINESS

In 1938 William Levitt, a UNC graduate student, followed his father "Uncle Sam" Levitt, a traveling salesman, to study "The Occupational Distribution of the Jews in North Carolina." He discovered, "In almost any small commercial town in North Carolina having a population over a thousand, there will be found at least one Jewish merchant." These "general merchandise" stores were like any other small-town stores, he noted, selling anything that people will buy. The storekeeper set prices by demand, age of product, and customer needs. Every store had tables piled with overalls, work shoes, and heavy clothing, but more stylish clothes, which sold quicker, were displayed in store windows. "Almost all the time," he noted, something is "on sale." Stores catered to low-income workers, both white and black. They engaged in "complex credit arrangements" through bartering or pawning. Credit was given on personal trust, buyer and seller knowing each other by first names, or on the "testimony of reliable customers." Rarely, Levitt observed, did merchants charge interest although items bought on credit may cost more than a cash sale. "People who paid us made payments faithfully and regularly," recalled New Bern's Elbert Lipman. "There was no interest in it." He could not recall his father ever turning down anybody for credit.[58]

Levitt surveyed 1,195 "gainfully occupied Jewish people" who lived in thirteen towns where the Jewish population exceeded one hundred. He found that professionals totaled 8.2 percent; "proprietors, managers and officials," 57.3 percent; clerical workers, 28.3 percent; and skilled workers, 5.2 percent; the remainder were unskilled workers, retirees, unemployed, or students. In towns with fewer than fifty Jews, they were engaged almost entirely in retail sales. Fayetteville listed thirty dry goods stores, and Raleigh had twenty-four. Every town, but one, had Jewish junk dealers, and eight had more than four. Asheville, Charlotte, and

Greensboro were wholesale distribution centers, and as transportation hubs they drew traveling salesmen and manufacturer representatives.

The occupational profiles indicate how Jews differed from other North Carolinians. The category of "unskilled workers" included one-quarter of the state's whites, almost two-thirds of its blacks, but only 0.2 percent of its Jews. "Proprietors, managers, and officials" accounted for 31.4 percent of whites, 21.1 percent of blacks, and 57.3 percent of Jews. Jews were almost three times more likely to be clerks than were whites, a field where blacks were hardly represented. Almost 10 percent of the Jews were professionals, a figure that was about 50 percent greater than it was for whites and almost four times greater than for blacks.[59] Levitt noted the Jews' upward mobility into the professions and "superior types" of ownership. In the state's thirteen largest communities, he found only two Jewish peddlers. He also observed that Jews were assisted financially and professionally by their families and the "community at large."[60]

Examining balance sheets, Levitt found no difference in the net worth or creditworthiness of Jewish and non-Jewish merchants. Both their incomes tended to be small, and they struggled to pay bills. Local conditions, such as the fluctuating price of cotton or tobacco, affected each alike. Jews had fewer merchants worth more than $100,000—1.1 percent versus 2.7 percent—but fewer worth less than $5,000—34.7 percent to 39.4 percent. More than half of each group was in the $5,000 to $50,000 range. Seventy-six percent of Jewish and non-Jewish businessmen alike were either "fair" or "prompt" in paying bills.[61]

Levitt listed textile mill owners in only four of the thirteen cities, dominated by Greensboro's Cone and Sternberger families. Yet, this statistic masked numbers of investors buying and building mills in rural towns where land and labor were cheaper. Moses Richter in Mount Gilead, Frank Goldberg in Bessemer City, and Karl Robbins in Hemp operated textile plants. Factories also brought Jewish managers, accountants, and salesmen.

Although Jews enjoyed warm relations with their customers, Levitt observed that their social circle consisted largely of other Jews who lived locally or in neighboring towns. The "Jew store," Levitt noted, was still regarded as "'different' in some slight and indefinable way." Jews born and raised locally were "accepted as part of the community," but a newly arrived merchant, especially an immigrant, bore the mark of "outsider." Jews more commonly enjoyed better personal relations with Christians in small towns than in larger cities where they lived among other Jews. "I allready [sic] lived here in Wilson 35 years," Michael Barker wrote a friend in 1942, "I love all Christain [sic] people white and colored I found 95 percent of the people is good and honest providing you deal honest with them."

PORTRAIT: MOSES RICHTER

Moses Richter started in North Carolina as an immigrant peddler and worked his way up to a department store in rural Mount Gilead. In 1926, while visiting family, Richter went to New York City to study the produce market. "I wanted to get out of the retail business, and I was living in the heart of the peach country," Richter recalled. "I had argued persistently with the growers that there had to be bigger and better ways of getting the peaches to market." Several years later, he helped form the Peach Cooperation of North Carolina. Shipping peaches in refrigerated rail cars and trucks, he dominated the New York market and expanded across America into Canada.

Richter became the "Peach King." He revolutionized the industry. Traditionally, growers shipped to a specific market. After packing his peaches on trucks and boxcars, Richter raced to his Charlotte office where as many as twenty men and women manned telephones to northern produce exchanges. On chalkboards they listed the hourly rising and falling prices of peaches. "If there was a half-cent difference per bushel between Albany and Providence . . ., Moses routed it to Rhode Island," Harry Golden explained. "Before the train pulled into the Pittsburgh terminal, Moses made his decision between Cincinnati and Cleveland markets."

In 1934, the Peach King sold his department store, but he was concerned that Mount Gilead was becoming "one of the vanishing Depression towns." Rallying local businessmen, he founded United Mills, a lingerie factory. By 1940 the mill employed several hundred. It was a family enterprise with his children and in-laws serving as executives. In 1965 United Mills merged with BVD. He was a generous benefactor. Mount Gilead honored him with Moses Richter Day. "I, Moses Richter, the immigrant peddler, have done very well," he recalled in a memoir. "My life has been very fulfilled."[1]

1. Harry Golden, *Our Southern Landsmen* (New York: G. P. Putnam's, 1974), 34; Charlotte Levin, "Belah and Jake: A Garden of Memories," typescript (1989), 112, JHFNC.

Older, native merchants upgraded their stores and catered to a "better class of trade," whereas newcomers, often northerners, opened pawnshops and second-hand stores.[62]

Jews themselves might be fierce rivals. Families split. In Mount Olive, Dan Satisky recalled, "Jewish people didn't talk to each, they were competitors." Resentments arose as merchants dissolved a partnership or competed to rent a propitious location. A peddler or salesman scouting a territory for a store might be told times were bad and pointed up the road. In Hendersonville, early Jewish merchants, the Pattersons and Lewises, were "fighting each other" as "friendly enemies." Morris Schas and Lou Sherman looked up the street "to see whose

PORTRAIT: FROM HEMP TO ROBBINS

In 1943 councilmen of Hemp in Moore County voted to change the town's name to Robbins, in honor of Karl Robbins, "prominent figure in the textile industry and the greatest benefactor that the town has had in its history."

Karl Robbins's story follows a familiar immigrant path. Born in Kiev in 1892, he came to America as a nine-year-old. His parents were storekeepers, but their son wholesaled fabric and invested in mills. In 1930 he purchased Pinehurst Silk Mills, renaming it Robbins Mills. Reinvesting profits, he kept the mill, the area's largest employer, humming during the Depression so that Hemp remained a "boomtown." Robbins built parks, playgrounds, and ball fields and supported public schools. Churches were repaired, and at Christmas ministers, Sunday School teachers, and the needy received gifts. One donation bought a fire truck, and another reduced town taxes. He provided workers health insurance and easy credit to buy homes. Robbins acquired plants in Aberdeen, Red Springs, and Rocky Mount and built a factory in Raeford before selling out to J. P. Stevens in 1954 to devote himself to philanthropy. "His many selfless acts brought the town of age," a newspaper explained. Robbins chaired the Research Triangle Committee in its formative years and purchased 4,000 acres to create the Research Triangle Park.

Robbins lived in both New York and Pinehurst, residing at the Carolina Hotel and joining the "exclusive Pinehurst Country Club" (which otherwise excluded Jews). Although not active in the state's Jewish community, Robbins helped found the Federation of Jewish Philanthropies in New York and endowed Yeshiva University. He may be a New Yorker, the *State* reported, but "we can also think of Karl Robbins as a North Carolinian."[1]

1. *State*, 14 Sept. 1943, 16, 18–19; *Pilot*, 27 June 1984.

Research Triangle Park entrepreneur Karl Robbins, third from left, next to Governor Luther B. Hodges. (North Carolina State Archives)

lights went out first," Morris Kaplan recalled, not wanting to close their stores first. One night Sherman left his lights on and went upstairs to sleep, leaving Schas up past midnight.[63]

Second-generation Jews, increasingly college graduates, were rising into the professions. Asheville, site of the nation's first sanatorium, had seven Jewish doctors while commercial Charlotte had but one. In 1931 physicians Sidney and

Maurice LeBauer, sons of a Greensboro mill owner, established a practice. In 1936 Sam Warshauer, son of an immigrant clothier, became Wilmington's first Jewish physician. Levitt also found eleven doctors in eight small towns. In 1938 Buxton and Hobgood each had one Jew, both of whom were physicians. Discrimination closed some doors to Jews, although the pattern varied by community. Greensboro had three Jewish public school teachers and Wilmington had four. Durham Jews felt the schools were closed to them. A Greensboro teacher, Sarah Brisker, received a letter from a superintendent informing her that she was qualified but would not feel welcome because of her "race." Jews in professional fields left the state, believing no job awaited them. This trend was not exclusively Jewish. Sociologist Wilson Gee reported in 1937 on "The 'Drag' of Talent Out of the South": the region "has been and is being depleted severely of its best talent to the enrichment of other parts and to its own impoverishment." Writers, lawyers, doctors, artists, and educators were leaving, many of them young Jews. "I went to Women's College in Greensboro, but I was never going to live in Wilmington," recalled Miriam Miller Warschauer. "Never."[64]

College was the route to occupational mobility. Although Jews were but 3.5 percent of the American population, they were about 10 percent of college enrollment. In contrast to northern campuses, where academic quotas prevailed, southern universities were more open. Jewish numbers were too small to pose a threat. Although hardly free of prejudice, campuses were bastions of the progressive South, often under assault from conservatives. In the 1930s the first Jews began enrolling at Wake Forest. Schools like High Point College, Meredith in Raleigh, or Biltmore in Asheville drew local Jewish youth. Duke University—expanded from Trinity College in 1924 after an endowment from the tobacco family—maintained a Jewish quota, although Durham Jews felt exempted. Statistics from 1930 to 1937 show that Duke undergraduate enrollment held at 3 percent. In 1933 79 of 3,214 students were Jews, 2.6 percent of the student body. The Medical School had a consistent Jewish enrollment of 15 percent, counting 28 of 170 students in 1933. The schools of choice for North Carolina Jews were UNC at Chapel Hill, which did not admit women until their junior years, and Women's College at Greensboro. In 1936 15 percent of UNC's entering class was Jewish, although Jews constituted less than one-quarter of 1 percent of the state's population.[65]

Parents expected sons, and often daughters, to attend college. Joe Kittner's father, an immigrant cobbler, told him "that I wasn't worth thirty-five cents in the business. I didn't know what a college was, but he said I should go to college." His father hitchhiked from Weldon to Goldsboro to obtain tuition money from the Sophie Einstein Student Loan Fund that the North Carolina Association of Jewish Women maintained for the state's Jewish students. Entering Chapel Hill in 1933,

Kittner worked three jobs, breaking rocks at the tennis court, selling drinks room to room, and "washing dishes and cleaning rooms and trying to study a little bit."[66] After he finished law school, he helped pay for his siblings' education.

On campus, Jewish students bore the mark of "Jew" yet participated, and sometimes excelled, in all aspects of campus life—captaining football teams, editing school newspapers, and winning academic honors. Herman Farber, who in 1930 became Wake Forest's first Jewish graduate, was nicknamed "Baptist Jew," but he was also elected class president. At UNC, Jewish students, not wanting to call attention to themselves, had an unwritten rule not to walk together as a group. "We wanted to be part of the scene without emphasis on the fact we were Jewish," E. J. Evans explained. Marshall Rauch, a New Yorker who came to Duke in 1940 to play basketball, was shocked that he could not join his teammates' fraternity. "There was a subtle discrimination with invisible guidelines," he discovered. "It was frustrating."[67]

Because Greek societies were closed, Jews created parallel institutions just as their parents did in their social lives. In 1924 a chapter of Tau Epsilon Phi formed in Chapel Hill, followed three years later by Zeta Beta Tau. Two more, Phi Alpha and Pi Lambda Phi, followed in the 1930s. Jews themselves drew exclusionary class lines. TEP drew East Europeans, whereas ZBT tended to be German. The ZBT house was owned by Ceasar Cone. At Duke, Pente fraternity, named for the five Jewish boys on campus, formed in 1926. Three years later it affiliated with

Phi Sigma Delta. Five years later, a ZBT fraternity chapter and Alpha Epsilon Phi sorority formed. By 1938, North Carolina State had enough Jewish students to form Sigma Alpha Mu.

Concerned about an assimilating youth, Sidney Stern of Greensboro and Rabbi Iser Freund of Goldsboro appealed in 1934 to B'nai B'rith, Hillel Foundation sponsors, to establish a program. A year later the North Carolina Association of Jewish Women (NCAJW) reported 100 Jewish students at Duke and 300 at UNC, 189 of whom were North Carolinians. Abram Sachar, national Hillel director, addressed the 1935 NCAJW meeting, which "voiced its enthusiasm." At a time of rising anti-Semitism, the organization wanted not only to provide for the students' Jewish needs but to lessen tensions. Sara Evans, reporting for a state Hillel committee, observed, "The Northern Jewish student, not being accustomed to the ways of the South, finds many difficulties in his path, and through misunderstanding, creates many more." On 9 October 1936, Hillel was dedicated in Chapel Hill. UNC president Frank Graham declared that "the University is a mingling of many currents and draws its strength from each." Rabbi Bernard Zeiger, the first director,

Tau Epsilon Phi fraternity, formed in Chapel Hill in 1924, included E. J. Evans, later Durham mayor (middle row, second from left); Leon Schneider, later Gastonia mayor (front row, second from right); and Harry Schwartz, captain of the UNC football team (back row, far left). (North Carolina Collection, University of North Carolina Library at Chapel Hill)

noted a "strange paradox." The University "warmly welcomed" Hillel, but Jewish students were indifferent. "The average college student knows little of Judaism and finds being a Jew a burden," the Rabbi noted. "He tries to hide his identity by imitating the non-Jew." Campus Judaism addressed American youth, holding Reform as well as Orthodox services. A Passover Seder drew 150 students, faculty, and townspeople, including President Graham.[68]

The ambivalent position of Jews was demonstrated in 1933 when Morris Krasny, a northerner married to a Durham woman, complained that UNC had rejected his application to medical school because of a Jewish quota. Krasny turned to President Graham, who called in medical school dean Isaac Manning for a "brief but frank and friendly discussion."[69] Manning admitted that he accepted but four Jewish students, 10 percent of enrollment, because Jews found it difficult to find places after attending UNC's two-year program. Manning, dean for twenty-eight years, did not regard the policy as prejudicial and claimed only out-of-state Jews were targeted. Manning's memoirs express concerns about a Jewish "problem." Some Jews he found "acceptable," but he believed "rigid measures" were needed to limit "exceedingly objectionable" Jewish students who changed their names or forged transcripts to gain admission. He did not want UNC to be overrun with Jews and felt that a Gentile would not want a Jew for a lab partner.

Publicly, Manning insisted he was defending academic freedom and standards. Manning won the support of alumni groups and all but one of the medical faculty. Graham told the dean, "I will have to overrule you, and the young man will be admitted to your school." Manning resigned as dean, although not from the faculty. The *New York Herald Tribune* praised Graham editorially, and his former student E. J. Evans wrote him that at a time when Nazis were grinding Jews under their heels, "your action brings a breath of joy to a despairing people."[70]

Jewish faculty certainly felt discrimination. When Edward Bernstein, a new Harvard Ph.D., interviewed at North Carolina State, a dean explained that the school had no Jewish faculty. The Economics Department would welcome him, but the dean was less sure of the trustees. Nonetheless, he was appointed associate professor. UNC Law School dean M. T. Van Hecke in 1932 doubted "the wisdom" of hiring an editor of the *Harvard Law Review* because he was a Jew. Few Jews held UNC posts in the 1920s and 1930s. Albert Suskin, a classics professor from 1936 to 1945, was the son of a New Bern immigrant storekeeper. Philosopher Louis Kattsoff and his wife were mentors of Hillel. The most distinguished was Milton Rosenau, who arrived in 1935 from Harvard. Rosenau, "one of the most eminent men of science in the United States," was founding dean of the School of Public Health. He served on national Jewish boards. UNC's Math and Physics Departments also had a Jewish influx in the 1930s, several of European origin. UNC included on its board of trustees North Carolina–born alumni, philanthropists, and politicians: Leslie Weil, Laura Weill Stern Cone, and Harriss Newman.[71]

The opening of Duke School of Medicine in 1930 first brought Jewish faculty to campus. Russian-born William Perlzweig, a nutritionist, was among the Johns Hopkins faculty recruited. His wife, Olga Marx translated classical literature and the writings of Martin Buber. She collaborated with an eccentric German-Jewish émigré scholar, Ernst Morwitz, who taught at both Duke and UNC, to translate German poet Stefan George. In 1938 a young physiologist, Philip Handler, embarked on a brilliant career that resulted in more than two hundred papers and the textbook, *Principles of Biochemistry*. At the urging of his friend Abram Sachar, he became Duke's informal Hillel advisor.

If universities imagined themselves to be citadels of the progressive South, they were still microcosms of a prejudicial society. "The native North Carolina Jew is an entirely different personality from those in the large cities," wrote state bar president attorney Kemp Battle in 1936 to UNC president Frank Graham in urging a Jewish quota. Battle included a letter from a southern "liberal," who explained that northern Jews came from Poland and Russia and "show the vices but not the

virtues of southern Jews who were "Sephardim [sic] Jews" from Spain, England, and Germany. He endorsed quotas on "the type of the Jew, known vulgarly as the Kike." UNC professor W. C. George, a renowned expert on blood, spoke as a social Darwinist in advocating a Jewish quota. He warned Graham that "restrictive measures" were necessary "to protect another race or racial culture." One race will "dominate and determine the nature of the civilization," George predicted, "and the other will be submissive or it will be exterminated." Such anthropologies

William Perlzweig, Duke Medical School.
(Duke University Medical Center Archives)

were scientific nonsense, but they expressed popular racial thinking that led to anti-Semitic discrimination.[72]

THREATENING THIRTIES

The Nazi drumbeat abroad echoed at home. Isolationist American Firsters saw Jewish hands controlling media and government. Roosevelt was damned for running a "Jew Deal." On radio Father Coughlin defended fascism and attacked Jews, although his national broadcasts resonated less loudly in the Protestant South. Edna Lichtenfels of Asheville observed, "The most scurrilous publications containing the vilest calumnies and libels about the Jewish people are scattered about the land."[73] The federal government in 1941, as it had in 1927, required enemy "aliens" to register. Immigrant Jews who were not yet naturalized, some escapees from Nazi Europe, were photographed and fingerprinted. Witnesses—often local Jews—signed affidavits attesting to their character.

The state's U.S. senators, Josiah Bailey and Robert Reynolds, opposed opening America to Jewish immigrants fleeing Hitler. "Our Bob" Reynolds was a bumptious mountaineer first elected in 1932 as a New Dealer, but he turned against Roosevelt and became venomously isolationist. He repeated canards about international Jewish conspiracies, and his *American Vindicator* newspaper gave voice to anti-Semites. A Nazi agent worked on his staff. Opposing the Wagner-Rogers Bill to admit refugee children, he told a pro-Nazi newspaper, "I am absolutely against the United States waging war for the purpose of protecting Jews anywhere in the world." North Carolina, he bragged, "had less aliens than any state." With its military camps and wartime industries, North Carolinians resisted Reynolds's isolationism. A "dump Reynolds" movement arose. Facing defeat, Reynolds did not seek reelection in 1944, putting an end, as a newspaper put it, to his "nauseating drivel."[74]

The notorious William Dudley Pelley, fashioning himself the "American Hitler," headquartered his Silver Shirt Legion in Asheville from 1932 to 1941. Pelley published a weekly filled with "scurrilous" attacks on Jews. In his 1933 Purim sermon, Asheville Rabbi Moses Jacobson, citing Hitler's rise in Germany, expressed fears that, though "the Jews as a body are respected here," they faced danger. In fact, Pelley, a New Englander, found little local support. Assisted by two Jews, Julius Levitch and attorney Alvin Kurtus, the sheriff arrested Pelley for stock fraud. Pelley relocated to Indiana, where he was jailed for sedition. In 1938 worshipers entering Wilmington's Temple of Israel were greeted by two large swastikas painted on its doors. Mayor Thomas Cooper personally supervised their removal and expressed "outrage." In 1944 a Jewish UNC student received a letter threatening to "show these Yankee Jews that they can't run this University as they damn please!" That year, two Jewish students were assaulted, and four students attacked Robert Rolnik, a campus activist, hospitalizing him.[75]

As the European Jewish crisis worsened, North Carolina Jews felt insecure. Nationally, Jews were divided, polls revealed, on easing immigration quotas, and significant numbers were isolationist. Jews could not sway public opinion or convince the Roosevelt administration to liberalize its policies. Jews feared provoking an anti-Semitic reaction if they pushed too aggressively. Isolationists accused Jews of dual loyalty and war mongering. In the late 1930s Jews enlisted the larger public in Jewish relief as they had in World War I. In Durham, Judge Marshall Spears chaired the United Jewish Appeals Campaign, and African American executives Asa Spaulding and J. H. Wheeler led a UJA drive in the black community. UNC president Graham lobbied Congress to open America to immigration. He gave his name to the Bergson Group, which advocated radical action, and cochaired the biracial Emergency Conference to Save the Jewish People of Europe.

WANTED

William Dudley Pelley

DESCRIPTION

Age, approximately fifty years; height, five feet, seven inches; weight, 130 pounds; has black hair mixed with gray; heavy eyebrows; wears mustache and a vandyke; has dark gray eyes, very penetrating; has straight Roman nose; wears nose glasses; dresses neatly; distinguished looking; good talker; highly educated; interested in physic research.

Capias has been issued by the Judge of the Superior Court of Buncombe County for the arrest of the above-named party for sentence on conviction of felony, making fraudulent representation, and also for violating the terms of a suspended sentence on another charge by failing to remain of good behavior, and by engaging in, among other things, UN-AMERICAN activities.

Arrest and notify
LAURENCE E. BROWN, Sheriff
Asheville, N. C.

1939

Wanted poster for fascist William Pelley, who was headquartered in Asheville. (Special Collections, D. Hiden Ramsey Library, University of North Carolina at Asheville)

The state's Jews were urged to use "the mediums of the press, radio and the platform to educate the public mind that the Jews are not a menace." The 1938 Seaboard Zionist Conference held in Durham was cosponsored by the Chamber of Commerce.[76]

Typically, a rabbi or civic leader acted as a "Jewish representative among the Christians," speaking as the voice of both local and global Jewry to civic clubs, church groups, and public schools. This ambassador or "ethnic broker" emphasized the Jews' Americanism and refuted the association of Jews with communism. Rabbis lectured on such themes as "Democracy's Hebrew Roots" or "Why the Jew Loves America." Commonly, they stressed Christianity's Jewish origins and traced America's deepest values to Israel's sacred history. The principal agency was the National Conference of Christians and Jews (NCCJ), founded in 1927. Six years later, in response to the "outbreak of intolerance abroad," the NCCJ launched a three-faith—Catholic, Protestant, Jew—national tour and inspired civic and religious leaders to act locally. Their Brotherhood Day expanded into Brotherhood Week in 1947. The ecumenical schedule was busy. In 1938 Greensboro attorney Herbert Falk addressed a Methodist Bible class on "What the Modern Jew Believes." The *American Jewish Times*, a statewide Jewish magazine, dedicated its February 1940 issue to "Brotherhood: Devoted to a Better Understanding between Christians and Jews, America's Hope." For Brotherhood Day in 1941, Winston-Salem's Rabbi Frank Rosenthal exchanged pulpits with the Moravian minister. Jewish groups joined Youth in Democracy patriotic rallies across the state. The Asheville and Buncombe County Ministerial Association invited Rabbi Stephen Wise of the Free Synagogue of New York to speak at the City Auditorium on the "persecuted Jews of Europe."[77]

At the behest of national Jewish organizations, North Carolina Jews turned to the airwaves. Governor Clyde Hoey's keynote address at a 1938 regional Zionist conference was broadcast over WDNC. A year later, Rabbi Robert Jacobs of Asheville began his weekly "Message of Israel" radio program. Greensboro's WBIG presented a rabbi, priest, and minister at an NCCJ forum on "The Present Crisis in Human Relations." For Brotherhood Week in 1941, Winston-Salem listeners of WSJS awakened to hear Rabbi Rosenthal intoning the morning prayer.[78]

Brotherhood teetered on the racial divide. In 1940 Greensboro's Temple Emanuel's assembly room overflowed for a choir concert by Bennett College, a black women's college, with the audience demanding "encore after encore." The Cone family donated the Hayes-Taylor YMCA to serve the African American community and named it for two "faithful" house servants. Three years later Durham's Rabbi Israel Mowshowitz spoke to the First Baptist Church, "On Common Ground," an NCCJ event described as "unique" for being interracial. In 1944

a white woman teaching a three-faiths class at a "colored school" in Asheville asked to bring her students to a Friday night service. They were "invited to attend and occupy the balcony seats in the temple."[79]

On campuses, too, Jews sought to establish a place for Judaism within the canon of Western civilization. In 1939 North Carolina State included in its English classes "Popular Studies in Judaism," published by the Reform movement. Four years later, Duke became the first southern university to create a full-time faculty position in Judaic studies. The Stern and Nachamson families, who lent financial support, wanted a teacher and scholar who would be a role model representing "the spirit of Judaism" to both Jewish and Christian students. At the time, universities debated whether Jewish studies belonged in a Semitic language department or the religious seminary, whether their mission was disinterested scholarship or ecumenical advocacy. Rabbi Stephen Wise of the Jewish Institute of Religion recommended to Duke Theodore Gaster of the University of London, a scholar of Canaanite texts. Duke, however, hired a rabbi, someone who could also take a community role. Conservative Rabbi Judah Goldin, ordained at Jewish Theological Seminary (JTS), taught courses in Hellenic Judaism and contemporary Judaism as a lecturer in Jewish Literature and Thought. After two years, feeling isolated and wanting a larger Jewish community for his family, Goldin left, embarking on a distinguished academic career at Yale and Penn and authoring the popular *Living Talmud*.[80]

URGE TO ORGANIZE

As it faced war and persecution, American Jewry was divided. Ethnically, Germans and East Europeans separated socially and institutionally. Religiously, Reform and Orthodox differed in their willingness to compromise with modernity, with Conservatives between them. Politically, Zionists and anti-Zionists contended at national philanthropic forums over policy and allocations. Organizations like the Joint Distribution Committee, which provided overseas relief, and the United Palestine Appeal conducted separate, and even competing, campaigns. Federations, beginning in Boston in 1895, unified local communities. In 1932 a national Council of Jewish Federations and Welfare Funds was pressured by the grass roots to consolidate the disparate appeals. In 1939, after Kristallnacht, as the European crisis worsened and the British government's White Paper limited immigration to Palestine, a United Jewish Appeal for Refugee and Overseas Needs brought the factions together.

North Carolina Jewish communities organized Federations and launched their own UJA campaigns, uniting their communities while linking them to global Jewry. In 1939 NCAJW president Edna Lichtenfels of Asheville wrote that she had "new faith in the future" as "all our Jewish organizations in North Carolina . . . have laid aside their external differences and have united to further the just cause of Israel." By 1943, at a B'nai B'rith state meeting in Charlotte, Chester Brown, editor of the *American Jewish Times*, was still arguing that "unity is essential to our religious survival." Brown pleaded, "The whole civilized world is waiting for the Jew to speak with one voice."[81] Prominent North Carolina Jews—Benjamin Cone, Julius Cone, Herbert Falk, Lionel Weil, Milton Rosenau—had served on national bodies of Jewish organizations. All were from well-established families of German origin, the plutocrats of American Jewry. Nationally, Jewish organizations were democratizing with the grass roots asserting leadership. More East European Jews participated. When an American Jewish Conference convened in 1944 to plan for postwar Jewry, E. J. Evans represented the state. The conference endorsed a Jewish state, which provoked the anti-Zionists to walk out.

Although the South is typically cast as non- or anti-Zionist, North Carolina Jews were, with exception, committed to Zionism. When Mrs. Phillip Katzin spoke before Winston-Salem's Council of Jewish Women in 1925 about her life in Palestine, she was "besieged with questions." In 1934 a state NCAJW-NCAJM conference featured Abram Sachar, national Hillel director, delivering an ardently

Zionist speech. The NCAJW pledged funds for European Jewry and the "upbuilding of Palestine." The religious Zionist society Mizrachi had chapters in Durham and Raleigh, towns with enclaves of Orthodox East European Jews. By 1933 Hadassah, with roots in secular Zionism, had eight chapters in North Carolina, more than any southern state. Asheville's Rabbi Moses Jacobson remained a fierce critic of a Jewish state. When the Central Conference of American Rabbis in 1936 considered a pro-Zionist platform, Jacobson led the opposition: "I regard Zionism as a supreme folly, a dire menace, and an outright iniquity." He felt that the "ballyhoo of Zionism" was weakening the "American Jewish Reform Cause." While Jacobson fulminated, a Zionist Organization of America chapter in Asheville counted 122 members by 1944. As Louis Brandeis had declared, Jews saw no incompatibility between Zionism and Americanism. With war beckoning, Jews spoke of Palestine at public forums as an "arsenal" on the "first lines of defense of democracy."[82]

The crisis of world Jewry and domestic anti-Semitism revitalized American Jewry, giving rise to a "culture of organization." NCAJW president Emma Edwards observed in 1937, "The urge to organize is inherent in the Jewish disposition." Asheville was described as the "most-organized Jewish community in the state" with Hadassah, Ladies Auxiliary, Jewish Book Club, sorority, Young Judea, and the NCAJW. Flora Stern of Greensboro formed National Council of Jewish Women chapters, while Sara Evans of Durham was known as Hadassah's "southern accent" for her leadership. By 1937 the state had twelve Hadassah chapters, four sections of the council, and ten Sisterhoods. B'nai B'rith Lodges formed or revived. The Hickory B'nai B'rith, formed in 1940, drew thirty-three members from a half-dozen towns. Asheville's Jews bought property for a Jewish Community Center. North Carolina women served on national boards, more so than any southern state. Fannie Berman Stein of Fayetteville joined the Hadassah board; Pearl Lichtenstein Oettinger of Wilson, the Temple Sisterhood; and Rebecca Seligman, the National Council of Jewish Women.[83]

Synagogue affiliation strengthened, too. From 1938 to 1941, Asheville's Beth Ha-Tephila grew from 73 to 113 members. In 1938 the rural towns of Wallace, Warsaw, Clinton, and Burgaw formed a Jewish Circle. Rabbi Thurman of Wilmington formed a second circle in Whiteville, Tabor City, and Fairmont. In 1939 Salisbury Jews organized a congregation, and five years later Burlington Jews planned a synagogue. The North Carolina response was consistent with national trends that revealed Jews responding to the crises of the 1930s and 1940s by affiliating in unprecedented numbers.[84]

Organizational efforts, as NCAJW president Min Klein put it, had an "accent on youth." The NCAJW spawned a youth group. B'nai B'rith Lodges formed chapters of Aleph Zadik Aleph, a fraternity for high school and college boys, starting in

Durham in 1940. Hillel Rabbi Bernard Zeiger had reported in 1935 that students regarded Judaism as a "burden" and wanted to assimilate, but his successor, Rabbi Maurice Schatz, observed that attendance at Friday night services strained the room. Students eagerly enrolled in classes in Zionism and European Jewry. UNC Hillel president Arthur Goldberg wrote in 1944 that the crisis engendered by the "sufferings of his people in Europe" and by "the bigoted groups which are behind the many manifestations of anti-Semitism in America has brought many Jewish students into organized Jewish life."[85]

Jews had maintained contact with their European families through letters, packages, and even visits. North Carolina families received pleading, heartrending letters from European cousins seeking sponsors to save them or their children from Nazi persecutions. Often the relatives were so distant as to be strangers. In 1941 Benjamin Cone convened a State Conference of the North Carolina Resettlement Committee in Greensboro.[86] The bureaucratic obstacles in both Germany and America were formidable. To bring a cousin to America, Greensboro attorney Sidney Stern had to supply affidavits documenting his income, worth, dependents, citizenship, and letters of credit. As sponsor, he had to prove that he could support or employ an applicant. He also had to document his relationship to his German relatives, their ages, locations, and occupations. Stern then had to lobby an array of governmental and refugee agencies.

Émigré stories attest to the European Jewish trauma. Hans Green had fled Germany for Holland and then France before relatives brought him to Greensboro in 1937. His sister Ruth joined him. Not knowing English, renaming himself John, he worked a bakery night shift and enrolled in business school. He sold programs, drinks, and ice cream at a ballpark. He found work at a salvage yard. When war erupted in 1941, he enlisted, landed at Normandy, and helped liberate the Dachau concentration camp. Furloughed to England, he met Ursula, a displaced German Jew. Returning to Winston-Salem, he proposed by mail, and she accepted. He purchased a scrapyard in Fayetteville, where John and Ursula Green became community and congregational pillars.[87]

For four generations Heinz Salomon's family had an optical business in Düsseldorf. In 1933 a Nazi stood before his store blocking customers. The police did nothing. Heinz realized, "I was not a German anymore." It took five years until visas arrived from an American cousin. Heinz's father hesitated, and when he decided to leave, quotas had shut the gates. He was sent to a concentration camp where he died of dysentery. In New York, Heinz Salomon became an American, Harry Sloan. Unable to find work, he placed an ad in a German newspaper, which was answered by optometrist Max Rones in High Point. "When the train stopped and the conductor told him to get off," his son Frank recalled, "he had no idea where he was." Grinding lenses, he began serving other optometrists. With a cousin, he formed the Southern Optical Company. There he met and married a Viennese émigré Edith, who had been brought to Durham by a cousin. She worked for Asa Spaulding, the African American insurance executive, who pointed her to a job in Greensboro. The Sloans brought to Greensboro his sister and her husband, Alice and Otto Loeb, who ran a boardinghouse for German Jewish immigrants.[88]

Southern universities courted academic refugees, more so in the sciences than in the liberal arts. In 1934 Edward R. Murrow, a Greensboro native, wrote to Duke president W. P. Few on behalf of the Emergency Committee in Aid of Displaced German Scholars. Few responded by offering positions to Louis Stern, director of the Psychological Institute of Hamburg, who had coined the term *intelligence quotient*. Heartbroken in exile, he died in 1938. Hillel Rabbi Zeiger recited kaddish at Duke Chapel. In 1934 Walter Kempner arrived at Duke Medical School, establishing a revolutionary diet program. Two distinguished German scientists joined the Physics Department, Lothar Nordheim in 1937 and Fritz London in 1939. London had left Frankfurt for Oxford and the Sorbonne, where chemist Paul Gross recruited him to Duke. In 1941 Raphael Lemkin, a Polish attorney and professor at the University of Warsaw, arrived at Duke. Professor Malcolm McDermott had met Lemkin in Warsaw and enlisted the local B'nai B'rith to sponsor him. Arriving with purloined Nazi documents, Lemkin wrote *Axis Rule in Occupied Europe*, coining the word "genocide" to describe the Nazi's mass murder. Lemkin, who lost forty-nine relatives, drafted the Genocide Convention. He remained at Duke but two years, as he embarked on a quixotic quest to have the United Nations adopt it.

Edith and Edward Bernstein worked with Quaker groups to bring émigrés to Chapel Hill. With funding from national refugee organizations, Dean Dudley Carroll and President Graham created positions. Irvin Hexner of Czechoslovakia and Franz Guttman of Germany joined the Economics Department. Mathematician Alfred Brauer had left the University of Berlin after Kristallnacht for the Institute of Advanced Studies in Princeton before coming to Chapel Hill. In 1934 Anne Hoffman, a graduate of the Leipzig Conservatory, began teaching voice and piano at Asheville Teacher's College, and five years later came another German émigré, Hilda Weiss.[89] On the faculty at Women's College was art historian Elizabeth Jastrow, whose resettlement was sponsored by the Greensboro community. In 1939 Ernst Manasse, bibliographer of Plato, arrived at North Carolina College for Negroes, among the scholars who found haven at southern black colleges. He had fled Germany for Italy and then England, while his wife Marianne escaped to

Since the early 1900s, Hugh MacCrae of Wilmington had wanted to settle European immigrants on his 40,000 acres in eastern North Carolina. His ambition was to create agrarian colonies based on progressive principles. Among his supporters was Alvin Johnson, a founder of New York's New School for Social Research, which granted refuge to Jewish scholars fleeing Nazi Europe. Johnson asked MacCrae about creating a colony for Jews. In 1939 Johnson solicited financier and statesman Bernard Baruch, who sent $2,500. Johnson convened a New York meeting of refugee activists, both Jews and Christians, to plan for Van Eeden, a farm co-op outside Burgaw. Each settler would be given ten acres, a cottage, and a cow, but equipment would be shared. That winter four families arrived, followed by another four in spring.

Their escapes were harrowing. Felix Willman, an Austrian, had been imprisoned in Dachau and Buchenwald. Max Wolf, a World War I veteran, had been beaten and tortured in a camp. Others had survived Kristallnacht in hiding. Their immigration was frustrated by bureaucracy in Germany and quotas in America.

The Van Eeden colonists were urban, cosmopolitan Germans and Austrians, and the transition to rural North Carolina—hot, humid, and swampy—was a cultural shock. Burgaw was not Berlin. Many came without basic English. Paula Willman, who had learned English from British teachers, could not at first understand her Pender County neighbors. Van Eeden children were welcomed, but occasionally taunted, at the Penderlea School. On Saturday afternoons, the Willmans invited teachers to their home where they played their opera records and served cheese and biscuits. Their cottage was compared to a Viennese coffeehouse. Virtually all were of Jewish origin, but several, like the Heimans, had assimilated into Christianity.

Most settlers had no or little experience living from the soil. Max Wolf had farmed a vineyard in Germany, but most others were professionals. Hubert Ladenburg held a doctorate in economics; Arthur Flatow was an architect, and members of Ursula Flatow's family were art dealers. "I think it is a general feeling that he is a fish out of water," an observer noted of Leonard Heiman, an executive. The colonists truck-farmed, selling eggs, milk,

Switzerland and then Brazil. Dr. James Shepard brought them to Durham, where he taught Latin, German, and philosophy for thirty years and she joined the Art Department. Other émigrés joined the faculty there too, including Hilda Weiss and Adolf Furth.[90]

Academic doors opened at the experimental Black Mountain College outside Montreat, which endured from 1933 to 1957. Founded on progressive, interdisciplinary principles, Black Mountain drew an artistic and intellectual avant-garde elite, including Fuller, Cage, Gropius, Cunningham, and Rauschenberg. Prominent Jews like artist Ben Shahn, photographer Aaron Siskind, poet Paul Goodman, nov-

and produce. "Our beans yielded low and proved unsalable, our spinach died after coming out of the ground," Ladenburg reported.

Visits to the movies or a drugstore in Burgaw were friendly, and local folk paid social calls or gave farm advice. Some suspected their "Germantalk," and a misunderstanding led to rumors of a Nazi agent. The colonists visited Wilmington to sell produce, buy supplies, or attend synagogue—and, for some, church. Wilmington families like the Newmans and Bluethenthals hosted them, and the Finkelsteins paid visits. Hubert Ladenburg and Felix Willman spoke at B'nai B'rith. Rabbi Thurman of the Temple of Israel mentored the families.

A few colonists grew fond of country life, but by the mid-1940s they began departing for the North, done in by snakes, mosquitoes, poor drainage, and inadequate farm skills. The Loebs became kosher bakers in Maryland. Paula Willman was a renowned sculptor in New York. Wolf Stein, an economist, became a shipping clerk in New York to finance his children's college education. The Rosenblums moved to a dairy farm in Pender County.[1]

1. Susan Taylor Block, *Van Eeden*, 27, 31, JHFNC. First published in Bulletin 40, no. 1, Lower Cape Fear Historical Society, 1995.

Émigrés from Nazi Europe at the Van Eeden farm commune.
(North Carolina Collection, University of North Carolina Library at Chapel Hill)

Harry and Edith Sloan, Alice and Otto Loeb, émigrés from Nazi Germany. (Tom Sloan)

elist Isaac Rosenfeld, and literary critic Alfred Kazin joined the faculty. Albert Einstein lectured there. European émigrés composed nearly half the faculty, most of whom were of Jewish origin like the textile artist Anni Albers and mathematician Max Dehn. German-born composer Stefan Wolpe and philosopher Ernst Straus had both settled in Palestine before coming to Black Mountain. Conductor Heinrich Jalowetz had been dismissed from the Cologne Opera as a non-Aryan. His wife Johanna, a voice teacher, was recalled as the college's "Jewish mother." Fritz Cohen, composer for the Joos Ballet, was stranded on tour when war broke out and could not return. He and his wife, dancer Elsa Kahl, found haven at Black Mountain.[91]

The school aspired to a democratic community that transcended religion and nationality. The émigrés, educated in the European tradition, formed a circle. Concerned that so many Europeans might challenge its open, American character, the school set a quota for Jews—not just for refugees—although it was apparently not enforced. In 1941, learning of the restriction, physicist Nathan Rosen, an American-born Jew, resigned and left for Chapel Hill.[92] Conservative North Carolinians saw the experimental College as an alien presence, politically radical and sexually libertine. Ashevillean Marilyn Blomberg Patton recalled riding on a northbound train listening to a man from Black Mountain curse all the damn Jews there.

STORY: REFUGE AT AN AFRICAN AMERICAN COLLEGE

In 1939 Dr. James E. Shepard, president of North Carolina College for Negroes, offered a post to philosopher Ernst Manasse, who had fled Nazi Germany. On North Carolina Central University's Founders Day in 1985, Manasse offered these remarks:

I was a refugee from racial persecution and was given a haven here at a racially segregated institution. . . . I became the first fully employed white teacher at this institution: I, the refugee from racial persecution had become the colleague and teacher of the members of an oppressed race, though not belonging to the oppressed group myself. But I was accepted, was given the opportunity to belong, to work as a member of a team as an equal. Helping the persecuted to establish a new home, what action could be more humanitarian than that[?][1]

1. Henry Landsberger and Christoph Schweitzer, eds., *They Fled Hitler's Germany and Found Refuge in North Carolina* (Chapel Hill: Academic Affairs Library, 1996), 48–49.

Ernst Manasse, a distinguished émigré philosopher, finds haven at a southern black college. (North Carolina Central University Archives)

CAMP TOWNS

"Durham was a peaceful town, then came the army," the newspaper reported. "It swarmed down the streets in a never-ending tide, growling like a tidal wave." The Roosevelt administration, for reasons of both national security and economic policy, bolstered the South's defense industries and military camps. The federal government rained $10 billion on North Carolina. Some 2 million soldiers served over 100 military facilities. New Bern and Wilmington built Liberty Ships. Campuses became military training centers. Camp Lejeune was situated on some 174 square miles between Wilmington and Morehead City. Fort Bragg, with adjoining Pope Air Force Base, was nearly twice as large. Fayetteville hosted 60,000 soldiers. Camp Butner, holding 50,000 soldiers, arose on 75,000 rural acres outside Durham. Jews arrived to both serve and service the camps. Rents skyrocketed, and stores were packed. War ended a prolonged strike at Wilmington's Block shirt factory, which converted from dress shirts to uniforms. Cone Mills won the Army-Navy "E" Award for wartime production, each employee wearing a victory lapel pin.[93]

Home-front Jews joined the general mobilization. North Carolinians were anxious. German U-boats attacked American ships so close to the coast that depth-charge explosions rattled windows. Burning ships could be seen from the coastline, and bodies washed ashore. Rumors of German landings spread panic, especially with thousands of German POWs in local camps. Fearing an anti-Semitic outburst and America's vulnerability, the Lindaus, Cone in-laws from Boston, built a mountain retreat at Gideon Ridge. Anxious Jews in Greensboro and New Bern removed their dead from Jewish cemeteries. Members of Raleigh's Jewish Women's Service Organization observed the skies for aircraft several hours each week at the Filter and Control Center. For the Red Cross, women knit, sewed, packed bandages, and made home nursing visits. As women volunteered for the United Service Organization (USO) and Red Cross, Jewish and gentile cooperation intensified. National unity was a civil religion that transcended ethnic and racial differences. Greensboro's B'nai B'rith sold more war bonds than all other civic groups combined.[94]

More than 500,000 Jews served in the armed services, and some 8,000 were killed. Their contribution was disproportionate. North Carolina's Jews answered the call. Five months after the war began, an "incomplete list" named 154 in uniform. Pulpits emptied. Rabbi Samuel Sandmel left UNC Hillel to become the navy's first Jewish chaplain, and Rabbi Elihu Michelson quit Charlotte's Hebrew United Brotherhood for chaplaincy school. Pinckney Bernstein, post commander at Camp Butner, became a brigadier general.[95]

On both battlefield and home front, Jews proved their Americanism. The sons of mill owners and storekeepers rose to officer ranks and earned battlefield commendations. From Gastonia alone, Lieutenant Alvin Witten won six stars in the Pacific, and Howard Lieber received a silver star for gallantry in Germany. Three Leinwand brothers from Whiteville served, with Robert earning a Purple Heart at Guadalcanal. Ensign Milton Sandes of Franklin, serving in the Royal Navy, was decorated by the king for entering "the flaming wreckage of a plane and coolly dismantling two bombs with a wrench and wire."[96]

With Nazi propaganda disparaging Jews as a race, each felt a representative of an entire people. At stake, wrote E. J. Londow in the *American Jewish Times*, was the "good name of the Jew." When Sgt. Jerome Levin was cited for bravery on a bombing mission, it was noted that "Charlotte Jewry may well feel proud." Gold Stars hung from Jewish homes, designating a fallen soldier. In Greensboro alone, Sigmund Pearl, Ted Myers, and Sanford Friedman made the "supreme sacrifice."[97] Hickory's Glenn Zerden went down with the *Dorchester* in the North Atlantic. Sydney Samet of Mount Airy was shot down over Hungary, and pilot Robert Rosenbloom of Rocky Mount died when his brakes failed in New Guinea. When Harry Freid's plane went down over Hungary, Weldon neighbors rushed to his home to comfort his grieving parents. After Freid was reported a prisoner of war, church bells tolled.

The Jewish Welfare Board (JWB), which had provided rabbis, prayer books, and kosher food to Jews in the armed forces during the previous war, revived in cooperation with the USO. The state JWB, chaired by Lionel Weil, formed in July 1941. Wilmington's JWB was dedicated by a Catholic priest, a Protestant minister, and a rabbi. A Methodist Church in Rockingham hosted a Yom Kippur service for Jewish soldiers. A consortium of men's and women's organizations—B'nai B'rith, Council of Jewish Women, Sisterhoods—sponsored meals and home hospitality for the servicemen and their visiting families. Synagogue social halls were turned into soldier lounges. At a state conference in 1943, Governor Melvin Broughton and a national JWB representative addressed more than 175 delegates representing twenty posts and communities. Nine Jewish chaplains served seven bases in the state. The governor saluted "men and women of varied faiths working together in the civilian community and on the battle fronts in a common cause."[98]

Although JWB public events might begin with a patriotic Four Freedoms Pageant, the real draws for boys in uniform were food and women. Junior Hadassah, the North Carolina Association of Jewish Youth, or college and high school students hosted dances, poured refreshments, played cards, and visited military hospitals. Raleigh's Jewish Woman's Club was pleased to report 250 soldiers attending weekly. Simchas Torah in Greensboro ended with a dance for the GIs and college girls. The soldiers were a pool of Jewish spouses. Starting in November 1941, when Hannah Lacob married Private Moses Malkin of New Jersey, communities announced engagements between local women and soldiers.[99] GI Morris Kaplan became a North Carolinian when his bunkmate, Sammy Williams,

The *American Jewish Times*, a North Carolina magazine, links Maccabis and GI Jews. (North Carolina Collection, University of North Carolina Library at Chapel Hill)

Sydney Samet of Mount Airy, here with his parents, was shot down over Hungary in 1945. (Jewish Heritage Foundation of North Carolina)

PORTRAIT: RABBI ALEXANDER GOODE

Rabbi Alexander Goode was born in 1911, son of Rev. Hyman Goodkowitz, who served the Kinston congregation. Rev. Goodkowitz and his brother Isaac were grocers, who moved between New York and North Carolina. Alexander, born in New York, spent parts of his youth in Kinston and High Point. In 1937 he was ordained at Hebrew Union College in Cincinnati, supported by the NCAJW's student loan fund, and three years later received a doctorate from Johns Hopkins University. In 1942 he was commissioned an army chaplain. Among his assignments was Seymour Johnson Field in Goldsboro. In 1943 a German U-boat torpedoed his troop ship, the *Dorchester*, in the North Atlantic. When the ship was struck at midnight, the 900 soldiers aboard panicked. Along with a Catholic priest and two Protestant ministers, the rabbi calmed and organized the desperate soldiers. When life vests ran out, the chaplains gave up their own. Lifeboats were inadequate, and 672 men went down. When last seen, the four chaplains were on deck, arms linked, joined in prayer. The ecumenical sacrifice of the Four Chaplains galvanized the nation as the embodiment of Americanism.[1]

1. The Four Chaplains Foundation, <http://four chaplains.org/story.html>, 22 July 2009.

Postage stamp honoring the Immortal Chaplains, including Rabbi Goode (far right). (American Jewish War Veterans)

showed him a photo of his sister Anne, and he was smitten. For the women who stayed behind, there was the anxiety of having their new GI beaux sent overseas in harm's way.

For homesick soldiers, Jewish food was hardly secondary. At the 1943 state JWB conference, Mrs. George Levine reported on "Brunch as an Effective Factor in Morale." In Greensboro, soldiers feasted on challah, gefilte fish, chicken soup with kneidlach, roast chicken, honey cake, all served with jokes and wisecracks to "the delight of the many New Yorkers." Deli owners sent soldiers back to base with cold cuts. Hundreds poured into Goldsboro and Burlington on weekends. In Charlotte, Shelley Silverstein recalled, Mr. Miller drove his delivery truck on Fridays to the local base, got out, and shouted "Landsmen." Hearing the Yiddish call, Jewish soldiers piled onto the truck for a weekend of home hospitality. One Yom Kippur eve, rows of military trucks, laden with hundreds of Jewish soldiers

on maneuvers, pulled up unannounced at Charlotte's Temple Israel. At Fayetteville's Friday night services, A. M. Fleishman asked each soldier to stand and then assigned him to a family for a Sabbath meal. On Passover soldiers marched in file to his home, where he led two seders. Sleeping soldiers covered floors and spilled into the yard.[100] Home hospitality was especially meaningful for urban northerners who had never before ventured beyond a Jewish community.

Florence Fleishman of Fayetteville offers USO hospitality to two GIs, including her future husband, Joseph Blumenstein (left), a German émigré. (David Moff)

DEATH AND REBIRTH

As early as April 1940, Rabbi A. J. Grossfeld of Raleigh wrote of the "great holocaust" facing European and Palestinian Jewry. In the state were first-person witnesses. Émigré scholar Raphael Lemkin lectured civic clubs on the tragedy, and European refugees spoke to the Wilmington B'nai B'rith. In December 1942, the *American Jewish Times* reported on the "hundreds of thousands" massacred "like helpless sheep" and a month later referred to Hitler's "execution chambers" and his "plan to annihilate every Jew in the occupied countries." The total was in the "millions." In October 1944 Winston-Salem Rabbi Frank Rosenthal sermonized on Treblinka and Oswiecim (Auschwitz).[101]

Six million—that number was established in 1946—was not abstract, particularly to the immigrant generation. "Everyone was in pain," recalled May Ornoff Segal of Durham. "We all had families." She lost grandparents. Louis Kittner in Weldon received a telegram from the Red Cross informing him that his parents were dead. One North Carolina Jew was a Holocaust victim. Therese Sternglanz had been born in Tarboro in 1881, but her parents returned to Germany in 1889 after suffering a bankruptcy. During the war Therese was deported from Munich and "disappeared" in Eastern Europe.[102]

The principal Holocaust remembrance, beyond personal mourning, was to rebuild the lives of the survivors. For the SOS (Save an Overseas Survivor) campaign shopkeepers kept boxes in their stores to collect clothes, medicine, and canned goods for displaced European Jews. In High Point, Leonard Kaplan remembered a concentration camp survivor who stood on the synagogue pulpit and rolled up his sleeve revealing a Star of David tattoo. "Look what they did to me," he said. "That was the total summation of the appeal," Kaplan recalled. "The whole crowd broke down in tears." The "outpouring was unbelievable," the giving "astronomical."

Through agencies like the Hebrew Immigrant Aid Society, local Jews sponsored survivors. The Meyerses in Enfield, after receiving a letter, took in a German mother and daughter although unsure how they were related. Simon Krynski, a Polish army veteran with advanced degrees from the University of Poznan, worked as a synagogue janitor before joining Duke's Slavic Languages Department. German-born Fred Hoffman, brought to Asheville by his Lichtenfels relatives, had met Hilde, a native of Leipzig, as an American soldier in England. Her father died during Kristallnacht, and her mother in a concentration camp. They married, and he brought her to Asheville. Anne LeVine of Windsor sponsored her brothers Sam and Meyer Scheib. Sam had escaped from a concentration camp to the woods where Meyer and their mother were hiding. The brothers opened clothing stores in Windsor and Ahoskie. Polish-born Markus Reich—a survivor of Auschwitz and a death march—was sent to Asheville by the Joint Distribution Committee in 1951. He lived at the YMCA, learned English by watching westerns, and ate at the S&W cafeteria, where, not knowing English, he could only point at the food. Walter Falk, saved by the Kindertransport, placed a stone on an empty grave in the Greensboro Hebrew Cemetery to memorialize his mother killed at Auschwitz.[103]

The Holocaust and Israel, death and rebirth, were the two pillars of postwar Jewish identity. If America was creating a new Jew in North Carolina so, too, was Israel. Zionism dominated community agendas. A prayer for the State of Israel was added to the liturgy, and Hebrew lessons replaced the cultural vacuum left by the decline of household Yiddish. Youth were taught Palestinian dances and songs at summer camps and religious schools. Junior Hadassah was the social in-group. Chapters of the Intercollegiate Zionist Federation formed at Duke and UNC. Adult discussion groups met to explore Zionist issues.

Emissaries of Zion arrived to speak at B'nai B'rith Lodges or Hadassah meetings. In the late 1940s and the 1950s touring the state were Ben Foreman, an *Exodus* crewman; Ruth Goldschmidt, a war correspondent from the Israeli Foreign Office; and Israeli labor minister Golda Meir. In 1943 Army Private J. B. Friedman, a New Yorker stationed in Davidson who had spent seven years in Palestine, spoke stirringly at Charlotte's Temple Beth-El on "the re-birth of a nation that has never died." When Rabbi Joseph Lookstein of Yeshiva University spoke at

Duke University for Mizrachi, the event was held at the football field to accommodate the crowd. At a 1944 Hadassah state gathering Rabbi Stephen Wise, head of the Zionist Organization of America, proclaimed North Carolina a "hotbed" of Zionism. In Charlotte, Hadassah grew so large that several chapters formed. The Rocky Mount B'nai B'rith Lodge purchased a jeep that was shipped to Palestine for the struggling Haganah, the prestate army. In a letter addressed to "Dear King Farouk," High Point haberdasher Sol Robinowitz appealed to the Egyptian monarch to assist an impoverished Jew trapped in Cairo after an anti-Jewish backlash provoked by Israel's founding.[104]

Jews enlisted political leaders in the Zionist cause. The typical forum was to honor a dignitary at a public dinner. In Goldsboro, Gertrude Weil and Morris Leder stood next to Eleanor Roosevelt as the former first lady signed a Zionist proclamation. Governor and later U.S. senator Kerr Scott was such a familiar presence that he affectionately referred to Zionist ladies as "Hadassies." One Friday night in 1947 a delegation of Christian ministers from Smithfield crowded into Raleigh's House of Jacob Synagogue to hear former ambassador and navy secretary Josephus Daniels, wearing a skull cap, deliver an impassioned Zionist speech. The Asheville Ministerial Association pledged "unanimous support" for a campaign, headed by an editor and an executive, to "mobilize the Christian community" to raise $55,000 for Palestine to resettle European Jewish refugees.[105]

RED SCARE

The McCarthy era marked another Red scare, which, as it had in the 1920s, alluded to Jewish conspiracies. In 1948 the Confederate Daughters of America chapter in Charlotte wrote its members to warn that "nearly all the Communists in America are Jews" and that "most of the funds and agitators used in stirring up your Southern Negroes are Jewish in origin." When E. J. Evans ran for Durham mayor in 1951, publisher W. O. "Wimpy" Jones printed *The Protocols of the Elders of Zion* in his *Public Appeal* newspaper, alleging an international Jewish conspiracy. He claimed that Evans was in cahoots with the "communist" NAACP. Nationally, Jews were especially anxious after Julius and Ethel Rosenberg were accused of passing atomic secrets to the Soviets.[106]

UNC had a tradition of campus radicalism. Student Sidney Rittenberg quit UNC in 1940, joined the Communist Party, and organized workers at textile mills. (Stationed with the U.S. Army in China in 1949, he remained after the communist revolution but was imprisoned during the Cultural Revolution.) Harry Lerner, son of a dry goods merchant in Lincolnton, recalled Chapel Hill radicalized him. He returned home one winter break to inform his father that he was going to Mexico to follow Trotsky. His father told him that he was needed in the store for the

Christmas season, and this is where he stayed. Austrian-born Hans Freistadt was a communist when the Atomic Energy Commission awarded him a UNC physics fellowship in 1949. He provoked a furor. His fellowship was revoked although he received a degree in 1950. The university trustees reacted by instituting an employee loyalty oath. In 1947 graduate student Leonard Bernstein claimed that the UNC History Department denied him admission to the Ph.D. program because of his Marxism, a case that drew the national media, including the communist *Daily Worker*. UNC physicist Nathan Rosen, who had once taught at the University of Kiev, was warned that an informant intended to cite his name before the House Un-American Activities Committee for a leftist affiliation from his student days at MIT. UNC promised to stand by Rosen, a collaborator with Einstein, but he left in 1953 for the Technion in Haifa, where he recruited blacklisted scientists to Israel and helped found a university in Beersheva.[107]

North Carolina's anxieties crystallized on the case of Junius Scales. In 1954 Scales became the only American convicted and imprisoned for violating the Smith Act, which forbade Communist Party membership. Although a patrician, Christian North Carolinian, Scales was twice married to Jewish women, and his Carrboro home was described as a "den of communism." The communist organizer for North Carolina was Bernard Friedland of New York, and academic Marxists spoke on campuses. After the state legislature in 1963 passed a Speaker Ban Law aimed at leftist radicals, students tested it by inviting Marxist historian Herbert Aptheker to campus.[108]

In 1955 newspapers reported that an informer at the Scales trial had named Eugene Feldman, a Sunday School teacher and B'nai B'rith youth counselor in Winston-Salem. The Lodge called a meeting, which lasted into the night. Feldman was asked to state that he was not a communist, to identify his friends, and to list his affiliations. Feldman refused. The next day the temple president took Feldman to the rabbi's study, where he was queried on his communist membership. He responded that "no American need answer such a question." Asked to resign as a Sunday School teacher, he again refused. He spoke stirringly of his faith in American democracy, "the Brotherhood of all men," and the Holy Torah. Although the president agreed that he was an "exemplary" teacher, he was asked to return his synagogue keys. Dropped off at work, Feldman was fired.

An ADL representative met with the B'nai B'rith Lodge. Feldman, a World War II veteran, spoke passionately. The FBI had offered no evidence. "The division in the lodge was very considerable," he observed. A member told him that "hurting a brother [is] an act which would bother the hell out of them for the rest of their lives." One member offered him a job, another meals at his restaurant, and still others, money. "People in the community immediately responded as democratic minded Americans," Feldman wrote, including "Jewish people, Gentiles, and Negroes." His employer offered to rehire him, and Feldman continued as a lodge member. He joined Temple Emanuel in Greensboro, where he taught Sunday School. Winston-Salem's Reform and Orthodox congregations both offered Torah honors, and he was invited to homes for New Year dinners. "We Jewish people must have unity," a Beth Jacob member assured him. "The people are with me and opposed to witch hunters," Feldman wrote.[109]

The hedging over Feldman reflected tensions Jews felt between their Jewish and American loyalties. "Such debates between anticommunism and defense of civil liberties wracked every liberal organization," historian Cheryl Greenberg notes. National Jewish defense agencies sought to dissociate themselves from suspected communists even as they opposed loyalty oaths. Liberal Harry Golden felt the congregation was right to fire Feldman because he was not under oath. Golden feared that "an entire community (Jewish) may conceivably be saddled with the views of a single member." He wished Feldman well.[110]

In the McCarthy era, Jews demonstrated their Americanism and their brotherhood as children of one God. The traumas of the Holocaust and the menace of a godless communism gave such efforts a special urgency. Rabbi Sidney Unger of Asheville, a military chaplain and American Legionnaire, was especially diligent. In 1956 Temple Beth Ha-Tephila hosted a musical pageant with a choir "representing different churches" that gave voice to the theme, "Have We Not All One Father; Hath Not One God Created Us All?" Nationally, brotherhood expanded from three-faith forums to an internationalism that embraced race and nationalities in the global family of man. In 1953, as the Korean War neared its end, Rabbi Unger chaired a Lion's Club Thanksgiving program with "representatives from the Cherokee Indians, the colored, the Catholic, Jewish and Protestant groups; and possibly representatives of the Chinese, Korean. . . ." Each would speak on "For What I am Thankful," and together they would sing "We Gather Together" and "America the Beautiful." The Rabbi organized Town Hall Meetings, citywide forums for youth. During an era of global, anticolonial movements, UNC Hillel Rabbi Efraim Rosenzweig was pleased that Hindus and Moslems came to Shabbat services. In the 1950s congregations organized a Festival of Holidays where non-Jews were invited to attend a program with displays and explanations of Jewish practices and observances.[111]

POSTWAR PROSPERITY

The postwar years marked an era of optimism. In 1949 Kerr Scott was elected governor in a "Go Forward" campaign. Veterans returned to raise families, start or expand businesses, buy homes, and erect synagogues. Always they declared that they were building for the future. Like other hyphenated ethnic Americans, Jews nationally were moving from cities into countrified suburbs that sprouted in the postwar housing boom.

By the 1940s a majority of American Jews were white-collar workers. As the ranks of factory workers diminished, the numbers of manufacturers swelled. Postwar prosperity again brought northern manufacturers south to take advantage of cheap land, taxes, and non-unionized labor. Local businesses expanded. High Point's Leonard Kaplan turned his father's janitorial supply service into industrial K-Chemicals. Robert Osterneck relocated from Philadelphia to Lumberton in 1950, opening a textile plant that would produce polypropylene yarn for newly popular leisure suits. New York lawyer Arthur Cassell arrived in High Point in 1945 to work for a High Point manufacturer, Stanley Taylor. He met native High Pointer Herman Bernard, and the two established Casard Furniture. In 1952 Ernest Mills moved his parachute factory from New York City to Asheville, drawn by nearby textile suppliers, cheap land, and skilled labor. With the Korean War, Mills Manufacturing became a major military contractor and expanded to sixty-five countries. Across North Carolina spinning mills, garment assemblers, handbag makers, and dry goods manufacturers of all sorts opened in small towns where land was cheap and labor plentiful. The Brenners, who had begun hauling wheelbarrows of scrap, expanded in the 1950s into Brenner Steel, national fabricators, and the Amarr Company, manufacturers of building products.[112]

Store owners expanded and upgraded their merchandise. Schulman's in Sylva, Steins in Fayetteville, or Margolis in Williamston were places to buy clothes with brand names that had cachet. Expanding radio and television stations presented new fields open to Jews. Oxford's Stan Fox, wanting to escape his father's mercantilism, began investing until he owned five radio stations in small-town markets. Jews also purchased radio stations in Charlotte and Lumberton.

Universities were the vanguard of North Carolina's social changes. Glass ceilings in law and medical schools had limited Jewish faculty, and Jews felt that their ethnicity, not their qualifications, often denied them deanships or faculty chairs. When the Duke law school considered hiring a second Jewish professor, Mel Shimm, who arrived in 1949, was told at a faculty reception that some elder professors felt "one Jew is enough." He observed that at the medical school, where his wife Cynia practiced, no Jew ever became a chief resident. Duke biochemist William Perlzweig, who had helped recruit the doctors who were later massacred at Hadassah Hospital in Jerusalem in 1948, once spoke on Israel at a campus forum; a Duke political scientist confronted him with an anti-Semitic harangue, arguing that Jews conspicuously ruined any place where they settled. A UNC professor told a Jewish Phi Beta Kappa student that he did excellent work, but his

PORTRAIT: FANNYE MARKS

"Fannye Is North Carolina's Fashion Dictator" read a newspaper headline describing Fannye Marks, whose dress shop in rural Roanoke Rapids outfitted the wives of governors for inaugural balls, socialites for European travels, and debutantes for cotillions.

Jewish merchants featured name brands, offering rural customers a taste of big-city fashion. Born in Kinston, Fannye was the daughter of an immigrant who had moved to Roanoke Rapids in 1907 to open a general store. She traveled to Paris, London, and Rome, where she sat in cafés, opera houses, and hotel lobbies taking fashion notes. Customers flew private planes to visit her store, and she shipped haute couture from her rural mill town to Asia, Europe, and Latin America.

"Clients" (never customers) did not simply walk into Fannye's but made appointments weeks ahead. "They didn't go to a rack and pick them out," her brother-in-law Robert Liverman explained, "We chose things for them and put them on." The client was given a bathrobe, seated in a dressing room, and served chili dogs from a nearby café for lunch. Fannye and her sister Marcella, dressed simply in black, draped the client in high fashion and "accessorized" her with jewelry and handbags. Fannye and Marcella then oohed and aahed, even applauded. Attorney Richard Allsbrook recalled that if he said a dress looked "nice" on his wife, Fannye replied it was "fabulous." If he remarked it was "cute," she answered it was "smashing." At this moment, too, the client learned the price. "Her color sense was magical," customer Lucia Peel Powe wrote in her novel *Roanoke Rock Muddle*, "She could dramatize the most mousy matron of any age. . . . [Fannye] was a psychiatrist of the first order."

A headline described the "Warm-Hearted Dress Shop Owner" who raised thousands for the Episcopal Parish House, where community groups met, and was quick for a loan to the needy, telling them to "forget it" rather than pay her back. She and her family were stalwarts of Weldon's Temple Emanu-El. Roanoke Rapids honored her with Fannye Marks Day.[1]

1. *Raleigh News & Observer*, 28 Jan. 1973; Lucia Peel Powe, *Roanoke Rock Muddle* (Raleigh: Ivy House, 2003), 170–79; North Carolina Clipping File-75, 42, NCC.

J. S. Mann's Store in Whiteville with Jewish star on sign. (Jack Steinberg)

policy was not to give a Jew an A. Fraternities and sororities still divided between Jewish and Christian houses. A UNC administrator assigned Jewish students to a single dormitory because he felt "certain people would prefer to be together"; when student Allard Lowenstein complained to President Graham, he ended the practice. In 1957 Eli Evans became the first Jew elected president of the student body, and seven years later David Kiel was the first awarded a prestigious Morehead Scholarship, until then a reserve of Christian gentlemen. UNC stopped asking students to state their religious preference on applications in 1955, the year the school integrated, and Duke followed in the 1960s. Jewish enrollment at Duke began skyrocketing.[113]

The situation for Jewish faculty changed first in medicine and the sciences and then in the liberal arts. Faculty bigots, who guarded academia as an Anglo-Saxon preserve, were supplanted by broad-minded leaders like Duke's medical school dean Eugene Stead, who introduced a meritocracy. Newly arriving Jewish faculty, often veterans educated on the GI Bill, did not feel pressured as did earlier generations to assimilate or veil their Judaism to advance their careers. Abraham Holtzman recalled only one other Jew at North Carolina State when he joined the Political Science Department in 1955. Each semester he began class by telling students that he was a Jew so that they could understand his perspective. Holtzman was secular but a passionate Yiddishist, and a year after his arrival, he became campus Hillel adviser, a post he held for nearly twenty years. Bernard Greenberg, who came to Chapel Hill in 1949 to found a biostatistics program, was both Zionist and Orthodox. At Duke, psychologist Martin Lakin was a graduate of the Hebrew University and a veteran of Haganah, while geneticist Sam Gross had attended Yeshiva Etz Chaim in Brooklyn. Other campuses opened to Jewish faculty, including Pembroke State College for Indians (now UNC-Pembroke), where Dr. Marter taught Shakespeare. Norman Sulkin arrived at Wake Forest's Bowman-Gray School of Medicine in 1952, followed three years later by Isadore Meschan, who chaired the Radiology Department.

"After the war it was like someone opened a cold steel door and left it ajar a bit, and said if you push it hard enough you might just get through," Gibby Katz of Durham reflected. North Carolina veterans, having witnessed the death toll of hatred, returned with broader experience of foreign places and peoples. A nascent civil rights movement cast prejudice as un-American. Barriers in workplaces, civic clubs, and residential neighborhoods began cracking. Brotherhood became America's civil religion. Americans spoke of their heritage more broadly as Judeo-Christian. Newly confident, Jews confronted discrimination. In 1955 the state's rabbis called for an end to classroom prayer and Bible readings, and Jews joined Seventh Day Adventists in Winston-Salem in opposing Easter crosses in public parks. Mr. Sutker, a Russian immigrant storekeeper was shocked to see a billboard reading "Randleman: Ku Klux Klan Country!" at the town's limits. He stormed into a Chamber of Commerce meeting and, in a thick Yiddish accent, demanded that the sign be removed, which it was. A 1946 national survey reported anti-Semitism was weaker in the South than in the North and in small towns than in larger cities, a profile that fit North Carolina.[114]

North Carolina Jews typically express warm feelings about their communities even as they acknowledged childhood taunting and adult social discrimination. "You sort of felt like an outsider," Herb Brenner of Winston-Salem reflected. "We knew there were doors closed to us—not just social, but economic doors as well." Not being able to join a country or downtown civic club was not just a question of social prejudice, Jerry Sternberg of Asheville felt, for these were the settings where the mill owner met the insurance agent, where the banker and realtor cut deals. "We would be invited to an event at this country club, and we would be the only Jewish people there," recalled Miriam Warshauer, whose husband Sam was president of the New Hanover County Medical Association in 1948. "We were very well accepted, but you always had a feeling of being a little on the outside." Jews spoke of the "five o'clock shadow" or a "segregation at sundown" that limited social relations between Jews and Christians to civic and mercantile activities in daylight hours. A 1962 national survey of 803 country clubs revealed more than half excluded Jews completely while more than a tenth had quotas.[115]

The new neighborhoods that sprouted in the postwar years were often off limits to Jews. This pattern was true not just of Charlotte or Winston-Salem, but also of small communities where a new golf course might spur development. Often these subdivisions contained anti-Jewish covenants, which the Supreme Court outlawed in 1948. In virtually all towns, Jews recounted slights. In High Point, Fred Swartzberg gave a realtor a deposit for a lot only to be told that "the guy that owns the property went around the neighborhood and they didn't want no Jews living there." In Pinehurst, covenants forbidding "sale or use by a Jew or a Negro, or any person affected by tuberculosis or consumption" were common. Resorts like Asheville's Grove Park Inn were considered closed, but none recall seeing the "No Jews Allowed" notices posted in Virginia, Maryland, or Florida. A forester in Asheville felt it best to hide his Judaism and remain unaffiliated because of his "bitterly anti-Semitic bosses."[116]

The pattern of discrimination varied widely. A study of Winston-Salem and Greensboro revealed different patterns. Elite clubs and societies were open to Jewish Cones in Greensboro, but closed to Episcopalian Cones in Winston-Salem. Greensboro with its Jewish industrialists and its Quaker legacy was regarded as somewhat different, although Jews felt sufficiently excluded that they led the move to form the Starmount club, which was heavily Jewish. Wilmington had an Old South legacy that reserved certain clubs to social elites. Jews felt Asheville and Charlotte were restrictive. In rural communities, with but a handful of Jewish families, Jews and Christians mixed more easily. In Hickory, Elaine and Marvin Zerden had for years a card circle consisting of Jewish and Christian couples who gathered in each other's homes. Harry Kramer of Wallace was "one of the guys," his daughter Muriel recalled, a fisherman, card shark, and ballplayer. Small-town shopkeepers joined cronies at local eateries, often owned by a Greek immigrant, to talk sports or politics. Clothier Ellis Farber held court among the old boys at Scotland Neck's Idle Hour Café. When a country club formed, he was a founder. Miles up the road in Weldon, which had a half-dozen Jewish families, Farbers and Freids could not play golf at the local club, although their homes bordered the course.[117]

When nominated for civic or country club memberships, Jews, some of whom were war veterans, often found themselves blackballed from a downtown Rotary or even an American Legion post. When industrialist Stanley Frank asked about joining the Sedgefield Country Club, "No one told me directly that I would be turned down because I was a Jew, but that was a clear signal." The daughter of the UNC Hillel director recalled the maitre d' asking her to leave the dining room of a Pinehurst country club although she was escorted by a Christian friend. Former Greensboro mayor Ben Cone Sr., married to a Christian, found doors open but conceded "there's always latent anti-Semitism, still is."[118] His son, Ben Jr., raised Episcopalian, discovered fraternity doors closed to him at Chapel Hill. A Christian friend who took him to the Roaring Gap country club was told not to invite "the Jew" again. In High Point, Zelda Bernard volunteered for civic societies, and Herman Bernard served on bank boards and headed hospital and redevelopment campaigns, but they could not join the country club.

The reasons that doors closed or opened, as they had in the past, varied by community and often owed to personalities as much as to structural factors. One bigot held the power to blackball. A token Jew or two might be allowed entry to places that were otherwise regarded as discriminatory. Wendy Block felt welcomed at Junior League in Wilmington but was reluctant to join when she moved to Winston-Salem because the "town had a reputation." Instead, she found "nicest . . . wonderful" friends. Debutante cotillions were exclusively gentile affairs, but Leah Levine's daughter in Raleigh came out in the 1960s. Harry Golden identified an "our Jew" phenomenon, an exceptionalism, where residents expressed warm feelings for the "Jew next door" even while they remain wary of the "mythical Jew." When Edward Martin Block died in Lexington in 1964 after serving as town physician for twenty-five years, stores and schools closed, and townspeople came to his funeral to hear a "real, live rabbi."[119]

Social circles in the South centered on the church. UNC sociologist John Shelton Reed noted that a "standard" opening gambit among southerners was, what church do you go to. Newly arriving Jews frequently took umbrage. "We're Jewish," Reed noted, was a "perfectly satisfactory response." North Carolina Jews repeatedly confirm this insight. Laverne Cohen, who worked at a Halifax County social services agency, was asked "'Are you a believer, do you go to church?' Once I told them that I was Jewish, and yes, I was active with Temple Emanu-El, that satisfied them." In Raleigh, Dan Satisky recalled, "a Jewish family kept their stores open on Yom Kippur, and the Gentile people questioned" them. Fayetteville's Joel Fleishman echoed, "It is important to southern Christians that Jews be Jews." Baptists saw Scotland Neck's Ellis Farber as one of God's "originals," and the bachelor took his niece Maralyn to country churches where she sang in Hebrew. "That's the Lord's language," Ellis told them. In Robeson County, David Weinstein blew the shofar at Baptist churches at High Holiday season.[120]

Marshall Rauch of Gastonia spoke for many Jews when he said, "I've never tasted a serious bit" of anti-Semitism in North Carolina, but then added, "Oh, there are some petty things . . . but those are likely to happen any place." Jews who experienced prejudice quickly named Christian friends who defended them.

Joan Samet recalled how the president of the High Point Arts Council, a Christian classmate of her husband's, stood up at Easter Sunday buffet to declare that she would not attend their annual ball if it were held at a restricted country club. Miriam Warschauer did not object that her music club had a prayer and a hymn, but a Christian friend did so on her behalf. Often well-meaning Christians expressed concerns about their unsaved Jewish friends' immortal souls. "I know I'm going to heaven," a hairdresser told Zelda Bernard, "but I don't know about you."

Slowly, doors opened. Country clubs, Jews felt, often solicited their membership for reasons of financial need rather than social equality. Durham's New Hope Country Club was insolvent, and Duke University agreed to help if it accepted Jewish faculty. Several Jewish doctors joined, and the club later held bar mitzvah parties. In High Point, the country club agreed to invite three Jewish families—they were "pushed into it," Zelda Bernard felt—but she and her husband declined. When a Winston-Salem club finally opened, Abe Brenner recalled a headline, "Jew Admitted to Country Club." Even in Greensboro, where the four prestigious clubs had some Jewish members, Jews were underrepresented on corporate boards, excepting those, like Cone Mills, of Jewish provenance.[121]

For Jews, their good name was important, as each felt to be a representative of the community. Businesses were built on trust, the storekeeper loaning a customer money until the mill's next payday or the next tobacco harvest. Merchants spoke disparagingly of other Jews who sold shoddy merchandise at inflated prices or re-collected merchandise sold on credit as damaging the community's good name. To see a Jew's name in a newspaper for tax evasion or economic crimes shamed the community. In Charlotte, two Jewish lawyers stepped forward in cases involving Jews to defend the community's honor.

RELIGIOUS REVIVAL

Postwar prosperity inspired a religious revival centered on the synagogue. "Young members had come back from the war, married, and new families with children were becoming part of our congregation," observed Ellis Farber of Weldon. As the economy boomed, annual national spending on churches and synagogues grew from $26 million in 1945 to $775 million in 1956. Jewish affiliation, which was 20 percent in the 1930s, rose to nearly 60 percent in the 1950s. Moreover, affiliation rates were higher in small and midsized cities than in metropolitan areas, a demographic that described North Carolina.[122] In 1948 a chapel was dedicated at Camp Lejeune to serve not only Jewish Marines but the nearby Jacksonville community. In 1951 a Hillel house arose a block from the UNC campus. New congregations formed in Hickory, Jacksonville, Whiteville, Wallace, and Durham. In communities with congregations, new or expanded synagogues arose in eighteen

Rocky Mount's Temple Beth El, a postwar synagogue. (Julian Preisler)

Camp Lejeune Jewish Chapel, Jacksonville, 1948. (Jewish Heritage Foundation of North Carolina)

communities. Annexes and social halls were added to accommodate new numbers and purposes.

Synagogues followed Jews into the suburbs. Typically, older downtown sanctuaries were abandoned. Durham's Beth El was near the members' stores, but the new synagogue bordered the Duke campus, where the community's future lay. Asheville's Beth Ha-Tephila moved with its members from the center city to the affluent northern suburbs. As "young marrieds" arrived, Charlotte's Walter Shapiro recalled, "we were all reaching out for a way to come together. Somehow the catalyst was the Temple." He added, "The need for socializing, that brought us together."[123] These buildings were designed to serve families, especially youth, not just the immigrant elders who had held congregational reins. The synagogue-centers, as they were often called, employed flexible floor plans for an adaptable Judaism. Folding doors allowed the sanctuary to expand into a catering hall for social events, dinners, dances, or school bazaars. Durham's Beth El included both a mikva for the observant and showers for basketball players. High Point's new B'nai Israel contained a boldly contemporary sanctuary and classroom wing as well as a mikva. Fayetteville's Temple Israel also relocated to the suburbs, but its first priority was to erect an educational building. Not one provided separate seating for women. Unlike the cathedral-style, downtown synagogues, postwar temples rarely replicated church architecture but were boldly modernist. Jews confidently expressed their difference.

A new edifice often brought a new name and religious identity. High Point Hebrew Congregation became B'nai Israel, and Asheville's Orthodox Bikur Cholim became Conservative Beth Israel and moved to the suburbs. In 1910 North Carolina had perhaps ten Orthodox congregations; in 1960 it had none. Conservative Judaism emerged after the war to become the nation's dominant Jewish religious movement. From 1955 to 1961 alone, it added 269 congregations nationally.[124] Orthodox Jews had once lived within walking distance of their shuls, but the new temples had parking lots for suburbanites. The children of Orthodox immigrants were affiliating with Reform and Conservative congregations in growing numbers.

Leadership was passing to a new generation. At Durham's Beth El, the longtime president S. H. Dworsky, a Polish-born Orthodox Jew with semicha (rabbinic ordination) from the Mir Yeshiva, handed leadership to E. J. Evans, an American-born UNC graduate who stumbled over Hebrew. Rabbis at Conservative synagogues, like Samuel Friedman in Asheville and Wilmington or Abe Schoen of Raleigh, were typically of Orthodox background. Freedman was born in Jerusalem and educated at a Mea Shearim yeshiva. The rabbinate similarly evolved. Traditionalist rabbis had to cope with the laxer, more liberal lifestyles of their congregants.

Rabbi Louis Tuchman resigned from Durham's Temple Beth El in 1958 when the Conservative movement permitted women to initiate divorces and Jews to drive to Sabbath services.

Conflict rended congregations as traditions loosened. Once Charlotte synagogue president Sol Levine was called at night by the police who had arrested a woman for swimming illegally in a city park. She needed a mikva. In Weldon, conflict arose when a Polish-born member objected after the congregation voted twenty-four to two for piano music at services. North Carolina rabbis convened a beth din (rabbinic court) to adjudicate the issue. The "primary factor in answering this question," the rabbis' advisory board ruled, "is the preservation of the unity of the congregation." Each community worked its own compromise. Charlotte's Conservative Beth Israel included an organ and choir on Friday nights, but not on Saturday mornings when the Orthodox attended. When Wilmington's B'nai Israel moved to its suburban center, which lacked a woman's balcony, the first two rows were reserved for men. Raleigh's Sam Glass was so upset when Raleigh's Conservative congregation introduced mixed seating that he took a reading stand, placed it by the wall, and never sat down again. "The 'Reform' group in our congregation has lost its early rigidity, and the 'Orthodox' group in our congregation has lost its scrupulous observance of the minutiae of Jewish law," wrote Rabbi Robert Jacobs of Asheville. "The two behavior-patterns have mellowed and blended.' . . . Within our Temple, an *American type of Judaism* is a-borning."[125]

Ethnic and social lines between those of German and East European origin were breached as differences of class, education, and acculturation lessened over generations. Although each group remained conscious of differences, marriages between them blurred divisions. Buddy Patton's German family in Asheville expressed displeasure when he became engaged to Marilyn Blomberg from a Russian family, but youth did not. Sternbergers, Meyers, and Bluethenthals married into East European families. North Carolina society was always far less given to social hierarchy than in Virginia or South Carolina. When the LeBauer family of Greensboro held a shiva (mourning period) in their home, Cone women rolled up their sleeves to help with the dishes. If Goldsboro's immigrant Orthodox Jews needed a tenth to make a minyan, Henry Weil gladly obliged. Whatever the differences of national origin, a blended southern Jewish ethnicity was evolving. When Leah Robinson married Morris Karpen of Brooklyn, her mother cried, not knowing "how she could relate to New Yorkers."[126]

Newcomers remarked how the South made them feel their Judaism even more. Very small numbers and the pervasive evangelical Protestantism of the South meant that Judaism could not be taken for granted as it often was in the northern communities they had left. "Having lived in the South really strengthened" my

Judaism, recalled Greenville's Morris Brody. "One thing about the Christians, they won't let you forget that you're a Jew." Christians were always curious, and "you have to know a lot about Judaism to answer their questions," he added. In a place with few Jews, without a resident rabbi, each individual was responsible for the community's survival. That pattern was true of small-town Jewish communities regardless of region. When Robert Liverman arrived in Roanoke Rapids from Boston, he was relatively unobservant, retaining "a little bit" of Hebrew from his bar mitzvah. As immigrant elders aged or passed away at Weldon's Temple Emanu-El, he stepped forward to lead services. He purchased a set of cantorial records, studied the liturgy, and became a longtime lay prayer leader, conducting funerals and weddings. "My life religiously was much richer after I moved to Roanoke Rapids than it ever had been," he reflected, echoing a common sentiment felt by newcomers settling in a region of more intense and pervasive religiosity.[127]

As historian Jonathan Sarna notes, Jews "gave every appearance of being 'at home' in America," but in fact lived in a "self-contained subculture, a parallel universe that shared many of the trappings of the larger society while standing apart from it." Denied entrance to civic or country clubs, Jews formed their own societies that largely imitated the very institutions that refused them. In Hendersonville, Jews created a southern Catskills. Five Jewish boardinghouses drew visitors from across the southeast to enjoy mountain air, gin games on the porch, and hefty portions of gefilte fish and tzimmes. In the evenings North Carolina Jewish kids gathered at the pavilion on Lake Osceola for big band dances, Milton Lurey recalled, joining other Jewish kids whose parents were staying at Mrs. Horowitz's or Rubin's Lake Osceola Inn. "It was the dancingest town in the world," added Ann Mottsman Michalove Kolodkin. The Osceola Inn hosted High Holiday services for visiting Floridians. After World War II, Charlotte Jews broke ground for the Amity Country Club. It evolved into a "Southern style Jewish country club" replete with restaurant, card rooms, pool, and sports fields. In Charlotte and High Point, chapters of the Jewish War Veterans organized, and in the latter city they erected their own monument.[128]

No event marked southern blending more than the annual Jewish Debutante Cotillion, first sponsored by the High Point chapter of the National Council of Jewish Women in 1942. The North Carolina Association of Jewish Youth gathered high school seniors from across the state for the event. Girls, adorned in long white dresses and clutching red roses, were escorted by Jewish boys. The setting was a decorated gymnasium. Maxine Schwartz Sellers of Wilmington, who attended the 1952 cotillion, recalled that it was "an imitation of the gentile debutante balls to which Jews were never invited." Her escort was a sophomore from her brother's TEP house at Chapel Hill. "Our parents pushed the North Carolina

Association of Jewish Youth happenings," Sellers realized, "because there were so few Jewish young people in any one town or city and this gave us a wider circle of Jewish friends."[129]

"We were very clannish," reflected Durham's Gibby Katz. Children were raised by the community. "I had thirty-seven parents," recalled Raleigh's David Glass. "It was a close knit community." As a counter to assimilation, Jews replicated their organizations for children. B'nai B'rith youth organizations, such as the fraternity Aleph Zadik Aleph and B'nai B'rith Girls, spread across the state. "We all belonged" to the North Carolina Association of Jewish Youth, recalled Raleigh's Burton Horwitz. "We were constantly going to conventions, which really were weekend socials." Lifelong friendships formed, marriages were spawned, and children were set on a path of Jewish organizational involvement.

Bonding North Carolina Jewry as a community was the B'nai B'rith Institutes

PORTRAIT:
I. D. AND HERMAN BLUMENTHAL

In 1924 I. D. "Dick" Blumenthal, a salesman, was driving his Packard from his native Savannah to Charlotte when the radiator sprung a leak. He pulled into a service station. Rather than a costly and time-consuming repair, Mr. Ray, the owner, poured in his homemade Solder Seal. Impressed, I. D. loaded his car with samples and peddled the product along the East Coast. He bought the company, Radiator Seal, and in 1937 summoned his younger brother Herman, a student at Chapel Hill, to join him. Next came a California rubber company which Herman managed after returning from four years in the wartime army. The brothers expanded into float balls, appliance hoses, safety vests, highway cones, and car products like Gunk and Liquid Wrench. Its three Charlotte area plants employed nearly 600, and its 2,000 products were sold in eighty-three countries.

I. D. (far right) and Madolyn (far left) Blumenthal flank scholars Solomon Grayzel and Mordecai Kaplan, with Maurice Weinstein, B'nai B'rith Institutes founder, in the middle. (Marcia W. Simon)

The brothers imbibed a lesson from their Orthodox immigrant parents: "If your community has been good to you, then you have an obligation to give something back to the community." That principle guided the brothers and their wives Madolyn and Anita in establishing the Blumenthal Foundation for Charity, Religion, Education, and Better Interfaith Relations in 1953. Beyond Jewish causes, the foundation gives to the arts, mental health, education, and the environment.

I. D., who called himself a junior partner of God, was a visionary who felt personally responsible for sustaining the state's Jewish community. In Charlotte he endowed temples, day schools, the Jewish Federation, and a community center. Perhaps his most notable venture was a retreat near Little Switzerland. In 1936 he heard that a 1,400-acre mountaintop, which once belonged to Klansman Thomas Dixon, was available from a Texas bankruptcy court. As he drove the court appraiser up the mountain road, fog descended, clouding the magnificent views. The panicky Texan quickly agreed. The retreat, named Wildacres, was legendary among the state's Jews as a communal gathering place for summer B'nai B'rith Institutes. In 1954 the foundation endowed the Circuit Riding Project. The mobile synagogue was novel, but the program seeded new congregations. The foundation also supported the Blumenthal Jewish Home for the Aged near Clemmons and financed the *American Jewish Times Outlook*, a statewide magazine.

Active in the NCCJ, the brothers founded Wildacres as an ecumenical retreat. It hosted groups as diverse as the Charlotte Choral Society and the University of North Carolina's Friday Scholars. Blumenthal Fellows were enrolled at Queens College. Concerned with the environment, Herman donated a coastal island to the Nature Conservancy. The brothers—exuberantly philanthropic Dick and quietly generous Herman—"led by example."[1]

1. <www.blumenthalfoundation.org/Director.htm.>, 10 Sept. 2008; M. S. Van Hecke, "I. D. and Herman Blumenthal," in Howard Covington and Marion Ellis, eds., *The North Carolina Century: Tar Heels Who Made a Difference, 1900–2000* (Charlotte: Levine Museum of the New South, 2002), 367.

of Judaism held at the Blumenthal family's Wildacres ecumenical retreat in Little Switzerland. Founded in 1948 by Charlotte lawyer Maurice Weinstein, the annual institutes promised "'Living Judaism'—a unique opportunity for a truly American-Jewish experience in a fellowship setting." The speakers were a who's who of American Jewry. The storekeeper from Reidsville and the housewife from Hickory heard Ludwig Lewisohn lecture on "Jewish Literature" or Mordecai Kaplan on "The Future of the American Jew." In 1954 Abraham Heschel expounded on "The Earth Is the Lord's." Other speakers included Jacob Rader Marcus, Leo Jung, Morris Adler, Arthur Lelyveld, Eugene Borowitz, and Louis Jacobs. Jews returned to their communities with a cosmopolitan perspective that countered the religious provincialism of their hometowns. As the sun set over the mountains, Jews gathered for communal prayer. "It was nice to be with other Jews," recalled Ruth Diamond, from Warrenton's lone Jewish family. "My son said that he didn't know that there were so many Jews in the world!"[130]

Organizational politics conferred community status, and Jews climbed into the global Jewish hierarchy. Weinstein's Institute expanded countrywide, and he was the founding national chair of the B'nai B'rith Continuing Jewish Education Commission and also chaired the B'nai B'rith International Council. Sara Evans rose from regional office to become national vice president of Hadassah. Industrialist Morris Speizman of Charlotte, after twice serving as national vice president of the United Synagogue of America, became two-term president of the World Council of Synagogues, the congress of the global Conservative movement. The presence of Jews from outside metropolitan areas, particularly New York, spoke to democrat trends in Jewish organizational life.

Living Judaism was a prescription to renegotiate the terms of American-Jewish identity. The prime consideration in hiring a rabbi would be his—and at the time, all were men—ability to relate to thoroughly American children. As Jews settled in the suburbs, their lifestyles did not markedly differ from that of their Christian neighbors, as they attended PTA meetings and gathered for backyard barbecues. Their children played sports and were elected class presidents. "I was just one of the kids around in the neighborhood," recalled Don Michalove of Hendersonville. "I wasn't any different." June Eisenberg, head cheerleader of Burlington High, was named Miss Daughter of the American Revolution, while Marcia Fleishman was elected Lumberton High Homecoming Queen. Marcia's brother Jay played football and basketball under the affectionate moniker of "Rabbi." The after-school supplementary religious program did not fit the schedule of children who attended student council meetings or played in the school band. Parents had religious expectations for their children that they did not have for themselves. If the immigrants were shaped by a habitual Yiddishkeit that led them to pray daily and observe dietary laws, parents were now less concerned with what they saw as the minutia of prayer. They wanted their children to have a Jewish heart, identity, or consciousness. "We weren't real observant," reflected Muriel Kramer Offerman of Wallace, "but we were known as a Jewish family."[131]

In 1952, when a first North Carolina Jewish Education Conference was held in High Point, the eighty-six attendees heard Dr. Azriel Eisenberg of the national Jewish Education Committee speak on "The Ideal Teacher." Gone were the rabbinic disciplinarians who rapped knuckles and pinched cheeks. Child psychology replaced the rote drilling for confirmation or bar mitzvah. "A child is an individual which must slowly be helped to develop," Eisenberg explained. "The teacher must be . . . self-effacing . . . to draw out the child's potentialities." Teacher training

Natalie Kramer, Wallace High drum majorette.
(Muriel Kramer Offerman)

institutes were planned at Wildacres. The 1955 meeting of North Carolina rabbis featured Jewish educational pioneer Emanuel Gamoran.[132]

To appeal to an American youth, national Jewish agencies produced filmstrips, textbooks, magazines, journals, phonograph records, and training material. Rabbi Jerome Tolochko, who served Kinston and Goldsboro, created his own prayer books that blended Jewish and American images. Colorful storybooks featured children with names like Jeremy and Judy. The curriculum borrowed from the public schools with coed classes, final exams, and sports teams. Children were awarded theater tickets and parties and picnics. Regional and national conferences on Jewish education drew lay leaders, often led by the rebbetzin (rabbi's wife), who in small congregations especially was responsible for education. Because boy and girls scouts were usually church based and conflicted with Hebrew school, synagogues organized their own troops.

Temple bulletins everywhere pleaded with parents to instill discipline in their children and to bring them to services. In Charlotte, Bob Speizman recalled, "What

STORY: BASKETBALL IMMORTALITY

Southerners were passionate sports fans, and Jews joined communities of true believers as Wolfpackers, Blue Devils, or Tar Heels. Colleges ran an underground railroad recruiting northern athletes, Jews among them, as they strove for national rankings. If North Carolinians worshiped a sport, basketball was their religion. For athletes like High Point's Fred Swartzberg, who, because of his war service, had the rare experience of playing for both UNC and North Carolina State, sports meant college scholarships.

No athlete was more venerated than UNC's Lennie Rosenbluth, who led the Tar Heels to an undefeated season and a national championship in 1957. A three-time all-American and national player of the year, Rosenbluth broke UNC's season and career scoring records. Coach Frank McGuire said of Rosenbluth: "He did a lot for his religion in the South. The more Rosenbluths we get down here the better."[1]

Not to be outdone, Duke won a recruiting war with UNC by signing New Yorker Art Heyman in 1961. Playing the jilted Tar Heels, a Duke coach recalled, "Every North Carolina guy that got near him called him every Jewish slur in the book, Christ killer, this and that." Heyman played for the U.S. Maccabiah team in Israel. A three time all-American and national player of the year in 1963, Heyman broke Duke scoring records. His combative play gave birth to the Duke Cameron Crazies fans. Sports loyalty trumped ethnic solidarity: when Duke played UNC in 1961, Heyman and Tar Heel guard Larry Brown, a fellow Long Islander, collided. The two Jewish boys came out swinging and benches cleared. As black players arrived, Horace Shelton of the Ku Klux Klan, unaware Heyman was a Jew,

saluted him as a white Christian exemplar.[2] The jerseys of Heyman and Rosenbluth were hung from arena rafters. Rosenbluth, who never lost his Bronx accent, was rousingly cheered in Chapel Hill a half century later.

1. *Raleigh News & Observer*, 10 Mar. 2009.
2. Will Blythe, *To Hate Like This Is to Be Happy Forever* (New York: HarperCollins, 2006), 201–2; <www.jewin sports.org/profile.asp?sport=basketball&ID=160>, 8 Oct. 2008.

Lennie Rosenbluth, national player of the year for the 1957 champion Tar Heels. (North Carolina Collection, University of North Carolina Library at Chapel Hill)

we learned in Hebrew school in the forties and early fifties was how to cuss and how to fight, a little bit how to read and write Hebrew, and a little about Jewish history." Kids dropped off at Hebrew school hid behind bushes and sneaked to the pool hall across the street. Once they locked the education director in a closet. A perennial complaint, as an Asheville temple bulletin reported, was the "great difficulty in obtaining teachers," who were usually parents untrained in pedagogy or Jewish literature. An Asheville bulletin appealed in 1951: "We would like to see greater attendance and participation on the part of all. . . . It is disheartening to come to a service on a Friday evening or Saturday morning and find some non Jews but Jews in absence." I. D. Blumenthal warned, "Jewish education alone is doomed to fail unless our homes implement the teachings of the classroom."[133]

To counter assimilation, Yiddish, Zionist, and religious movements formed summer camps, notably the Conservative Ramah camps in the 1940s. Camping, which once aspired to turn young Jews into Native Americans, had a new purpose. Georgian Herman Popkin and his brothers Harry and Ben, who had worked as B'nai B'rith and Zionist youth activists, founded Camp Blue Star in 1948, the year of Israel's statehood. Two years later, it located on 740 Blue Ridge acres near Hendersonville. Outside Wilmington, Zionist camp Tel Yehuda was held in 1959. Two years after that, Camp Judea, which had begun as a program at Blue Star, purchased 118 acres and became one of Hadassah's five national camps. Camp Judea's mission was for children to have a "FUN summer that enhances that camper's Jewish identity and love for Israel." Gerry Katz Taratoot recalled, "Coming from Statesville with only twenty-two Jewish families, Young Judea was really my link to Judaism."[134]

PORTRAIT: CAMP BLUE STAR

For Jewish kids scattered across the small-town South with few, if any, Jewish companions, Camp Blue Star was a unique immersion into Jewish time and community.

The camp traces to three brothers—Harry, Herman, and Ben Popkin—who after serving in World War II had worked in Zionist and B'nai B'rith youth movements. They started in 1948 with a leased facility, moving in 1950 to 600 acres outside Hendersonville. The camp grew from sixty boys and twenty counselors to 750 coed campers and a staff of 300. Their 1948 mission statement declared that the camping would be based on an "understanding and appreciation of American and Jewish values."[1] They built a synagogue without walls open to nature. Campers learned Israeli folk dances and canoed whitewater streams.

The camp's origins coincided with the birth of Israel. "We lived through the founding of the state," recalled camper Lynda Wachsteter, "There was a real halutz (Israeli pioneer) spirit. We thought we were the pioneers." Israeli counselors served as models of independence and self-assurance. Miles Kuttler, a camp coordinator, recalled, "You'd see one thousand Jewish kids in the hills of North Carolina singing Hebrew songs. There's no way to describe it." Stuart Eizenstat, later a diplomat and

cabinet officer, got his political start as Teen Village mayor, and Federal Reserve Chairman Ben Bernanke was another camper.[2]

Blue Star evolved with American Jewry. In the 1950s it hosted a two-week Camp Judea program, and in 1961 the Hadassah-sponsored Zionist camp purchased its own property nearby. In 1969 Blue Star created a Camping Unlimited Program for children of different races, classes, and religions. Among them were children of Martin Luther King Jr., Ralph Abernathy, and Andrew Young. Jewish camps were laboratories of Jewish innovation. Director Rodger Popkin spoke of a Judaism "without dogma," and former camper Walter Solomon described how "it opened me to a different form of worship." Campers created their own services that included both the traditional amidah (standing prayer) and "Put a Little Love in Your Heart." As Uncle Herman and Uncle Harry intended, campers took their Jewish and Zionist experiences back to their homes and communities.

1. Herman Popkin, *Once Upon a Summer* (Fort Lauderdale: Venture Press, 1997), 9.
2. Jewish Telegraphic Agency, 1 May 1998, <http://www.jweekly.com/article/full/8204/for-50-years-southern-camp-serves-as-jewish-summer-home/>, 8, 9 Oct. 2008.

I. D. Blumenthal took a visionary view of North Carolina Jewry. He saw Jews living in myriad places across a distant landscape beyond the reach of the Jewish urban revival. Blumenthal noted that Methodist circuit riders traveled to rural churches. In 1953, as president of the North Carolina Association of Jewish Men (NCAJM), he proposed a Circuit Rabbi Project to serve some 300 dispersed families. The goals were to teach children, provide rabbinic services for worship and pastoral care, organize adult study, plan Sunday school curriculum, train lay leaders,

and improve public relations with church and civic groups. A rabbi would travel
to communities without organized congregations. A trailer would be outfitted
as a portable synagogue, complete with a library and a classroom. A projector
would show movies and filmstrips. To support the project, every congregational
member was asked to donate one dollar. He wanted the synagogue to be "hitting
on all cylinders . . . in the spring of 1954."[135] Ten small towns were designated for
visits.

The project spread Jewish revival into the countryside. Committees met to
finance the project. Whiteville, Herman Leder reported, "shall go along 100%."
Statesville, Dr. S. W. Hoffman wrote, was inspired "to reactivate Congregation
Emanuel which has been defunct for many years." The 1892 Temple, "restored to
its original beauty," held High Holiday services in 1955, and, with new Jews drawn
by growing industries, the congregation revived. Fifteen families in the Weldon–
Roanoke Rapids area, who had raised $33,000 to purchase a synagogue, joined
the project after receiving a letter from Blumenthal telling them a building was
insufficient: "You must include God in your plans if you propose to serve him and

RELIGION

CIRCUIT RIDING RABBI

IN WALLACE, N.C., WHERE HE SERVES 12 FAMILIES, RABBI FRIEDMAN TREATS HIS RELIGION CLASS TO EXTRACURRICULAR BUS RIDE AROUND THE BLOCK

Traveling Synagogue

NORTH CAROLINA RABBI HOLDS SERVICE IN BUS

In many of the small communities and rural areas of North Carolina, Jewish families have been remote from synagogues and have grown remote from their faith. Now the synagogue comes to them in the form of a specially designed bus which is equipped with everything from a lending library of 60 volumes on Judaism to a battery-powered eternal light.

This rolling synagogue is driven by Rabbi Harold Friedman, who tours a 1,200-mile circuit each fortnight and stops in 10 different communities to lead religious instruction and conduct services for some 300 families. Rabbi Friedman's sponsors, the North Carolina Association of Jewish Men, believe the $14,000 bus is succeeding in its mission of serving and reviving Jewish faith in the area. One community has already gotten together to build a new synagogue, and three others are now busily raising money to put up their own centers.

DISTRIBUTING CAPS to be worn in bus, Rabbi Friedman greets worshiper in Jacksonville, N.C.

CONTINUED

do His will."[136] Lumberton built a new Temple in 1956, soon followed by Hickory, Whiteville, and Jacksonville. In 1972 circuit rider Rabbi David Kraus gathered fifteen Jews at the home of Professor Sheldon Hanft of Appalachian State University, which led to the Boone Jewish Community. In addition to ten towns, twenty-two smaller communities were served.

Circuit rider Rabbi Harold Friedman listed his qualifications: "I am 36 years of age, American born, married, a graduate and ordained rabbi." He knew small towns through pulpits in New York and West Virginia. He had met his Austrian-born wife Miriam in Israel and had Zionist credentials. The rebbetzin was to teach youth, lead music, work with sisterhoods, and keep the books. In March 1955 a unique dedication was held at Charlotte's Amity Club not for a trailer but for a bus outfitted as a synagogue. It contained ten seats, a library, and a portable ark. A Judaica gift shop sold books and records so that Judaism could live in the home. Rabbis gave blessings. At the dedication ten children from each community recited the "Shema Yisrael." Blumenthal placed a Torah in the ark. The North Carolina Council of Churches offered greetings. Abram Sachar, now president of Brandeis University, spoke of Judaism as an "ambulatory religion." In sermons and speeches, the bus was compared to the Holy Tabernacle carried by the Children of Israel through Sinai. Rabbi Friedman declared, "Jews of this state demonstrated that they are part of Klal Yisrael (community of Israel) and want to show their ties with our religion and people even though they are far from centers of Jewish life." The closing hymn was "America." *Life* magazine featured the bus, and Walt Disney filmed it for national television. The "Eternal Light" radio show broadcast a drama, "Synagogue on Wheels."[137]

Every two weeks the rabbi traveled a 1,200-mile circuit. Once a state trooper pulled him over not to give the rabbi a ticket but to provide a police escort with a siren. Excited children, wanting joy rides, greeted the bus. The rabbi and his wife tutored children and trained Sunday School teachers. "When I came to Statesville on Tuesday," Rabbi Friedman recalled, "it was Sabbath on Tuesday." Afterward, adults gathered for study using the popular text, *Pathways through the Bible*. When the rabbi built a sukkah, one worshiper wrote that she had "never been in nor had I ever seen" one before, noting "so many members of our congregation have had no more actual Jewish upbringing than I have." Circuit rider Reuben Kesner described a day in Lumberton that began with a Sunday School, fried-chicken picnic, followed by prayer with a man awaiting surgery, a baccalaureate service, and a baby naming. Zionism was also on the rabbinic agenda. Each community sent a telegram to Secretary of State John Foster Dulles protesting arms sales to Arab states. In Hendersonville, the rabbi enlisted the local VFW post.[138]

Circuit riders had difficulty accommodating to small-town Jewish life. The project continued without a rabbi from 1959 to 1962. In 1971 Rabbi Philip Fried refused to perform a Jewish-Christian intermarriage in Rocky Mount. He complained of another congregation that held Torah services with only six men attending, "an open violation of 1900 years of Halacha." Turnover was high, often a year or two. Hiring a rabbi willing to travel and to serve Jews of all kinds proved thorny. The circuit was broken into Southeast, Piedmont, and Northeast districts. Executive director Dr. William Furie was a well-respected and much-beloved educator but without ordination. The program continued into the 1970s and then faded.[139]

CIVIL SOCIETY AND CIVIL RIGHTS

The postwar years saw doors open to politics. Franklin Roosevelt had brought Jews into federal government. Race and gender barriers fell as blacks and women won appointment to state boards and election to city councils. Governor Kerr Scott, a gruff, cigar-chomping dairy farmer, brought an African American to the state education board and a woman to superior court. He appointed Frank Graham, the South's leading liberal, to the U.S. Senate. Scott, always willing to lend his name to Jewish causes, nurtured a generation of progressive politicians.

The state had traditionally been led by a paternalistic plutocracy of businessmen who were progressive on matters of internal improvement but avoided underlying issues of race. Textile magnates Julius Cone served on the Greensboro City Council for nearly twenty years, and Benjamin Cone Sr. served from 1949 to 1956 and as mayor from 1952 to 1954. Cone was a member of a downtown club that groomed its favored sons for leadership. After the war, a new generation

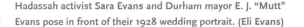

of Jewish politicians emerged, the children of immigrants. In Charlotte, Arthur Goodman was elected to represent Mecklenburg County in the state legislature in 1945, 1953, and 1955, followed by his son Arthur Goodman Jr. in 1965. The Goodmans were lawyers, and the father's firm was notable for hiring Jews. E. J. "Mutt" Evans won six terms as Durham's mayor (1951–63), his brother Monroe Evans two terms as Fayetteville's mayor (1965–69), and their brother-in-law Leo Schneider one term as Gastonia's mayor (1955–57).

These Jews were downtown merchants with long civic resumes. "Mutt" Evans, who headed civic and hospital drives in both black and white communities, was president of the Merchant's Association. Arthur Goodman founded animal welfare and handicapped-children organizations. Hannah Block, the first woman elected to the Wilmington City Council, had been active in the wartime USO and Red Cross and served as the state's first female head lifeguard. In 1947 she co-founded the Azalea Festival for Wilmington and produced its first pageant. Voted Wilmington's Woman of the Year in 1953, she became mayor pro tem. Clothier Fred Swartzberg, elected four times to High Point's city council, had been state Jaycee president and was a local YMCA sports hero.[140]

Jews elected to office publicly identified themselves as Jewish communal leaders. Although he was intermarried and unobservant, Ben Cone chaired state Israel Bonds and UJA Campaigns. Mel Schwartz observed of his father, Wilmington's mayor, "It was an easy step for him to go from the synagogue and the Jewish charities to the community charities and to city council and mayor." Gastonia's Leo Schneider had been a synagogue president. When campaigning, Mutt Evans advertised his UJA and synagogue service believing that "people down here respect church work." He quipped publicly that town council meetings were a pleasure compared to his synagogue board.[141]

Jewish politicians experienced anti-Semitism both overt and subtle. Mutt Evans—a tall, athletic, courtly southerner—defied stereotypes, yet handbills were printed, "Do We want a Goldberg or an Evans? What's the Difference? They're All Alike." When Art Shain, a soft-spoken native North Carolinian, ran for mayor of Lumberton with a black campaign manager, rumors spread that he was a New York Jew. He lost. The Gaston County Democratic chair suggested to Marshall Rauch that he not seek reelection to city council since another Jew, Leon Schneider, intended to run for mayor. He was offended but withdrew. Schneider won in a landslide.[142]

CIVIL RIGHTS

Jews seeking office sought and enjoyed support from African Americans. Often their political careers were launched through biracial councils. E. J. Evans was a member of Durham's biracial Citizens for Good Government Committee, when black banker John Wheeler asked him to run for mayor. Evans ran under the banner, "Equal Representation to All People," and won one black district by 1,241 to 64. The newspaper headlined, "Negro Vote Elects E. J. Evans." "I was for the civil rights," explained Wilmington's mayor pro-tem Hannah Block.

After the Supreme Court's 1954 decision ending public school segregation, North Carolina—in contrast to its sister southern states—earned a reputation for moderation. Political and business leaders, not wanting to jeopardize economic progress, acted to preserve public order. In 1956 the state elected governor not a massive resistor like Orval Faubus of Arkansas but bank president Luther Hodges. In 1958 Albert Vorspan, reporting for the Commission on Social Action of Reform Judaism, cautioned against generalizing about the South: "North Carolina, for example, is a state where the KKK is a discredited and despised crew, repudiated and condemned by the Governor, political leaders, the press, clergy and virtually the entire power structure." Yet, the Klan had more Klaverns in North Carolina than any other state, and into the 1960s its membership exceeded that of all other southern states together.[143]

Tokenism proved a stronger deterrent to integration than resistance. The legislature proposed to keep public schools open yet support whites who sought alternatives. In 1966 165 of the state's 170 school districts were "in compliance," yet just 5 percent of black children attended integrated schools. Not until the 1970s did integration take hold. Under court order, Chapel Hill had become the first white southern state college to admit blacks in 1955, but Duke and Davidson did not do so until 1961. On 1 February 1960, four black students from North Carolina A&T College in Greensboro sat down at a Woolworth's lunch counter igniting a sit-in movement across the South. Sit-ins erupted in Durham and Winston-Salem, followed by Charlotte, Salisbury, and Chapel Hill. Students at Shaw University in Raleigh organized a militant Student Nonviolent Coordinating Committee that pressed for nonnegotiable action. Integration now proceeded not through courts but through confrontation.[144]

National Jewish organizations like the Anti-Defamation League and American Jewish Congress (AJC) had filed court briefs in support of integration, and Jews were disproportionate among the white activists. In 1966 Kivie Kaplan, the last white national NAACP president, presided at the group's annual state meeting in Raleigh. White southerners long blamed the push to integrate not on native blacks but on "outside agitators" and pointed fingers at Jews. When an interracial Journey of Reconciliation arrived in Chapel Hill in 1947 to test segregation, a judge sentenced bus rider Igal Roodenko to thirty days on a road gang, but he assessed "misled" black protestor Bayard Rustin only court costs. The judge explained, "I presume you're Jewish, Mr. Rodenky, well, it's about time you Jews from New York learned that you can't come down here bringing your nigras with you to upset the customs of the South." UNC trustee John Clark, protesting plans to integrate North Carolina State, blamed not Chief Justice Warren and President Eisenhower but "the Rosenwald crowd" and "old Frankfurter and his gang."[145]

Fearing "a storm of hatred," southern Jews traveled to ADL and AJC headquarters asking them to "quietly withdraw" civil rights briefs. In 1952 Charlotte leaders Alfred Smith and Morris Speizman met with the AJC in New York to "express grave concern." AJC's David Petegorsky wrote, "They were fearful that the Supreme Court would in one fell swoop eliminate segregation and that the Jews would be blamed for it." They threatened to cut Charlotte's AJC allocation. Harry Golden offered to solicit sympathetic Jews to compensate. Two years later Smith and Speizman, joined by Joe Hanchrow of Wilson, met with the ADL in New York "to present the Southern Jewish point of view." In Greensboro, an ADL representative attended a house meeting where Ceasar Cone explained that local race relations were good and northerners were causing racial problems. When Freedom Riders arrived by bus in Raleigh in 1961, Rabbi Abe Schoen publicly welcomed the rabbis among them even as he privately disdained them as "publicity seekers." He felt that, not understanding the local situation, they created a mess that they left others to clean up. A lifelong Jewish resident of Henderson complained that out-of-town Jewish activists "started all the problems here."[146]

"For the most part," civil rights advocate Albert Vorspan reported, the state's Jews did not advocate integration. Yet, he added, "They seemed to appreciate my participation and were even willing to discuss the possibilities of positive social action programs—the very suggestion of which is anathema to many of our leaders in the other parts of the South." Jews were less segregationist than gradualist, identifying with the moderation typical of the state generally. At a 1958 UNC student debate, David Evans of Fayetteville noted that "it is impossible to disregard a tradition in one abrupt step that we have had for hundreds of years. I believe that integration will take place, but it must proceed at a rather slow pace, so as to give the people of the South time to accept it." Charlotte's Alfred Smith, a member of the ADL's Southern Regional Board, argued that "men of good will—and we are certainly in that category—want with utmost sincerity to see an extension of the democratic principle of equal civil rights in all fields," even as he urged the ADL to reconsider filing briefs.[147]

In contrast to the "quiet voices" of the southern rabbinate, North Carolina rabbis spoke out. In 1955 Governor Hodges broadcast a "Report to the State" calling on both races to continue segregation on a "voluntary basis." Blacks were outraged. Within a month, fourteen desegregation suits were filed, and NAACP membership swelled. The North Carolina Association of Rabbis passed a resolution declaring "its whole-hearted support of the Supreme Court decision for de-segregation in the Public Schools." They asked the governor to act "without undue delay." Invoking "the Fatherhood of God" and the "true Brotherhood of Man," the rabbis proclaimed, "We dare not permit the existence of laws which discriminate against any human being." A year later, as the legislature debated, the rabbis again called for "a swift end to segregation." They had Christian cover. Baptist, Episcopal, Quaker, and Unitarian groups had acted, and Roman Catholics integrated their schools. In 1955 the North Carolina Council of Churches resolved "in the spirit of Christ to realize an integrated school system."[148]

Typically, southern rabbis expressed liberal views from pulpits but did not cross into civil disobedience. Charlotte's Rabbi Israel Gerber spoke for many when he said, "All I did was lend my voice." Nationally, Reform Jews, North Carolinians among them, held an annual Race Relations Sabbath. Conservative and Orthodox rabbis expressed similar views. One week after *Brown v. Board of Education of Topeka*, Conservative Rabbi Simcha Kling of Greensboro sermonized, "Anti-Negro prejudice . . . is absolutely unfounded and is unequivocally irreligious. One cannot be prejudiced and be true to God!" On Hanukkah 1957, Rabbi Louis Tuchman, Durham's last Orthodox rabbi, addressed the "problem of integration," calling upon Jews to "thrust ourselves into the fray" in defense of "God given right." Rabbi Kling observed that "not one of my members has ever criticized me, to my knowledge, because of this stand; in fact, the majority have agreed with me." Raleigh's Rabbi Schoen heard an occasional voice to "tone it down," but none had his tenure threatened.[149]

As demonstrations struck Greensboro in 1963, Rabbi Joseph Asher of Temple Emanuel was the only white clergyman invited by a black church and civil rights coalition to address a mass protest meeting. He explained to the 1,200 African Americans who overflowed the auditorium that "I am here because I am a Jew." He spoke as a "living witness" to God's covenant at Sinai. The Temple board "tolerated" his activism. Five years later, when the Greensboro Day School asked to rent Temple space, the board agreed only if a minority student were awarded a scholarship. With Episcopal and Presbyterian churches, the Temple in 1968 hosted a program to feed and tutor underprivileged children.[150]

Rabbis forged links with African Americans through pulpit exchanges, ministerial associations, and college teaching. In 1949 Rabbi Simon Glustrom of Durham invited a black congregation to a Sabbath service. Rabbi Gerber welcomed black choirs and speakers to Temple Beth El in Charlotte. In 1957 Rabbi Sidney Unger of Asheville opened his temple to an interracial student group for a NCCJ program. The students sat together for an integrated luncheon. Commonly in towns with black colleges, rabbis taught courses in Hebrew Bible. The first and only whites to be designated professor emeriti at North Carolina Central University were both Jews, Ernst Manasse and Nell Hirshberg.

Rabbis joined ministerial associations, which were agencies of integration. In Greensboro, ministerial groups, both black and white, endorsed sit-ins. As head of Wilmington's Ministerial Association, Rabbi Samuel Friedman, with Orthodox ordination, spoke often in black churches. When a black mail carrier was unjustly fired, the Rabbi interceded at the post office until he was reinstated. Rabbi Fredrick Rypins of Greensboro happily converted Vickie Kilmanjaro, an African American woman engaged to a black Jew, John Kilmanjaro. In 1956, when churches were still rigidly segregated, the Kilmanjaros had a Temple wedding. "The Temple environment has always been warm and welcoming for me and my family," Vickie Kilmanjaro recalled. A member for a half century, she served as temple librarian for two decades, while her husband taught religious school. Other congregations also had African American members, among them, Ada Fisher, who was the daughter of a prominent Durham minister. African American Jews, like their coreligionists, tended to be well-educated professionals. Fisher was a physician, and Kilmanjaro published the *Carolina Peacemaker*, which gave voice to the black community.[151]

A Durham storekeeper put it, "No matter how much we may have sympathized with the blacks, we had to protect our own positions first." "Jews didn't get involved," a merchant in Wilson observed. "They had enough problems being Jewish." Their livelihoods depended on the goodwill of customers, both white and black. Accustomed to fitting in, they feared taking positions that might jeopardize their personal or financial security. Storekeeper Leonard Guyes was "scared to death" during the Woolworth sit-in by white racists who stormed to town to bait blacks. Business "just dried up," he recalled. Obedience to law was a core Jewish value. Greensboro activist Joanne Bluethenthal recalled that Jews were "very reticent"; "they don't ever want to attract attention." Morris Speizman of Charlotte advised Christian ministers that Jews would take a "visible" position only after white southern Protestants had committed themselves. When invited to the black protest rally, Rabbi Asher and his temple board agreed to the "wisdom" of asking a white Protestant minister to accompany him.[152]

Harry Golden, whose *Carolina Israelite* ridiculed racism and segregation, decried his fellow Jews as the "Trembling Tribes of Israel." Surely, not all Jews held liberal views. For many Jews, a black was always a shvartzer (a black)—a house servant, a yardman, a store employee. As mill owners, Jews like other manufacturers came south in search of cheap labor, and several Jewish industrialists found themselves entangled in long and bitter labor disputes with their low-paid, mostly black work forces. In at least one community, Jews were accused of being slumlords, charges that they vigorously denied. When UNC Hillel Rabbi Efraim Rosenzweig hired a black woman as a secretary in the 1950s, B'nai B'rith members threatened to fire him.[153]

Jewish fears were not unfounded. Bombs were planted, and sometimes detonated, at synagogues in Atlanta, Miami, Jacksonville, and Birmingham, regardless of whether Jews were involved. In 1957, as forty women were meeting at Charlotte's Temple Beth El, a janitor discovered six sticks of dynamite. A year later a policeman walking past Gastonia's Temple Emanuel noticed a valise on its front step. Inside were thirty sticks of dynamite, enough to destroy a city block. Its fuse was within an inch of detonating. Police stood guard at services and Sunday Schools. A bomb blasted the entrance of Wilmington's B'nai Israel. The 1955 state B'nai B'rith convention featured civil rights attorney Morris Abram speaking on "How to Stop Violence: Intimidation in Your Community."[154]

Even when victimized, Jews were reluctant to go public. Charlotte's Temple Beth El, on advice of the police chief, suppressed the news of the attempted bombing, labeling it a "boyish prank or the act of a lunatic." The Conservative congregation was enraged, "blasting the 'indifference of the general community'"—especially the Ministerial Association and the Reform temple—for not publicizing the incident. Contrarily, Gastonia Jews went public. Civic and church groups expressed "profound shock" and posted a reward. Wilmington's alleged bomber was acquitted, but clergy rallied to the Jews.[155]

To lessen tensions, municipalities in the 1950s and 1960s appointed biracial citizen councils, often including a Jew. Rabbi Arnold Task, who chaired Greensboro's Human Relations Council, was motivated by Jeremiah's admonition to "seek the welfare of the city." Rabbi Samuel Friedman of Wilmington cited the biblical adage "Ger Ezrach," a stranger is a native, in explaining why he joined the Wilmington and New Hanover Community Council. The intent of these councils was dialogue. Arnold Schiffman Sr., who owned a jewelry store across from the Greensboro Woolworth's, had been president of the Merchant's Association when he was asked in 1960 to join the Human Relations Council. Believing that integration "needed to be tempered with time," Schiffman endorsed gradualism. Integration would be achieved through reasoned negotiation with middle-class black ministers and educators, Schiffman believed, not by "rabble rousers" with their demonstrations and civil disobedience. Martin Luther King Jr. denounced such gradualism in his Letter from a Birmingham Jail, contending that the "great stumbling block" was not the Klan but the "white moderate" whose primary concern was "order." A disconnect opened between Jews who sought mutual understanding through dialogue and African Americans who demanded direct action.[156]

Jews were intermediaries. When a Charlotte high school integrated in 1957, the principal chose the only nonsoutherner, Irving Edelman, as the black student's homeroom teacher. Although other Jews warned Marshall Rauch not to "rock the boat," he agreed to chair Gastonia's twenty-three-member Human Relations Committee. "Marshall was the liaison between the white establishment and the black community," a publisher recalled. "His Jewish heritage probably helped in this area. He was the single harmonizing force among the diverse groups." He worked to integrate restaurants, theaters, and the YMCA. A black member described Rauch as "color blind."[157]

Historian Clive Webb emphasizes the "diversity" of southern Jewish responses to civil rights. Most were "frightened into silence," but a "conspicuous minority" risked their security to overthrow the racial status quo. Attorney Adam Stein and his law partner Julius Chambers, an African American, led legal efforts to desegregate Charlotte. Dr. Maurice LeBauer, who opened a medical practice in Greensboro in 1931, kept an integrated waiting room, contrary to common practice. Friendly with the president of North Carolina A&T, he arranged for students to work in the family's home in exchange for college tuition. The LeBauers maintained a lifelong friendship with one student, Curtis Day, who became a superintendent of schools. If Greensboro protestors were denied service at Woolworth's, across the street at Lane's Pharmacy Bill and Dave Stang sat blacks and whites alike at their lunch counter. The owner of the Mayfair Cafeteria stood in his doorway blocking blacks from entering, but next-door Sol Jacobs welcomed them to his deli. Told that the integrated snack bar at his department store was illegal, E. J. Evans removed the seats since the law said nothing about a stand-up counter. In Chapel Hill, Harry and Sybil Macklin's Jewish-style deli, perhaps the first restaurant in the state to integrate, became the command post for civil rights strategists, and pro-segregation radio announcer Jesse Helms denounced the place.[158]

In many towns, Jews were the first to hire black sales clerks, a pattern repeated across the South. "When I hired my first black in my store, some of these white people tried to boycott my store, but that passed," recalled Harry Freid in Weldon. In his Asheville department store, Harry Winner promoted an elevator attendant, an African American woman, to clerk, the first in town. He then went store to store urging others to do the same. He also placed a black fashion manikin in his window. Dan and Alice Satisky not only took the bold step of hiring a black saleslady at their high-fashion Raleigh dress shop, but when they retired, they turned the business over to her. When Howard and Lillian Lee moved to Chapel Hill in 1960—he later became the South's first black mayor of a majority white town— the one realtor willing to show them homes was Melvin Rashkis. In Charlotte I. D. Blumenthal offered to hire a black civil rights worker fired from her job because of her activism. In Charlotte, only three whites were NAACP members—Harry Golden, Marion Cannon, and Herman Cohen—and all were of Jewish origin.[159]

For émigrés from Nazi Europe, racial segregation spoke to their experience. In the 1950s Ernst Manasse invited a black colleague from North Carolina College to his home for coffee. "I was called to come to the rental office," he recalled. "The neighbors complained." Six weeks later, after again hosting the colleague, he was told that "the neighbors won't stand for this" and was warned next time his colleague would be shot. Other émigrés committed to social justice and welfare. John Green founded a school for handicapped black children in Fayetteville. Mill owner Fred Stern joined Rabbi Israel Gerber as a member of the Charlotte-Mecklenburg Council on Human Relations in 1963. For Fayetteville Rabbi Henry Ucko, civil violence reawakened fears of his native Germany. As a personal protest against segregation, he rode the black-owned bus line, but he also questioned a black woman who wanted to convert to Judaism. Why, he wanted to know, would she want to be doubly burdened? When Black Mountain faculty debated integrating the college in 1944, Nazi émigré Ernst Straus opposed it, finding blacks "strange."[160]

As elsewhere in the South, middle-class Jewish women, who, unlike their husbands had less fear of an economic backlash, were often leading activists. In Greensboro, women like Joanne Bluethenthal and Leah Tannenbaum created social justice programs in public housing projects. Bluethenthal, a Philadelphian, was "astounded and horrified by segregation" when she moved south. Her husband Arthur, Gertrude Weil's nephew, had once walked out of a business luncheon when he learned the restaurant was segregated. With Shirley Frye, an African American educator and civic activist, Joanne Bluethenthal raised funds and held open houses and retreats to prepare the schools for integration. She visited black homes and organized residents of public housing projects. A UNC faculty spouse, Charlotte Levin, raised in rural Troy, joined the multiracial Panel of American Women which conducted civil rights forums before civic and religious groups. Bigots told her "all Jews are nigger-lovers," and she received threatening mail. Jewish activists recalled arguments over civil rights, but as Joanne Bluethenthal observed, "We didn't lose any friends over it. . . . Basically, Jewish people kept quiet."[161]

"Each community has its own story," explained Greensboro's Rabbi Arnold Task. Raleigh was a university town and the state capital. Jewish store owners there did not feel threatened by their clientele, who included students, professors, and bureaucrats, not "rednecks." In Fayetteville, Jewish merchants served Fort Bragg's black soldiers, who were treated respectfully. In Chapel Hill, Hillel Rabbi Rosenzweig felt emboldened to join Jewish faculty picketing a segregated theater, while in nearby working-class Durham Rabbi Herbert Berger felt constrained about marching with Dr. King. Yet, Durham was also the Negro Wall Street, and African American bankers, professors, and executives were a moderating force. The town's establishment, led by the Jewish mayor E. J. Evans, cooperated with the black middle class, knowing that behind them were militant student groups.

In rural towns, Jews faced difficult situations. Jewish storekeepers had built relations with black customers, outfitting grandparents for church and their grandchildren for school. Jews found their stores picketed by young protestors who threatened boycotts if merchants pulled their children from schools or did not hire blacks. Harry Kittner as a Weldon school board member worked with African American educators to integrate schools but still had his store picketed. His children and nieces attended the newly integrated school. "It was definitely strange to go to tenth grade and suddenly it was a 70 percent black school," his son Ben recalled. His sister Bert heard "Jew" taunts. Their friend Maralyn Farber was given the choice of attending the formerly all black high school or the white academy. On principle, she chose the integrated school, but fights, racial tensions, and bomb threats disrupted learning. Concerned about SAT scores and college admission, she transferred to Halifax Academy for her final year. In Durham and Greensboro, rabbis and professors sent their children to integrated schools. Grant Kornberg, son of a Duke political scientist, was the lone white student at Durham's Hillside High.[162]

In the early 1970s, as public schools in Charlotte and Greensboro integrated, Jewish day schools opened alongside white Christian academies. Amanda Stang, who attended Greensboro's B'nai Shalom school, recalled later confronting her mother on whether she "didn't want me to go to an integrated school." Her mother responded, "It wasn't so much white flight, but a fear that the school would be pretty chaotic." She added that the move for a Jewish school came from a "group of people interested in a more comprehensive Jewish education."

If legal segregation was distinctly southern, racism was not. The national Jewish defense agencies that advocated civil rights did not necessarily represent popular Jewish feeling, although national surveys revealed Jews to be less biased than other whites. In Detroit, Chicago, and New York, lingering black resentments against allegedly exploitative Jewish landlords, employers, and storekeepers erupted into riots. In 1955 Bennett Bobrow, a UNC student from New York, drafted a petition calling upon the state legislature to resist court-ordered desegregation. Although a Jewish "Yankee," he acted on behalf of the "overwhelming majority of the people of this state." Opposing him was Ron Levin, a Jewish student from Williamston, who organized a counter-petition urging the legislature to "uphold this decision" as a "lesson in freedom and the democratic way of life." Levin was taunted as a "n—— loving Red and told to go back where I came from," which, as he noted, was a swamp town in eastern North Carolina. The national media picked up the story.[163]

Campuses hosted Jewish activists. UNC sociologist Richard Kramer was the first faculty adviser to the UNC's chapter of the NAACP. Professor Dan Okun, chair of the Committee of Concerned Citizens, was called upon to mediate between the Congress of Racial Equality (CORE) and Chapel Hill to open public accommodations. Nor were Jewish students complacent as they were on many southern campuses. When a Chapel Hill judge sentenced protestors to jail in 1964, Joseph Tieger, a Duke student, counted twenty-three arrests for civil disobedience, in the judge's words, "the dubious distinction of having the most arrests in Orange County." CORE organizer Rosemary Ezra, a Californian, was sentenced to six months in Women's Prison, the "first Jewess ever to be locked up there." She had mortgaged her car and home to finance her activism and could not pay the $500 fine. After

UNC student Paul Wellstone saw Klansmen spit on demonstrators, he led a strike of black underpaid cafeteria workers that brought the state police to campus.[164]

Jewish mayors who were elected as racial moderates were caught in the cross-fire. As riots tore apart the urban north, fears spread that racial violence would become epidemic. In 1967 the state passed antiterrorism laws aimed at extremists of both races. Mutt Evans, Durham's mayor from 1951 to 1963, and his brother Monroe Evans, Fayetteville's mayor from 1965 to 1969, confronted both the Klan and black militants. As Durham mayor, Evans had appointed the city's first black firemen, policemen, and supervisors, and his urban renewal program replaced slums with low-income housing. One night the police called to inform him of a sit-in at Woolworth's. He rushed downtown to assure the protestors that he would represent their demands. They left, but that night windows were smashed on Main Street. Monroe Evans let the Klan and black protestors alike know that his police were armed to protect public order.

North Carolina was the battlefield of two of the South's most vocal civil rights champions: Harry Golden and Allard Lowenstein. The *Carolina Israelite* mocked segregation with various Golden Plans that reduced racism to absurdity. Dr. King praised Golden by name when writing from the Birmingham jail, and Golden introduced King when he spoke in Charlotte. Jews felt ambivalently about Golden—"I just wish he would go away," wrote one rabbi—yet, his speaking calendar also reveals him to be a popular speaker at state B'nai B'rith Lodges, and scarcely a Jewish home was without the *Israelite*.[165]

Allard Lowenstein, a New Yorker who enrolled at UNC in 1945, threw himself into liberal causes, rising to the presidency of the National Students Association. At the 1945 state student legislature in Raleigh—a meeting of college student governments—Lowenstein and his friends introduced a resolution to desegregate the group. When the resolution carried by a two to one margin, public cries arose against communists and outside agitators. In 1962 Lowenstein returned to teach at North Carolina State. He invited to Raleigh Angie Brooks, Liberia's United Nations ambassador, and with a multiracial group attempted to integrate hotels and eating places. Media attention embarrassed the country at a time when America and the Soviet Union contended for influence in postcolonial Africa. Pressed by city merchants, Governor Terry Sanford agreed to negotiate the city's desegregation.[166]

In the late 1960s the civil rights movement grew militant as young black-power advocates asserted themselves. Integrationists like Dr. King confronted separatists like Stokely Carmichael, who scorned white patronage. Robert Williams of Monroe became a nationally known fugitive when he urged blacks to arm in self-defense. Jews on biracial councils or school boards who had met comfortably

PORTRAIT: HARRY GOLDEN

Harry Golden may lay claim to being North Carolina's most *famous* Jew if not its most typical. Born Herschel Goldhirsch in Galicia in 1903, he was raised in New York's Lower East Side. Like many young New York Jews, he attended City College, which sharpened his socialist instincts. After a stint as a soapbox radical, he opened a bucket shop, a brokerage that speculated with other people's money. When it failed, he was arrested for fraud and spent three years in the Atlanta penitentiary. Upon release, he renamed himself Harry Golden, and in 1941 he moved to Charlotte, settled in a mill village, and wrote for the *Labor Journal*.

In 1942 Golden started his own newspaper, the *Carolina Israelite*. He wrote about labor, Jews, Zionism, civil rights, Jewish-Christian relations, literature, and history. Mostly he wrote about himself, and his voice was that of a streetwise ghetto kid. He advocated for Israel, explained New Yorkers to southerners and southerners to New Yorkers. He rhapsodized on kosher pickles and the U.S. Constitution. His writing was both insightful and sentimental. The *Carolina Israelite* endured for twenty-four years, and its circulation surged to

Harry Golden stands before his home and office. (Harry Golden Papers, J. Murrey Atkins Library, University of North Carolina at Charlotte)

with middle-class blacks now faced young militants who picketed their stores or threatened violence. Jeweler Bill Kingoff, who chaired Wilmington's Bi-Racial Committee and the New Hanover Human Relations Commission, confronted a black leader who, dissatisfied with dialogue, led a walk out. When Harry Golden ended the *Carolina Israelite* in 1968, he cited his disenchantment with a civil rights movement grown bitter and bigoted. Once he had found racism absurd, but in his final editorial he wrote, "There is nothing funny about it anymore nor do I attempt to find its humor."[167]

30,000 worldwide. At one time he had two essay collections, *Only in America* and *For 2¢ Plain*, on the best-seller list. His books were translated into eight languages. Golden became a national celebrity, a favorite of television talk shows. Among his friends were Carl Sandburg and John and Robert Kennedy and North Carolinians Frank Graham, Kerr Scott, and Billy Graham.

Golden's reputation rests on his civil rights advocacy. He sought to undermine racism through ridicule, most notably his various Golden Integration Plans, such as putting out-of-order signs on white water fountains, which would force everyone to drink from black ones. Noting that African American nannies attended segregated theaters with white children, he suggested distributing white plastic babies to black theatergoers. His most famous was the Vertical Negro Plan. Observing that blacks and whites could stand but not sit down together, he advocated removing chairs from schools as a way to desegregate them. Martin Luther King Jr. lauded Harry Golden in his "Letter from Birmingham Jail." In 1960, when Dr. King addressed 2,700 NAACP delegates in Charlotte, Golden introduced him. Racial extremists targeted him. "Let me tell you, fat boy, there wouldn't be so much anti-semitism if there weren't so much Semi-

tism," wrote a man from Pinehurst. A 1962 phone call warned, "Are you Harry Golden? I intend to come over there and shoot you right between the eyes, you Nigger lover."[1]

Golden received mixed reviews from his fellow Jews. His newspaper was well read, even loved. He organized brotherhood dinners for the NCCJ where a prominent citizen, like Governor Kerr Scott or activist Gertrude Weil, was honored with a Carolina Israelite Award. His charm and humor won over enemies. But for people who found comfort and security by fitting in, Golden wore his Jewishness too loudly, and his public advocacy of unpopular causes jeopardized their status as solid, middle-class Americans. He admonished southern Jews for being too fearful during the civil rights crisis.

In 1968 Golden closed the *Carolina Israelite*. The civil rights movement was now in the hands of black-power advocates. His Lower East Side nostalgia no longer appealed to a new generation of suburban Jews. Golden died in 1981, and his celebrity faded.

1. Stephen Whitfield, "The 'Golden' Era of Civil Rights: Consequences of *The Carolina Israelite*," 14, no. 3 (Fall 2008): 29; Raymond E. North to Harry Golden, 15 Feb. 196[?], HGP; Harry Golden to FBI, 30 Aug. 1962, HGP.

A COMMUNITY LEGACY

Jews were in the vanguard of North Carolina's progress from the 1920s to the 1960s. Their upward mobility was also in lockstep with Jews nationally. Downtown cathedral-style synagogues testified to affluence and permanence. The modernist temples that replaced them were symbols of social as well as religious change. Mill and market towns, with their small-town hospitality, were yielding to a suburban society more typically American. Coming to a stormy end was the most potent element of southern distinctiveness, legal racial segregation.

Jews felt uncommonly welcome in North Carolina. To be sure, the local Klan and pulpit-thumping evangelists discomfited them. An elite anti-Semitism closed some social, academic, and occupational doors. North Carolina Jews felt, too, the national challenges of nativism, Naziism, and race prejudice although perhaps not so severely as their cousins in the North. Jewish southern acculturation proceeded quickly as the immigrant generation yielded to a native-born, secularly educated youth. Most North Carolina Jews were relative newcomers to the South, and the civil rights crisis tested their acculturation, targeted their insecurities, and heightened their feelings of difference. Yet, as a community, Jews prospered, and most recall small-town life as friendly and neighborly despite slights, discrimination, and, more rarely, violence.

Jews remained ethnically and nostalgically Jewish even as they blended into their communities. If no longer kosher, they still gathered at local delis for pastrami and kibitzing. They lost fluency in Yiddish but held onto Yiddishisms. They enrolled their children in religious schools even if they attended synagogue infrequently. Kinship and landsmen ties across a scattered landscape bonded them as an extended family. "North Carolina is in reality a large neighborhood," NCAJW leader Emma Edwards wrote in 1937.[168] Familial, commercial, and institutional networks linked them to distant Jewries. They organized to save an endangered European Jewry and to rebuild Zion.

If belief and ritual eroded, they affirmed Jewish values. These renegotiated values were based not on deference to the authority of halacha, Jewish law, but to ethical codes that they saw as rooted in Judaism, consonant with America's founding principles. In 1942 Raleigh Young Judeans pledged both to serve American Jewry and to rebuild Palestine by emphasizing "anew the ideal of democracy, a vital part of our Jewish heritage." Jews had faith in America. A "cult of synthesis" held Judaism and Americanism not to be "competing allegiances" but mutually reinforcing. America's heritage was no longer exclusively Christian, but Judeo-Christian. All joined under the banner of brotherhood. They could be Jews, Americans, and southerners without contradiction.[169]

1968–2009

When Judith Schindler left New York for Charlotte in 1998, she confessed the move "was a leap of faith," like getting married or becoming a rabbi. Three years earlier she had been ordained at Hebrew Union College in New York. She had intended to be a clinical psychologist but felt spiritually drawn to a profession which historically had been closed to women. While serving as an associate rabbi in Scarsdale, New York, she had met Chip Wallach, a banker, and they decided to marry.

"He lived down here in Charlotte, and I lived in New York where he grew up," the Rabbi recalled. "We had to make the decision about where is the best place to raise a family." Their ambition, like many of their generation, was to be a two-career family. When they considered Wall Street for him and a New York synagogue for her, they felt uncomfortable with big-city pressures. They decided that they "could have a better lifestyle working as a rabbi and in the banking world here in Charlotte." Chip Wallach was a loan executive at the Bank of America, the nation's largest commercial bank. Rabbi Schindler was hired as Associate Rabbi at Temple Beth El. Five years later she became Senior Rabbi. By 2005 Charlotte had more than 10,000 Jews.

The rabbinate may not have been a typical career choice, but women now entered fields once denied them. As gender barriers shattered, women found jobs in research laboratories, executive offices, and university classrooms. And North Carolina with its booming economy was inviting for two-career families, especially when one's spouse was also a professional. The Rabbi and her husband reflected generational changes among Jews. By 1980 Jews divided evenly between "wage-earning professionals" and "managers, agents, or retailers," and two-career families were normative.[1] Like earlier generations, they were drawn south by economic opportunity, not as poor, unskilled immigrant peddlers or scrap collectors, but as well-educated, third- and fourth-generation Americans pursuing high-paying positions in academia, medicine, research, or finance. They flocked to a region hailed by the media for its temperate climate and relaxed life-

style, its heat and humidity now cooled by air conditioning. Retirees, too, flooded into golf communities, college towns, and coastal and mountain resorts.

In 1968 a new word entered the national lexicon: Sunbelt. A South once benighted by poverty, racism, disease, and illiteracy was now celebrated as the brightest of the nation's regions. Historian C. Vann Woodward proclaimed a "bulldozer revolution" as Old South plantations and battlefields were leveled for shopping malls and suburban subdivisions. As a matter of policy, North Carolina encouraged a "decentralized" system of community colleges and public universities to spread development. Just as railroads had once inspired urban growth, now interstate highways were economic lifelines. By 2000 nearly three-quarters of all North Carolinians resided within fifteen miles of an interstate highway. A third of the state's people lived adjacent to I-85 from Gastonia to Charlotte to Greensboro to Durham. The North Carolina map was dominated by sprawling metropolitan clusters: Greater Charlotte, Triangle (Raleigh–Durham–Chapel Hill), and Triad (Greensboro–High Point–Winston-Salem). Mountain Asheville and coastal Wilmington, linked by I-40, also thrived.[2]

The Sunbelt reinvented the southern cityscape. Downtowns declined as retail centers, and Jewish stores were displaced by urban renewal. Parking decks, government centers, arts venues, and office complexes replaced once vibrant shopping districts. A *Durham Sun* headline in 1975 read, "Site of Gladstein's Inc. on Mangum to Become Parking Lot, Another Block of Downtown Business Must Move Out."[3] Pedestrian friendly streets were replaced with one-way thoroughfares to hurry cars from downtown to suburbs. Like spokes of a wheel, roads extended to highway loops that circled the city. Residential and commercial life increasingly took place in suburban rims where housing developments, shopping malls, industrial parks, and corporate and business campuses proliferated. Starting with Raleigh's Cameron Village in 1949, malls "popped up like wild onions" at city gateways. In 1961 a newspaper reporter counted more than a dozen malls in Charlotte. In 1970 came Southpark, with a retail area covering 1 million square feet.[4]

The independent, downtown merchant could not compete with Sears, Walmart, and big-box chain stores. Storekeepers faced the choice of closing shop or joining the suburban exodus. "We didn't have the capital to build the store in a shopping center," reflected Dennis Winner, whose parents owned a downtown Asheville department store. The chains ran perpetual sales with constant markdowns. Winner's father said he would rather quit than open seven days a week like Sears. They sold out, and the store went under two years later. Other owners found their way to malls or highway strips. Jerry Levin organized a rearguard fight against Charlotte's redevelopment plans, but his Lebo's Store, a downtown fixture, gave way to a Radisson Hotel and reopened on a boulevard. Others, too, joined the flight. Freedmans of Durham and Rosenbachers of Winston-Salem brought their men's stores into malls. Brody's Department Store anchored a Greenville mall. The Cohens of Greensboro and Zimmers of Wilmington opened jewelry store chains, Carlisles and Reeds respectively, in malls across the region.

Rural small-town storekeepers boarded up no less than their city kinsmen. We were "tired of losing money," as one merchant's wife put it. "Hickory without Zerden's? You are kidding me, right?" read a headline. "We had people come in who said how sorry they were," Elbert Lipman of New Bern reflected on his store closing. "It was an institution for them." An elderly customer told Sarah Kittner when their Weldon store closed, "Oh my Lord. My daddy always said a town without a Jew ain't no town at all." When Sol Schulman closed his Sylva store after sixty years, folklorists recorded memories of clerks and customers. News correspondent Drew Levinson and Professor Melinda Weinstein returned to their Robeson County hometowns to film *Lasting Impressions* of empty storefronts and vanished communities.[5]

Although, as Eli Evans noted, fathers built businesses for sons who did not want them, more commonly parents sacrificed so that their children could aspire

THE MAN WHO LIVED ON MAIN STREET

Stories By and About Sol Schulman

Collected and Edited by
Jan Schochet and Sharon Fahrer

to a life that offered more than storekeeping. "My father didn't want me to come back to the family business," recalled Drew Levinson of Fairmont. "He saw the little towns dying." Hy and Ruth Diamond closed their store in Warrenton in 1981, telling their children to do "better things." Joe Reznick's music shop in Winston-Salem was magical for his son Steven, but when he expressed interest, his father threatened to burn it down. The son earned a Ph.D. and chaired the Psychology Department at Chapel Hill.[6]

The rare downtown Jewish stores that survived into the twenty-first century were remnants of a dying breed. Since 1916 Joe Sugar's clothing store anchored downtown St. Pauls, but the third-generation owners sold its small and large men's clothing nationally through its "world's largest selection" Web site. In rural Whiteville, whose main street once had a row of Jewish stores, J. S. Mann's Store held on, a star of David adorning its front as it had since the 1920s. Miller's was the lone Jewish dry goods store left in downtown Winston-Salem, and its rarity attracted filmmaker Donna Schatz to memorialize *The Southern Jewish Store*. In rural towns, stores like Stadiem's in Kinston, Sherman's in Hendersonville, or Leinwand's in Elizabethtown defied Walmarts through customer loyalty and niche lines. Lebo's in Charlotte featured a unique Tutu Boutique and a Boot Hill western wear shop.

POSTINDUSTRIAL NORTH CAROLINA

No longer could merchants count on workers streaming from their factories on paydays or farmers arriving for seasonal markets. Labor strikes and foreign competition devastated textiles, and antismoking campaigns ravaged tobacco. Durham, which once had thirteen tobacco markets, had none. Wilson's tobacco warehouses were bulldozed. Jews who had built textile mills either sold out to conglomerates or closed as the industry consolidated and moved overseas. Cone Mills, once a family-owned concern, had gone public in 1951. After a series of corporate mergers, it was no longer economically viable. Gastonia's Rauch Industries, world's largest manufacturer of satin Christmas ornaments, was sold to Syratech Corporation in 1996. Heilig & Meyers Co., founded in Goldsboro in 1913, expanded from fourteen stores in eastern North Carolina in 1965 to 662 stores in twenty-four states, but its focus on rural towns brought it to bankruptcy by 2000.

North Carolina's growth was spurred by a diversified, postindustrial, high-tech economy. Tobacco-town Durham reinvented itself as the City of Medicine, and its largest employers became the Duke and the Veterans Administration hospitals. "When I was a kid, we had no Jewish doctor," Joe Reznick recalled, but as Wake Forest University Baptist Medical Center expanded, Jewish medical professionals flocked to Winston-Salem. Storekeepers and mill owners had once dominated

Gastonia's Temple Emanuel. In 2008 its president, Jason Gluck, was an electronics engineer and its lay prayer leader, Charles Brown, was a clinical psychologist. Charlotte was second only to New York as a national banking center.

National corporations redrew local economies. Firms identified with Jewish founders like Dell Computers and Google built major facilities, and Home Depot ranked among the state's largest employers. Economies that once depended on weekly paychecks of mill workers or crop liens of farmers now relied on million dollar payouts in federal funds. Duke, North Carolina State, and the University of North Carolina were corners of a Research Triangle Park, founded in 1958. Mammoth facilities arose for the Environmental Protection Agency and the National Institute for Health Sciences. The Park grew to some 7,000 acres with 170 firms employing 42,000. Similar parks rose outside Charlotte and the Triad. Outside Concord, the North Carolina Biotechnology Center drew investment in the hundreds of millions. Wilmington's Screen Gems Studios was among the largest east of Hollywood, the site of some 300 feature films and 8 television serials.

Jews made the transition into the new economy by investing in real estate or new technologies. Civic-minded entrepreneur Karl Robbins, who had sold his textile mill in 1954, purchased 4,000 acres of farmland to create the Research Triangle Park. With the economic landscape changing, Stanley Tanger of Greensboro, starting in Burlington in 1981, developed a national chain of thirty-one brand-name outlet shopping centers focused on boomtowns and tourist destinations. In 1993 it became the first outlet center listed on the New York Stock Exchange.[7]

The North Carolina mantra was "globalization." The Research Triangle Park included French, British, Swedish, Japanese, and German corporations. British pharmaceutical giant GlaxoSmithKline had its American headquarters there. From his Charlotte headquarters, evangelist Billy Graham, a farmer's son, operated an international ministry in seven countries. The North Carolina National Bank grew into the global Bank of America. Airports, considered essential to economic viability, offered nonstop flights from Charlotte to Frankfurt and London and from Raleigh-Durham to Paris and London. In the 1990s a Global TransPark with a jetport and Foreign Trade Zone was established in Lenoir County to lure multinational corporations to an economically depressed rural region. The World Wide Web ended the sense of living in the provinces. A survey indicated that 50 percent of North Carolinians saw themselves as "linked to people around the world" as opposed to 29 percent who persisted in seeing themselves as "different from non-southerners." UNC anthropologist James Peacock explained, "It seems what the South is doing is thinking globally."[8]

Since colonial days, Jews had traded in global markets. Junk peddler Louis Gordon's descendants in Statesville were now recyclers exporting metal to China.

The Brenners' Amarr Corporation evolved into a company with four factories, including one in Mexico, and sixty distribution centers in thirty-one states and three countries. Greensboro's Chico Sabbah, using models developed by Lloyd's of London, created the Fortress Re reinsurance corporation. It held bonds on the planes that crashed on September 11, 2001, and found itself financially embroiled with Japanese banks.

Just as the New South had welcomed the Jewish peddler, storekeeper, and industrialist, so, too, did the Sunbelt extend warm greetings to the Jewish doctor, engineer, scientist, professor, and entrepreneur. According to the 1987 *American Jewish Yearbook*, "Jewish population growth occurred precisely in those areas of the country that were experiencing the greatest economic development," particularly in places that made the transition into the "post-industrial 'high-tech' economy." In their demography Jews were following other Americans into the Sunbelt. In 1980 an estimated 15 percent of American Jews lived in the South. That percentage grew to 22 in 1990 and to 27 in 2001.[9] Although major influxes to Atlanta and south Florida skewed these figures, the trend could be seen in the Charlotte, Triad, and Triangle metropolitan areas and also in Asheville and Wilmington. Towns that a generation earlier had counted Jews in the hundreds now did so in the thousands.

North Carolina Jewry equaled or exceeded demographic changes transforming both the state's population and American Jewry. Sixty-seven percent of Charlotte's Jews had college or graduate degrees. In the 1990s 51 percent of American Jews could make such a claim, compared to 26 percent of Americans, and 22.5 percent of North Carolinians. In the medical, research, and academic community of Durham–Chapel Hill, a survey revealed 23 percent of employed Jews were professors, 18 percent were dentists or physicians, and 8 percent were psychologists or social workers. Even small-town demographics reflected such trends. In 1938 industrial High Point had four Jewish professionals; a 2005 survey revealed twenty-three, including five lawyers and six doctors, among the sixty congregants, more than a third of the community. Only ten had retail stores.[10]

MULTICULTURAL SOUTH

As the South blended into the national cultural mainstream, mass media, particularly television, brought Jewishness into living rooms. Jewish content was disproportionate in American culture. From comedians like Sid Caesar or Milton Berle in the 1950s through Jerry Seinfeld and Jon Stewart in the 2000s, ethnic Jewishness became common currency. Yiddishisms like "kibitz," "schlep," "chutzpah" and "schmooze" were used in contexts and by people that had nothing to do with Jews. Bagels were everywhere—on supermarket shelves, in college din-

STORY: BISCUITS AND BLINTZES

Native southerner Steve Schewel, publisher of Durham's alternative newspaper the Independent, *reflects on how food expresses the contradictions of his southern-Jewish identity.*

So here I am in this holy season struggling with this question: What does it mean that a committed Jew loves to eat pig so much? Oh! For a slab of hard, salty country ham or dripping strips of bacon from Breadman's. Or, best of all, barbecue—chopped or sliced, it doesn't matter—once every coupla weeks from Bullocks. . . .

Presiding at the Passover table, Grandpa Abe taught us that Jews were a people apart, chosen, supposed to act with a special ethical quality. We were different, and the difference was good. . . . Two decades later, it is still food through which I embrace the Southern Jewish paradox. During the Passover season I forego eating bread in favor of matzoh all week long. That week, though, I'm also likely to lunch on pig meat and greens at Big Ed's.

Friday nights my family gathers round to kindle the Sabbath lights, bless the wine and the challah. At breakfast the next morning, during the heart of the Jewish day of rest, you're likely as not to find that same family slurping down pork sausage at the Waffle Shop . . .

There are important similarities between my two cultures, the Jewish and the southern. Each has a sense of its chosenness, each a sense of its historic burden of defeat and suffering—the Jews' centuries-long exile from Jerusalem; the Southern history of slavery and the Lost Cause.

Too heavy? Then let's do what we've always done; join around a table of good food to make it right. If you're a Southerner, slather your biscuit with butter. If you're a Jew, bathe your rye bread in schmaltz. If you're like me, you can do both.[1]

1. Steve Schewel, "Biscuits and Blintzes: Growing Up Jewish in the Fatback South," *Independent* 10, no. 41 (7 Oct. 1992): 10–11, 13.

ing halls, in motel lobbies—while the traditional biscuit was consigned to ethnic southern eateries. At Raleigh's legendary Upstairs deli, Leah Levine presided over a lunchtime crowd of judges, legislators, and politicians, including the governor, who savored chicken soup and matzo balls, pastrami, and cheese cake, all prepared by African American cooks. An appreciation of Jewish ethnicity supplemented the religious philo-Semitism engrained in southern Christianity. Jews were not so strange.

The metropolitan South where most Jews settled differed little from the places they had left. The Sunbelt's generic landscape of subdivisions, chain stores, fast-food outlets, and shopping malls expressed no regional identity. The Carolina Panthers and Charlotte Bobcats competed in national sports leagues, and the Carolina Hurricanes won an ice hockey world championship playing in a Raleigh arena named for a Canadian bank. Skyscrapers suggested that Charlotte had left Mayberry far behind. Scholars of southern identity debated whether regional differences persisted, often lamenting what they observed to be their attenuation if not absolute demise. Charlotte's international airport featured rocking chairs in its modernist atrium so that jet set travelers could enjoy front-porch southern hospitality. Such gestures were symbolic of a grace and gentility rapidly passing.

Not only was the North coming south, but southern culture was pervading America. The elections of Lyndon Johnson, Jimmy Carter, and Bill Clinton suggested that southern politics were no longer outside the national consensus. NASCAR, whose origins trace to moonshiners on dirt roads, was covered in the *New York Times*. Country was a national music. Jews, once reluctant to move south, no longer felt they were moving into an alien, unfamiliar territory.

Being southern was a matter of ethnicity even more than geography. With the civil rights revolution and influx of outsiders, southern identity itself was "destabilized," surveys revealed. "Its meanings are now fluid and ambiguous, and its bearers are now likely to be quite diverse." The South continued to differ from the nation in its "poverty, evangelical Protestantism, and political conservatism," but its culture had largely merged into the American mainstream. Some 96 percent of Jews who were "lifelong southerners with regional accents" identified as southerners, same as Protestants. "Of course, I'm a southerner," Carolyn Weill LeBauer drawled. "What else would I be? I was born in Greensboro." Yet, native Jews were outnumbered by "unacculturated geographic southerners," who were mostly transplants lacking southern ancestry. Southern identity was largely a matter of self-identification. "I'm not really a Southerner," Robert Liverman said in his Massachusetts accent, "except I consider myself a Southerner" after a half century in rural Roanoke Rapids.[11]

Newcomers noted how the South had slowed them, how they had adopted southern manners if not the speech. "Everybody was so kind and polite," Maurice "Chico" Sabbah reflected, when he and his wife Zmira stepped from a New York flight. "I think we both felt—after the initial getting used to, which wasn't very long—in love with North Carolina." Commonly, Jews like the Sabbahs contrasted the laidback lifestyle with the harried pace of urban northern life. On the irreverent "BBQ Jew" Web site, native North Carolinian Porky Le Swine and New Jersey transplant The Rib Rabbi reviewed roadside joints convinced "that the Promised Land is not flowing with milk and honey but barbecue and hush puppies."[12] Such self-conscious southern-Jewish blending was an extreme example of how quickly and congenially Jews acculturated to the South. Jews were normative southerners. As a third-generation North Carolinian growing up in Statesville,

Barry Gordon reflected, "I didn't feel any different than the Baptist child, or the Presbyterian, or the Methodist. . . . We enjoyed rock-n-roll, going to the drive-in, Friday-night football games, the total American experience."

Jews were now thoroughly integrated into a diverse corporate economy, no longer fitting in an ethnic niche. Jews found places in boardrooms and executive offices. Larry Brown coached the Charlotte Bobcats while Chuck Lieberman of Deep Gap headed the Association of Jewish Christmas Tree Growers. The state's military bases drew Jewish career soldiers. Brothers Paul and Irving Barker of Wilson, sons of an immigrant storekeeper, were veterans of three wars who rose to the rank of colonel. As the state promoted itself as a research and science center, it proudly touted its four Nobel Prize winners, two of whom were recently transplanted northern Jews. Research Triangle scientists Gertrude Elion and Martin Rodbell won Nobels in Physiology in 1988 and 1994 respectively. The stereotype of the southern Jew as a downtown storekeeper was gone.

MULTICULTURAL NORTH CAROLINA

Not merely in its global trade relations but in its own composition North Carolina was rapidly becoming a multicultural society like mainstream America. The nation's regions were distinguished by their ethnicities—Asians and Hispanics in the Far West, blacks in the South, Hispanics and Native Americans in the Southwest. In the North, with its European immigrant legacy, the primary marker of white identity was ethnicity—Italian, Polish, Irish, Slavic, or Jewish. North Carolina held historically a Protestant people divided along a black and white racial line, but the Sunbelt redrew this distinction. With new migrations Jews were increasingly joined by descendants of other hyphenated ethnic groups. Roman Catholic dioceses reported exponential growth. From 1971 to 2000 the percentage of Catholics in the Triangle area grew from 2.5 to almost 7.0 percent, while the percentage of Southern Baptists declined from about 24 percent to about 13 percent. From 1995 to 2000 North Carolina gained about 338,000 residents from other states. From 2000 to 2005 52,012 New Yorkers moved to North Carolina. In 1980 24 percent of North Carolinians were born out of state. In places like Wake County (Raleigh) and Mecklenburg County (Charlotte), about half made that claim. With legal segregation ended, African Americans who generations ago had fled the South for the urban north began a reverse migration that totaled more than 100,000 from 1970 to 1980 alone.[13]

As North Carolina grew multicultural, it returned in measure to its colonial legacy as an immigrant, polyglot society. In 1990 2 percent of North Carolina's population was foreign born; by 2000 that rose to more than 5 percent. Eight percent of its people spoke a language other than English in their homes. With the

Julian Rauch kicks winning field goal for Appalachian State against Michigan. (Marshall Rauch)

arrival of Asian, Arab, and Hispanic peoples, Jews were no longer the region's most conspicuous aliens. Hispanics composed almost 7 percent of the state's population, and Asians almost 2 percent. In 2008 the state held thirty-four mosques in seventeen cities.[14] Churches conducted Korean, Spanish, Ukrainian, and Polish services. When Greenville's Bayt Shalom Synagogue moved to a new sanctuary, its former home became a Hindu temple.

As white people, well educated and middle class, Jews broke through glass ceilings. Just as Jews had once concentrated in dry good trades, so, too, did new immigrants establish ethnic economies. Chains of family-owned Mexican tiendas and restaurants extended into small towns. Palestinians and Lebanese operated convenience stores, and Pakistanis and Indians owned motels. Highly

PORTRAIT: MISS NORTH CAROLINA

For Jews the beauty queen represented Anglo-Saxon values. She was to be not merely chaste and virtuous but also blonde, blue-eyed, and pale-skinned. The selection of Bess Myerson as Miss America in 1945 was a milestone for the nation's Jews, a validation after the Nazi racial degradations. Southerners had long placed women on pedestals. Jewish girls, too, aspired to be Junior Miss Azaleas or high school May Queens. When Hannah Block, a former nightclub singer who created the pageant for Wilmington's Azalea Festival, was asked what was involved in training a beauty queen, the daughter of Lithuanian Jewish immigrants responded, "I taught them that good, old fashioned southern charm."

In 1970 Miss North Carolina was a brown-eyed, olive skinned, dark-haired beauty from Asheville, Connie Lerner, the daughter of Auschwitz survivors. She dated only Jewish boys, she told reporters, not wanting to "open myself up to complications I couldn't handle." She was photographed demonstrating with United Synagogue Youth at a Charlotte courthouse on behalf of Soviet Jewry and listed among her credentials her regional presidency of B'nai B'rith Girls.[1] Lerner represented the state at the Miss America pageant in Atlantic City. For North Carolina Jews her selection confirmed that North Carolina was embracing a more tolerant and inclusive southern identity than lily white Christian. That year an African American was a runner up.

1. Eli Evans, *The Lonely Days Were Sundays* (Jackson: University Press of Mississippi, 1993), 37–38.

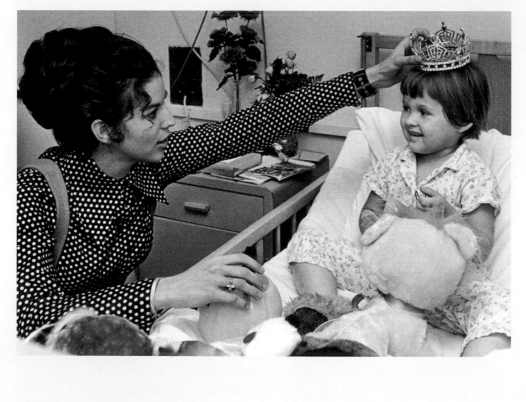

Connie Lerner, Miss North Carolina 1970, visits a hospital. (Carpenter Archives, Wake Forest University School of Medicine)

educated immigrants of all nations were found in research laboratories, college classrooms, and high-tech entrepreneurial centers. When Karl Straus as president of the Asheville bar spoke at a citizenship ceremony, he emotionally told the immigrants that he had stood in their place a half century earlier as a refugee from Nazi Europe.

With multiculturalism, Jews were more willing to assert their Jewishness in the public sphere by placing a Hanukkiah in public squares or wearing a skullcap at school or work. The universalism of brotherhood was supplanted by a celebration of differences. The "influx of people from different areas" led to broader thinking, Sandra Levine observed. "Charlotte in particular has become a much more accepting city of diversity, especially in the past fifteen years."[15]

With racial integration, the paternalism that had governed race relations yielded to a greater egalitarianism. Rather than as a yardman or nanny, Jews now knew African Americans as colleagues at work, personal bankers, or school-teachers. In the 1980s the national black-Jewish civil rights alliance broke under the stresses of affirmative action, the anti-Semitism of Louis Farrakhan, and Israeli relations with apartheid South Africa. In the urban north, Jews and blacks locked in bitter territorial disputes over political redistricting and local control of schools. Multiculturalism also spawned an identity politics that pitted groups against each other. Occasional tensions were felt in North Carolina, too. A black labor leader asserted, without evidence, that Jewish administrators were blocking black progress at Duke Hospital. Black Muslim students at historically African American campuses echoed Farrakhan's rhetoric about Jews as "Children of the Devil." When philosopher Ernst Manasse taught a class on "black power" at North Carolina College, he found a "tension . . . as there had never been before." Militant and moderate students argued, and half walked out.[16] Yet, Jewish-black relations in North Carolina were not embittered, and the conditions that fermented urban black-Jewish conflict were little in evidence. Blacks who ran for political office in North Carolina, notably Charlotte mayor and senatorial candidate Harvey Gantt, enjoyed public and widespread support among Jews. Generally, Jews who won elections did so with black backing.

Concerned with worsening black-Jewish relations nationally, Jews in Durham–Chapel Hill created a Black-Jewish Roundtable in 1985 to discuss issues like apartheid and affirmative action. The black and Jewish politicians and professors discovered that they shared similar liberal views. In 1990 the group met with school superintendents in an African American church to discuss gifted-child programs, which blacks felt unfairly tracked their children. Jews found difficulties identifying black leadership for such programs, and the elites who met did not always reflect the grass roots of a diverse African American community. Class divisions continued to separate Jews and blacks. However much Jews continued to view themselves as a victimized, minority people, they were from a black perspective members of the white elite. By income and education Jews were statistically a privileged people. What Jews and blacks continued to share from a national perspective was a commitment to liberal politics.

Jews and blacks remained largely apart socially and residentially, reflecting white and black relations generally. Contacts tended to be through individual advocacy or congregational efforts. In Whiteville, circuit rider Reuben Kesner established the Columbus County Community Center, the 4-C's club, which became a hang-out for both white and black kids, who called him "Rab" or "Ruby Baby."[17] He persisted despite public resistance to the race-mixing evident there. With the Reform movement's legacy of social activism, rabbis in Charlotte, Durham, and Greensboro maintained warm personal friendships with black clergy. In 2000 Durham's Judea Reform joined with the First Presbyterian Church and Fisher Memorial United Holy Church, an African American congregation, on a multiracial, multireligious tour of Israel.

Although the tenor of racism ameliorated, extremists continued to target Jews and blacks. White supremacist groups like the Christian Knights of the Ku Klux Klan or Confederate Knights of America called North Carolina home. When elderly Laura Weill Stern Cone donated money for a statue of Martin Luther King Jr. in Greensboro, she received death threats. Periodically, fliers or mailings appeared denouncing "the Jewish establishment and their pet Negroes in the NAACP." In 1979 members of the Communist Workers Party drove from Durham to Greensboro to join an anti-Klan, anti-Nazi rally. Jim Waller, Mike Nathan, and Paul Bermanzohn were community activists who had organized black workers and provided medical services to low-income African Americans. Nathan served as a pediatrician at a black community clinic. As they marched, armed Klansmen ambushed them, killing Nathan and Waller and wounding Bermanzohn. The Jewish community had little sympathy for their politics, but the shootings shocked them, even more so when the Klansmen were acquitted. The victims, however, saw themselves as Jewish radicals. Bermanzohn's parents were Holocaust survivors, and Nathan's widow appealed to Jewish groups for support.[18]

Historically, local and state politics were marked by conflicts between progressive and conservative forces. The state that repeatedly sent Jesse Helms to the U.S. Senate, often by narrow margins, also elected James B. Hunt Jr., four times to the governorship. Jews were especially close to Hunt. Greensboro's Arthur Cassell served as his finance director during his celebrated 1984 senatorial race against Helms, the most expensive in history. Jews who sought office most often ran as moderates or progressives, less often as conservatives. Ada Fisher was a noted

African American member of the Republican National Committee, and Thomas Roberg ran unsuccessfully for Congress as a conservative Republican in 1998 from the Research Triangle area. The plutocracy of white Anglo-Saxon businessmen yielded to "citizen-power" coalitions, and blacks, women, and ethnic minorities won local and statewide office.[19] When Governor Hunt appointed longtime adviser Muriel Offerman secretary of the Department of Revenue, she became the first Jew in the Council of State.

In the 1970s Jewish politicians were still entangled in racial identity politics. In 1972 Benjamin Schwartz was elected Wilmington's mayor just as the town faced international scrutiny over the racially incendiary case of Rev. Ben Chavis and the Wilmington Ten. Violence erupted after Chavis had led church-related activists in a boycott of segregated city schools. Two died. A Schwartz store burned. Amnesty International regarded the Ten's trial and prison sentences as unjust, and the convictions were overturned. Mayor Schwartz positioned himself as a reconciler, convincing a Klan leader to sit down with a black editor. "He's too nice a guy," a conservative newsman complained. The Rights of White People threatened to tear down the mayor's house. "We must resolve our differences by being vocal, not violent," Schwartz explained.[20] Schwartz went to the state legislature,

PORTRAIT: MARSHALL RAUCH

"Can a tall, dark and handsome Jew from New York City survive and prosper as an aspiring politician and manufacturer (of Christmas ornaments, no less) in rural, agricultural prominently Protestant North Carolina?" a Raleigh newspaper asked in 1970. The reporter answered his own question: "It's what's happening."

Marshall Rauch left Long Island for Duke University in 1940, less to realize his father's ambition to become a doctor than to play basketball. At Duke, he met a coed from Gastonia, Jeanne Goldberg, the daughter of immigrants who had prospered in the textile industry. After war broke out, Rauch joined the army. He returned with five combat medals, married the girl he left behind, and went to work in the textile industry. In 1963 he received a patent for satin Christmas ornaments, and Rauch Industries grew into the world's largest producer.

In 1955 he first ran for Gastonia city council, winning two terms with African American support. In 1966 he was elected to the State Senate from Cleveland and Gaston County, although he fared badly in Klan precincts. In Cherryville, a Rauch billboard was defaced with "Jew." Once he approached a farmer

Marshall Rauch with his daughter at the state legislature. (Marshall Rauch)

and in the 1980s his brother Bill was elected mayor. Bill Schwartz had political experience as a city councilman, chair of the United Way, and president of B'nai B'rith. Another councilman, Irv Fogler, had the distinction of serving as president of both the Reform and Conservative congregations.

As mayor of Lumberton, a small eastern town, David Weinstein also found himself embroiled in racial-identity politics. Robeson County, where his family had lived since 1897, divided among whites, blacks, and Indians, primarily the mixed-race Lumbees. Racial divisions meant three school systems, three water fountains. In 1988 a Tuscarora Indian seized hostages to protest alleged police plowing behind his mule, who asked Rauch if he were "Hebrewish." When he said that he was, he won his vote.

Rauch was elected for twelve terms until defeated by the Republican tide of 1990. Elected to the state Senate, Rauch was touched when it amended its rules, without his asking, to permit hats to be worn in the chamber so that even rabbis could serve as Senate chaplains.

Rauch's reputation as a legislative "watchdog" earned him chair of the Finance and Appropriations Committees. A fiscal conservative and a social liberal, he supported improved migrant-labor camps and tax fairness for the poor and elderly. His opposition to the equal rights amendment for women, despite a personal phone call from President Jimmy Carter, proved contentious. Rauch was one of the state's most powerful politicians in "influence and effectiveness."

Rauch's public service paralleled Jewish leadership. He supported legislation to create the Holocaust Council and pushed forward a bill to have Yom Kippur recognized as a holiday. President of Gastonia's Temple Emanuel and B'nai B'rith Lodge and a Sunday School teacher, Rauch also headed the state's United Jewish Appeal and Lubavitch Hasidic organization. The Rauch Family Foundation endowed buildings, professorships, and athletic facilities at community colleges and universities across the state, most notably in Gaston County. Political journalist Paul O'Connor commented, "He deserves the title of Mr. Public Servant."[1]

1. Ned Cline, *Success Is a Team Sport: The Marshall Rauch Family Story* (Gastonia: Rauch Family Foundation, 2004), 153, 163, 172, 165; *Raleigh News & Observer*, 1 Mar. 1970.

corruption. Shortly thereafter a Lumbee judicial candidate was murdered. The governor intervened, and world media focused on the rural town. Weinstein—described as a "courtly, distinguished" southerner—explained to the *New York Times*, "We have a tri-racial community here, and I'm a Jewish Mayor presiding over a city in the heart of the white Bible Belt, with three blacks and one Indian on the City Council." Weinstein's politics placed him among business progressives: "Economic development and human relations are the big issues in the city and the county," he explained. "If you don't get along, you're not going to get industry." A dissenting Indian editor described Weinstein as "one of my favorite people."[21] Weinstein went from the mayor's office to the state senate.

Five-term state representative Stan Fox came from Oxford, a town that received notoriety after a black veteran was shot to death in 1970, and the murderer was acquitted. He ran in a majority African American district, and a black educator volunteered to serve as his campaign manager. Campaigning in black churches, Fox defeated a black physician from a neighboring town. His winning margins subsequently increased, and in his last two terms he was unopposed.

By the 1980s being Jewish was rarely a political issue as it had been for an earlier generation of Jewish politicians. In the foothill town of Morganton, native son Melvin Cohen was first elected mayor in 1985. He won nine terms, serving twenty-two years, "with crushing margins over his opponents." Often he was unopposed. His efforts to revive downtown with greenways and festivals were appreciated. In mountain Hendersonville, Don Michalove served sixteen years on the city council, twelve of them as mayor. When the Ku Klux Klan asked him for a permit to march, he granted it but told them, "I'm Jewish." The "fun part" was when he sent them to the police chief, who was black. Kenneth Michalove was elected mayor of Asheville after lengthy service as city manager and town councilman during which he played a central role in downtown urban renewal. His resume included presidency of the Jewish Community Center and an executive post with Opportunity Corporation, working to improve schools and public housing as the city integrated. In Elizabethtown, a heavily black eastern hamlet of 4,000, clothier Wallace Leinwand served six years as mayor in the 1990s. The *Bladen Daily Journal*, saluting him as "a positive force," identified him as the son of "a proud Jewish immigrant," who had come in the 1930s.[22] In Holly Ridge, grocer Alfred Popkin was mayor. They, too, were "our Jews."

In socially conservative North Carolina, politics meant accommodation. After two prominent Jewish legislators voted against the equal rights amendment, a female senator confronted them, telling them pointedly that a "person of your race" should support it. Surveys showed southern Jews to be less liberal than northern Jews on racial and political issues, but more liberal than other southern whites. To appease conservatives, Mayor B. D. Schwartz gave presidential candidate George Wallace the keys to the city when he campaigned in Wilmington but then was accused of a "great betrayal" for commuting the jail term of a teenaged black protestor. When Boone councilman Saul Chase, a school principal, ran for reelection in 1990, an opponent passed out unsigned fliers accusing him of having "a goal to wipe out Christian influence from our town." Chases's wife had published op-ed pieces expressing her discomfort as an "outsider" in the Bible Belt.[23]

In the college town of Chapel Hill, politics were liberal. Ken Broun, who was elected mayor in 1991, was a former dean of the UNC Law School who had worked for legal rights in South Africa. The town also elected Joe Herzenberg to its town council. A socialist and civil rights activist, Herzenberg won renown as the first openly gay elected official in the South. That Broun and Herzenberg were Jews was not noted.

Jews were elected to the state legislature in disproportionate numbers. Dennis Winner and Leslie Winner were the only brother and sister in the legislature's history to serve simultaneously. Senator Franklin Block was the son of Wilmington's mayor pro tem. New Jerseyan Jerry Popkin ran a populist campaign to upset a popular incumbent from Onslow County in 1976. Rick Glazier, a labor lawyer, listed his experience as a Sunday School teacher and president of Temple Israel in winning three terms in religiously conservative Cumberland County. An advocate of social programs, he was unopposed for a fourth term. In the bedroom suburb of Cary, Jennifer Weiss cited her background as a lawyer and stay-at-home mother when she ran for the legislature from Wake County. Winston-Salem's Ted Kaplan served six years in the State House and ten in the Senate, where he was twice elected majority leader as one who could work across party lines.

MULTICULTURAL JEWS

In some measure the multiculturalism transforming North Carolina society generally was felt within the Jewish community. Jews were a global people, and the blending of the various ethnic strands of Jews in Israel—Ashkenazi, Mizrahi, Sephardic, Ethiopian—had its counterpart in American Jewish culture. Jewish food at a wedding or bat mitzvah now consisted not just of bagels and lox but also Israeli humus, tabouleh, and falafel. A trickle of the larger migrations of Jews from Arab lands, Cuba, Israel, and, most especially, the former Soviet Union arrived in North Carolina. In the latter case numbers were sufficient to form subcommunities. The aftershocks of the Holocaust were still felt as European émigrés and their children continued to arrive, like other Jews, for retirement or career opportunities.

Jews from Arab lands were displaced after the founding of Israel in 1948. These émigrés integrated generally into the Jewish community. Iraqi Ezra Meir was an engineer who worked on the Duke campus before moving to Wilmington. Professor Jack Sasson, raised in Lebanon, was a distinguished scholar of Assyrian in UNC's Religion Department who regularly lectured on his Syrian heritage before Jewish groups. At his Passover seders, he walked around the table, a bag of matzo slung over his back, as his ancestors had for generations. Eve Gelfand of Winston-Salem recalled her family's dislocation from Egypt in 1948. The textile industry drew Denise and Herb Somekh, natives of Iraq, to Greensboro. Conscious of their lost heritages, they otherwise lived typically middle-class suburban Jewish lives. Esther M. Grosswald was raised in Brooklyn's Syrian community but had married an Ashkenazi Jew. In Charlotte, she enjoyed speaking Arabic with the occasional Middle Eastern visitor. The leader of Fayetteville's Temple Israel was Rabbi Yosef Levanon, whose family had left Turkey for Jerusalem in 1948. With a doctorate in Jewish studies, Rabbi Levanon was an authority on Sephardic culture. The benefactor of Greensboro's American Hebrew Academy, Maurice "Chico" Sabbah, embodied an emerging global Jewish identity. His father was a Greek Jew from

Rhodes, and his mother was of Russian ancestry. His parents were joined by their Zionism, and Sabbah married an Israeli. Intramarrying with Ashkenazi Jews, Jews of Mediterranean origin had broken from tightly knit ethnic enclaves.

Israelis also formed a subcommunity. UNC psychologists Amnon and Aviva Rapoport, Israeli nationals, recalled that "from 1961 to 1966 hardly any attention was paid to us by the Jewish community," but after the 1967 war they became suddenly popular. Israeli academics took positions on campuses and in research laboratories. Israelis owned chains of souvenir shops along the Carolina coast. The airways between Israel and North Carolina were busy ones, and for most Israelis immigration was not a rupture from the Jewish homeland but, with the advent of multiculturalism, an added nationality. Israelis taught Hebrew and Jewish studies in day schools and at congregations.

Latino Jews, like their Jewish neighbors, tended to have family roots in Eastern Europe. Rosa Perelmuter, a professor of Romance Languages in Chapel Hill, wrote about the dislocations that took her family from Poland to Cuba to America. In Charlotte, Cubans formed a subcommunity. After the Castro takeover, several extended families—Baicovitz, Kaplan-Wojnowich, Rosenberg, Luski, and Kier— arrived to reestablish themselves in the textile industry. They were drawn by business contacts with Speizman Industries, a distributor of textile machinery. The cultures of these families of East European origin were deeply rooted in Yiddishkeit, and they blended easily into the Ashkenazi community. Their Jewish bonding was heightened by Holocaust experiences. Their narratives were sagas of the twentieth-century's Jewish traumas. Lithuanian-born Suly Chenkin survived the German occupation as an infant when her parents placed her in a sack and threw her over the ghetto fence. A Christian family found and raised her. Surviving the war, the family scattered to three continents until they reunited in Cuba. These Jubans, as they were called, retained vestiges of their Latino acculturation, gathering to share Cuban memories and Spanish conversation and retaining a certain culinary fondness for beans and rice. Yet, their lifestyles were indistinguishable from those of other Jewish suburbanites. Abraham and Isaac Luski contributed to Charlotte's development through Shamrock Realty as brokers and operators of office, residential, and shopping complexes.

In 1964 a national Student Struggle for Soviet Jewry organized demonstrations before the United Nations in New York to demand that the Soviets end the "spiritual genocide" against the Jewish people. Four years later Elie Wiesel published *The Jews of Silence*, which revealed the surprising persistence of a living Judaism in the communist state. A forgotten community was thrust into the forefront. Recalling the failures to save Nazi-threatened Jewry, Jewish youth pushed to found in 1971 the National Conference on Soviet Jewry to save the remnant.

Charlotte Jews
welcoming émigrés
from the Soviet Union.
(Charlotte Jewish
Historical Society)

Soviet Jewish emigration was an issue in America's Cold War policy—the Jackson-Vanik amendment linked Soviet relations to Jewish immigration—and Jews began leaving in the thousands and then tens of thousands monthly for Israel and America. Charlotte's Gorelick family traveled to the Soviet Union to meet its Russian relatives, who pleaded, "Get us out of here." The Russians showed their cousins decades of letters they had saved from their American family.

In 1974 Walter Klein, a Charlotte public relations executive, read an article in the *Jewish Post* about the need to find homes for Russian Jews and contacted the Hebrew Immigrant Aid Society. With the support of his B'nai B'rith Lodge and its Women's Auxiliary, he rallied the Charlotte Jewish Federation to sponsor a half-dozen families. Local Jewish federations in Durham, Raleigh, and Greensboro also formed resettlement committees so that engineers, musicians, scientists, and doctors could find housing and jobs. A concert violinist might start as a deliveryman until his English and skills were sufficient for a professional position. Most families, once they had acculturated, moved on.

The global Jewish politics of resettling Soviet Jews hit Charlotte. Federation leaders argued that immigrants should be directed to Israel, not America, and ended the funding. The B'nai B'rith Women then took responsibility to find homes and jobs and teach skills. Soviets sent to North Carolina tended to be professionals. The first in Charlotte, Boris and Irene Rozovskii, were professors from Moscow State University, who arrived in 1988. Boris, a coveted mathematician, took a position at UNC–Charlotte. He acknowledged "humiliating" anti-Semitism in the Soviet Union, but his main reasons for emigrating were "political and in some sense scientific." By 1990 eight families had been sent to Charlotte, including five engineers, a doctor, a nursing student, a computer programmer, and a violin teacher. In Durham–Chapel Hill a subcommittee of the federation, led by UNC Sovietologist Joel Schwartz and his wife Myrna, oversaw the resettlement. By 1999 Durham–Chapel Hill had thirty-seven families. These émigrés were thoroughly immersed in Russian culture, and many families consisted of Jews intermarried with ethnic Russians. Iosif Vaisman's family had been "nonpracticing" Jews in the Ukraine, but "genetic memory" led him back to the "tradition of my ancestors," and he created the Yiddish cultural Web site Shtetl. The Russians formed their own social circles. They adorned their homes with New Year trees in celebration of a secular holiday and enrolled their children in Russian-language programs.[24]

European-born Jews, displaced by the Holocaust, were drawn to North Carolina for retirement or career opportunity. Fort Bragg physician John Gimesh had burned his yellow star when the Budapest ghetto was liberated, but he kept his sister's framed as a remembrance. Czechoslovakian-born Julius Blum had survived a slave labor camp and served in Israel's Haganah army before coming to Asheville in 1966 to open a textile mill. Several of the state's rabbis—Frank Fischer of Chapel Hill, Henry Ucko of Fayetteville, Karl Rosenthal of Wilmington, and Joseph Asher of Greensboro—were displaced Germans. Rosenthal, briefly imprisoned in the Sachsenhausen concentration camp, lost one son in the Holocaust and another who died while serving with the U.S. Army. When escaping Germany, Ucko's ship was torpedoed in the English Channel, and he spent a night in the cold sea clinging to an overturned lifeboat. He found refuge in the Dominican Republic before taking a rabbinic post in Fayetteville.

European-born Jewish North Carolinians themselves embraced a multicultural identity that reflected the state's globalization. UNC computer scientist Henry Fuchs, whose family had fled Hungary in 1956, returned to his native Tokaj to assist in the restoration of the synagogue where his grandfather had once presided. He located a Tokaj Torah—which an Orthodox priest had hidden during the Holocaust—in Beersheva, Israel, and took possession of it, loaning it to local congregations. His mother Ilona, an Auschwitz survivor, taught the traditional Hungarian art of weaving Torah crowns from flowers. At the invitation of the German government, Jewish émigrés returned to their hometowns, where they were appropriately honored. *Look* magazine published Rabbi Asher's moving account

Attorney Morris Kiel
(back center) with
North Carolinians (left
to right) Carlton Raper,
U.S. Army liberator;
Shelley Weiner, Polish
Holocaust survivor;
Elias Mordechai;
Lillian Andorn, born
in a displaced persons
camp; and Esther
Mordechai, wife of
Elias and, like him,
a Greek survivor
with a concentration
camp tattoo. (Joseph
Rodriguez/*News &
Record*)

of his return to his German hometown, where he reconciled with a classmate, a former Nazi youth. The rabbi provoked controversy by advocating forgiveness and reconciliation, which earned him a Grand Cross of Merit from the German government. UNC sociologist Henry Landsberger helped raise funds for the restoration of the Dresden synagogue where his grandfather had been rabbi. Hanna and Howard Adler of Statesville visited her hometown of Darmstadt in 1982 as guests of the government. Although deeply moved by the German government's efforts to restore Jewish life, Hanna Adler explained, "We have planted our roots very deeply in America."[25]

Holocaust memorialization remained a defining element of Jewish identity. At first, efforts to honor the victims and learn from their example were largely personal. At Weldon's temple, Bernard Szabo showed children the scars from his beatings in labor camps in the Ukraine. Hickory's Marvin Zerden, a war veteran, placed above his store's clothing racks large Holocaust posters distributed by B'nai B'rith to educate his customers. Morris Kiel, an attorney at the Nuremberg trials who had worked to rehabilitate survivors, embarked on a personal crusade of Holocaust education. Yom HaShoah, Holocaust memorial day, made its way onto Jewish liturgical calendars, and the community-wide observances were among the best attended events on the calendar. Synagogues gave honored places in their Holy Arks to Holocaust Torahs redeemed from Nazi Europe through London's Westminster Torah Fund. Communities researched the scrolls, even traveling to their towns of origins.

Public Holocaust observance gained momentum starting in the 1960s and 1970s when Jewish consciousness was aroused in the aftermath of the Eichmann trial and Israel's Six Day War. In 1980 the U.S. Congress created the United States Holocaust Memorial Council, and a year later Governor James B. Hunt Jr., by executive order created the North Carolina Council on the Holocaust. In 1985 it became the first such state council to be established by legislative decree. The council's founding chair was Dr. B. Elmo Scoggin, a retired professor of Hebrew and Old Testament at the Southeastern Baptist Theological Seminary. An indefatigable friend of the Jewish people, Scoggins was well known as a biblical archaeologist and opponent of anti-Semitism. This effort, like that of the United States Holocaust Memorial Museum in Washington, recast the Holocaust as an American tragedy, making it relevant not as an "alien experience" but as an event that touched the lives and basic values of the nation itself—in fact, of all humanity. Thus, according to the North Carolina mission statement, "through its education programs and annual commemorations, the Council strives to help prevent atrocities similar to the systematic program of mass murder by the Nazis of six million Jews and others." Jewish suffering was universalized, placed alongside ongoing genocides globally. In a politics of victimization, Jews staked a place along with Native and African Americans. A Raleigh museum displayed an Anne Frank exhibition for two years.[26]

The council's primary purpose was educational, and it sponsored filmstrips, books, speakers, workshops, and school curricula. Its videotape *The Holocaust: A Personal North Carolina Story* featured interviews with survivors and liberators. The council held an annual Holocaust Memorial service with a survivor or a ranking scholar delivering a keynote address. Educational consultant Linda Scher, accompanied by a survivor or an academic expert, held teacher workshops. In rural communities she had to overcome not prejudice but ignorance. At one such workshop, a teacher asked if Nazi concentration camp medical experiments had not in fact benefited humanity. A frequent council speaker, Auschwitz survivor Gizella Abramson of Raleigh told students at the University of North Carolina at Pembroke, "I'm here because of you young people." At a Salisbury middle school, Dr. Susan Cernyak-Spatz, a native of Vienna, rolled up her sleeve to show her tattooed concentration camp number. A language professor at the University of North Carolina at Charlotte, Cernyak-Spatz wrote a memoir *Protective Custody: Prisoner 34042*. Another literature professor, Lilian Furst of Chapel Hill described her family's ordeal to escape Nazi Vienna in *Home Is Somewhere Else*, depicting herself as living in perpetual exile. Simone Weil Lipman had spent the war years in her native France, rescuing Jewish children in the guise of a Catholic social worker. She continued to hear from these children at her Chapel Hill home.

In Asheville, the Center for Diversity Education created in 1999 "Choosing to Remember: From the Shoah to the Mountains." The center hosted programs that focused on the Holocaust as a touchstone for the teaching of racial, religious, and ethnic tolerance. An oral history project recorded more than twenty-five survivors and witnesses in western North Carolina and created an online archive. These cosmopolitans had left their native Germany, Hungary, or Czechoslovakia and found refuge in England, Australia, or Palestine before migrating to the United States. They came to Asheville like other Jews to retire, join their children, or advance their careers.[27]

If the Holocaust was one pillar of American Jewry's postwar identity, then Israel was the other. Yom HaAtzmaut (Israel Independence Day) and Yom HaZikaron (Israel Memorial Day) entered liturgical calendars. The response of North Carolina, relative to its Jewish numbers, was outsized.

Israel's 1967 Six Day War, Jonathan Sarna observes, "jolted the American Jewish community from [its] universalistic agenda." Fears of a second Holocaust turned to euphoria as Israel defeated the massed armies of three Arab nations. In 1968 North Carolina's annual Institute of Judaism changed its focus from its usual programs on Jewish belief and practice to "The State of Israel." Greensboro's Temple Emanuel had raised funds to build a new school building but instead donated the money to Israel. Those who had been Jewishly ambivalent asserted a newfound pride, and philanthropy reached record levels. In 1967 American Jewry donated a record $240 million to Israel and purchased $190 million in Israel bonds, more than doubling the previous year's totals. The 1973 Yom Kippur War, when Israel's existence again seemed threatened, inspired another outpouring. Jews unfamiliar with Talmudic sages could speak knowledgeably about Israeli politicians and generals, and rabbis were expected to be Zionist spokespersons. Raising funds for Israel, celebrating its history, and lobbying politically on its behalf were integral to Jewish agendas and calendars. Jews in Charlotte and Greensboro especially were linked to AIPAC, the American Israel Public Affairs Committee, which by the 1970s had become a nationally powerful lobbying organization. When Al Gore contemplated running for president, he attended an AIPAC meeting at the home of Paul and Sara Lee Saperstein in Greensboro. North Carolina Jews participated in a coordinated national lobbying effort. "Israel is the heart of the Jewish people," Charlotte's Bill Gorelick explained, the last refuge of a perpetually endangered Jewish people, even though he acknowledged "we have built a wonderful Jewish community here."[28]

A small but significant aliyah (immigration) of Jews flowed to Israel. They

Ricky Leinwand of Elizabethtown with Prime Minister Shimon Peres in Israel. (Ricky Leinwand)

ranged from leftist, secular kibbutzniks to right-wing, Orthodox West Bank settlers. Youth, inspired by the 1960s counterculture, were drawn to Israel by the kibbutz movement with its promise of utopian, communal living and return to the soil. Lee Siegel left a Chapel Hill communal house, the Bayit, to farm on Kibbutz Gezer. Others, raised in suburban synagogues that they found spiritually lacking, had turned Orthodox and felt that only in Israel could they live fully Jewish lives. Avi and Ilana Kleiman moved from a north Raleigh suburb to Efrat on the West Bank. The son of Holocaust survivors, Kleiman, a technology consultant, claimed to be closing a historical "loop" in settling land he knew as Judea and Samaria. One poignant émigré was Greg Barry, raised in an interfaith Chapel Hill home. Drawn to Judaism, he became a Young Judea leader, visited Israel, and in 1981 joined a kibbutz. Called into the army, he was killed early in the Lebanese war. "At that moment I realized how strongly connected I was to the Jewish community," his mother Pat Fischer recalled. She became federation president, married a rabbi, and purchased a second home in Haifa.[29]

Academic exchanges tightened bonds. UNC's Cecil Sheps visited Israel twenty-eight times to build a medical program at Ben-Gurion University and his colleague Morton Teichner advised Bar Ilan University on its school of social work. Israeli professors Bernard Avishai and Yaron Ezrahi held appointments at Duke University. UNC archaeologist Jodi Magness returned regularly for digs. Duke in

Israel, led by the husband and wife professorial team of Carol and Eric Meyers, directed archaeological expeditions and encouraged cooperative efforts between Duke and Israeli universities. The program drew a thousand students.

In 1994 Governor Jim Hunt created a commission to stimulate relations with Israel, which led two years later to the North Carolina–Israel Partnership. It encouraged trade, science, education, technology, and cultural exchanges. More than 100 North Carolina officials and employees traveled to Israel. Although the formal program broke down, by 2006 the state had exported nearly $1.5 billion in goods to Israel. UNC professor Lee Marcus, working with Israeli first lady Leah Rabin, offered technical assistance for the diagnosis and treatment of autism. The Guilford County schools tailored the Israeli YACHAD ("Together") peer-tutoring program to its students. More than eighty North Carolina firms conducted business with Israel. Tom Sloan of Greensboro's Southern Optical worked with a kibbutz factory and a Jerusalem incubator to put Russian émigré scientists to work. Universities, high-tech firms, and agricultural companies established cooperative agreements on research and technology.[30]

Federations twinned their communities with Israeli towns. Charlotte and Hadera, an industrial city in Israel's north, created "bonds of friendship and understanding," linking groups by professional interest and developing communications. The Charlotte Jewish Federation underwrote tutoring programs for immigrant youth, a self-help project for Ethiopians, and a gifted children's project at a technology center. Another program brought together Charlotte and Hadera teenagers for visits to the two countries. Concerned by national surveys that showed American Jews' declining attachment to Israel and their growing rates of intermarriage—Charlotte demonstrated both trends notably—national Jewish philanthropists in 2000 created Birthright Israel, which provided free trips for Jewish youth to the Jewish state. For youth, Zionism was intended as a counterforce to assimilation.

The conflicts in Israeli politics—between left and right, between peace-process opponents and proponents—that divided the American Jewish community were felt in North Carolina, too, although, given the smaller Jewish numbers and southern civility, not as bitterly as in metropolitan Jewish communities. Newspapers regularly featured skirmishes in their editorial pages at each successive Israeli crisis: the intifadas, Lebanese wars, territorial withdrawals, peace process negotiations and breakdowns. With exception, the North Carolina Jewish community was unified in its allegiance to Israel, however differently that was interpreted. Local Arabs occasionally intoned in newspapers and public forums, but communal fears focused more on those whose anti-Zionism was regarded as latently anti-Semitic. After the Yom Kippur War, bumper stickers appeared in

Charlotte reading, "We need oil, not Jews." A prominent local contractor testified before a congressional committee calling upon the United States to honor the Arab boycott of Israel. Archconservative Jesse Helms called for "shutting down Israeli aid," and pro-Israeli supporters flocked to his opponent, Jim Hunt, in the infamous 1984 senatorial election.[31]

Evangelical Christians rooted their faith in Zion. Christians, on issues like trading occupied Palestinian land for a peace, sometimes exceeded Jews in their zeal for Zion. The Abundant Life Baptist Church of Goldsboro flew an Israeli as well as an American flag. Accompanied by North Carolina Jews, Jesse Helms visited Israel in 1985 after his near defeat. Visiting the Western Wall in Jerusalem, adorned in a skullcap, he reversed direction and proclaimed his support of Israel. Billy Graham, who repeatedly apologized for anti-Semitic remarks made in the Nixon years, spoke of his "love of the Jewish people," and his daughter volunteered on a kibbutz. The Billy Graham Evangelical Association produced a documentary on Israel titled, *His Land*. When Greensboro's Zmira Sabbah visited farms to pick vegetables, the farmers, noticing her accent, would ask where she was from. When they learned Israel, "they fell in love with her," her husband Chico recalled. They brought out their Bibles and assured her that God had promised Israel to the Jews, not to the Arabs.[32] Fundamentalists whom Jews had regarded warily for their intolerance now saw Israel's ingathering of exiles as a prelude to the Second Coming. This Christian dispensationalism discomfited Jews, although some welcomed Christian support for the Jewish state, believing beleaguered Israel should welcome friends wherever they were to be found.

North Carolina Jews, no less than those nationally, directed their ire toward the media for their allegedly anti-Israeli bias. In Charlotte, attorney Mark Bernstein in 1985 sat down with columnist Frye Gaillard of the *Charlotte Observer*, who expressed his "openness and willingness to discuss the issues," adding that he "deeply resents accusations by certain members of the community" who suggested he was anti-Semitic. Having visited Israel, Gaillard expressed "high regard" for the Jewish state. Durham–Chapel Hill Jews who confronted Claude Sitton, editor of the *Raleigh News & Observer*, received a similar response. Jewish delegations regularly lobbied elected officials in support of Israel. Community Relations Councils published addresses of media and government representatives with the admonition, "Once again, Israel faces an hour of need. WRITE YOUR LETTERS NOW!!"[33] Israel's consul in Atlanta traveled a southeast circuit to meet with local groups and address public forums. Speaking schedules brought Israeli diplomats and spokespersons.

The range of opinion found in North Carolina reflected the diversity within the American Jewish community rather than any specifically regional feeling, especially as newcomers arrived. In college towns, radical left-wing Jews rankled the community in their Palestinian advocacy. In 2004 the Palestine Solidarity Movement held its fourth annual conference at Duke. Jewish groups expressed outrage, but Duke president Richard Brodhead stood for free speech and academic freedom. Jews—joined by political and campus leaders (including Brodhead)—responded with an antiterrorism concert, a lecture by neoconservative Daniel Pipes, a teach-in with former Knesset speaker Avraham Burg, and a display of a bombed Israeli bus. The conference itself was a microcosm: the fifty attendees included bearded anti-Zionist Hasidim, Palestinians, leftist Israelis, and student activists. Observing local members of Jews to End the Occupation as well as counterprotestors from New York, Duke vice provost Judith Ruderman noted, "The Jews in this country don't speak with one voice." UNC Hillel director Or Mars observed that most campus anti-Zionism came not from Muslim societies but from academic leftists, many of Jewish origin.[34]

Media and public quarrels on Israel were often intramural squabbles among Jews. When Durham Rabbi John Friedman, an outspoken peace advocate, editorialized in the *Raleigh News & Observer* on "Israel's stake in the Palestinians," Susan Behrend of Raleigh responded with a letter in "Israel's Defense," noting that it is "ironic indeed to see Jewish leaders" promoting a dialogue with Palestinians who deny Israel's right to exist. A chapter of Americans for Peace Now, a support group for the Israeli peace movement, arose in Durham–Chapel Hill. Ten North Carolina rabbis from five communities joined 400 rabbis nationally who signed a 2006 *New York Times* letter on behalf of Brit Tzedek v'Shalom, the Jewish Alliance for Justice and Peace. Hendersonville's Rabbi Philip Bentley opined in his local newspaper that "Israel is a secular democracy and . . . the Zionist movement includes many different philosophies, religious and secular."[35]

Middle Eastern politics also had implications for Jews seeking to define their place on the multicultural spectrum. On campuses Jewish-Muslim dialogue groups organized. When Duke hired a Muslim chaplain in 2008, he was welcomed during Ramadan to a "Jewish iftar" at the Center for Jewish Life. The Levine Museum of the New South in Charlotte created the "Families of Abraham," a folkloric exhibit that "celebrated" through photographs and narratives the "life and faith traditions of Jewish, Christian and Muslim families." The focus was both roots "we share" as descendants of a common ancestor and what remains "distinctive." It included panels on the Torah, Bible, and Koran. Rabbi Murray Ezring of Temple Israel saluted it for "opening doors of understanding between people of many faiths and ethnic backgrounds." Imam Khalil Akbar of Charlotte praised it as a "powerful tool for understanding."[36]

Although such programming responded to a national multicultural agenda, native Jews and Arabs cite neighborly relations shaped by their southern acculturation. The Gordons of Statesville held multigenerational relationships with the Palestinian Kutteh family, one of whom was the town's mayor. The Jewish Kittners and the Lebanese Rabils of Weldon were old family friends. Noting Christian and Muslim Arabs on his Boy's Club executive board, Barry Gordon felt, "That's part of growing up in the South—it just doesn't matter."

CHANGING JEWISH LANDSCAPE

The Jewish map of North Carolina reflected economic changes. While Charlotte Jews were building an expansive Jewish campus at Shalom Park, synagogues—nearly a century old—were shuttering in Tarboro, Weldon, Wilson, Lumberton, Jacksonville, and Goldsboro. The fortunes of these eastern North Carolina towns were tied to tobacco and textiles. Merchants' children who had gone to college to study law or accounting headed to Charlotte, Greensboro, or Durham–Chapel Hill, where they could find careers and Jewish community. Often their parents joined them in retirement. The decline of these communities owed less to assimilation than to general economic conditions. These towns were losing populations, and churches, too, closed or lost members.

Jews continued to be an urban people, and the major growth was in the Sunbelt metropolitan centers. In large measure the Sunbelt migration was from suburb to suburb, and the move from Great Neck, Long Island, to Myers Park in Charlotte did not entail a cultural cataclysm. These migrants "fit into the Southern urban environment comfortably because the Southern city is really a suburb," observes David Goldfield, UNC-Charlotte's historian of southern urbanism. The Charlotte and Triangle metropolitan areas each held more than 10,000 Jews. Durham–Chapel Hill saw its Jewish population rise from 545 in 1964 to more than 6,000 in 2008. Greensboro, Asheville, Wilmington, and Winston-Salem also successfully made transitions into a postindustrial economy, and their Jewish populations also burgeoned.[37]

Despite the growth of metropolitan Triads and Triangles, the state held to its historic landscape. Although North Carolina was the tenth-most-populated state, its largest city, Charlotte, still ranked only twentieth in the nation in 2005. As the coast, Triad, Triangle, and Charlotte areas grew exponentially, the northeastern counties lost population. Census data confirm two North Carolinas, a declining agrarian and industrial region and a prospering suburban, postindustrial Sunbelt. Historian Lee Shai Weissbach notes a national pattern: of the 490 small-town Jewish communities he identified in 1927, 253 had "disappeared" by 1983. Others had grown into metropolitan communities.[38] The Jews of the New South mill and market towns did not so much die as move to emerging Sunbelt centers.

STORY: CLOSING A TEMPLE

When Weldon's congregation closed its doors in the early 2000s after nearly a century, Harry Kittner, whose immigrant parents were among its earliest members, reflected on its legacy.

Harry Kittner, farewell to the Weldon temple.
(Chris Seward, Raleigh News & Observer)

What's to happen to our Temple? What's going to happen to the scrolls, the Torahs, the stained-glass windows? But the big thing is, what will happen to the memorial plaques, the *yahrzeit* tablets? In the Jewish religion, in the synagogues, you erect a memorial tablet with a nameplate of a person saying when they were born and whey they died. On the anniversary of that person's death, a candle is lit, usually for 24 hours. You say a memorial prayer, the *kaddish*, a prayer praising God. I would like to give all our artifacts and funds to a new small congregation that needs them. Maybe they would preserve our memorial plaques and say a prayer in memory of our dead.[1]

1. *Raleigh News & Observer*, 14 Mar. 1999.

Small-town Jewish communities were born, or dying ones were revitalized, in academic, resort, and retirement centers as well as in the exurbs of metropolitan areas. Places that once had no or negligible Jewish settlement suddenly had Jewish communities.

As universities dropped their discriminatory practices and Jews flocked to academia, college towns saw their Jewish communities explode. This trend was national, as Madison, Ann Arbor, and Berkeley also experienced dramatic rises. Nearly a quarter of those responding to a Durham–Chapel Hill survey listed their occupation as "professor."[39] As congregations closed or struggled in nearby Kinston, Weldon, and Goldsboro, a new congregation organized in 1986 in Greenville, site of East Carolina University, with its newly established medical school. In Boone, home of Appalachian State University, Jews were searching for land in 2008 to erect a synagogue that would also serve as a campus Hillel. Asheville, Charlotte, Raleigh, Greensboro, Wilmington, and Winston-Salem held rapidly expanding university campuses, drawing Jewish faculty and administrators. UNC-

Charlotte was growing into the largest in the state system. Retirees were drawn to college towns, some through alumni ties, but most by medical facilities and cultural and educational opportunities.

North Carolina, with its mild climate, gained a national reputation as a retirement center. Jews, like other Americans, settled in resort towns from coast to mountains. New communities formed in Brevard, Franklin, Kitty Hawk, Lake Norman, and Pinehurst, while established communities in Asheville, Boone, Hendersonville, New Bern, and Wilmington were revived. Retirees in the golfing resort of Pinehurst organized the Sandhills Jewish Cultural Group in 1981; by 2002 they were worshiping in their own synagogue, Temple Beth Shalom, with a resident rabbi, also a retiree. Retirees needed health care as well as financial and mercantile services, all of which created a prosperity that drew young Jewish families. Floridians with summer homes supported the Mountain Synagogue in Franklin, founded in 1979, which grew to more than a hundred members. Retirees revitalized Agudas Israel in Hendersonville and created the Brevard Jewish Community. B'nai Scholem in New Bern was near closing with 15 households in 1972, but in 2008 the temple celebrated its centennial with 121 households from six counties. The Jewish Community of the Outer Banks met in Kitty Hawk for holiday and Friday-night services. At Fearrington Village, a retirement community

Barbara Thiede, founder of Concord's Temple Or Olam. (Kate Lord)

near Chapel Hill, a havurah, a small fellowship group, of sixty families gathered, and at St. James Plantation, a gated community in coastal Brunswick County, a group organized in 2002 to hold yahrzeit (memorial) services and celebrate holidays.

As congestion and housing prices made metropolitan areas less desirable, Jews settled in exurbs from which they commuted to jobs in metropolitan areas. Those employed in Raleigh and the Research Triangle Park created a community in Cary, once a country town but now a sprawling suburb. Beth Shalom Congregation organized there in 1983, drawing members from the even more distant Apex, Fuquay-Varina, and Holly Springs as development spread into forest and pasture. In Concord, a former mill town on I-85 twenty-one miles northeast of Charlotte, Jews raised funds to construct Temple Or Olam, which first formed as a havurah in 2003. A havurah in the exurb of Matthews grew into a congregation. Lake Norman, twenty miles north of Charlotte, drew both retirees and commuters. Two congregations formed there.[40]

The wave of new arrivals meant that native Jews were a subcommunity of their own hometowns. In the 1980s and 1990s—with the aging of the mercantile generation, the departure of youth, and the arrival of new families—congregations confronted change. The circle was broken. The B'nai B'rith clubrooms where Jews gathered for card-playing camaraderie closed, and the downtown delis where storekeepers schmoozed over lunch shut their doors. The *American Jewish-Times Outlook*, a monthly magazine which reported on the state's Jewish community for more than half a century, ceased publication in the 1990s. Once National Council of Jewish Women chapters were the social and welfare centers of communities; now North Carolina had not one chapter. "There wasn't that oneness anymore," Sam Margolis of Durham lamented.[41]

REVIVAL OR SURVIVAL

In the postwar years brotherhood was America's civil religion, but its gospel of universalism yielded in the late 1960s to an era of personalism.[42] A youthful counterculture promoted self-fulfillment through drugs and enlightenment through Eastern spiritualisms like yoga, zen, or transcendental meditation. Feminists demanded a rewriting of history and tradition that included women in the narrative. Antiestablishment feelings were intensified by a Vietnam War protest movement that questioned authority and sought to tear down, sometimes violently, hierarchies. Century-old traditions were disdained as racist, sexist, or Eurocentric. Being gay became a matter of culture and politics, not just biology. Brotherhood with its three-faith dialogues yielded to a multicultural agenda that advanced race and ethnicity as markers of identity. America was reconceived as a stew rather than a melting pot. If the seventies and eighties were marked by spiritual upheavals, the nineties were marked by an ethnic awareness, a search for roots in a mobile society grown blandly suburban. Jews once committed to universal causes like civil rights or antiwar movements now applied themselves diligently to rescuing Soviet Jewry or engaging with Israel.

Student movements provided much of the energy and creativity transforming American Judaism. Youths who attended summer camps or innovative college programs brought their experiences home. In 1973 *The First Jewish Catalog: A Do-It-Yourself Kit* offered creative approaches to Judaism, infusing holidays with new meanings sensitive to the environment, social justice, and artistic expression. A Jewish handicraft movement inspired creative Hanukkah lamps, Torah mantels, prayer shawls, and marriage contracts. Colorful skullcaps replaced standard black, and Hasidic and Sephardic melodies enlivened liturgies. In 1970s Hillel rabbi Robert Seigel—who, dressed in black leather, rode a motorcycle with a dog perched on its handlebars—instituted a Free Jewish University at Duke and UNC that described a "community-in-formation," raising "questions of identity, feeling, and knowledge." The students studied "kabbalistic mystics" on gathering sparks of divinity to repair the world, a concept of spiritual renewal known as tikkun olam.[43]

Youths experimented with new communal structures based on egalitarian principles. The Bayit commune organized in Chapel Hill. In the 1970s a Progressive Jewish Network of several hundred arose in the Research Triangle, affiliated with the politically activist New Jewish Agenda. It marched in Gay Pride parades and lobbied against apartheid. By the 1990s it had evolved into a havurah—meeting for peace seders, antisexist Purim parties, and Yom Kippur meditations. Such groups were dynamic, and by the late 1990s they faded away. These Jews were attuned to national rather than regional movements.

In the 1960s the havurah became popular for study, worship, socializing, or, in a few cases, living arrangements. The term derived from ancient Pharisaic days, but it also evoked the immigrant chevra. When Jews first organized in Concord and Matthews in the 1990s, they took havurah as a title. Established congregations, Reform and Conservative alike, formed their own havurot, grouping people by ages or interests. The intent was to create community as congregations grew larger with people who lacked local roots or family. Often the havurah consisted of a gathering for a monthly Shabbat dinner.

The institution building of the postwar years yielded to a renewed theological interest, inspired by the neo-Hasidic writings of Martin Buber and Abraham Heschel. Another student innovation that became mainstream in the 1970s was the Shabbaton, a communal gathering that featured a weekend of workshops, worship, and discussion. In 1973 Durham's Judea Reform hosted a "Communal Jew: Getting It All Together," where, as the rabbi sat and listened, congregants proposed a new ten commandments that would enshrine social activism, "mystical relationships with God," and "getting into nature." In place of communal faith commandments, Judaism was becoming personal, democratic, and participatory. Increasingly, Jews described the essence of Judaism as tikkun olam, a cabalistic concept of spiritual renewal that was reinterpreted as a commandment to engage in social and environmental action to fix a broken world. As one Shabbaton participant put it, being a Jew meant becoming "the very best Human Being one could be." The Institute of Judaism held at Wildacres in 1972 chose as its theme, "Relevant Judaism for To-Day and the Future," featuring Arthur Green, a founder of the pioneering Havurat Shalom, and Rabbi Robert Seigel, the North Carolina Hillel director.[44]

Observers of American Jewry gave conflicting interpretations as they studied data collected every decade by the National Jewish Population Surveys. (They also contended on the reliability of that data.) Some proclaimed a Jewish revival or renaissance. They cited the burgeoning day school movement, growth of institutions outside the framework of congregations, and the creativity and commitment of a rising generation. They saw a community transformed, renegotiating the American-Jewish equation and reinventing Judaism for a new age committed to the environment, social justice, and new spiritualisms. In concert with national efforts, North Carolina Jews created new institutions—day schools, summer camps, Jewish studies programs, and new Hillel buildings on campuses—to ensure continuity. Newly expanded synagogues experimented with new worship styles. Film festivals and street fairs drew unaffiliated Jews. Several surveys showed younger Jews more "ritually active" and better Jewishly educated than their elders.[45]

Other observers, deploring rates of Jewish intermarriage and assimilation, saw a Judaism emptying itself of the traditional content that had preserved Jews as one people over generations. In all the liturgical experimentation and religious diversity, they questioned a Judaism that had transgressed boundaries of identity, too willing to blend into the environment. Jewish personalism, the quest for self-fulfillment, threatened bonds of community and tradition. Jews were consumers shopping in a religious marketplace, and Jewish fitness centers, meditation workshops, or Kiddush Cup golf tournaments were no substitute for attending a Sabbath service or studying Talmud. A minority of Jews were synagogue members, and Jews had the lowest rate of weekly worship attendance among religious denominations. A 1998 national survey revealed that only about one-half of American Jews agreed that Jews were an "extended family" and that they as individuals had a "special responsibility" to care for Jews elsewhere.[46] Such feelings had once been the very essence of what it means to be Jewish.

With the flood of new migrants, North Carolina Jewry more resembled national demography. Where once traditionalist congregations debated fiercely the membership of intermarried Jews or even converted spouses, now all tended toward inclusivity. The changing profile of American families, the rise of divorce and single-parent families, shaped congregational dynamics. A 1992 survey of Durham–Chapel Hill Jews showed more than one-quarter living alone. Gays also created a new constituency. In their mission statements congregations echoed messages similar to that of Greensboro's Conservative Beth David: "Our congregation warmly welcomes Jews from all backgrounds and levels of observance. Singles, families, empty nesters, retirees, born Jews, Jews-by-choice and intermarried couples will all find members of our synagogue waiting to help you feel at home."

Especially targeted were interfaith families. They constituted perhaps 10 percent of the membership of Durham's Judea Reform congregation in 1980; by 1992

Rabbi John Friedman estimated it was approaching 30 percent. A 1997 Charlotte Jewish survey of married couples found that 47 percent were intermarriages, 44 percent involved two born Jews. Charlotte's intermarriage rate placed it at the top of forty-one cities surveyed nationally. The situation was more extreme in small communities. At one point B'nai Israel of High Point observed that only two of twenty-four children in its religious school came from homes with two Jewish parents.[47]

Responding to national outreach programs begun in the late 1970s, congregations instituted programs to bring interfaith families into the fold. In Charlotte 34 percent of the children in interfaith families were being raised Jewish while another 20 percent were being raised in two religions. Congregations and federations responded with workshops, seminars, and counseling. Counselors noted that interfaith family problems were heightened in the South, where the likelihood was greater that the non-Jewish spouse was a committed Christian. Conservative and Orthodox rabbis categorically did not perform mixed marriages, whereas Reform rabbis might do so under certain circumstances, as would those who identified as Reconstructionist, a pluralistic movement positioned between Reform and Conservative. A dividing line between the movements arose when Reform and Reconstructionist movements agreed to accept patrilineal, not just traditional maternal, descent as a Jewish qualification. In towns with both Reform and Conservative congregations, the Reform was always the larger and faster growing. Smaller, one-congregation towns were Reform or independent.

If conversion to Judaism had once been rare, now it became commonplace. Often the conversion involved a marriage. In Charlotte 10 percent of Jewish couples reported that one spouse was a convert compared to a national average of 3 percent. Statistics suggest that the rate of Jewish conversion was slowing in the 1990s as acceptance of patrilineal Jews lessened the need to convert to raise Jewish children. A Protestant, Barbara Barrett, who served as president of the Greensboro Jewish day school PTA, observed, "Everybody knows that I'm not Jewish, and nobody seems to care."[48] Moreover, intermarriage no longer carried a stigma. In congregations that would once not accept intermarried Jews as members, they now served as officers and prayer leaders.

The changing family profile reshaped community organizations. Two-career families were less likely to have the freedom to volunteer, and women who had provided a cadre of community activists now were preoccupied with their own careers. In smaller communities individuals by necessity had taken responsibility for group survival. With community growth, that was no longer true. Organizations like the NCAJW, B'nai B'rith, B'nai B'rith Youth Organization (BBYO), and the Wildacres institutes reinforced communal bonds. Children knew each other

North Carolina Association of Jewish Youth. (Steven Leder)

from BBYO and NCAJY dances and meetings, and their parents met at Wildacres and Hadassah or B'nai B'rith conventions. Hadassah remained vital with eleven chapters, and Wildacres continued its institutes, but the camaraderie that had marked B'nai B'rith lodges faded as their core constituency of downtown merchants declined. The thirteen lodges listed in the state, like other service organizations, struggled to enlist youth and define their purpose. The NCAJW and NCAJM evolved into the Carolina Association of Jewish Women and Men before disappearing altogether, preserving its student loan fund. The Blumenthal Home for the Jewish Aged saw its Jewish enrollment decline, and in the 1990s it sold its building as it evolved into a Blumenthal Jewish Home Foundation for Senior Services. It sought ways to assist the state's scattered elderly locally, some of whom resided at the Blumenthal Jewish Nursing and Rehabilitation Center in Greensboro. Membership declined at Charlotte's Amity Club, where Jews had gathered to eat, dance, swim, and play cards. In 1974, with its finances imperiled, members turned it over to the Jewish Community Center (JCC).

Jewish communities were undergoing an institutional realignment consonant with both local needs and national trends. When the Amity Club became a Jewish Community Center, it grew from 130 members to 375. The JCC and the federation became central Jewish addresses. In a previous era, ethnic brokers personally represented the community. Now the approaches became institutional. The Council of Jewish Federations (CJF) linked Jewish communities to a national and international network, and its General Assembly gave place to the grass roots in the plenum of the Jewish people. The theme of "We Are One People" united Jews in Hickory or Whiteville to those in Kiev or Netanya. A significant federation donation conferred community status, and federation dinners and celebrations were community building events. In an effort to unify competing philanthropic efforts, the CJF, the United Jewish Appeal, and the United Israel Appeal merged in 1999 to form the United Jewish Communities (UJC) which enlisted 155 federations and 400 independent communities. Asheville, Charlotte, Durham–Chapel Hill, Greensboro, and Raleigh-Cary all supported their own federations, while eleven other communities were listed as "networks."[49]

Under the federation umbrella were a family services agency and the Community Relations Council. The federations oversaw philanthropy for the community, Israel, and overseas Jewish relief, and its allocations, which often provoked controversy, expressed community values. Increasingly, federations focused their funds on serving local needs rather than sending it abroad to Israel. In 2008 the Jewish Federation of Greater Charlotte raised more than $3 million, of which about $900,000 was for "Israel and Overseas." The bulk of funds supported the local activities of the federation, community center, family services, Shalom Park, and the day and high schools.[50] The federation allowed Jews to affiliate with the community outside the synagogue. Newcomers from metropolitan Jewish communities brought their federation experience with them, and their involvement was welcomed. While synagogues debated roles for women, women assumed leadership positions in federations. When Durham–Chapel Hill organized its federation in 1976, Gladys Siegel became its first president. North Carolina Jews climbed in the national organizational hierarchy. Greensboro's Kathy Manning rose to the national chair of the board of UJC, and Wilmington's Wendy Block chaired its national network.

Statistically, synagogue membership remained the primary agency of Jewish affiliation. Yet, culturally Jews also now had other means to associate beyond the communal structures of synagogue and federation. A 2008 national religious survey revealed that Jews have "group passions and energies . . . invested in causes and institutions which have no genuine parallels among major American religious groups."[51] Asheville maintained a Jewish Business Forum, while Durham–Chapel Hill had a Maimonides Society for doctors. Chapters of MOSAIC drew hikers and lovers of the great outdoors. Asheville, Charlotte, the Triangle, and the Triad sponsored Jewish film festivals, which were nationally popular since San Francisco held its first in 1980. The French, German, and Israeli films featured at these festivals brought cosmopolitan Jewish cultures into local communities, often exploring such issues as gay Jews or Palestinian-Israeli relations. Asheville's annual Hard Lox Festival drew as many as 10,000 into downtown streets to nosh on Jewish foods, listen to klezmer, and stroll among vendors advertising merchandise or community services. UNC's Carolina Center for Jewish Studies sent its faculty into communities. Crowds in Asheville or Greensboro came to hear Marcie Cohen Ferris, author of *Matzoh Ball Gumbo*, lecture on southern-Jewish foodways or Holocaust scholar Christopher Browning present his research on Jewish resistance. The Jewish Heritage Foundation of North Carolina, founded in 1998, sought to validate Jewish roots in the state. Folklorists Sharon Fahrer and Jan Schochet created "The Family Store" exhibition that displayed panels at former sites of Jewish-owned stores in Asheville. Cultural Jewishness appealed to ethnic or secular Jews beyond Judaism itself.

North Carolina communities had lacked the critical mass to create Jewish Community Centers. In 1940 Asheville had laid claim to being the smallest Jewish community in the country to support a JCC, and in 1994 it was demolished to build a new facility with preschool classrooms, a playground, a kosher kitchen, and a gymnasium–social hall. Raleigh purchased rural land with a lake for a day camp and built a pool, recreation facilities, and a multiuse center. Durham–Chapel Hill embarked on a campaign to build its own center.

Two capital developments attested to North Carolina's presence on the global Jewish map: Charlotte's Shalom Park and Greensboro's American Hebrew Academy.

Charlotte's Jews, at a total cost of some $100 million, erected a Jewish campus on fifty-four acres in an upscale suburban neighborhood. After the Amity country club burned in 1983, Charlotte Jews purchased land on Providence Road as a "place for prayer and play." Shalom Park opened in 1986 as a "unifying" center to serve an estimated 10,000 Jews. The site included Reform Temple Beth El, with more than 1,030 families; Conservative Temple Israel, with 760 households; the Levine Jewish Community Center; a pool and athletic fields; a children's Camp Mindy; federation and Jewish Family Service offices. The Levine-Sklut Media Resource Center provided technical assistance to Jewish religious schools across the state through its Carolina Agency for Jewish Education. Nearly a third of the Park's visitors were not Jewish. The enormous scale of the project served as a national model.

The Shalom Park campus in Charlotte, a place to play and pray, is laid out as a menorah. (Mecklenburg County GIS)

Visionary Greensboro philanthropist Chico Sabbah invested some $150 million in creating the American Hebrew Academy (AHA) on 200 rolling acres in Guilford County. AHA was the first pluralistic Jewish boarding school in the world. The scenic Piedmont campus, designed by a Frank Lloyd Wright protégé, featured advanced technology and environmental engineering, all finished in Jerusalem stone. Students debated American politics in Hebrew, overseen by an Israeli teacher. The school held simultaneous prayer services to accommodate both the Orthodox Jew from Mexico City and the Reconstructionist from Vermont. The college preparatory school intended to create a Jewishly literate, committed elite, and it pursued a dual curriculum in secular arts and sciences as well as Jewish studies. One trimester was spent in Israel. The school's founders anticipated that its enrollment would come globally from Jews in isolated communities, but the original impetus came from Sabbah's recognition that Greensboro Jews alone lacked numbers for a Jewish secondary school. Designed for as many as 1,000 students, AHA enrolled 140 by 2007 from twenty-eight states and ten countries. Nearly 40 percent were Conservative: others were evenly divided between Reform and Orthodox.[52] AHA testified both to a pluralistic Judaism and to a global North Carolina.

AHA reflected the Jewish continuity agenda of national philanthropists to refocus resources on Jewish youth. Survey data confirmed summer camping as a formative Jewish experience, especially in socializing youth into Jewish community commitment. While Camp Blue Star and Young Judea flourished, in 1997 North Carolina philanthropist Leonard Kaplan helped endow Camp Ramah Darom just across the state line in Georgia as part of the Conservative movement's national camp program. At Young Judea, camp officer Elyssa Gaffin noted that southern Jewish camps have a different purpose than those in the urban north: "It's all about giving your kids a chance to be surrounded by Jews." A Young Judaea Continuity Study reported in 1998 that camp alumni had low rates of intermarriage and high rates of synagogue affiliation and organizational leadership.[53]

Responding to surveys that suggested supplementary Sunday and Hebrew schools were inadequate to inspire Jewish commitment, philanthropic efforts were directed toward education. Kaplan led a move to erect a new state Hillel headquarters in Chapel Hill, and his son Randall chaired International Hillel. Duke opened the Freeman Center for Jewish Life, which also hosted a Hillel. The Schusterman and Steinhardt Foundations in New York helped underwrite the Jewish Community Day School Network. By 2003 the country supported 759 Jewish day schools enrolling 205,000 students. North Carolina Jewish day schools affiliated with newly formed national organizations like the Partnership for Excellence in Jewish Education and Ravsak: The Jewish Community Day School Network, which offered grants, technical assistance, and educational resources.

The first North Carolina Jewish day school was the Hebrew Academy established in Charlotte in 1971. I. D. Blumenthal rallied the Charlotte community to fund a Solomon Schechter School affiliated with the national Conservative day school movement. It opened with twenty-one students. Over the years, the school went through several permutations as it sought to find qualified Hebrew teachers, secure its finances, and negotiate movement identity. In the 1970s, parents wanting a more comprehensive Jewish education for their children organized the

B'nai Shalom Jewish Day School in Greensboro. Amanda Stang, an early student, found a "comfortable place to be a Jewish kid as opposed to public school where Christians surrounded us."

The state's Jewish day schools were conceived as pluralistic and community-centered rather than movement affiliated. Small numbers and limited resources dictated unity and compromise. Parent and board meetings were often contentious as common ground was sought between those who did not want the school to be "too Jewish" and those looking for firmer adherence to Jewish law. As Asheville stated, "We reach out across denominational borders to attract Reform, Conservative, and Orthodox families; religious and secular; affiliated and unaffiliated." In 1990 the Charlotte Jewish Day School reorganized, and it was opened to "all levels of observance" although children identified as Conservative were a plurality. In Raleigh and Charlotte, Lubavitcher Hasidim operated the schools as community-based leadership faltered.[54]

Typically, the schools began in rented congregational spaces, sometimes adding a trailer, before raising the funds to erect buildings of their own. After first meeting in churches and synagogues, Greensboro's B'nai Shalom Day School erected a building and grew into a program extending to eighth grade. In 1992 twenty parents met to plan a Jewish Community Day School in Durham–Chapel Hill. Three years later a school opened with thirteen students in space rented from Judea Reform Congregation. In 1998 the group dedicated the 14,000-square-foot Lerner Jewish Community Day School, which grew to 136 students in an expanded facility. In 2004 a half-dozen families in Asheville each contributed $500 as seed money to start the Maccabi Academy. They visited Jewish Day Schools across the state and country, and a year later their numbers had grown tenfold. In 2006 the academy began with seven kindergarteners and first graders, and a year later it enrolled twenty. Raleigh's Jewish Academy of Wake County, opened in 2008, was the successor of several day school efforts.

In 1998 North Carolina had thirty-one Jewish congregations; by 2008 that number had grown to more than forty, despite the closing of several small-town ones. Beyond numbers, North Carolina Jewry reflected the pluralism that had become perhaps the most salient feature of American Judaism. Each movement in itself bore such internal diversity that a congregation's affiliation did not precisely describe local ritual practices. High Point used a Reform prayer book on Friday nights, when liberal Jews more commonly attended, and a Conservative one on Saturday mornings, with its traditional Torah service. Indeed, High Point had marched through all the movements from Orthodoxy to Conservatism to Reconstructionism and then to Reform. By 2000 virtually every Jewish orientation—Reform, Conservative, Orthodox, Reconstructionist, Hasidic, Jewish Renewal, humanist—had a presence in the state. On Rosh Hashana, black-coated Lubavitch Hasidim davened in gender-segregated services, while counterculture Jews from an artists' colony blew homemade shofars from Mount Mitchell.

The Reform movement, renamed the Union for Reform Judaism in 2003, grew into the nation's largest Jewish movement with more than 900 congregations and 1.5 million members. Much of its growth was attributed to its more open attitude toward interfaith families and its acceptance of Jews of patrilineal descent. In 1990 41 percent of American Jews identified themselves as Reform, 36 percent as Conservative, 6 percent as Orthodox, and a lesser percentage as Reconstructionist. Yet, surveys also showed decreasing percentages of Jews defining their beliefs

Jews from mountain communities near Penland gather for the annual sunrise shofar blowing on Mount Mitchell on Jewish New Year. (Warren Gentry)

or practices in movement terms. In 1990 13 percent identified themselves as "Just Jewish"; by 2000 that figure had risen to 20 percent. Observers began speaking of a trans- or postdenominational Judaism. "Whom are you affiliated with?" asked Concord's new Temple Or Olam on its Web site. "Judaism," it answered, defining itself as "trans-denominational." These trends were apparently even more pronounced in North Carolina. In 1997 in Charlotte 32 percent defined themselves as "Just Jewish" compared to 26 percent nationally. They were also somewhat more likely to define themselves as Reform, less likely as Conservative, and far less likely as Orthodox. "Religious switching" typified Christian life, too, with 44 percent of Protestants reporting a changed affiliation as they increasingly defined themselves as "nondenominational."[55]

American Judaism was undergoing a historic reinvention, "sometimes, paradoxically," Jonathan Sarna notes, "by promoting radical discontinuities." Judaism was entering a post-rabbinic phase as most self-identifying Jews lived outside the frameworks of traditional law and authority, choosing to follow only those commandments and observe those rituals that spoke to their own moral conscience, spiritual yearning, or social and family needs. The notion of a normative Judaism was open to question. Jews were autonomous and even contradictory in their religious behaviors. A national religious survey revealed that Jews resembled "the religiously Unaffiliated" in being "far less certain about belief in God" than Evangelical Protestants, Mainline Protestants, or Catholics.[56]

Lines between movements blurred. Reform Jews polled in the 1970s called for more liturgy and communal bonding even as services became more democratic and participatory with rabbis deferring to lay leaders. Classical Reform yielded to a neotraditionalism. Pushing forward change was Union of Reform Judaism president Rabbi Eric Yoffie, whose first pulpit was Durham's Judea Reform Congregation. Unlike his predecessor at Judea Reform, Yoffie wore a skullcap and prayer shawl during services and would not officiate at interfaith weddings. The bar and bat mitzvah replaced confirmation as the focus of the children's educational program. When Rabbi Thomas Liebschutz arrived in Winston-Salem as a "traditional rabbi," he moved the congregation from "very Reform" by introducing more Hebrew into worship.[57]

Neotraditionalism challenged Jews raised in classical Reform Judaism. When Rabbi Israel Gerber of Charlotte's Temple Beth El donned a cantorial hat and brought more Hebrew, the congregation splintered. In 1972 Greensboro's Temple Emanuel replaced the *Union Prayer Book* with *The Gates of Prayer*, a flexible siddur that offered liturgical choices. The congregation was torn, and older Jews rebelled. Edward Benjamin of Greensboro complained that children would never learn Hebrew, and he left the congregation and Judaism. To accommodate those who did not know Hebrew, especially as perhaps a quarter of his members were interfaith, Rabbi Fred Guttman passed out transliterated prayer sheets. The congregation also gave non-Jewish spouses worship honors. As the Reform movement grew more traditional, the Conservative movement was moving leftward on gay, gender, and ritual issues, causing turmoil at its Jewish Theological Seminary. Nationally, the Conservative movement, once the nation's largest, was losing members as well as affiliates. Its membership was aging, and its ideology of being modern but rooted in Jewish law compromised its clarity.[58]

A Reconstructionist movement, inspired by the writings of Rabbi Mordecai Kaplan of the Jewish Theological Seminary, had some North Carolina presence, too, in Matthews and Chapel Hill congregations and, briefly, in High Point. Kaplan described Judaism not theologically but as "the evolving civilization of the Jewish people." The movement reinterpreted Jewish practices and reinvented traditions so that they were consonant with liberal, American values. In 1968 it established its own rabbinical college in Philadelphia. Originally focused on communalism and social action, Reconstructionists increasingly emphasized "personal growth and spirituality," evolving from naturalism to neo-Hasidism. A Triangle Congregation for Humanistic Judaism, led by madrikha (lay rabbi) Lois Alpern, also formed.

Following the rationalistic Judaism promulgated by Rabbi Sherwin Wine, founder of the Society for Humanistic Judaism, it appealed to secular, self-identifying Jews still committed to Jewish culture, tradition, and community if not belief. Its liturgy and educational program were expunged of god language.[59]

As movement differences lessened, local demography, even more than affiliation, set the character of congregations. Pluralism had been a historical legacy of small-town Judaism. When Dale Fuerst was asked if Rocky Mount's Beth El was Reform, Conservative, or Orthodox, she answered, "Why yes." Her husband Herbert responded, "People didn't know what they were." Elaine Solomon Zerden of Hickory recalled that "whoever was at the bimah chose the service." Dennis Barker observed of Wilson, "In a small community where you have fifteen families, you're going to have a mixture of everything. We did our own services."[60] Greenville's Bayt Shalom affiliated with both Reform and Conservative movements to maintain household peace. Rural congregations held several sets of prayer books. They were grateful to have prayer quorums, and small numbers dictated unity. A dissident Jew had nowhere else to go.

"Diversity" was the word increasingly employed to describe Jewish practice. "The word 'diversity' may get over-used," noted Winston-Salem's Al Davis, "but I genuinely feel we have a diversity in the congregation we have never enjoyed." President Jerrold Pinsker of Greensboro described Temple Emanuel as "spiritually diverse." The means of accommodating diversity varied by community. At a minyan at Fayetteville's independent Beth Israel, Rabbi Levanon stood next to one worshiper guiding him through the Hebrew book while a neighbor, wrapped in tefillin and tallis, swayed as he davened. At Durham's Conservative Beth El, Rabbi Steven Sager, ordained at the Reconstructionist seminary, created an Orthodox minyan in a basement chapel while leading a Conservative service upstairs. When Greensboro's Temple Emanuel built its resplendent suburban campus in 2002, elderly members lamented the move from the historic downtown Temple that was the treasury of their memories. The change was more than geographic, for the new temple introduced Reform neotraditional services. They formed a corporation to purchase the old building, and the congregation agreed to hold a monthly Friday night service there in classical mode with an organ.[61]

Jews coalesced on consensual issues focusing on youth, social justice, and Israel. In contrast to the rote drilling of past generations, bar and bat mitzvah ceremonies now marked not just the child's ability to read from the Torah and chant the haftarah, but also to complete a mitzvah project for community betterment. "We are teaching them personal responsibility for their own actions and that means a religious requirement to help others," explained Rabbi Murray Ezring of Charlotte's Temple Israel. In Charlotte, Sammy Lerner filled tote bags with toys for special-needs children, and in Greensboro Maya Weinberg collected books for a rural public school. Max Grad of Boone paid weekly visits to children at Baptist Hospital.[62] Banners in support of refugees in Darfur appeared on synagogue lawns, and on the Yom Kippur fast day Jews brought cereals and tuna cans for food banks.

Just as earlier women's movements had a transforming effect on American Judaism, so, too, did the feminism of the late twentieth century. Duke religion professor Carol Meyers's books *Discovering Eve*, *Households and Holiness: The Religious Culture of Israelite Women*, and *Women in Scripture* provided scholarly foundations to a larger effort to write women into the Jewish narrative. Judaism's rituals, beliefs, and theology were reshaped, and lay and spiritual leadership reconfigured. Women had usually taken traditional domestic roles in congregational affairs: their sisterhoods raised funds for social welfare, sponsored community celebrations, supported education, and furnished the kitchen and interior decoration. After World War II, sisterhood presidents joined congregational boards, and as officers, they were often secretaries. In the 1980s women in both Reform and Conservative congregations began serving as congregational presidents. These trends reflected the national mainstream, especially as newcomers brought new perspectives into their congregations.

As women asserted their place, worship became more egalitarian and participatory. The boy's brit milah (circumcision ritual) was joined by a covenantal naming ceremony for girls. By the 1990s congregations adopted gender-inclusive prayer books that the movements were increasingly producing. Blessings were now said not just in the names of the patriarchs but also in those of the matriarchs. Women gathered to hold their own pre-Passover seders. Reform Judaism, with its willingness to rewrite tradition, did not have to contend with legal barriers to gender equality, while Conservative Judaism wrestled with the competing needs to accommodate both lifestyles and commandments. In 1973 the Conservative movement made the momentous decision to count women equally in the prayer quorum. Not every congregation was convinced. Charlotte's Temple Israel, at Rabbi Rocklin's insistence, decided to "maintain the tradition" of male worship, a position he later regretted. Although the Orthodox worshipers were unrelenting, they, too, became more sensitive and accommodating to women's needs than they had historically been. The local Lubavitch Hasidim separated worship spaces for men and women more equitably side by side, and the rebbetzin (rabbi's wife) led study and prayer groups for women.

The final barrier fell as women entered the rabbinate. In 1972 Reform Judaism ordained its first female rabbi, followed by the Reconstructionists two years later, but the Conservative movement did not follow until 1985. Not only men but women with traditional upbringings had difficulties accepting a female rabbi. In 1982 when Rabbi Amy Scheinerman arrived at Weldon's Temple Emanu-El as a student rabbi, she was greeted politely but hesitantly. She had expected as much. Hebrew Union College assigned students without regard to gender. "After the first service, Erev Rosh Hashana, and the first sermon, the ice melted entirely, completely," Rabbi Scheinerman recalled, "and all their warmth, affection, and loveliness were there." She was hired as a monthly rabbi. When Rabbi Lucy Dinner arrived at Temple Beth Or in 1993 as the first woman to serve as a full-time rabbi in the state, some 325 women already held synagogue pulpits nationally. Leah Levine, a member for more than half a century, felt for an older generation "it would have been too difficult to accept." Rabbi Dinner saw herself as a "feminist," but she insisted that her "agenda as a rabbi has always been Judaism first." Indeed, her hiring also owed to the comfort the congregants felt for her as a native southerner and a Chapel Hill alumna. In her first six months, fifty new families joined Beth Or. The assistant rabbi was also a woman. Three years later, Winston-Salem's Temple Emanuel hired Rabbi Marla Joy Subeck, followed two years after that by Rabbi Schindler in Charlotte. By the 1990s women constituted the majority of students at the Reform, Conservative, and Reconstructionist seminaries. Greenville's Bayt Shalom hired Rabbi Alysa Stanton, ordained by Hebrew Union College, who was not only a woman and a Jew by choice, but an African American, a "historic first" in Jewish annals. Women also served in Asheville, Chapel Hill, Durham, and High Point. Rabbi Dinner's son asked if boys could grow up to be rabbis, too.[63]

JEWISH NEIGHBORLINESS

A common refrain among North Carolina Jews was—that in contrast to the divisions that wracked northern, urban communities—Reform, Conservative, and Orthodox Jews enjoyed unusual harmony. Greensboro's Harry Samet noted that "we have a wonderful feeling of Klal Yisrael [community of Israel] here unlike in bigger communities." Certainly congregations competed for members, but in communities with multiple congregations, warm feelings generally prevailed. Small numbers meant that Jews had little choice but to get along. When Rabbi John Friedman arrived at Durham's Judea Reform in 1980, he wrote in the bulletin of Conservative Beth El, "After all, there are not so many Jews in our community that we can remain strangers for very long. . . . The unusually congenial spirit which exists between our two congregations is most refreshing. As many of you know, this is generally not the case in many metropolitan areas." The congregations held a joint yearly service and cooperated on Midrasha, a supplementary program for high-school students. Rabbi Lucy Dinner and Lubavitch Rabbi Pinhas

Rabbi Lucy Dinner, shown here with her son Jacob, in 1993 became the first full-time female rabbi in North Carolina. (Evan A. Pike)

Herman enjoyed harmonious relations not typically found between Reform and Orthodox in the urban Jewish world. Although the Hasidic rabbi did not recognize her rabbinic authority, Rabbi Dinner found him "welcoming and gracious . . . ready to reach for commonalities."[64] Living in such a strongly and pervasively Christian society led Jews to lessen differences. The goodwill also owed to a southern ethos, that sense of neighborliness that persisted even in a changing Sunbelt. Newcomers often commented on how welcome they felt.

Yet, many congregations suffered some initial discord as newcomers overwhelmed natives whose families had held sinecures for generations. The pulpits, Torah mantles, and stained-glass windows bore the names of their parents and grandparents, and families held leadership roles and ritual honors as legacies. When Rabbi Steven Sager arrived at Durham's Beth El in 1976, he observed, "The socially cohesive community that built the building started to recede. An academic community that didn't feel it had any roots here became prominent." Families that had held sinecures on High Holiday honors or as synagogue officers suddenly found themselves challenged. Older members sat through services feeling as if they were strangers in the very congregations that their parents and grandparents had sacrificed to create. "I really don't feel at home in the Temple anymore," explained Raleigh's Alice Satisky, whose husband had served forty years as treasurer. "There's so few people that I know."

Yet, old-timers also expressed joy to see communities rejuvenated that had faced waning memberships after their own children had departed. Suddenly, they found themselves confronting problems of growth. "There was something very special about the closeness that was there long ago, but what I see today is really impressive," noted Al Davis, a longtime member of Winston-Salem's Temple Emanuel, "The younger members are incredibly sharp, bright, knowledgeable, good to and with each other, and Jewish . . . in a really lovely way." He added, "Twenty-five, thirty years ago was a wonderful time, today is better."[65]

Living in a mobile society that was anonymously suburban, distant from extended family and without generational roots, Jews sought association with other Jews. "We create family," Greensboro rabbi Fred Guttman explained. Among the best-observed holidays were celebratory, family-oriented festivals like Purim, Sukkot, Passover, or Hanukkah. Tu Bish'vat, the new year of the trees, was recast as an earth day celebration observed with a seder, a ritual meal. A common denominator drawing Jews together was nostalgia for Jewish food, and synagogue tables were laden with chopped liver and bagels and lox. One continuity from the older community was the significance of the synagogue kitchen as a social setting—with the added presence of men.

In the 1990s and early 2000s, the state experienced a flurry of synagogue construction such as had occurred in the 1920s and 1950s. And the sanctuaries arising in Charlotte, Durham, Greensboro, Raleigh, and Winston-Salem were not just flexible plan buildings but sprawling complexes with educational wings, multiple chapels, and catering facilities for congregations numbering in the many hundreds. Charlotte's Beth El totaled more than 1,000 households, putting it in the mega-church category. New synagogues also arose in the smaller communities of Asheville, Hendersonville, Hickory, and Pinehurst. The Chapel Hill Kehillah

Maya and Benjamin Stang Weinberg of Chapel Hill at Purim with hamantaschen. (Howard Weinberg)

purchased the former sanctuary of the Chapel Hill Bible Church in 2001 as that town's first community synagogue.

The preference for affiliation with one congregation or another in communities that had more than one often had less to do with belief or practice than with the synagogue's location, the rabbi's personality, social circles, or nostalgia for the worship of one's youth. Conservative Judaism was losing affiliates nationally. The percentage of American Jews who identified as Conservative declined from 36 percent in 1990 to 26 percent in 2001.[66] In 2008 North Carolina had nineteen Reform congregations but only six Conservative ones (including Greenville's Bayt Shalom, which affiliated with both movements). Two were Reconstructionist. Formerly Conservative congregations in Fayetteville, Salisbury, and Wilmington were now independent, a growing national trend. Traditional congregations in Hickory and Gastonia were now Reform.

Orthodox congregations, which had expired by 1960, enjoyed a modest local revival, as they did nationally. In small measure the movement was inspired by older, traditional Jews never pleased with their congregations' evolution from their parents' Orthodoxy to Conservatism. Traditional Jews at Wilmington's B'nai Israel demanded that their rabbi put away his guitar on Saturday mornings for the Torah service. The Durham Orthodox Kehillah was led by Leon Dworsky, whose father had been a pillar of traditional Judaism, but he was joined by younger, observant Orthodox Jews arriving in growing numbers at Duke University. In 1979 sufficient numbers of Orthodox Jews arrived in Raleigh to establish Sha'arei Israel. Orthodoxy struggled to establish a footing. Out-of-state foundations sent rabbis to build communities in a region where kosher food was not always readily available, and suburban sprawl worked against Sabbath observance.

In 1980 the Lubavitcher Rebbe in New York dispatched Rabbi Yossi Groner as a shaliach (an emissary) to North Carolina. His presence was part of a worldwide campaign to establish local Jewish centers that would not just provide places for Orthodox Jews to worship but to encourage Jewish commitment among secular and less observant Jews. The Lubavitcher pattern of congregational development resembled that of the new Christian churches in contrast to the grassroots gatherings that typically marked other Jewish congregational formations: a charismatic spiritual leader arrived in a community and inspired a flock to gather around him. Beginning in Charlotte, Rabbi Groner, supported by local philanthropists, began outreach programs from children's camps to adult education. A year after arriving, the Lubavitchers began holding Shabbat services and constructed a mikva. In 1989 the Lubavitchers acquired Congregation Sha'arei Israel in Raleigh, and new Chabad Houses followed in Durham–Chapel Hill in 1998 and in Asheville in 2006. Chabad congregations in Raleigh and Charlotte resumed twice-daily weekday services, a practice not available in the state for at least a half century. In 1991 the Lubavitchers purchased 4.5 acres in Charlotte as state headquarters. A preschool opened in 1993 and a day school two years later.

More typically, the new Jewish groups that arose in the 1990s and early 2000s did so spontaneously and were most often independent. A typical process began with a chance meeting of Jews, a newspaper ad or article, a series of phone calls, and home meetings. They grew by word of mouth. School principal Norman Bossert, living in mountain Pisgah Forest an hour from the nearest synagogues, hoped to gather five or six people to his home for a Friday night service. He placed an ad in the *Transylvania Times*, "Are you Jewish? If so call Norman Bossert." He was "really shocked" to receive some seventy calls. Most were retirees, some had attended a Unitarian church. They were seeking "Jewish association," Bossert explained, "to be able to get together with some landsmen every Friday night. . . . that's very important." After meeting at homes, the newly organized Brevard Jewish Community rented church space. A lay cantor led High Holidays, and they took possession of a Torah. Using *Gateway to Prayer*, a Reform siddur, the group held services that were "hamish," "relaxing" and "collegial" with much discussion and kibitzing. Pinehurst's Sandhills Jewish Congregation began in 1981 as a "social and cultural gathering," and not until seventeen years later did it introduce Shabbat and holiday services. In 2001 Pinehurst, a place that once had re-

stricted Jews, had a Reform temple. In 1996 Ed Grad of Beech Mountain placed an ad in the *Mountain Times* asking for anyone interested in klezmer music or Yiddish stories to call him: "To his surprise the phone started ringing and in a short while there were twenty-six people sitting in his living room. That was the birth of the Havurah of the High Country." Twelve years later the group was seeking land to build a synagogue.[67]

This process was repeated in a dozen locales from the Jewish Community of the Outer Banks in Kitty Hawk to the Mountain Synagogue in Franklin. Kitty Hawk was "an unaffiliated group of Jewish individuals and families who want to maintain their traditional Jewish identity through social and spiritual activities." These new, independent groups market themselves as "welcoming." A Lake Norman congregation advertised, "Beth Shalom has something for everyone." Typically, the groups lack a movement identity and include Jews of diverse interests and orientations. Some, like the Fearrington Havurah in a retirement village in Chatham County, are social and cultural and avoid worship. More commonly, they begin with Friday night services and holiday observances, especially Purim, Passover, or Hanukkah, which have a social, celebratory aspect. Some, like the Mountain Synagogue in Franklin, which is supported by summering Floridians, meet only seasonally and remain as congregations without walls. In several communities, groups form as alternatives to established congregations, sometimes in response to rabbinic conflicts or synagogue politics. Chapel Hill's Etz Chayim sponsored social gatherings and periodic services, importing a cantor from New Jersey for High Holiday services.

Loosely structured and organized, these groups are often in flux, sometimes fading away only to reemerge when new leaders move into the community. With community growth, groups in Chapel Hill, Concord, Greenville, Lake Norman, and Pinehurst planted the seeds of formal congregations with rabbis and synagogue buildings. Lake Norman Jewry grew so large that it spawned Reform and Conservative groups. Beth Shalom became a satellite of Charlotte's Temple Israel. In 2006 the Lake Norman Jewish Congregation organized "to answer the community's desire for Reform-based spiritually enriching religious services." After being served by a Hebrew Union College rabbinic intern, it hired Rabbi Michael Shields as a "full time spiritual leader."[68] Rabbinic students or retired rabbis were pressed into service. English professor Andrew Ettin of Wake Forest University received ordination from Aleph–The Alliance for Jewish Renewal and served as a pulpit rabbi at congregations in Concord, Salisbury, Lake Norman, and Winston-Salem. In Pinehurst, Rabbi Floyd Herman, who had retired to the golfing community, took the pulpit.

Very often, the congregations were lay led, with members Jewishly educating themselves or by attending programs from the movements or from groups like the Coalition for the Advancement of Jewish Education, the Florence Melton Jewish Leadership Institute, or the National Havurah Committee. Marilyn Stern, a Jew by choice, was the prayer leader of New Bern's B'nai Scholem. Dr. Barbara Thiede of the Concord Havurah was inspired to pursue rabbinic ordination through Jewish Renewal. Services were often do-it-yourself Judaism, an eclectic blend with non-liturgical readings and discussions. In Brevard, either Hebrew or English could predominate, depending on who led.

These Sunbelt congregations arose as older communities declined in New South mill and market towns. Jewish congregations followed the changing economic fortunes of the collapsing textile and tobacco industries. Especially hard hit were the depressed inland eastern counties. Congregations closed in Wilson, Goldsboro, Jacksonville, Lumberton, and Tarboro. Tarboro—which in the 1880s had a congregation, a YMHA, a Jewish literary society, and a B'nai B'rith—had but one Jew a century later. Its synagogue, dating to the early 1900s, was rented to a church. Its roof collapsed, and it was demolished. In the late 1990s the Wilson temple, built in the 1950s, was sold and converted into a private home. "We've seen this coming for years," remarked Hyman Barshay, a member, "We knew it was a matter of time."[69] Lumberton's Temple Beth El was sold to a Baptist Church. Goldsboro's historic Oheb Sholom, built in 1886, no longer held a congregation, but David and Emily Weil, descended from a founding family, preserved the building in the hope that it could be reused. Congregations in Rocky Mount, Kinston, and Salisbury teetered as memberships declined to elderly members. They managed to hold an occasional Shabbat and High Holiday service. Whiteville was an anomaly. Its main street still had Jewish stores that persisted into a second and third generation. A core of knowledgeable Jews sustained services, but its future was uncertain. Weldon struggled to sustain its congregation, which dated to 1912. As elderly members left to join children in Norfolk or Raleigh, they argued over who would be the last to turn out the lights. It was finally sold to an African American church.

The material culture of shuttered synagogues, like the people themselves, was recycled into new congregations. Dennis Barker of Wilson took two Torah scrolls, including one that his immigrant grandfather had brought from New York in 1921, and placed them at Raleigh's Temple Beth Or. He watched children read the very scroll from which he had conducted his own bar mitzvah almost forty years earlier. Weldon's Judaica was moved to a Temple Emanu-El chapel in the new Chapel Hill synagogue, and its Torah was reinstalled at a new havurah in Concord in an emotional ceremony. "The Torah was asleep," remarked Harry Kittner. "Now it is awake again." At a bar mitzvah, Weldon Jews were given synagogue honors. Lumberton's Judaica also found a home in Chapel Hill.

A common refrain among northern newcomers, as Duke student Tandy Solomon observed, was that "the South makes you feel your Jewishness stronger and you also—because of the environment—you have to fight to keep it up." Compared to Jews in other regions, surveys revealed that southern Christians had higher rates of religious affiliation even among the well educated, a profile that fit Jews. "You make a whole series of compromises down South that one does not need to make up North," reflected Rabbi Eric Yoffie. Certain issues were perennial: conflicts over scheduling events on Jewish holidays, Christian prayer invocations at public gatherings, Christmas trees in dormitories at state universities. . . . When thirteen-year-old Brad Selig wore a skull cap to Cary's Green Hope High School in 2006, he was suspended for a week.[70]

In religion no less than on racial issues, Old and New Souths contended. In 1980 Rev. Bailey Smith of the Southern Baptist Convention said that "God Almighty does not hear the prayer of a Jew." Historian David Goldfield described "religious orthodoxy" as the South's "new racism." Yet, after Smith's remarks North Carolina rabbis found their mailboxes filled with letters from ministers dissociating themselves from Smith's comments. The Baptist State Convention passed a resolution regretting the statement and declaring that "God has chosen to speak to and through the children of Abraham."[71] Without his asking, legislator Stan Fox was handed a Tanakh (Hebrew Bible) when Bibles were distributed in the general assembly.

Commonly, when Jews organized, churches opened their doors. Rabbi Michael Cain of Bayt Shalom in Greenville joked that his biggest problem with the Christian community was having to choose among the churches that insisted on offering hospitality to the newly formed Jewish congregation. The first meeting of the Boone Jewish Community was at the Methodist Student Center. When members arrived, they found pinned to the door a note from the Episcopal priest inviting them to a Holocaust memorial service at his church. Unitarian Universalists offered space in Kitty Hawk. Catholic priest Father Carl laughed heartily when Brevard's Jews called themselves the Sacred Heart Synagogue in honor of the church's hospitality.

The advent of a multicultural society encouraged an awareness of the complexity and ambiguity of identity not only between but within individuals. Where blood once divided people, now it was a unifying force as ideals of pure races yielded to the reality, confirmed by DNA testing, of mixed heritage. Identity was no longer an essence, determined by the biology of one's race or skin color, but was constructed socially. With growing recognition that Americans typically traced their origins to multiple heritages, identities were now freely chosen rather than imposed by others.

All Jews, in some sense, were Jews by choice, not just those who converted from other religions. In a spirit of racial reconciliation, southern whites and blacks met at plantations like Midway or Somerset to trace their common heritage and ancestry. Durham's Katya Gibel Azoulay, an Israeli of Afro-Caribbean origins, penned a memoir, *Black, Jewish, and Interracial: It's Not the Color of Your Skin, But the Race of Your Kin and Other Myths of Identity*. Descendants of the Moses and Mordecai families had intermarried and given birth to numerous progeny, and Christian North Carolinians both black and white claimed Jewish ancestry. African American families like the Riveras of Durham County traced bloodlines to early North Carolina Jews. Abraham Moses' and Solomon Simons's descendants included leading families like Belk, Bennett, and McCauley. The Mordecais had married into the state's first families, and descendants bore Old South names like Cheshire and Grimes. In Raleigh, Jacob Mordecai's portrait hung in the living room of a descendant whose family had long assimilated into Christianity, and the restored Mordecai-Lane House was set in a park as a model of Old South life. Some Christians embraced their Jewish heritage, especially when family folklore pointed to an ancestor of Jewish origin, sometimes through a name or a tombstone inscription. The Loflins from rural Montgomery County cherished a family Bible inscribed by Elizabeth "Janie" Marks Loflin, born in Germany in 1842. According to family legend, grandfather Loflin, walking home from the Civil War, had met and married a Jewish woman to the distress of her family. In her memory, a descendant donated to the Deep Creek Baptist Church in Yadkinville a stained-glass window inscribed "Shalom."[72]

Religious mobility raised questions of Jewish borders and boundaries. One piercing issue concerned Jews for Jesus and Messianic Jews. These Christians, often but not always of Jewish origin, still regarded themselves as Jews although the organized Jewish community did not. Indeed, one marker of Jewish identity was "not Christian." UNC Professor of Religion Yaakov Ariel in *Evangelizing the Chosen People* boldly characterized such Christian converts not as Jewish apostates but as sincere spiritual seekers. Tensions arose when a messianic Jew might appear at a Jewish gathering or religious service to give testimony. One Shabbat, some visitors "hoodwinked" the rabbi at Charlotte's Temple Beth El and attempted to deliver a "conversion pitch" from the pulpit. When Concord's Havurat Olam wrote its bylaws, it included an article specifically excluding messianic Jews or Jews for Jesus as members. Of the some 300 messianic congregations in the country, 7 were listed in North Carolina. Three were in Charlotte, where evangelical Christianity had an especially strong presence. Their members were a mix of born Jews, most often intermarried, and born Christians seeking what they saw as a more authentic religious experience.[73]

A strain of Christian fundamentalism sought to recover Jewish roots, and synagogues in communities with strong evangelical presences frequently received inquiries from spiritual seekers. One high-profile adherent was all-pro football star Reggie White, a small-town North Carolinian who retired to Charlotte. A lay preacher, he stopped attending church and devoted himself to "go back and research the Scripture in its original language." He traveled to Israel, engaged a Hebrew instructor, and returned to North Carolina to devote himself to Torah study. White rejected Christmas worship but celebrated Hanukkah. He even dreamed in Hebrew.[74] Country churches flew Israeli flags before their chapels. When Arnold Leder closed his Goldsboro store, he rented it to the Harvest Fellowship Church. Rev. Pete Norris saw God's hand at work, and he placed in the window of his storefront church a menorah and a prayer shawl.

Children of intermarried parents negotiated between two faiths. Barry Gordon of Statesville "raised my boys Jewish, but I made them aware that their mother came from a Christian background." Both Jewish and Christian holidays were celebrated. "They understand both religions," he added. "They kind of co-mingle all of it." Benjamin Cone Jr.'s religious journey was emblematic. His intermarried Jewish father was unobservant, and he had been raised Episcopalian, serving as an acolyte. Turned down by fraternities at Chapel Hill and rejected at a country club, he came to see himself as a Jew. The Six Day War inspired him further. After formally converting to Judaism, Cone asked his father to lead a family seder, but his father confessed that he had never attended one. Both his sisters married Jews, and one also converted to Judaism. He cherished a letter that his ancestor Herman Kahn had brought to America in 1846 admonishing him to remember the faith of his fathers. Mainline churches drew Jewish members who were most frequently intermarried.

Other spiritualisms drew Jews, too. The counterculture's fascination with eastern religions was especially evident in the mountains and college towns, which were havens for spiritual seekers. Floridian Bo Lozoff established a commune outside Chapel Hill for his Human Kindness Foundation. There he practiced a spiritual healing ministry for convicts based on the teachings of "the great sages of all religions." His guru was Neem Karoli Baba, whom he had never met except in a dream. In the 1980s the former wife of a prominent Jewish Charlottean became entangled with the guru Bagwhan Shree Rajneesh. A Hadassah activist from an Orthodox Jewish home, she renamed herself Vindanta Hanya and with her son Swami David joined the guru's Oregon commune. Hanya drew headlines when she rented a plane from the Charlotte airport to abet the guru's escape from America after he was charged with immigration fraud. "I was what I thought an American Jewish housewife should be," Hanya explained, until she realized "there was something in me that was not that." In Charlotte "I only knew Jewish people," but the guru's taped discourses made her feel that religion was not "sitting in a synagogue," but that "we are all the same."[75]

NORTH CAROLINA REINVENTED

North Carolina's universities were the engines of the state's economic growth. Davidson College, Wake Forest University, and Duke University were ranked among the nation's elite, and the sixteen-campus state university system, led by its flagship campuses in Raleigh and Chapel Hill, was also highly regarded. The University of North Carolina at Charlotte, founded after World War II, grew into a doctoral-granting research institution with 900 faculty and more than 22,000 students. Jews advanced from academic outsiders to insiders. Starting with Terry Sanford's presidency, Jewish enrollment at Duke nearly doubled from 6.5 percent in 1971 to about 12 percent in 2000.[76] As Jewish student and faculty bodies grew, Jewish studies secured its place in the curriculum.

The cracking of discriminatory barriers was occasionally noisy. In 1977 Davidson College was thrust into the national media when it withdrew its offer to historian Ronald Linden of Swarthmore. The school had a "Christian tenure policy," and Linden said that he could not honor the school's "church-related" mission.

Students and faculty marched in protest, and radio-station owner Harriet Kaplan, a Jewish member of the college's advisory board, promised to bring the issue to the trustees. The North Carolina General Assembly threatened to draft legislation to deny tax money to any school that had "discriminatory policies."[77]

Universities anticipated larger social changes that for the most part ended occupational discrimination for Jews and later for blacks and women. As Wake Forest University positioned itself as a national liberal arts college, Jews joined the faculty, particularly the distinguished Bowman Gray Medical School, but also in the liberal arts. Rabbi Andrew Ettin served on its English faculty, and Herbert Brenner, a synagogue president, sat on its board. The Duke hospital and medical school that once had quotas or glass ceilings for Jews saw Ralph Snyderman become president of Duke Health Care Systems in the 1980s. In 1991 when UNC named a research center for Vice Chancellor Cecil Sheps, who had come to the school of public health in 1947, he thanked officials for "starting his medical career at a time when Jewish people were not always welcome in university communities."[78] Law schools where anti-Semites once locked doors now had Jewish deans, Ken Broun at UNC and David Levi at Duke. Rick Glazier was a law professor at Campbell University, a conservative Christian school. In 1991 Dr. Sam Schuman, a professor of English and American literature, was installed as chancellor of the University of North Carolina at Asheville. Delivering the invocation and benediction was Rabbi Jonathan Malino, a professor at Guilford College.

Certainly Jewish academics included assimilationists who found meaning and community in science or cosmopolitan cultures and had tangential, if any relation at all, to things Jewish. Duke feminist Eve Kosofsky Sedgwick spoke of herself "in some regimes a Jew" but rejected "the Jewish choice of a minority politics based on a conservative reinscription of gender roles." Her colleague Alice Kaplan thought Yiddish was a language of "bad memories," and she needed to "think in French." Deconstructionists and academic Marxists did not always have use for a Jewish identity that confined them ideologically or separated them from other classes or ethnicities.[79] Duke writer Ariel Dorfman acknowledged his Jewish ancestry but as a native Chilean identified culturally as a Latino.

Yet, faculty members who had the widest influence in North Carolina, if not in the academic world, tended to be Jews who publicly identified as such. Fayetteville native Joel Fleishman, founding director of the Terry Sanford Institute of Policy Sciences, was a synagogue cantor prominent in national Jewish philanthropic circles. Political scientist Abe Holtzman of North Carolina State mentored a generation of state leaders. One devoted Holtzman protégé, a farmer's son from Wilson named James B. Hunt Jr., served four terms as a progressive governor, notably appointing Jews to state office and instituting public programs on the

Professor Abe Holtzman of North Carolina State University. (Jim Wilson, *Raleigh News & Observer*)

Holocaust and Israel. UNC political scientist Joel Schwartz counted among his former students judges, legislators, and a U.S. senator. Richard Levin, who headed MBA and executive training programs at the UNC Business School for more than forty years, lent his name and philanthropy to Jewish causes. His former students included the state's banking and corporate elite, who honored him with an endowed chair. A 1961 UNC graduate, Jonathan Yardley—later an editor and journalist—noted that "urban Jews" were the formative influence of his college years.[80]

A significant measure of Jewish integration was the proliferation of Jewish study programs. In the late 1960s and 1970s, historian Paula Hyman notes, such programs were "virtually impossible," and specialists tended to come from Jewish institutions. A quarter century later, Jewish studies were thoroughly integrated into the broader liberal arts curriculum. Rather than focus on Jewish advocacy, the courses offered critical and pluralistic perspectives on Jewish history and

Duke archaeologists Eric and Carol Meyers pose for *People* magazine as raiders of the lost ark. (Eric M. Meyers)

culture, and the approach was interdisciplinary.[81] A course in archaeology might question the biblical account of the Exodus or place Jewish immigration in the context of other ethnic peoples. Jewish studies were part of a national effort to find a place for marginal cultures in the larger narratives of American history and Western civilization. Jewish subjects were listed in catalogs along with courses in Asian, Hispanic, African American, and American regional studies. In seeking to strengthen the Jewish campus presence, university development offices were not unmindful, too, of their Jewish alumni and donor bases.

Duke University had pioneered Jewish Studies in 1943, but the program had faded until it revived in 1972 with the support of the Evans and Stern families and the Z. Smith Reynolds Foundation. Duke's Center for Judaic Studies enrolled some 500 students by the 1980s, and the catalog listed a dozen faculty teaching courses ranging from archaeology to Yiddish. Its founding director Eric Meyers with his wife Carol Meyers received international recognition for their archaeological excavations of the oldest known ark of the covenant and the Mona Lisa of the Galilee mosaic. UNC-Chapel Hill's Jewish studies was originally conceived as a joint program with Duke, but they disengaged administratively. In 2003 UNC created the Carolina Center for Jewish Studies and launched an ambitious development plan to build on faculty teaching Jewish subjects in religion, history, and literature. Endowed professorships drew ranking scholars in archaeology, rabbinics, and Holocaust studies. Marcie Cohen Ferris offered a course, "Shalom Y'All: The Jewish Experience in the American South." More than 1,000 students enrolled in the center's classes by 2008.

Other state campuses, too, followed the national trend to incorporate Jewish studies among proliferating ethnic and multicultural academic programs. UNC-Asheville's Center for Jewish Studies, founded in 1982, described its mission to be "part of the University and a part of the Community." Its director, Richard Chess, created a curriculum in Jewish history and literature and launched a public program of lectures, concerts, and films. The university library housed an archive dedicated to Jewish life in the region. East Carolina University also included Jewish Americans in its ethnic studies program, although the school had but seventy Jewish students. Appalachian State University founded its Center for Judaic, Holocaust, and Peace Studies in 2002 with the intent to create both academic majors and public outreach. Its faculty included Zohara Boyd, who had survived the Holocaust as a child, and Rosemary Horowitz, a daughter of survivors. UNC-Wilmington created an endowed chair for the Charles and Hannah Block Distinguished Professor of Jewish History, while UNC-Greensboro offered a Jewish studies major under the tutelage of rabbinic scholar Marc Bergman, who held an endowed chair. Elon University near Burlington, whose sports teams were formerly the Fighting Christians, now enrolled more than 200 Jewish students, created a campus Hillel, and held a "strategic plan" meeting on "Envisioning the Future of Jewish Life at Elon." On its faculty was Holocaust scholar David Crowe, biographer of Oskar Schindler. Not only Jews but North Carolina itself was establishing a place in the canon of Western civilization.

As North Carolina reinvented its economy, it promoted itself as the State of the Arts, and the Jewish contribution in art, film, music, and literature was outsized locally as it was nationally. The Jewish impact on the performing arts was felt from Tin Pan Alley, to Broadway, to Carnegie Hall. In the 1950s the two dominant strands in American literature were southern and Jewish writing. Jews were realizing their ambitions largely in the realms of high culture, and their settings were the museum, university, and concert hall. The Jewish presence countered H. L. Mencken's stereotype of the South as the Sahara of the Bozart.

North Carolina was a breeding ground for writers, and native Jews wrote in a southern idiom. Novelist Lawrence Naumoff, son of a Charlotte physician, penned comic tales of southern dysfunction in *Rootie Kazootie* and *Silk Home, N.C.* His nonfiction *A Southern Tragedy in Crimson and Yellow* took a critical look at a tragic fire at a rural chicken processing plant. In *The Past Is Never Dead*, Ashevillean

David Schulman created a murder mystery featuring detective Gritz Goldberg. The promising career of Durham-born Amanda Davis ended in a plane crash while on a book tour for her novel, *Wonder When You'll Miss Me*. Davis, daughter of a Duke doctor, attributed her writing to a southern upbringing: "[T]he thing about growing up in the South is that every time anyone answers you a question, they answer it with a story—everyone . . . I definitely feel like I absorbed and loved and drank in." When she died, she was working on a "Jewish Southern gothic novel" about a peddler.[82] New Jersey transplant Maureen Sherbondy explored her southern discomfort in poems of "A Jew in the South." Charlotte's Judy Goldman considered three generations of a southern Jewish family in her novel *The Slow Way Back*. The dean of southern literature was Chapel Hill English professor Louis Rubin Jr., who not only mentored a generation of southern writers as a teacher but was a pioneer publisher as founder of Algonquin Books of Chapel Hill. The author or editor of nearly sixty books, Rubin wrote a memoir, *My Father's People: A Family of Southern Jews*.

Eli Evans, son of the Durham mayor, was the acknowledged spokesperson of southern Jewry. His book, *The Provincials: A Personal History of Jews in the South*, first published in 1973, colorfully portrayed a people who had largely lacked definition until he described a uniquely southern Jewish consciousness. The best seller—it appeared in three editions—was a coming of age memoir and a travelogue to unexpected places and people. He followed it with *The Lonely Days Were Sundays: Recollections of a Jewish Southerner* and *Judah P. Benjamin: Jewish Confederate*.

Universities gave positions to creative writers, most of whom were transplanted northerners. North Carolina State English Professor Lawrence Rudner explored Russian Jewish roots in his novels *The Magic We Do Here* and *Memory's Tailor*. Poets Richard Chess at UNC-Asheville and Alan Shapiro at UNC-Chapel Hill turned to Jewish subjects and themes in their writings. Chess published poetry collections *Tekiah* and *Third Temple*. In "Rabbi Gets Around" he observed, "Asheville: it's a long way from Jerusalem," adding in another poem, "But you are free in Buncombe County to believe whatever you choose, Jew."[83]

Two principals in North Carolina's dance renaissance were Melissa Hayden and Robert Weiss. Born Mildred Herman in Toronto, Hayden had danced with the New York City Ballet under legendary choreographer George Balanchine. In 1983 she came to the North Carolina School of Arts, where she taught until her death in 2003. New Yorker Robert Weiss started dancing for Balanchine's company at seventeen, rising to principal dancer. In 1997 when the Carolina Ballet was launched in Raleigh, Weiss was hired as artistic director. Assembling dancers worldwide and choreographing his own ballets, Weiss led the company to critical success, exciting the New York critics. Carolina Ballet—along with the Ameri-

can Dance Festival, whose dance troupes included those of Anna Halprin, Lar
Lubovitch, and Israel's Batsheva Dance—gave North Carolina cultural cachet. The
state's larger ambition was to play on a global rather than a regional stage culturally as well as economically.

Raised in musical homes and college educated, Jews aspired to high culture.
Their contribution was disproportionate locally as it was nationally. Audrey
and Jacques Brourman served as pianist and conductor for the Charlotte Symphony. Miriam Warshauer was first violinist for the Wilmington Symphony and
led its Concert Association. Her daughter Maxine was a noted composer on Jewish themes. Steven Jaffe, composer in residence at Duke, wrote "Three Yiddish
Songs" as well as "Poetry of the Piedmont." Hinda Honigman, president of the
National Federation of Music Clubs, guided the Brevard Music Center, where a
library, scholarship, composer's award, and amphitheater bear her name. David
Effron served as its director. Sheldon Morgenstern was the founding musical director of Greensboro's Eastern Music Festival. He was the son of a furniture salesman drawn to the area in the 1930s by his cousins, the LeBauers. In his memoir,
he traced the festival's origins to Herman Cone Jr., its first president, and Leah
Tannenbaum, its "spiritual mother." He credited its survival to President Samuel
LeBauer, who rallied leaders to secure its financial position. Now led by Gerard
Schwarz, the festival draws international artists for its institutes and performances.

The klezmer revival that became a global musical phenomenon drew inspiration from young urban Jews who came to ethnic Jewish music through American roots music. Si Kahn, who came South for the civil rights movement, settled in Charlotte, where he mixed social justice with Appalachian rhythms. Every North Carolina city had at least one klezmer ensemble which played at Jewish celebrations and folklife festivals. Most bands, true to klezmer's eclectic roots, offered a multicultural mélange and included both Jewish and gentile musicians. In the Triangle was the Magnolia Klezmer Band, which played jazz, polka, and Balkan music and featured a Yiddish lead singer. Asheville's Bandana Klezmer Band, with a steel guitar among its fiddles and clarinets, included musicians from mountain communities. Greensboro's Sinai Mountain Ramblers described their music as "Jew-grass." Charlotte's Viva Klezmer included musicians from the Charlotte Symphony.

Like the musicians, Jewish painters were cosmopolitans who drew inspiration well beyond local colors. German-born Edith London had come to North Carolina when her physicist husband took a position at Duke in the 1930s. An abstractionist, London created collages and oil paintings, and her work was collected by the North Carolina Museum of Art. Raleigh's Alice Ehrlich was the daughter of the immigrant schochet Rev. Rubinstein, but her artistic sensibilities were entirely modernist. She wielded large influence as a teacher. Henry Pearson's artistic career is a North Carolina Jewish odyssey. Born in 1914 in Kinston to an immigrant storekeeper, he attended UNC-Chapel Hill and Yale before his army career took him to Japan. A student at the Art Students League and a teacher at the New School for Social Research, Pearson created geometric abstractions that were collected by elite museums internationally. The North Carolina Museum of Art dedicated a one-man show to him. He occasionally worked in Jewish themes.

The Penland School of Crafts had a cadre of Jewish artists, including a director, Ken Botnick. Potter Norman Schulman, metalsmith Fred Fenster, and textile artist Ruth Gaynes crafted Judaica. In the 1960s glassblowers Bill and Kathie Bernstein had arrived from New Jersey in a station wagon as card-carrying hippies. After teaching at Penland, they opened a studio in the mountain community of Burnsville. Curiously, they found themselves living among a community of Jewish glassblowers: David Goldhagen, Robert Levin, Jeff Todd, and Yaffa Sikorsky. Yaffa Sikorsky was the daughter of Holocaust émigrés who had first settled in Israel. Each crafted Judaica. Levin made mezzuzot and Elijah cups; Sikorsky, dreidels; and the Bernsteins, hanukkiot and Kiddush cups. When Levin told mountain folks that he was Jewish, he observed one of two reactions: either they scratched their heads in perplexity or were exceedingly curious.

The North Carolina Museum of Art in Raleigh was one of two state art mu-

STORY: NORTH CAROLINA KLEZMORIM

If the globul klezmer revival had a birthplace, it might have been the Blue Ridge homes of Tommy Jarrell and Fred Cockerham, master fiddlers and banjo players. In 1976 aspiring musician and folklorist Henry Sapoznik joined other young New York Jews at Jarrell's Mount Airy home to swig corn liquor from a Clorox jug and learn fiddle tunes. The Brooklyn-born Sapoznik, son of Holocaust survivors, became the leading impresario of the klezmer revival through his work with the Yiddish Radio Project, Living Traditions, and the YIVO Institute for Jewish Research.

We were equally exotic to one another. They to me; living in the model of "Mayberry RFD" and Tommy couldn't understand how these northern city boys would want to play their music. He was actually pretty sophisticated for a guy from around there, I mean he had been up north and met other kinds of people, he was no Aborigine, and he knew that we were, you know, Jews and all. We had this long relationship of trying to puzzle each other out. At one point he had been making breakfast, and I was a vegetarian at the time and he was making you know, bacon, eggs fried in bacon fat and probably the coffee had a bacon base. I wasn't eating any of this stuff and Tommy is pushing it on me, "Come on Hank! Eat up," more like a Jewish mother than a southern fiddler. And I wasn't eating this stuff and at one point he goes "Come on Hank, what are you? A damn Jew?!!" I was so totally taken aback, I couldn't tell if I was more taken aback at the statement or the fact that he . . . understood . . . the laws of Kashruth (kosher food) enough to know what Jews eat. Well, that got us started. "Well yes, Tommy I AM a damn Jew." We started talking about it, and it opened up this line of communication for which there was no context.

And he asked me "Don't your people got none of your own music?"

. . . When Tommy put that bug in my ear about my people having their own music, I got to thinking, well, was there an equivalent to old time string band music in the Jewish world?[1]

1. Mark Rubin, "Henry (Hank) Sapoznik," *Banjo Newsletter*, <http://www.markrubin.com/sapoznik.html>, 17 Oct. 2008.

seums nationally to house a permanent Judaica display. Its inspiration came from Dr. Abram Kanof, a local pediatrician and authority on Jewish ritual art, who donated its core collection and guided its acquisitions. The gallery opened in 1983 featuring candlesticks, a seder plate, and charity box. The collection's focus was aesthetic rather than cultural, and it included artisanal pieces from Jerusalem's Bezalel Workshop and North Carolina's Penland, from eighteenth-century Holland and nineteenth-century Galicia. Forging a relationship with the Jewish Museum of New York, the gallery expanded its exhibition space in a new building.[84]

Jews gained entry into the arts well before other civic doors opened. Sam Gala-

bow served as president of Charlotte's Mint Museum of Art in 1954, a post held
by Morris Speizman for three years starting in 1972. Herbert Cohen, a nationally
recognized potter, served as a curator and director of the Mint in the 1960s. Justus
Bier was the second director of the North Carolina Museum of Art in Raleigh.
Museums canonized the place of Judaism with blockbuster exhibitions. In 1996
the North Carolina Museum of Art hosted "Sephoris in Galilee: Crosscurrents of
Culture" that featured archaeological displays. An exhibition of Dead Sea Scrolls
from the Israel Museum in Jerusalem drew crowds to museums in Charlotte and
Raleigh. For North Carolina Christians, these exhibitions affirmed the rootedness
of their own religion in Judaism and strengthened their attachment to the Holy
Land. For Jews it confirmed their place in both southern society and culture.

The arts figured prominently in the reinvention of North Carolina's downtowns. With the closing of factories and suburban sprawl, main streets had lost
their viability. Downtowns that survived urban renewal enjoyed a rebirth in the
1990s. Durham's tobacco warehouses and Asheville's textile factories were turned
into loft apartments and upscale boutique malls. Shoe stores were now sushi
bars. Jewish entrepreneurs joined the revitalization efforts. Frequently anchoring
these developments was a museum or arts center. A store on Greensboro's Elm
Street expressed these larger transformations. Sylvia Gray, a daughter of East

Bill and Katherine
Bernstein, glassblowers
of Burnsville. (William
Bernstein)

European immigrants raised in Mount Airy, had operated a novelty secondhand shop crammed with several floors of merchandise: used books, fabric, toys, buttons, ribbons, military surplus, etc. After her death in the 1990s, the store had remained shuttered until her grandson George Scheer took proprietorship. Scheer, a graduate of Penn and Duke, turned the store into the Elsewhere Arts Collaborative. Artists from around the globe were invited to create sculptures using his grandmother's merchandise on condition that nothing was brought in or taken out. Doll parts formed a cornucopia. Army surplus was stacked into a maze. Regarding his grandmother as an artist of merchandise, Scheer reconceived the store as studio and gallery. Elsewhere expressed materially the economic and cultural changes of both Jews and North Carolinians alike in the evolution from grandmother to grandson, from storekeeper to art entrepreneur.

GIVING BACK

Jews as a community were prosperous. National profiles suggested that "Jews have the highest levels of affluence" among ethnic groups. Although no such statistics exist for North Carolina Jews, their philanthropies offer anecdotal evidence. Jews who had achieved wealth often expressed gratitude for their communities. Sandra Levine expressed an oft-repeated Jewish sentiment in observing of her husband Leon, "It was very important to him to give back to the community that made him successful." This giving back could be seen small and large, from

the storekeeper who did not demand payment from the farmer after a poor harvest to the philanthropist who endowed hospitals. High Point's Fred Swartzberg cited his mother, rather than the Talmudic source, in explaining "that a good name is more to be desired than fame or money."[85]

Health care was a special beneficiary of largesse. Nationally, Jews have increasingly directed giving to social, cultural, and environmental causes rather than Jewish ones. In Greensboro, Moses Cone Hospital, which grew into a health-care system, was established by Cone's widow, Bertha Lindau Cone, when she bequeathed a $15 million endowment in 1947. In Greenville, the Brody family donated more than $22 million to establish a medical school at East Carolina University, which was named for them in 1999. They were the university's largest donors. The family also endowed the J. S. "Sammy" Brody Scholars Medical Program, which assisted students with scholarships. Recalling his father Morris and uncles Leo and Sammy, Hyman Brody explained, "Eastern North Carolina has been so good to our family. We wanted to do something meaningful that would

PORTRAIT: LEON LEVINE

The Leon Levine saga is a classic North Carolina Jewish story writ large. His father, Harry Levine, was drawn from Russia to America by his brother Max, who had arrived in Baltimore in 1907. The brothers settled in Rockingham where they opened The New York Bargain House. On a buying trip to Poughkeepsie, New York, Harry met a secretary at a warehouse, Minnie Ginsberg. They wed in 1922 and would raise four children in Rockingham. "I became a businessman at a pretty early age," Leon Levine recalled. After his father died in 1949, his mother ran the store, which became a second home. At fifteen, while his brother was serving in Korea, Leon titled himself "executive vice president," and a year later created the store's bargain basement. As a college student, Leon, with his brother Sherman, bought a bedspread factory.

Like many small-towners, the three Levine brothers saw Charlotte as a "growing town" and relocated there. Alvin opened Pic 'N Pay Shoes in 1957, and two years later Leon started his first Family Dollar Store with his cousin Bernard Richter

First Family Dollar Store. (Leon Levine)

touch a lot of people and make their lives better." Levine Children's Hospital in Charlotte and Brenner Children's Hospital in Winston-Salem were also endowed by long-standing local families. "If we leave behind a thank you to 'our' city," Herbert Brenner reflected at a Chamber of Commerce testimonial dinner in 1989, "it's our family's way of letting Winston-Salem know that the three sons of a Jewish immigrant father passed through, and we are grateful to you for letting us stay for a while."[86]

Philanthropists traced their charity to Jewish values, remembering parents and grandparents who set examples before them. "We were reared seeing charity boxes on our mother's kitchen wall—where coins were placed each Sabbath eve-of Mount Gilead as a partner. They bought factory close outs, odd lots, and overruns, pricing nothing higher than two dollars. Focusing on a strategy of opening stores in small markets where major discounts chains would not go, Family Dollar expanded from 50 stores in 1959 to 400 in 1981 to 2,500 in 1996 to 6,200 in 2006. Leon Levine scouted locations by looking for oil spots on the parking lot asphalt. "If they were there, it was our kind of place because it meant people were driving old cars," Sherman Levine explained, "Our customers didn't drive Cadillacs." Motor oil was their biggest seller. In 1979 Family Dollar was listed on the New York Stock Exchange, and it became a Fortune 500 company. From nine national distribution centers, fleets of Family Dollar trailer trucks delivered merchandise from Arizona to Maine. Leon's brother Alvin built his Pic 'N Pay chain to 459 stores, selling 8.5 million pairs of shoes annually before selling out in 1980. Turning to philanthropy, Alvin Levine served as president of the Charlotte Jewish Foundation.

Leon Levine had a reputation as a tough negotiator, but he insisted on delivering fair value. Ivy League business schools used Family Dollar as a case study. Levine cousins, in-laws, and children took positions, revolving in and out as company fortunes rose and fell. With his small-town southern roots, he retained a common touch. In a city where Jews had once been excluded from power elites, Levine counted bank presidents as friends. When Charlotte won a National Football League franchise, Levine became part owner of the Panthers.

Levine philanthropies to Jewish, medical, and educational institutions total in the tens of millions. The Jewish Community Center at Shalom Park was named for Sandra and Leon Levine. Having lost his first wife and daughter Mindy to cancer, Levine has contributed especially to medicine, including the Levine Children's Hospital in Charlotte and the Leon Levine Research Center at Duke University. Also bearing the Levine name are the Museum of the New South, a Senior Center in Matthews, and a campus at Central Piedmont Community College as well as scholarships for need-based students. "Leon Levine," said Museum director Emily Zimmern, "is a New South success story."[1]

1. *Charlotte Observer*, 3 Oct. 2002; Bea Quirk, *Leon Levine and Family Dollar: An American Success Story* (Charlotte: Knight, 1997), 31.

Leon and Sandra Levine with Duke president Keith Brodie (left) at Levine Science Research Center. (Leon Levine)

Brody School of
Medicine, East Carolina
University. (East
Carolina University
News Services)

ning," Herbert Brenner told the Chamber members. The Brenners were quick
with loans for the worker who needed to pay rent or tuition for a daughter's
nursing school. "Well, I've always liked to help people," clothier Sol Schulman
of Sylva explained when he slipped a Walmart clerk some money to attend her
mother's funeral. "My biggest mission in life is to have what they call in Jewish a
'mitzvah.'" The First Methodist Church held a Sol Schulman Day after he donated
land, and in awarding him an honorary doctorate for endowing scholarships,
the president of Western Carolina University noted that his funds often came
with a handwritten note, "Do not need to be identified as it is a pleasure to help."
In Hendersonville Morris Kaplan oversaw for more than fifty years a Kiwanis
program that sent poorly shod schoolchildren to Sherman's Sporting Goods to
receive shoes and socks. His partner Becky Banadyga recalled washing the feet
of a child whose rotting shoes left him covered with sores. Every Christmas in
Asheville storekeeper Lou Pollock gave away shoes to needy children. A Joe Sugar
Memorial Park in St. Pauls or a Leinwand Field in Elizabethtown testified to small-
town Jews who laid down southern roots.[87]

Lou Pollock
Christmas shoe
giveaway, Asheville.
(Ada and Louis Pollock
Collection, Special
Collections, D. Hiden
Ramsey Library,
University of North
Carolina at Asheville)

SUNBELT LEGACY

In the early 1900s North Carolina was one of the most illiterate and impoverished states. In the early 2000s it had by numerous measures caught and even exceeded national norms with a diversified economy, growing population, and expansive research and academic centers. This upward trajectory parallels the course of the Jewish people over generations as they rose in social and occupational status from poor immigrants peddling the countryside to merchants and industrialists in mill and market towns to professionals in postindustrial research, academic, and financial centers.

With its progress, Sunbelt North Carolina was ironically returning to the condition of its earliest years when it was a multinational society linked to a global marketplace. If few Jews could claim the multigenerational rootedness of native

Durham-born Lena Gordon Goldman, 101, writes her own Torah. (Temple Emanuel, Greensboro)

North Carolinians, increasingly neither could their neighbors. One in twelve southerners was northern born in 1950; by 1980 it was one in five.[88] The state's population rose from fewer than 2 million in 1900 to more than 8 million in 2000. Along with its numbers, the state's character was also being redefined. The conservatism and provincialism that had typified so much of its history was yielding as the small, agrarian mill and market towns were being outshone by the expansive Sunbelt communities. In 2008 its electoral politics turned from red to blue as women were elected governor and U.S. senator and an African American won the presidential vote. Jews were agents of that change. If Jews were coming in ever-increasing numbers, they were doing so because they found a diverse society and economy that was congruent with their needs, talents, and values.

The feelings of community that had once bound North Carolina Jews as an extended family had attenuated even as North Carolinians no longer constituted a cohesive Protestant society. Jews blended into their American environment even as they insisted on their difference. Indeed, Judaism's survival owed not to an inflexible adherence to tradition but to a liberality that embraced diverse belief and practice. Rabbinic authority yielded to grass-roots Judaism. Women reading from the Torah, yoga and meditation classes, and patrilineal Jews were discontinuities from the Jewish past. If religion was the bond that served as a Jewish nexus, its content was negotiable and its boundaries were permeable. As a group, though certainly not for every individual, Jews resisted a blending that would have led to a complete assimilation. They remained Jews. In North Carolina, the survival of the Jewish community seemed less threatened than its unity. Efforts like the multimedia project, "Down Home: Jewish Life in North Carolina," attempted to validate Jewish roots in North Carolina, to create a narrative that gathered Jews once again into a community, to give Jews a heritage as well as a history.

Shalom Park, American Hebrew Academy, day schools, summer camps, Hillel centers, Judaic studies programs, and new synagogues testify to an unprecedentedly large and prosperous Jewish community. The new Jewish groups constantly arising in unexpected places like the Blue Ridge and Outer Banks point to seismic shifts in the American Jewish landscape. The mobility that has brought new Jews to North Carolina has made the state's Jews as varied as Jews globally. If North Carolina Jewry is new and diverse, if its community is discontinuous with its past, so is the North Carolina they call home.

NOTES

ABBREVIATIONS

AJA   American Jewish Archives, Cincinnati, Ohio

AJHS   American Jewish Historical Society, New York, N.Y.

BLHC   Baker Library Historical Collections, Harvard Business School, Boston, Mass.

BRC   Bill Reaves Collection, New Hanover County Public Library, Wilmington, N.C.

CJHS   Charlotte Jewish Historical Society, Levine-Sklut Judaic Library and Media Resource Center, Shalom Park, Charlotte, N.C.

Duke   Rare Books, Manuscripts, and Special Collections Library, Duke University, Durham, N.C.

HGP   Harry Golden Papers, Special Collections, J. Murrey Atkins Library, University of North Carolina at Charlotte

IRO   Industrial Removal Office, American Jewish Historical Society, New York, N.Y.

JHFNC   Jewish Heritage Foundation of North Carolina, Durham, N.C.

MFP   Mordecai Family Papers, Southern Historical Collection, University of North Carolina at Chapel Hill

NCC   North Carolina Collection, Wilson Library, University of North Carolina at Chapel Hill

NCSA   North Carolina State Archives, Raleigh

NHCPL   North Carolina Room, New Hanover County Public Library, Wilmington, N.C.

SHC   Southern Historical Collection, Wilson Library, University of North Carolina at Chapel Hill

UNC-A   Special Collections, D. Hiden Ramsey Library, University of North Carolina at Asheville

UNC-C   Special Collections, J. Murrey Atkins Library, University of North Carolina at Charlotte

INTRODUCTION

1. Mark Bauman, *The Southerner as American: Jewish Style* (Cincinnati: American Jewish Archives, 1996), 5, 29. Beth Wenger, *In Search of American Jewish Heritage* (Ann Arbor: Jean and Samuel Frankel Center for Judaic Studies, 2008), 9. I thank Mark Bauman and Stephen J. Whitfield for clarifying the arguments of this introduction.

2. William S. Powell, ed., *Encyclopedia of North Caro-lina* (Chapel Hill: University of North Carolina Press, 2006), 1157; Lee Shai Weissbach, *Jewish Life in Small-Town America: A History* (New Haven: Yale University Press, 2005), 350.

3. Rob Christensen, *The Paradox of Tar Heel Politics* (Chapel Hill: University of North Carolina Press, 2008), 311.

4. See Eli Evans, *The Provincials: A Personal History of Jews in the South* (Chapel Hill: University of North Carolina Press, 2005).

5. Ronald Schecter, *Obstinate Hebrews: Representations of Jews in France, 1715–1815* (Berkeley: University of California Press, 2003), 12; Sander Gilman, *Multiculturalism and the Jews* (New York: Routledge, 2006), x; Stephen J. Whitfield, "Declarations of Independence: American Jewish Culture in the Twentieth Century," in David Biale, ed., *The Culture of the Jews: A New History* (New York: Schocken, 2002), 1100. This double process is also described as coalescence and compartmentalization. See Sylvia Barack Fishman, *Jewish Life and American Culture* (Albany: State University of New York Press, 1999), 1.

6. W. J. Cash, *The Mind of the South* (New York: Vintage, 1969), 342.

7. Henry Feingold, *Bearing Witness: How America and Its Jews Responded to the Holocaust* (Syracuse: Syracuse University Press, 1995), 253.

8. This discussion owes much to Stephen J. Whitfield, "The Paradoxes of American Jewish Culture," in Deborah Dash Moore, ed., *American Jewish Identity Politics* (Ann Arbor: University of Michigan Press, 2008), 243–62.

CHAPTER 1

1. See James Shapiro, *Shakespeare and the Jews* (New York: Columbia University Press, 1996), for a discussion on Jews in Elizabethan England.

2. Eli Faber, *A Time for Planting: The First Migration, 1654–1820* (Baltimore: Johns Hopkins University Press, 1992), 4–8; Malcolm Stern, "New Light on the Jewish Settlement of Savannah," in Abraham Karp, ed., *The Jewish Experience in America*, vol. 1 (New York: Ktav, 1969), 70.

3. In 1664 English Barbadians established the colony of Charles Town on the Cape Fear River. It grew to 800 residents before being abandoned in 1667. Its constitu-

tion granted freedom of religion. Whether Barbadian Jews joined the colony is unknown. See Lindley Butler, "Charles Towne," in William S. Powell, ed., *Encyclopedia of North Carolina* (Chapel Hill: University of North Carolina Press, 2006), 200. Simon Fernandez, a ship's pilot, sailed the Carolina coast in 1578 and returned for the Lost Colony expedition of 1587. Converted to Protestantism in England, he was thought to have been a Portuguese Jew who adopted Christianity publicly if not privately. See E. Thomas Shields and Charles Ewen, eds., *Searching for the Roanoke Colonies: An Interdisciplinary Collection* (Raleigh: Office of Cultural Resources, 2003), 70; Ira Rosenwaike, *On the Edge of Greatness: A Portrait of American Jewry in the Early National Period* (Cincinnati: American Jewish Archives, 1985), 1; Melvin Urofsky, *Commonwealth and Community: The Jewish Experience in Virginia* (Richmond: Virginia Historical Society, 1997), 1; Mark Greenberg, "A 'Haven of Benignty,'" in Mark Bauman, ed., *Dixie Diaspora: An Anthology of Southern Jewish History* (Tuscaloosa: University of Alabama Press, 2006), 14.

4. Jacob R. Marcus, "The American Colonial Jew: A Study in Acculturation," in Jonathan Sarna, ed., *The American Jewish Experience* (New York: Holmes & Meier, 1997), 6, 7.

5. Elizabeth Fenn and Peter Wood, "Natives and Newcomers: North Carolina before 1770," in Joe Mobley, ed., *The Way We Lived in North Carolina* (Chapel Hill: University of North Carolina Press, 2003), 30, 38; Malcolm Stern, "New Light on the Jewish Settlement of Savannah," in Karp, *The Jewish Experience in America*, 1:72.

6. Milton Ready, *The Tar Heel State: A History of North Carolina* (Columbia: University of South Carolina Press, 2005), 39.

7. Fenn and Wood, "Natives and Newcomers," 72; Ready, *The Tar Heel State*, 54; Powell, *Encyclopedia of North Carolina*, 112.

8. John Malcolm, ed., *Scottish Notes and Queries*, vol. 6 (Aberdeen: D. Wyllie and Son, 1893), 61 (Sept. 1892); Jonathan Sarna, *Jacksonian Jew: The Two Worlds of Mordecai Noah* (New York: Holmes & Meier, 1981), 62.

9. William Saunders, ed., *The Colonial Records of North Carolina*, (Wilmington: Broadfoot, 1993), 1:639; Kimberly Sims, "Wilmington Jewry: 1800–1914" (Honors Program thesis, History Department, University of North Carolina at Wilmington, Apr. 1999), 3. Sims cites other Jewish names, the carpenters Philip David and his son David David, whose names appear on records from 1738–55. David Goldberg, "An Historical Community Study of Wil-

mington Jewry, 1738–1925" (History Seminar, University of North Carolina at Chapel Hill, Spring 1976), 1. Zachariah Jacobs appears in Wilmington in 1772; Saunders, *Colonial Records*, 5:977. For Jacob Franks, see Jacob R. Marcus, *The Colonial American Jew, 1492–1776* (Detroit: Wayne State University Press, 1970), 712–16. See also Leon Huhner, *Jews in Colonial and Revolutionary Times: A Memorial Album* (New York: Gertz, 1959), 141; Stanley Chyet, *Lopez of Newport: Colonial American Merchant Prince* (Detroit: Wayne State University Press, 1970), 54; Morris Speizman, *The Jews of Charlotte* (Charlotte: McNally & Loftin, 1978), 3; Steven Hertzberg, "Unsettled Jews: Geographic Mobility in a Nineteenth Century City," *American Jewish History Quarterly* 67, no. 2 (Dec. 1977): 142; Leonard Rogoff, *Homelands: Southern Jewish Identity in Durham and Chapel Hill, North Carolina* (Tuscaloosa: University of Alabama Press, 2001), 9; Saunders, *Colonial Records*, 7:733. Huhner, *Jews in Colonial and Revolutionary Times*, 137–148, lists many with Jewish-sounding names whose origins cannot be confirmed. Some names were also prevalent among the English and Pennsylvania Germans who settled colonial North Carolina. They include Cone, Coan, Cohon, Hendricks, Hays, Levi, Moses, Aaron, Emanuel, Gabriel, Isaacs, Nathan, Israel, Solomon, Jacobs, and Myars. The 1790 Federal Census, Huhner notes, in addition to Abram Moses of Halifax, lists Isaac Aaron of Halifax and David Moses of Fayette, Anson County. In 1768 William Levy of Orange County added his name to a petition of grievances addressed to the "Governor & Councill" that warned of a "discontent growing," but nothing but his name suggests Jewish origins. These Regulators, protesting unfair fees and taxes, rose in armed rebellion two years later, anticipating the Revolution. Histories of Wilmington Jewry begin by citing the presence of David, Philip, and Jane David in 1738, but again no evidence documents them as Jews. Zachariah Jacobs is also listed as an early settler, Martin Ettinger was a gunsmith in 1799, and Abraham Judah sold candles to the Episcopal church in 1819; see Goldberg, "An Historical Community Study," 9–10.

10. Chyet, *Lopez of Newport*, 178; Virginia Beaver Platt, "Tar, Staves, and New England Rum: The Trade of Aaron Lopez of Newport, Rhode Island, with Colonial North Carolina," *North Carolina Historical Review* 48, no. 1 (Jan. 1971): 21; Griffith J. McRee, *Life and Correspondence of James Iredell* (New York: Appleton, 1858), 28, 584.

11. Chyet, *Lopez of Newport*, 128, 134, 198–99. See also Malcolm Stern, *First American Jewish Families: 600 Gene-*

alogies, 1654-1977 (Cincinnati and Waltham: American Jewish Archives and American Jewish Historical Society, 1978), 38, 85, 151, 175, 312.

12. William Byrd, *William Byrd's Histories of the Dividing Line betwixt Virginia and North Carolina*, ed. William Boyd (Raleigh: North Carolina Historical Commission, 1929), 72.

13. Hugh Lefler and William S. Powell, *Colonial North Carolina: A History* (New York: Scribner's Sons, 1973), 192.

14. Harry Watson, "An Independent People: North Carolina, 1770-1820," in Mobley, *The Way We Lived in North Carolina*, 201, 216.

15. Saunders, *Colonial Records*, 7:544, 9:103.

16. The early synagogues in Newport, Charleston, and New York presented popular neoclassical facades on their exteriors while replicating the architecture of their mother congregations in London and Amsterdam on their interiors.

17. Jonathan Sarna, *American Judaism* (New Haven: Yale University Press, 2004), 12-15; Chyet, *Lopez of Newport*, 23.

18. Hasia Diner, *The Jews of the United States, 1654-200* (Berkeley: University of California Press, 2004), 33; Platt, "Tar, Staves, and Rum," 11; Sarna, *American Judaism*, 18, 12-13, 26.

19. Watson, "An Independent People," 107; Byrd, *Histories of the Dividing Line*, 74.

CHAPTER 2

1. Judith Mordecai to "My Dear Parents," 19 Dec. 1792, MFP; Emily Bingham, *Mordecai: An Early American Family* (New York: Hill and Wang, 2003), 18-21; Jacob Rader Marcus, *Memoirs of American Jews: 1775-1865*, vol. 1 (Philadelphia: Jewish Publication Society of America, 1955), 218.

2. Statistics derive from Jacob Rader Marcus, *To Count a People: American Jewish Population Data, 1585-1984* (Lanham: University Press of America, 1990).

3. Malcolm Stern, "The 1820s: American Jewry Comes of Age," in Jonathan Sarna, ed., *The American Jewish Experience* (New York: Holmes & Meier, 1997), 31; Frederic Cople Jaher, "American Jews in the Revolutionary and Early National Periods," in Stephen Norwood and Eunice Pollack, eds., *Encyclopedia of American Jewish History*, vol. 1 (Santa Barbara: ABC-CLIO, 2008), 15-16; Betty Camin, *North Carolina Naturalization Index, 1792-1862* (Mount Airy: B. J. Camin, 1989), NCSA.

4. Jaher, "American Jews," 17.

5. Morris Speizman, *The Jews of Charlotte, North Carolina* (Charlotte: McNally and Loftin, 1978), 3. Moses Stern enlisted in 1777 in Major Ashe's company and was paid $100 in bounty in 1781, when his term expired; Harry Golden, *Our Southern Landsmen* (New York: G. P. Putnam's, 1974), 177.

6. Leon Huhner, *Jews in Colonial and Revolutionary Times: A Memorial Album* (New York: Gertz, 1959), 142, 144; Jacob Rader Marcus, *Early American Jewry*, vol. 2 (Philadelphia: Jewish Publication Society, 1953). See Colonel John Walker Papers, 1736-1909, 274, NCSA. Levy's spelling of widow suggests German origins; William Saunders, ed., *The Colonial Records of North Carolina* (Wilmington: Broadfoot, 1994), 17:18, 89. Lt. Col. David Franks is not to be confused with the Tory of the same name, who once employed Jacob Mordecai in New York; Marcie Cohen Ferris and Mark Greenberg, eds., *Jewish Roots in Southern Soil: A New History* (Waltham: Brandeis University Press, 2006), 36.

7. Jacob Rader Marcus, *Early American Jewry, 1655-1790* (Philadelphia: Jewish Publication Society, 1953), 252; William S. Powell, *North Carolina through Four Centuries* (Chapel Hill: University of North Carolina Press, 1989), 236.

8. Harry Watson, "An Independent People: North Carolina, 1770-1820," in Joe Mobley, ed., *The Way We Lived in North Carolina* (Chapel Hill: University of North Carolina Press, 2003), 113, 176, 184.

9. Ibid., 171, 161; Milton Ready, *The Tar Heel State: A History of North Carolina* (Columbia: University of South Carolina Press, 2005), 160, 161, 164; Powell, *North Carolina through Four Centuries*, 247, 248; Hugh Lefler, *History of North Carolina* (New York: Lewis Historical Publishing, 1956), 320.

10. Powell, *North Carolina through Four Centuries*, 250; Ira Rosenwaike, "An Estimate and Analysis of the Jewish Population of the United States in 1790," *Publications of the American Jewish Historical Society* 50, no. 1 (Sept. 1960): 99-104.

11. See Rosenwaike, "An Estimate and Analysis," 99-104.

12. Memorandum of an Agreement between Simon R. Oliveira and Benjamin Nicholls, 28 Sept. 1826, NCSA; *North-Carolina Gazette*, 15 Apr. 1790; Stephen F. Miller, "Recollections of Newbern Fifty Years Ago with an Appendix" (Sept. 1873), typescript, NCSA. I thank Yitzhak Kremer of the Hebrew University for explaining the origins of Abroo's name. Jacob Rader Marcus, *United States Jewry, 1776-1985* (Detroit: Wayne State University Press, 1989), 320. Stern, "The 1820s," 85. I thank Richard Wyndham, who uncovered this case. It is documented

on America's Historical Newspapers database: see *Pennsylvania Packet and Daily Advertiser*, 12 Dec. 1787; *Massachusetts Centinel*, 26 Dec. 1787; *Charleston City Gazette and Daily Advertiser*, 16, 26 June 1788; *Newport Herald*, 3, 8 July 1788; *Columbian Herald*, 15, 19 Nov. 1787; *State Gazette of South-Carolina*, 22 Nov. 1787, <http://www.newsbank.com/readex/?content=96>.

13. See Stern, "The 1820s," 85.

14. Diane Cashman, *Cape Fear Adventure: An Illustrated History of Wilmington* (Woodland Hills: Windsor, 1982), 47; *Wilmington Gazette*, 31 Dec. 1801; Kimberly Sims, "Wilmington Jewry: 1800-1914" (Honors Program thesis, History Department, University of North Carolina at Wilmington, Apr. 1999), 6.

15. "Diary Kept by John Osborn in Union County, North Carolina, January 1, 1800-October 2, 1802," 49, 74, 98, 103, 106, typescript, Mecklenburg County Public Library, Charlotte, North Carolina. See Camin, *North Carolina Naturalization Index*; Golden, *Our Southern Landsmen*, 177; Monroe Evans, *A History of Beth Israel Congregation and the Jewish Community in Cumberland County, North Carolina* (Fayetteville, 2002), 7.

16. Huhner, *Jews in Colonial and Revolutionary Times*, 142; Theodore Rosengarten and Dale Rosengarten, *A Portion of the People: Three Hundred Years of Southern Jewish Life* (Columbia: University of South Carolina Press, 2002), 81; Melvin Urofsky, *Commonwealth and Community: The Jewish Experience in Virginia* (Richmond: Virginia Historical Society and Jewish Community Federation of Richmond, 1997), 11.

17. William S. Powell, ed., *Encyclopedia of North Carolina* (Chapel Hill: University of North Carolina Press, 2006), 85; Sims, "Wilmington Jewry: 1800-1914," 5; *Wilmington Gazette*, 18 Mar. 1802.

18. *Gazette*, 8 Sept. 1785; Charles Sydnor, *The Development of Southern Sectionalism, 1819-1848* (Baton Rouge: Louisiana State University Press, 1968), 117-18.

19. Thomas Clayton, "Close to the Land: North Carolina, 1820-1870," in Mobley, *The Way We Lived in North Carolina*, 270.

20. Holly Snyder, "Queens of the Household: The Jewish Women of British America, 1700-1800," in Pam Nadell and Jonathan Sarna, eds., *Women and American Judaism: Historical Perspectives* (Hanover: Brandeis University Press), 178-80; Joseph Blau and Salo Baron, *The Jews of the United States, 1790-1840: A Documentary History*, vol. 1 (New York: Columbia University Press, 1963), 65.

21. Lefler, *History of North Carolina*, 300; Guion Johnson, *Ante-Bellum North Carolina: A Social History* (Chapel Hill: University of North Carolina Press, 1937), 164-65; Powell, *North Carolina through Four Centuries*, 258.

22. Snyder, "Queens of the Household," 407; David Goldberg, "An Historical Community Study of Wilmington Jewry, 1738-1925" (History Seminar, University of North Carolina at Chapel Hill, Spring 1976), 10. New Bern members included Jacob Henry, Abraham Cutten, Samuel Hart, and Jacob Sabiston, and Wilmington's St. John's Lodge included Joseph and Benjamin Jacobs as wardens; Speizman, *The Jews of Charlotte*, 3; Goldberg, "An Historical Community Study," 10.

23. Penny Leigh Richards, "'A Thousand Images Painfully Pleasing': Complicating Histories of the Mordecai School, Warrenton, North Carolina, 1809-1818" (Ph.D. diss., University of North Carolina at Chapel Hill, 1996). Richards refutes claims that the Mordecai curriculum was progressive or protofeminist. Elizabeth Fox-Genovese and Eugene Genovese, *The Mind of the Master Class: History and Faith in Southern Slaveholders' Worldview* (Cambridge: Cambridge University Press, 2005), 257; Richards, "'A Thousand Images,'" 194, 195, 197, 201, 202, 203.

24. Bingham, *Mordecai*, 64-69.

25. Ibid., 66-69, 144-45. As Bingham notes, Edgeworth's liberality was limited: the novel's American Jewess Berenice has a Christian mother, is not a practicing Jew, and marries a Christian.

26. Eli Faber, *Jews, Slaves, and the Slave Trade* (New York: New York University Press, 1998), 134-36; Bertram Korn "Jews and Negro Slavery in the Old South, 1789-1865," in Leonard Dinnerstein and Mary Dale Palsson, eds., *Jews in the South* (Baton Rouge: Louisiana State University Press, 1973), 96; Rosenwaike, "An Estimate and Analysis," 68.

27. Watson, "An Independent People," 149; Rosenwaike, "An Estimate and Analysis," 70; Ira Rosenwaike, "Further Light on Jacob Henry," *American Jewish Archives* 23 (Nov. 1970): 117.

28. Rachel Lazarus to Ellen Mordecai, 25 Aug. 1822; Rachel Lazarus to Ellen Mordecai, 22 Oct. 1822; Rachel Lazarus to Ellen Mordecai, 14 Oct. 1821, SHC; Bingham, *Mordecai*, 130-31.

29. Bingham, *Mordecai*, 107-8.

30. Ibid., 25; Jacob Mordecai to Moses Mordecai, 20 July 1797, MFP, SHC.

31. Myron Berman, *Richmond's Jewry, 1769-1976: Shabbat*

in *Shockoe* (Charlottesville: University Press of Virginia, 1979), 207; Letter from Jacob Mordecai to Aaron and Rachel Mordecai Lazarus, 8 Jan. 1827, JHFNC.

32. Ready, *The Tar Heel State*, 157; Rachel Mordecai to Sam Mordecai, 16 Dec. 1810, Pattie Mordecai Papers, NCSA; Jacob Mordecai to Rachel Mordecai, 13 Aug. 1797, MFP, SHC.

33. Watson, "An Independent People," 140; Joel Martin, "Native American Religion," in Samuel Hill, ed., *Religion*, vol. 1 of *The New Encyclopedia of Southern Culture*, Charles Reagan Wilson, gen. ed. (Chapel Hill: University of North Carolina Press, 2006), 103; Robert Calhoon, "Ethnic Protestantism," in Hill, *Religion*, 62.

34. Thomas Frazier, "Women and Religion," in Hill, *Religion*, 160–61.

35. Bingham, *Mordecai*, 118; Rachel Mordecai Lazarus to Ellen Mordecai, 7 Oct. 1821, Duke.

36. Jacob Mordecai to Esther Cohen, 16 Oct. 1797, MFP, SHC; Bingham, *Mordecai*, 46–48.

37. Jacob Mordecai to Dear & Respectable Brethern, 27 Jan. 1796, Pattie Mordecai Papers, NCSA; Bingham, *Mordecai*, 47–48, 24; Rachel Mordecai to Sam Mordecai, 8 May 1814; Rachel Mordecai to Ellen Mordecai, 12 Dec. 1813, MFP, SHC.

38. Sims, "Wilmington Jewry: 1800–1914," 9, 45; Jacob R. Marcus, "Light on Early Connecticut Jewry," in *Studies in American Jewish History* (Cincinnati: Hebrew Union College, 1969), 90–91; Elizabeth Murray, "Mordecai, [Miss] Ellen," in William S. Powell, ed., *Dictionary of North Carolina Biography*, vol. 4 (Chapel Hill: University of North Carolina Press, 1991), 314; Goldberg, "An Historical Community Study," 15.

39. Bingham, *Mordecai*, 135; Goldberg, "An Historical Community Study," 12; Solomon Breibart, *Explorations in Charleston's Jewish History* (Charleston: History Press, 2005), 140; "Moses, Abraham," Mecklenburg County Wills, 1749–1967, NCSA; Joel Henry Last Will and Testament, NCSA.

40. Goldberg, "An Historical Community Study," 12, 13; Samuel Mordecai to Rachel Mordecai, 16 Sept. 1805, Duke; Rachel Mordecai to Samuel Mordecai, 19 Sept. 1814, Pattie Mordecai Papers, NCSA. This letter was written from Warrenton.

41. Bingham, *Mordecai*, 161, 128.

42. Ibid., 134–36, 196.

43. Ibid., 194, 220–21. For Emma Mordecai's articles in the *Occident*, see <www.jewish-history.com/Occident/ volume2/jan1845/duty.htm> and <www.jewish-history .com/Occident/volume5/jul1847/essay.html>.

44. Blau and Baron, *The Jews of the United States*, 17; Griffith McRee, ed., *Life and Correspondence of James Iredell* (New York: Appleton, 1857), 339.

45. Morton Borden, *Jews, Turks, and Infidels* (Chapel Hill: University of North Carolina Press, 1984), 13–15.

46. Watson, "An Independent People," 200; *Colonial and State Records of North Carolina*, Minutes of the North Carolina House of Commons, North Carolina General Assembly (Oct. 22, 1784–Nov. 26, 1784), <http://docsouth.unc .edu/csr/index.html/document/csr19-007>, 784. Laney argued that Haryon cheated him.

47. Ronald Schechter, *Obstinate Hebrews: Representation of Jews in France, 1715–1815* (Berkeley: University of California Press, 2003), 8.

48. Amendment I (Religion). Debate in North Carolina Ratifying Convention, <http:presspubs.uchicago.edu/ founders/documents/amendI_religions52.html>, 8; Huhner, *Jews in Colonial and Revolutionary Times*, 7–8; Ready, *The Tar Heel State*, 150.

49. Mills's resolution against Jacob Henry, 5 Dec. 1809, House of Commons, Session 1809, Lp. 236, NCSA.

50. Faber, *The Time for Planting*, 136–37.

51. Huhner, *Jews in Colonial and Revolutionary Times*, 17–18; "Gaston's Address," *Proceedings and Debates of the Convention of North Carolina (1835)* (Raleigh: J. Gales, 1836), 266–68; Mary Hollis Barnes, "Jacob Henry's Role in the Fight for Religious Freedom in North Carolina" (19 Mar. 1984), typescript, NCSA.

52. For a text of the full speech, see Blau and Baron, *The Jews of the United States*, 29–32.

53. Gilman, *Multiculturalism and the Jews*, xi.

54. "An Appeal by he Jews of Maryland," in Blau and Baron, *The Jews of the United States*, 50–52; Huhner, *Jews in Colonial and Revolutionary Times*, 15.

55. Huhner, *Jews in Colonial and Revolutionary Times*, 16; "Gaston's Address," 275.

56. Huhner, *Jews in Colonial and Revolutionary Times*, 21–23.

57. Richards, "'A Thousand Images," 20; Gratz Mordecai, *Publications of the American Jewish Historical Society* 6 (1897): 40–57; Rosengarten and Rosengarten, *A Portion of the People*, 75.

CHAPTER 3

1. Avraham Barkai, *Branching Out: German Jewish Immigration to the United States, 1820–1924* (New York: Holmes & Meier, 1994), 11; Jonathan Sarna, *American Judaism: A History* (New Haven: Yale University Press, 2004), 64.

2. Barkai, *Branching Out*, 3; Sarna, *American Judaism*, 64; Kimberly Sims, "Wilmington Jewry: 1800–1914" (Honors Program thesis, History Department, University of North Carolina at Wilmington, Apr. 1999), 11; *Carolina Israelite*, Apr. 1950.

3. Leon Jick, *The Americanization of the Synagogue, 1820–1870* (Hanover: Brandeis University Press, 1992), 29–30; Herbert Ezekiel and Gaston Lichtenstein, *The History of the Jews of Richmond from 1796 to 1917* (Richmond: Herbert T. Ezekiel, 1917), 95, 301; Barkai, *Branching Out*, 1; Sarna, *American Judaism*, 65; Sims, "Wilmington Jewry: 1800–1914," 12.

4. Milton Ready, *The Tar Heel State: A History of North Carolina* (Columbia: University of South Carolina Press, 2005), 185; Daniel Grant, *Alumni History of the University of North Carolina, 1795-1924* (Chapel Hill: University of North Carolina Press, 1924), 47, 362, 553.

5. Thomas Clayton, "Close to the Land: North Carolina, 1820–1870," in Joe Mobley, ed., *The Way We Lived in North Carolina* (Chapel Hill: University of North Carolina Press, 2003), 319.

6. William S. Powell, *North Carolina through Four Centuries* (Chapel Hill: University of North Carolina Press, 2003), 31; Ready, *The Tar Heel State*, 183–84; William S. Powell, ed., *Encyclopedia of North Carolina* (Chapel Hill: University of North Carolina Press, 2006), 937.

7. Clayton, "Close to the Land," 331.

8. Quoted in Hugh Lefler, *History of North Carolina* (New York: Lewis Historical Publishing, 1956), 468.

9. Adam Mendelsohn, "Old Clo' in the Old South: The International Dimensions of the Southern Jewish Clothing Trade" (paper presented at the Southern Jewish Historical Society Annual Conference, 2 Nov. 2008).

10. David Goldberg, "An Historical Community Study of Wilmington Jewry, 1738-1925" (History Seminar, University of North Carolina at Chapel Hill, Spring 1976), 22; *Newbernian*, 21 May 1844; North Carolina, vol. 7 p. 47, R. G. Dun & Co. Collection, Baker Library Historical Collections, Harvard Business School.

11. Clayton, "Close to the Land," 289.

12. John Alexander, *History of Mecklenburg Co. and the City of Charlotte from 1740 to 1903* (Charlotte, 1902), 379; *Carolina Israelite*, Apr. 1950. The statistical source is C. C.

Crittenden of the North Carolina Department of History; Lee Shai Weissbach, *Jewish Life in Small-Town America* (New Haven: Yale University Press, 2005), 39.

13. *Raleigh Register*, 3 June 1854; North Carolina, vol. 25, p. 1e; vol. 22, pp. 36P, 365, R. G. Dun & Co. Collection, BLHC. Powell, *North Carolina through Four Centuries*, 312;

14. Walter Klein, "Past Masters," *Confederate Veteran* 3 (2001): 29, 30–31; Sims, "Wilmington Jewry: 1800–1914," 17–18.

15. North Carolina, vol. 15, p. 114, R. G. Dun & Co. Collection, BLHC.

16. *Old North State*, 9 Feb. 1850; *Rowan Whig and Western Advocate*, 27 Oct. 1854; North Carolina, vol. 4, p. 139, R. G. Dun & Co. Collection, BLHC.

17. Hasia Diner, "Entering the Mainstream of Modern Jewish History: Peddlers and the American Jewish South," in Marcie Cohen Ferris and Mark Greenberg, eds., *Jewish Roots in Southern Soil: A New History* (Waltham: Brandeis University Press, 2006), 86, 90, 95; Lu Ann Jones, *Mama Learned Us to Work: Farm Women in the New South* (Chapel Hill: University of North Carolina Press, 2002), 29–31.

18. Guion Johnson, *Ante-Bellum North Carolina: A Social History* (Chapel Hill: University of North Carolina Press, 1937), 532; Deborah Weiner, *Coalfield Jews: An Appalachian History* (Urbana: University of Illinois Press, 2006) 24, 82–90; Diner, "Entering the Mainstream of Modern Jewish History," 99; Charles Sydnor, *The Development of Southern Sectionalism, 1819-1848* (Baton Rouge: Louisiana State University Press, 1948), 117.

19. North Carolina, vol. 11, p. 1; vol. 7, p. 35, R. G. Dun & Co. Collection, BLHC; Lewis Atherton, "Itinerant Merchandising in the Antebellum South," *Bulletin of the Business Historical Society* 19 (Apr. 1945): 35–59.

20. North Carolina, vol. 20, p. 283; vol. 5, p. 194; vol. 17, p. 119, R. G. Dun & Co. Collection, BLHC; Goldberg, "An Historical Community Study," 23.

21. North Carolina, vol. 16, p. 102B; vol. 4, p. 122; vol. 20, p. 283; vol. 9, p. 26, R. G. Dun & Co. Collection, BLHC.

22. North Carolina, vol. 5, p. 206; vol. 19, p. 256; vol. 7, p. 5; vol. 8, p. 406, R. G. Dun & Co. Collection, BLHC.

23. North Carolina, vol. 16, pp. 28, 93, R. G. Dun & Co. Collection, BLHC.

24. Sydnor, *The Development of Southern Sectionalism*, xi; John Hope Franklin, "As for Our History . . . ," in Charles Sellers Jr., ed., *The Southerner as American* (Chapel Hill: University of North Carolina Press, 1960), 4–5. Maria Buttner to Albert Butner, 13 Sept. 1852, Duke.

25. Marcia Horowitz, "The Jewish Community of

Greensboro: Its Experience in a Progressive City" (M.A. thesis, University of North Carolina at Greensboro, 1993), 113; Henry Belden and Arthur Hudson, eds., *The Frank C. Brown Collection of North Carolina Folklore*, vol. 2 (Durham: Duke University Press, 1952), 155–60; *The Life Confession and Execution Jew and Jewess, Gustavus Linderhoff, Fanny Victoria Talzingler Who Were in Ashville, North Carolina Oct. 27, 1854* (Baltimore: A. R. Orton, 1855).

26. Moses Rountree, *Strangers in the Land: The Story of Jacob Weil's Tribe* (Philadelphia: Dorrance, 1969), 5.

27. *Newbernian*, 21 May 1844; Chatham County, North Carolina, vol. 5, p. 209, Dun & Co.

28. Clayton, "Close to the Land," 246; Goldberg, "An Historical Community Study," 21–22; Handbill for Slave Sale, Warrenton, N.C., 1859, Division of Archives and History, Raleigh, North Carolina; Lindsey Butler and Alan Watson, eds., *The North Carolina Experience: An Interpretive and Documentary History* (Chapel Hill: University of North Carolina Press, 1984), 193.

29. Robert Fogel and Stanley Engerman, *Time on the Cross: The Economics of American Negro Slavery* (New York: Norton, 1974), 73–74; *Salisbury Rowan Whig and Western Advocate*, 11 Feb., 2 Sept., 1853.

30. Bertram Korn, "Jews and Negro Slavery in the Old South, 1789–1865," in Leonard Dinnerstein and Mary Dale Palsson, eds., *Jews in the South* (Baton Rouge: Louisiana State University Press, 1973), 104; Johnson, *Ante-Bellum North Carolina*, 533; North Carolina, vol. 24, p. 37, R. G. Dun & Co. Collection, BLHC; Clarice Elias Auerbach, "Recollections of the Early Jewish Residents of Raleigh, North Carolina," undated typescript, AJA.

31. Korn, "Jews and Negro Slavery," 130–31; *Dial 1* (1860): 219–28.

32. Hasia Diner, *A Time for Gathering: The Second Migration, 1820–1880* (Baltimore: Johns Hopkins University Press, 1992), 25–26.

33. Barkai, *Branching Out*, 112; Jick, *Americanization of the Synagogue*, 41; Jacob Rader Marcus, *This I Believe: Documents of American Jewish Life* (Northvale: Jason Aronson, 1990), 79–81. Maria Buttner to Albert Butner, 13 Sept. 1852, Duke.

34. Jick, *Americanization of the Synagogue*, 47; Jeffrey Gurock, *Orthodoxy in Charleston* (Charleston: College of Charleston, 2004), 3.

35. Jick, *Americanization of the Synagogue*, 55–56; Sarna, *American Judaism*, 91, 94.

36. Sarna, *American Judaism*, 89, 90, 111.

37. Barkai, *Branching Out*, 66; Sarna, *American Judaism*,

69, 70–71, 74; Elizabeth K. Berman, "M. S. Polack's Circumcision Record Book," *Generations* (Fall 1989): 10–16; Martin Weitz, *Biblio . . . Temple of Israel, Wilmington* (Wilmington, 1976), 12; Record of Marriages by Rev. Dr. Hochheimer, Baltimore Hebrew Congregation, 1850–1900, AJA.

38. Sarna, *American Judaism*, 74.

39. Harry Watson, "An Independent People: North Carolina, 1770–1820," in Mobley, *The Way We Lived in North Carolina* 279; Ready, *Tar Heel State*, 188; *Hillsborough Recorder*, 15 Nov. 1851.

40. Sarna, *American Judaism*, 76.

41. Ibid., 98.

42. *Occident* IV, 8 (Nov. 1846) <http://www.jewish-history.com/ocident/volume4/nov1846/news/html>; Jick, *Americanization of the Synagogue*, 43.

43. *Wilmington Journal*, 29 Mar. 1852; Sims, "Wilmington Jewry: 1800–1914," 23–24; Weitz, *Biblio*, 12, 13.

44. Isaac Leeser, "Jewish Emancipation," *Occident*, 3 June 1845; Morton Borden, *Jews, Turks, and Infidels* (Chapel Hill: University of North Carolina Press, 1984), 48.

45. Borden, *Jews, Turks, and Infidels*, 49; Goldberg, "An Historical Community Study," 21–22.

46. Borden, *Jews, Turks, and Infidels*, 49.

47. Powell, *Encyclopedia of North Carolina*, 236, 1016; Ready, *Tar Heel State*, 216–17; Korn, "Jews and Negro Slavery," 119; Larry Logue, "Jews and the Civil War," in Stephen Norwood and Eunice Pollack, eds., *Encyclopedia of American Jewish History* (Santa Barbara: ABC-CLIO, 2008), 324.

48. Bingham, *Mordecai*, 224; Emma Mordecai to Emma Mordecai II, 21 Apr. 1861; Matthew Karres, "Mordecai, Alfred," in William S. Powell, ed., *Dictionary of North Carolina Biography*, vol. 4 (Chapel Hill: University of North Carolina Press, 1991), 313.

49. Speizman, *Jews of Charlotte*, 4; *Charleston Daily Courier*, 24 June 1861.

50. Mel Young, *Where They Lie* (Lanham: University Press of America, 1991)169.

51. Harry Simonhoff, *Jewish Participants in the Civil War* (New York: Arco, 1963), 107.

52. Ready, *Tar Heel State*, 236; Powell, *North Carolina through Four Centuries*, 364; James Sprunt, *Tales of the Cape Fear Blockade* (Wilmington: Charles Towne Preservation Trust, 1960), 88; Goldberg, "An Historical Community Study," 23, 25–26; Beverly Tetterton, Helen Solomon, and JoAnn Fogler, eds., *History of the Temple of Israel* (Wilmington, 2001), 5; "General B. F. Butler and the Israelites," *Jew-*

ish *Messenger*, <http://www.jewish-history.com/civilwar/ general.htm>, 21 Oct. 2008.

53. Goldberg, "An Historical Community Study," 25; Barkai, *Branching Out*, 114, 115–17.

54. L. Leon, *Diary of a Tar Heel Confederate* (Charlotte: Stone Publishing, 1913), 70.

55. Ibid., 41, 14.

56. Robert Rosen, *Jewish Confederates* (Columbia: University of South Carolina Press, 2000), 2–3, 4; Albert Moses Luria, Diary, 1861–1862, 32, SHC.

57. Rosen, *Jewish Confederates*, 50.

58. Leon, *Diary of a Tar Heel Confederate*, 6, 70; Luria, Diary, 31.

59. Rosen, *Jewish Confederates*, 9; Luria, Diary, 6, 29, 30, 31.

60. Maurice Weinstein, ed., *Zebulon Vance and "The Scattered Nation"* (Charlotte: Wildacres Press, 1995), 39; Thomas Clayton, "Close to the Land," 342.

61. Weinstein, *Zebulon Vance*, 40–41.

62. See Young, *Where They Lie*, 175–270; Ezekiel and Lichtenstein, *History of the Jews*, 194–95; Simon Wolf, *The American Jew as Patriot, Soldier and Citizen* (Philadelphia: Levytype, 1895), 303.

63. Leon, *Diary of a Tar Heel Confederate*, 71.

64. Korn, "Jews and Negro Slavery," 30.

65. Ready, *Tar Heel State*, 250.

66. Ibid., 250.

67. *Board of Delegates of American Israelites Proceedings at the Session for 5627* (New York: J. Davis Printer, 1867), appendix, 19, 20, AJHS.

68. *Occident* 6, Sept. 1866; Ready, *Tar Heel State*, 257; Borden, *Jews, Turks, and Infidels*, 50.

69. Sims, "Wilmington Jewry: 1800–1914," 35; *Wilmington Daily Journal*, 24 Apr. 1868; W. McKee Evans, *Ballots and Fence Rails: Reconstruction on the Lower Cape Fear* (Chapel Hill: University of North Carolina Press, 1967), 124; Rountree, *Strangers in the Land*, 30–31.

70. Laurie Gunst, *Off White: A Memoir* (New York: Soho Press, 2005), 257; North Carolina, vol. 9, p. 473; vol. 7, p. 187, R. G. Dun & Co. Collection, BLHC; *Wilmington Star*, 13 Mar. 1878.

71. Rountree, *Strangers in the Land*, 30–31; North Carolina, vol. 9, p. 473; vol. 16, p. 466, R. G. Dun & Co. Collection, BLHC; Auerbach, "Recollections," 4–5.

72. Weinstein, *Zebulon Vance*, 64, 74, 82–84, 88, 89; *Wilmington Morning Star*, 16 July 1875.

73. Barkai, *Branching Out*, 126, 127.

74. Ibid., 130–31, 136.

75. Leonard Rogoff, *Homelands: Southern Jewish Identity in Durham and Chapel Hill, North Carolina* (Tuscaloosa: University of Alabama Press, 2001), 46.

76. Lefler, *History of North Carolina*, 587, 388–89, 590–92; *Durham Herald*, 22 Mar. 1876; Harry Golden, *Our Southern Landsmen* (New York: G. P. Putnam's, 1974), 180.

77. Lefler, *History of North Carolina*, 594–95; Ready, *Tar Heel State*, 267.

78. Ready, *Tar Heel State*, 267.

79. Rogoff, *Homelands*, 16; North Carolina, vol. 19, p. 70L, R. G. Dun & Co. Collection, BLHC; Goldberg, "An Historical Community Study," 26–27.

80. Weinstein, *Zebulon Vance*, 82; North Carolina, vol. 6, p. 374; vol. 24, p. 140; vol. 14, p. 215; vol. 10, p. 17; vol. 9, p. 504, R. G. Dun & Co. Collection, BLHC.

81. North Carolina, vol. 24, p. 82; vol. 24, p. 166; vol. 9, p. 137, R. G. Dun & Co. Collection, BLHC; *Index of North Carolina Bankrupts: Acts of 1800, 1841, & 1867*, William Bennett, ed. (Raleigh, 1994), NCSA; Goldberg, "An Historical Community Study," 28.

82. North Carolina, vol. 16, p. 102; vol. 17, p. 550, R. G. Dun & Co. Collection, BLHC; Rountree, *Strangers in the Land*, 10; *Warrenton Gazette*, 14 June 1873.

83. Allen W. Trelease, *The North Carolina Railroad, 1849–1871, and the Modernization of North Carolina* (Chapel Hill: University of North Carolina Press, 1991), 348; North Carolina, vol. 14, p. 14, R. G. Dun & Co. Collection, BLHC.

84. Emil Rosenthal Ledger, 1868–1875, SHC; North Carolina, vol. 9, p. 446, R. G. Dun & Co. Collection, BLHC; Mary Bayard Clarke to Willie Clarke, 1 Jan. 1837, New Bern Public Library.

85. *Wilmington Star*, 24 Sept. 1875; Rountree, *Strangers in the Land*, 19, 16; *Kinston Free Press*, 17 Aug. 1918; Rebecca Cohen, Album, JHFNC; North Carolina, vol. 9, p. 446, R. G. Dun & Co., Collection, BLHC.

86. Stephen J. Whitfield, *In Search of American Jewish Culture* (Waltham: Brandeis University Press, 1999), 33; *Wilmington Star*, 2 Feb. 1873, 29 Apr. 1874, BRC.

87. *Daily Charlotte Observer*, 22 Mar. 1878; <http://www .ajhs.org/hai/entry.cfm?id=26>, 12 Jan. 2009.

88. Mary B. Jacobs, "A Sketch of the Bear Family in North Carolina," Apr. 1938, JHFNC.

89. *Occident*, 8 Nov. 1867.

90. Sarna, *American Judaism*, 124; Barkai, *Branching Out*, 135.

91. Rountree, *Strangers in the Land*, 32–33; *Wilmington Weekly Star*, 28 Sept. 1877; Rogoff, *Homelands*, 34.

92. *Occident*, 8 Mar. 1860; Robert Kravitz, "An Early

History of Lodge #364 from the Original Minutes of that Lodge" (history paper for Dr. J. R. Marcus, Hebrew Union College, Fall 1973).

93. *The Heritage of Iredell County* (Statesville: Genealogical Society of Iredell County, 1980), 532.

94. Sims, "Wilmington Jewry: 1800–1914," 26; *Evening Star*, 23 Sept. 1867; *Wilmington Journal*, 28 Sept. 1867.

95. Sims, "Wilmington Jewry: 1800–1914," 28; *Wilmington Star*, 30 Sept. 1868, 17 Sept. 1871, BRC.

96. Karla Goldman, *Beyond the Synagogue Gallery: Finding a Place for Women in American Judaism* (Cambridge, Mass.: Harvard University Press, 2001), 59–68; Helen Solomon, "History of the Ladies Concordia Society of the Temple of Israel Wilmington, North Carolina," in Tetterton, Solomon, and Fogel, *History of the Temple of Israel*, 33.

97. *Wilmington Star*, 11 Apr. 1875; Goldberg, "An Historical Community Study," 33.

98. Cornelia Wilhelm, "Shaping the American Jewish Community: The Independent Order of B'nai B'rith, 1843–1914," Christof Mauch and Joseph Salmons, eds., *German Jewish Identities in America* (Madison: Max Kade Institute, 2003), 72; *Wilmington Morning Star*, 16 July 1875.

99. Weitz, *Biblio*, 19. Sarna, *American Judaism*, 125; *Wilmington Weekly Star*, 28 May, 1875.

100. *Wilmington Star*, 7 Apr. 1876.

CHAPTER 4

1. Min Klein, *This I Remember*, 22E, JHFNC.

2. Deborah Weiner, "Filling the Peddler's Pack: Southern Jews and Jacob Epstein's Baltimore Bargain House" (paper delivered at the Southern Jewish Historical Society Conference, Baltimore, 5 Nov. 2005); Deborah Weiner, *Coalfield Jews: An Appalachian Story* (Urbana: University of Illinois Press, 2006), 24–25.

3. Leonard Rogoff, *A History of Temple Emanu-El: An Extended Family, Weldon, North Carolina* (Durham: Jewish Heritage Foundation of North Carolina, 2007), 5; Charlotte Levin, "Belah and Jake: A Garden of Memories," typescript (1989), JHFNC.

4. Jennie Nachamson, ". . . always be good to each other," 6, typescript (1968), Duke.

5. Levin, "Belah and Jake," 4; Leonard Rogoff, *Homelands: Southern Jewish Identity in Durham and Chapel Hill, North Carolina* (Tuscaloosa: University of Alabama Press, 2001), 60–61; Ned Cline, *Success Is a Team Sport: The Marshall Rauch Family Story* (Gastonia: Rauch Family Foundation, 2004), 35.

6. Harry Stein, *Pathway to a Future* (New York: Carlton Press, 1980), 40; Barry Brodsky, *Temple Emanuel: A History of the First Seventy-five Years of Judaism in Gastonia* (n.p., n.d.)

7. Nachamson, ". . . always be good," 6; Mimi Cunningham, *The Joys of Politics: A Biography of B. D. Schwartz* (Wilmington, 1989), 15, Southeastern North Carolina Collection, William Madison Randall Library, University of North Carolina at Wilmington.

8. Monroe Evans, *A History of Beth Israel Congregation and the Jewish Community in Cumberland County* (Fayetteville, 2002), 46; Charlotte Litwack, "Recollections," 35, typescript (1976), JHFNC; Pearson, "The Morris Pearson Story," typescript, JHFNC.

9. Rogoff, *Homelands*, 56–57.

10. Letter from Miriam Weil, Feb. 1910, Weil Papers, NCSA; Charlotte Schiff Simmonds to Jacob Schiff, 16 Nov. 1905, IRO; Henry Feingold, "German Jews and the American-Jewish Synthesis," in Christof Mauch and Joseph Salmons, eds., *German Jewish Identities in America* (Madison: Max Kade Institute, 2003), 9.

11. B. Aronson to David Bressler, 19 July 1914; Bernard Nevelson to David Bressler, 22 Apr. 1905; Michael Kirschbaum to A. Solomon, 22 Oct. 1913, AJHS.

12. Marcia Horowitz, "The Jewish Community of Greensboro: Its Experience in a Progressive City" (M.A. thesis, University of North Carolina at Greensboro, 1993), 73–74; Robert Cain, "Immigrant Colonies," in William S. Powell, ed., *Encyclopedia of North Carolina* (Chapel Hill: University of North Carolina Press, 2006), 602.

13. "Land for Jewish Exiles," *Philadelphia Herald*, 22 Feb. 1882; Henry Katussowiski to Calvin Cowles, 2 Mar. 1882, NCSA; *Wilmington Star*, 29 May, 5 Sept. 1891; *Wilmington Messenger*, 27 Aug. 1891.

14. Rogoff, *Homelands*, 39, 57; Leonard Rogoff, "Is the Jew White? The Racial Place of the Southern Jew," in Mark Bauman, ed., *Dixie Diaspora: An Anthology of Southern Jewish History* (Tuscaloosa: University of Alabama Press, 2006), 394–95.

15. Paul Gaston, *The New South Creed: A Study in Southern Myth-Making* (Baton Rouge: Louisiana State University Press, 1976), 4.

16. Hugh Lefler, *History of North Carolina* (New York: Lewis Historical Publishing, 1956), 613; Robert Durden, "North Carolina in the New South," in Lindley Butler and Alan Watson, eds., *The North Carolina Experience: An Interpretive History* (Chapel Hill: University of North Carolina Press, 1984), 314–15.

17. Benjamin Cone Papers, MS Coll no. 25, box 3,

folder 1, Greensboro Historical Museum Archive, Greensboro, N.C.

18. Horowitz, "The Jewish Community of Greensboro," 49; *Greensboro Daily News*, 10 Sept. 1963; Lefler, *History of North Carolina*, 613; Milton Ready, *The Tar Heel State: A History of North Carolina* (Columbia: University of South Carolina Press, 2005), 267.

19. Lefler, *History of North Carolina*, 618, 619.

20. Ibid., 748, 750.

21. Ibid., 614, 619, 737.

22. Rogoff, *Homelands*, 42.

23. Ibid., 43.

24. Ibid., 43, 47.

25. Ibid., 47, 48.

26. Hiram Paul, *History of the Town of Durham, North Carolina* (Raleigh: Edwards and Broughton, 1884), 117–18; *Raleigh News & Observer*, 15 Sept. 1886.

27. A. Solomon to David Bressler, 19 Mar., 23 Mar. 1913, IRO, AJHS.

28. Horowitz, "The Jewish Community of Greensboro," 84–85, 86; <http://www.livingplaces.com/NC/Davidson_County/Lexington_City/Erlanger_Mill_ Village_Historic_District.html>, 3 Aug. 2008.

29. Deborah Weiner, *Coalfield Jews: An Appalachian History* (Urbana: University of Illinois Press, 2006), 24, 82; Gary Freeze, "Roots, Barks, Berries, and Jews: The Herb Trade in Gilded-Age North Carolina," in William Childs, ed., *Essays in Economic and Business History* (Columbus: Ohio State University, 1995), 113, 114.

30. Freeze, "Roots, Barks, Berries, and Jews," 118, 115.

31. Ibid., 117, 114, 116.

32. *The Landmark Trade Edition*, 20 May 1890, AJA; *Wilmington Messenger*, 14 June 1905; Marni Davis, "Bottoms Up: The Whiskey Trade and Southern Jewish Mobility," Southern Jewish Historical Society Annual Conference, Atlanta, Nov. 2008.

33. Lee Shai Weissbach, *Jewish Life in Small-Town America* (New Haven: Yale University Press, 2005), 26.

34. A. Solomon to David Bressler, 14, 16 Mar. 1913, IRO, AJHS.

35. Levin, "Belah and Jake," 9–10.

36. Evans, *History of Beth Israel Congregation*, 36.

37. C. Vann Woodward, *The Burden of Southern History* (Baton Rouge: Louisiana State University Press, 1968), 18; Rogoff, *Homelands*, 48.

38. Levin, "Jake and Belah," 115; Rogoff, *A History of Temple Emanu-El*, 7; *Raleigh News & Observer*, 10 Oct. 1997.

39. Litwack, "Recollections," 66; Rogoff, *A History of Temple Emanu-El*, 44; Irving Howe and Kenneth Libo, *How We Lived: A Documentary History of Immigrant Jews in America, 1880–1930* (New York: Richard Marek, 1979), 327–28.

40. *Laws and Resolutions of the State of North Carolina, 1879* (Raleigh: The Observer, 1879), p. 90, sec. 22; *Laws and Resolutions of the State of North Carolina, Session of 1885* (Raleigh: P. M. Hale, the State Printer), 283, 608.

41. *Wilmington Dispatch*, 23 Nov. 1900; *Wilmington Star*, 10 Feb. 1909, BRC.

42. *Durham Sun*, 21 Sept. 1901; *Raleigh News & Observer*, 14 July 1894; W. F. Shelton, *The Day the Black Rain Fell* (Louisburg: W. F. Shelton, 1984), 7–12.

43. Hugh B. Johnston Jr., "Oettinger's The Dependable Store," typescript, Wilson County Public Library, Wilson.

44. *Durham Sun*, 14 May 1904; Evans, *History of Beth Israel Congregation*, 18.

45. Litwack, "Recollections," 104.

46. Ibid., 67.

47. Rogoff, *Homelands*, 73.

48. Powell, *Encyclopedia of North Carolina*, 93; Morris Speizman, *The Jews of Charlotte, North Carolina* (Charlotte: McNally and Loftin, 1978), 83; *Kinston, N.C. Directory, 1908* (Richmond: Hill's Directory, 1908); Kimberly Sims, "Wilmington Jewry: 1800–1914" (Honors Program thesis, History Department, University of North Carolina at Wilmington, Apr. 1999), 39; Agudas Israel archives, Hendersonville, JHFNC.

49. R. D. W. Connor, *North Carolina: Rebuilding an Ancient Commonwealth, 1584–1925* (Chicago: American Historical Society, 1929), 63; Jan Schochet and Sharon Fahrer, *The Family Store: A History of Jewish Businesses, 1880–1990* (Asheville: History@Hand, 2006), 15–16; Harry Golden speculates, without corroboration, that David Ovens, partner of J. B. Ivey in a department store chain, was a secret Jew named Ovinsky. See Harry Golden, *Our Southern Landsmen* (New York: G. P. Putnam, 1974), 26–27; Dorothy Coplon, "The Coplons of North Carolina," *American Jewish Times-Outlook*, July–Aug. 1987, 4.

50. Lee Shai Weissbach, "Stability and Mobility in the Small Jewish Community: Examples from Kentucky History," *American Jewish History* 79, no. 3 (Spring 1990): 361, 371; *Durham Morning Herald*, 6 Jan. 1911; Anne and Morris Kaplan interview with Jill Savitt, 6 Mar. 1997, Agudas Israel archives, Hendersonville; Ed Patterson interview with Jill Savitt, Agudas Israel archives, Hendersonville.

51. Rogoff, *Homelands*, 78; Litwack, "Recollections," 68–69.

52. Schochet and Fahrer, *The Family Store*, 18.

53. Whitfield, *In Search of American Jewish Culture*, 51–52; Nachamson, ". . . always be good," 44.

54. *Durham Morning Herald*, 4 Dec. 1910; A. Solomon to David Bressler, 14 Mar. 1913, IRO, AJHS; "Sidney J. Stern," typescript, JHFNC.

55. Sims, "Wilmington Jewry: 1800–1914," 30; David Goldberg, "An Historical Community Study of Wilmington Jewry, 1738–1925" (History Seminar, University of North Carolina at Chapel Hill, Spring 1976), 28; Horowitz, "The Jewish Community of Greensboro," 53.

56. *Our State*, Oct. 1996, 3; Max Shevel, Durham County Probate Records, Will Book 3, 16 Mar. 1917, Durham County Courthouse, Durham; Wake County Real Estate Records, <http:rodwcb02.co.wake.nc.us/books/pr/prePrint.asp>, 27 June 2007.

57. Rountree, *Strangers in the Land*, 2; Letter from Harry Pearson to Louis Pearson, 28 May 1911, JHFNC.

58. *Wilmington Messenger*, 7 Dec. 1892, BRC.

59. Amy Crow, "'In Memory of the Confederate Dead': Masculinity and the Politics of Memorial Work in Goldsboro, North Carolina, 1894–1895," *North Carolina Historical Review* 83, no. 1 (Jan. 2006): 31; *Wilmington Morning Star*, 25 Feb. 1904; Seth Epstein, "Tolerance and Redemption: Zebulon Vance's 'The Scattered Nation' and Post-Reconstruction North Carolina" (paper presented at the Southern Jewish Historical Society annual conference, Atlanta, 4 Nov. 2008).

60. Goldberg, "An Historical Community Study," 30; Sims, "Wilmington Jewry: 1800–1914," 33–34; Rountree, *Strangers in the Land*, 103.

61. Auerbach, "Recollections," 18; Goldberg, "An Historical Community Study," 30; *Wilmington Messenger*, 12 Nov. 1895, Bill Reaves Collection, NHCPL.

62. *Durham Morning Herald*, 27 Mar. 1913.

63. Howard Rabinowitz, "Nativism, Bigotry, and Anti-Semitism in the South," in Mark Bauman, ed., *Dixie Diaspora: An Anthology of Southern Jewish History* (Tuscaloosa: University of Alabama Press, 2006), 279; *New Bern Daily Journal*, 28 June 1888; Goldberg, "An Historical Community Study," 22; *Winston-Salem Journal*, 25 Nov. 1885.

64. Goldberg, "An Historical Community Study," 32–33, 36; Rogoff, *Homelands*, 64–65.

65. Rogoff, *A History of Temple Emanu-El*, 6; Levin, "Belah and Jake," 116; Golden, *Our Southern Landsmen*, 160; Sydney Nathans, "The Quest for Progress: North Carolina, 1870–1920," in Joe Mobley, ed., *The Way We Lived in*

North Carolina (Chapel Hill: University of North Carolina Press, 2003), 446.

66. *Wilmington Star*, 27 Mar. 1904, 17 May 1911; *Wilmington Messenger*, 13 Nov. 1887; *NC Crossroads* 5, no. 2 (Apr./May 2001).

67. Nachamson, ". . . always be good," 40; *Wilmington Star*, 18 Feb. 1914; *Raleigh News & Observer*, 2 Apr. 1972; Thomas Wolfe, *Look Homeward, Angel* (New York: Modern Library, 1929), 96–97.

68. Speizman, *Jews of Charlotte*, 17; Wolfe, *Look Homeward, Angel*, 96.

69. *High Point Enterprise*, 13, 24 Sept. 1909; Goldberg, "An Historical Community Study," 22; Rogoff, *Homelands*, 107–9.

70. Letter from Morris Pearson to Louis Pearson, 7 Apr. 1913, JHFNC.

71. Ibid.; Goldberg, "An Historical Community Study," 31.

72. *New York Times*, 3 Mar. 1884; *Wilmington Star*, 3 Apr. 1891; Amy Grant, typescript (n.d.), JHFNC.

73. *Wilmington Dispatch*, 20 Feb. 1900, BRC; *Wilmington Star*, 17 Mar. 1912.

74. *Durham Morning Herald*, 7 Jan. 1914; *Wilmington Star*, 20 Mar. 1906, BRC.

75. Lefler, *History of North Carolina*, 651; Levin, "Belah and Jake," 51–52.

76. *Raleigh News & Observer*, 2 Apr. 1972; Cunningham, *The Joys of Politics*, 18; Rogoff, *Homelands*, 55–56; Goldsboro B'nai B'rith Leopold Zunz Lodge 364 Minutes, 15 Oct. 1913, 9 Jan. 1919, AJA; Wolfe, *Look Homeward Angel*, 95–97, 234; Paul Green, *Paul Green's Wordbook: An Alphabet of Reminiscence* (Boone: Appalachian Conservancy, 1990), 604; *American Jewish Times* 10 (Dec. 1944): 3; Jan Schochet and Sharon Fahrer, eds., *The Man Who Lived on Main Street: Stories by and about Sol Schulman* (Asheville: History@Hand, 2003), 11, 12.

77. Lefler, *History of North Carolina*, 655; Auerbach, "Recollections"; Clarice Elias. "Recollections of the Early Jewish Residents of Raleigh, North Carolina," typescript (n.d.), AJA.

78. Alice Cotton, "Lichtenstein, Gaston," in William S. Powell, ed., *Dictionary of North Carolina Biography*, vol. 4 (Chapel Hill: University of North Carolina Press, 1991), 64.

79. R. C. Lawrence, "Lionel Weil," *State* 11, no. 39 (26 Feb. 1944): 2.

80. *Chanticleer* (Durham: Organizations of Trinity Colleges, 1916).

81. Terri Leith, "Pre-eminently Practical," *NC State*,

June 1996, 6; Litwack, "Recollections," 106; Rogoff, Homelands, 85; Golden, My Southern Landsmen, 222.

82. Rogoff, Homelands, 95; Nachamson, ". . . always be good," 38, 44, 47.

83. Rogoff, Homelands, 95–96.

84. Ibid., 96–97.

85. Wilmington Messenger, 20, 30 Dec. 1900; Wilmington Star, 13 Jan. 1901.

86. Tobacco Plant, 11 Dec. 1888; North Carolina: Rebuilding an Ancient Commonwealth, 31.

87. Arthur T. Abernethy, A Jew a Negro, Being a Study of the Jewish Ancestry from an Impartial Standpoint (Moravian Falls: Dixie Publishing Co., 1910), 11, 107.

88. Sims, "Wilmington Jewry: 1800–1914," 43.

89. New York Times, 9 June 1903.

90. Rogoff, Homelands, 56; "1898 Wilmington Race Riot—Final Report, 31 May 2006," 631, 681, <http://www.history.ncdcr.gov/1898-wrrc/report/report.htm>, 25 Sept., 2008.

91. Lefler, History of North Carolina, 69; New Berne Weekly, 25, 28 Oct. 1898.

92. Eric Goldstein, The Price of Whiteness: Jews, Race, and American Identity (Princeton: Princeton University Press, 2006), 58; Messenger, 21 Nov. 1895, 28, 31 March 1898; Laurie Gunst, Off White: A Memoir (New York: Soho Press, 2005), 258.

93. "1898 Wilmington Race Riot—Final Report," 98.

94. Ibid., 964–95, 105; Goldberg, "An Historical Community Study," 35; Raleigh News & Observer, 8 Oct. 1898.

95. "1898 Wilmington Race Riot—Final Report," 114; "Signatures to Resolutions Passed at Citizens Meeting held Nov. 9/98," A. M. Waddell Papers, SHC.

96. Jewish South, 24 Nov. 1898.

97. North Carolina, vol. 7, pp. 62, 139, Dun & Co. Collection, Baker Library Historical Collections, Harvard Business School.

98. New Bern Journal, 28 Oct. 1898.

99. Charles Chesnutt, The Marrow of Tradition (New York: Penguin Books, 1993), 33.

100. New Bern Daily Journal, 27, 29, 30 Oct., 5, 10 Nov. 1898; Raleigh News & Observer, 30 Oct. 1898.

101. New Bern Daily Journal, 12 Nov. 1898, 14 Sept. 1899.

102. New Bern Daily Journal, 30 Oct. 1898; Gunst, Off-White: A Memoir, 257–58; Chesnutt, The Marrow of Tradition, 289–90.

103. Hasia Diner, A Time for Gathering: The Second Migration, 1820–1880 (Baltimore: Johns Hopkins University Press, 1992), 144–45.

104. Raleigh News & Observer, 17 Nov. 1906; Sims, "Wilmington Jewry: 1800–1914," 36; Diner, A Time for Gathering, 144–45.

105. "1898 Wilmington Race Riot—Final Report," 698.

106. Roanoke News, 24 Feb. 1898; Rogoff, A History of Temple Emanu-El, 3–4; Raleigh News & Observer, 3 Jan. 1896.

107. Rogoff, Homelands, 98–99.

108. Gary Zola, "The Ascendancy of Reform Judaism in the American South during the Nineteenth Century," in Marcie Cohen Ferris and Mark Greenberg, eds., Jewish Roots in Southern Soil: A New History (Waltham: Brandeis University Press, 2006), 156.

109. Statesville Landmark Trade Edition, 22 May 1890. Charlotte's German Jews were exceptional in not creating a synagogue.

110. Goldsboro Argus, 1 Jan. 1887; Rountree, Strangers in the Land, 64; Sims, "Wilmington Jewry: 1800–1914," 42.

111. Beverly Tetterton, Helen Solomon, and JoAnn Fogler, eds., History of the Temple of Israel (Wilmington, 2001), 14–15; Kinston Free Press, 17 Aug. 1918; Letter from Rev. Charles Arik to Dear Friends, 2 June 1910, AJA; Speizman, Jews of Charlotte, 15.

112. Rountree, Strangers in the Land, 52, 58–60; Herbert Ezekiel and Gaston Lichtenstein, The History of the Jews of Richmond 1769 to 1917 (Richmond: Herbert Ezekiel, 1917), 277.

113. Wilmington Messenger, 13 Jan., 5 Feb. 1893.

114. "Twenty-Second Annual Report, Proceedings of the Executive Board of the Union of American Hebrew Congregations" (Dec. 1895), 3433, AJA; Greensboro News-Record, 9 Sept. 2007.

115. Digest of the Minutes of Oheb Sholom Congregation, 1883–1958, AJA; [Tarboro] Congregation B'nai Israel Congregational Minutes, 6 July 1884, AJA; The Golden Book of Memoirs: Fiftieth Anniversary of Congregation Beth Ha-Tephila (Asheville, 1941), 7.

116. Rogoff, Homelands, 66–67, 102; Sarna, American Judaism, 159.

117. Sarna, American Judaism, 185, 186, 191.

118. Brodsky, Temple Emanuel.

119. Leonard Rogoff, "Synagogue and Jewish Church: A Congregational History of North Carolina," Southern Jewish History 1 (1998): 65; Litwack, "Recollections," 118.

120. Digest of the Minutes of Oheb Sholom Congregation 1883–1958, AJA; Rogoff, Homelands, 111, 107; Evans, History of Beth Israel Congregation, 26–27.

121. Rogoff, Homelands, 102, 142; Minutes, B'nai Israel, 1909, JHFNC.

122. "The Winston-Salem Hebrew Congregation," *American Jewish Times* (suppl., 1932), 13; Report from A. Solomon to Industrial Removal Office, 14 Mar. 1913 IRO, AJHS; Rogoff, *Homelands*, 103.

123. *Wilmington Morning Star*, 21 Jan. 1898.

124. A. Solomon to David Bressler, 23 Mar. 1913, IRO, AJHS; Jacob Rader Marcus, *United States Jewry, 1776–1985* (Detroit: Wayne State University Press, 1989–93), 689.

125. A. Rossman, "History of the Jewish Community of Greensboro," *American Jewish Times* (suppl. 1932), 10; "A History of Temple Beth Or" (n.d.), 10, JHFNC; *Golden Book of Memoirs*, 21.

126. Sarna, *American Judaism*, 197; *Golden Book of Memoirs* 7, 52.

127. Sarna, *American Judaism*, 164; Rogoff, *Homelands*, 141; Karla Goldman, *Beyond the Synagogue Gallery: Finding a Place for Women in American Judaism* (Cambridge, Mass.: Harvard University Press, 2000), 202; Annual Statement of the Charity Work Done by the Jewish Ladies Aid Society of Asheville, North Carolina, August, 1916, UNC-A.

128. Annual Statement of the Charity Work; Mrs. L. H. Pollock to the Jewish Ladies Aid Society, undated, UNC-A; Auerbach, "Recollections," 13; Emma Schiff Simmonds to David Bressler, 25 Nov. 1905, AJHS; *Wilmington Messenger*, 8 Nov. 1895, BRC.

129. A. Solomon to David Bressler, 14 Mar. 1913; Rogoff, *Homelands*, 101.

130. Samuel Mayerberg, *Chronicle of an American Crusader* (New York: Bloch, 1944), 5; Michael Barker Ledger, JHFNC, courtesy of Michelle Leder; Rabbi L. A. Peres Papers, JHFNC, courtesy of Sara Ziskin.

131. A. Solomon to David Bressler, 19 Mar. 1913, IRO, AJHS; Mayerberg, *Chronicle of an American Crusader*, 5; Leon Finkelstein, *Leo Finkelstein and the Poor Man's Bank* (Boone: Center for Appalachian Studies, 1998), 39.

132. Sam Pearson to Louis Pearson, 27 Mar. 1911, JHFNC.

133. *Temple Emanuel: The First Fifty Years, 1907–1957* (Greensboro, 1958), JHFNC.

134. Emma Schiff Simmonds to Nathan Schiff, 16 Nov. 1905, AJHS.

135. *Wilmington Star*, 24 Sept. 1914; *Wilmington Dispatch*, 1 Feb. 1918, BRC, NHCPL.

136. Levin, "Belah and Jake," 30; *Report of the Building Committee of the Beth-El Congregation* (Durham, 1921), 6; *Rockingham Post-Dispatch*, 9 Oct. 1919; William S. Powell, "Mendelsohn, Charles Jastrow," in Powell, *Dictionary of North Carolina Biography*, vol. 4, 251–52.

137. James Seymour, ed., *Memorial Volume of the American Field Service in France* (Boston: American Field Service, 1921), 102; *Raleigh News & Observer*, 7 Mar. 1958; *Statesville Landmark*, 2 Sept. 1918.

138. Auerbach, "Recollections," 14–15; *Charlotte Observer*, 30 Sept. 1934.

139. Rogoff, "Synagogue and Jewish Church," 59.

140. Lionel Weil to J. H. Hoffmann, 29 July 1918, Lionel Weil Papers, NCSA.

141. W. B. Council to Lionel Weil, 12 Aug. 1918; J. M Gamell to Lionel Weil, 17 Aug. 1918; J. W. Williams to Lionel Weil, 15 Aug. 1918, Lionel Weil Papers, NCSA.

142. W. R. Allen on Jewish War Relief, n.d., Lionel Weil Papers, NCSA; *Raleigh News & Observer*, 18 Aug. 1918.

143. *Kinston Free Press*, 17 August 1918.

144. Cunningham, *Joys of Politics*, 85.

145. Rountree, *Strangers in the Land*, 103–9.

146. Martin Raffel, "History of Israel Advocacy," in Alan Mittleman, Jonathan Sarna, and Robert Licht, eds., *Jewish Polity and American Civil Society* (Lanham: Rowman and Littlefield, 2002), 106; Nachamson, ". . . always be good," 52; *Asheville Times*, 8 Apr. 1916.

147. Sylvia Barack Fishman, *Jewish Life and American Culture* (Albany: State University of New York Press, 2000), 1; George B. Tindall, *The Ethnic Southerner* (Baton Rouge: Louisiana State University Press, 1976), 11.

CHAPTER 5

1. Lee Shai Weissbach, *Jewish Life in Small-Town America* (New Haven: Yale University Press, 2005), 1, 18, 30; William Levitt, "The Occupational Distribution of the Jews in North Carolina" (Master's thesis, University of North Carolina, 1938), 2, 13.

2. Weissbach, *Jewish Life in Small-Town America*, 350; *American Jewish Yearbook* (Philadelphia: Jewish Publication Society, 1927), 910–91.

3. John Kobler, "Why They Don't Hate Harry," *Saturday Evening Post*, 20 Sept. 1958, 126; *Carolina Israelite*, Aug. 1957.

4. Levitt, "The Occupational Distribution of the Jews," 29.

5. Henry Feingold, *A Time for Searching: Entering the Mainstream, 1920–1945* (Baltimore: Johns Hopkins University Press, 1992), 125–26; *Whiteville News Reporter*, 21 June 1945.

6. Durham County Tax Rolls, 1910, 1925, Durham County Courthouse.

7. *Greensboro Record*, 5, 6 June 1923; "Sidney J. Stern,

Correspondence from 1936–1944," Sidney J. Stern to Herbert Bluethenthal, 1 Mar. 1939, JHFNC.

8. Leon Finkelstein, *Leo Finkelstein and the Poor Man's Bank* (Boone: Center for Appalachian Studies, 1998), 31–32; "Memories of New Bern," Elbert Lipman with Dr. Joseph Patterson, New Bern Oral History Project No. 4751, SHC, UNC-CH.

9. Leonard Rogoff, *Homelands: Southern Jewish Identity in Durham and Chapel Hill, North Carolina* (Tuscaloosa: University of Alabama Press, 2001), 147–48; Jonathan Sarna, *American Judaism* (New Haven: Yale University Press, 2004), 218; Finkelstein, *Leo Finkelstein's Asheville*, 25.

10. Rogoff, *Homelands*, 132–33; *Durham Morning Herald*, 25 Jan. 1922; 7 Sept. 1927.

11. Jan Schochet and Sharon Fahrer, eds., *The Man Who Lived on Main Street: Stories by and about Sol Schulman* (Asheville: History@Hand, 2003), 11, 12; *American Jewish Times* 10, no. 4 (Dec. 1944): 3; letter from Leonard Lewis to Morris Kaplan, 26 Apr. 1983; Ed Patterson interview with Jill Savitt, 7 Mar. 1997, Agudas Israel archives, Hendersonville.

12. Rogoff, *Homelands*, 88, 147; David Citron, Temple Israel interview, CJHS.

13. James Baker, "The Battle of Elizabeth City: Christ and Antichrist in North Carolina," *North Carolina Historical Review* 54, no. 4 (Oct. 1977): 401.

14. W. O. Saunders, *The Book of Ham* (Elizabeth City: Independent, 1932), 3; Edward E. Ham, *50 Years on the Battle Front with Christ: A Biography of Mordecai F. Ham* (Louisville: Old Kentucky Home Revivalist, 1950), 165.

15. Thomas Parramore, "Express Lanes and Country Roads: North Carolina, 1920–1001," in Joe Mobley, ed., *The Way We Lived in North Carolina* (Chapel Hill: University of North Carolina Press, 2003), 554.

16. *Williamston Enterprise*, 27 Mar., 7 May 1925; *Kinston Daily Free Press*, 3 Apr. 1925.

17. *Kinston Daily Free Press*, 30 Mar. 1925; *Williamston Enterprise*, 12 May 1925.

18. *Kinston Daily Free Press*, 4 Apr., 20 Mar. 1925.

19. Rogoff, *Homelands*, 131–32; Thomas Wolfe, *Look Homeward, Angel* (New York: Modern Library, 1929), 234–35. Vann Newkirk, *Lynching in North Carolina: A History, 1865–1941* (Jefferson: MacFarland, 2009), 86, 93.

20. Levitt, "The Occupational Distribution of the Jews," 74; Emma Edwards, "A History of North Carolina's Association of Jewish Women," *American Jewish Times*, Apr. 1936, 13; Charlotte Levin, "Belah and Jake: A Garden of Memories," 109, typescript (1989), JHFNC.

21. Leonard Rogoff, *A History of Temple Emanu-El, Weldon, North Carolina* (Durham: Jewish Heritage Foundation of North Carolina, 2007), 34; *Winston-Salem Journal*, 15 Oct. 1989.

22. Deborah Dash Moore, ed., *American Jewish Identity Politics* (Ann Arbor: University of Michigan Press, 2008), 6; Sarna, *American Judaism*, 226.

23. Rogoff, *Homelands*, 201; Hebrew School Committee, Hendersonville, 5 Jan. 1927, Agudas Israel archives, Hendersonville.

24. Frederick Block, *Tales of a Shirtmaker: A Jewish Upbringing in North Carolina* (Wilmington: Winoca Press, 2005), 19; Jeffrey Gurock, "The Orthodox Synagogue," in Jack Wertheimer, ed., *The American Synagogue: A Sanctuary Transformed* (New York: Cambridge University Press, 1987), 52; Rogoff, *Homelands*, 143.

25. Richard Zweigenhaft and G. W. Domhoff, *Jews in the Protestant Establishment* (New York: Praeger, 1982), 81.

26. Samuel Wrubel, "What Camp Life Really Means," *American Jewish Times*, Aug. 1938, 5, 6; "Osceola Well-Equipped for Boy Building," *American Jewish Times*, Aug. 1938, 5, 6.

27. Quoted in Rogoff, *Homelands*, 137; Elsie Samet, "Mama Needs a Shul," typescript, JHFNC.

28. Morris Speizman, *The Jews of Charlotte, North Carolina* (Charlotte: McNally and Loftin, 1978), 19–20; Agudas Israel Minutes, 29 Dec. 1926, JHFNC; Rogoff, *Homelands*, 182.

29. Anna Goldberg Shain, *The Story of Anna* (n.p.: privately printed, n.d.), JHFNC.

30. Ida Smith, Charlotte Oral History, 2, CJHS; Block, *Tales of a Shirtmaker*, 37; Monroe Evans, *A History of Beth Israel Congregation and the Jewish Community in Cumberland County, North Carolina* (Fayetteville, 2002), 63.

31. Hasia Diner, *A Time for Gathering: The Second Migration, 1820-1880* (Baltimore: Johns Hopkins University Press, 1992), 249; Sarna, *American Judaism*, 254.

32. *The Golden Book of Memoirs: Fiftieth Anniversary of Congregation Beth Ha-Tephila* (Asheville, 1941), 22–24.

33. Rabbi William Greenburg, interview with Wendy Cooper, Temple Israel, CJHS; *American Jewish Times*, Apr. 1938, 41.

34. Richard Levin, *Growing Up: A Personal History* (Chapel Hill: Professional Press, 2007), 39.

35. Charlotte Litwack, "Recollections," 52, typescript (1976), JHFNC.

36. Arthur Goodman Jr., Temple Israel interview; Jerry

Levin, Temple Israel interview, CJHS. *Down Home: Jewish Life in North Carolina* (documentary film produced by Steven Channing and Henry A. Greene, 2009).

37. Evans, *A History of Beth Israel Congregation*, 61; Block, *Tales of a Shirtmaker*, 4; Karla Goldman, *Beyond the Synagogue Gallery* (Cambridge, Mass.: Harvard University Press, 2001), 202. Goldman's generalization about the nineteenth century holds true for the twentieth.

38. Digest of the Minutes of Oheb Sholom Congregation, 1883–1958, AJA.

39. Marcia Horowitz, "The Jewish Community of Greensboro: Its Experience in a Progressive City" (M.A. thesis, University of North Carolina at Greensboro, 1993), 95; Kurt Lauenstein, *Temple Emanuel Greensboro, 1907–2007*, 24, JHFNC; *American Jewish Times*, May 1938; *North Carolina: Rebuilding an Ancient Commonwealth*, American Historical Society III (1928), 63, AJA.

40. Levin, "Belah and Jake," 88, 97; Mark Bauman, "Role Theory and History," in Mark Bauman, ed., *Dixie Diaspora* (Tuscaloosa: University of Alabama Press, 2006), 242.

41. Rogoff, *Homelands*, 173.

42. Morris Speizman, *The Jews of Charlotte, North Carolina* (Charlotte: McNally and Loftin, 1978), 92–93.

43. Ibid., 94, 95–96.

44. *Winston-Salem Journal*, 10 July 2007.

45. Jon Bradshaw, *Dreams That Money Can Buy: The Tragic Life of Libby Holman* (New York: William Morrow, 1985), 301; *Winston-Salem Journal*, 12 July 2007.

46. *Winston-Salem Journal*, 12 July 2007.

47. *Down Home: Jewish Life in North Carolina* (documentary film).

48. Ron Levin, *The Long Journey Home* (Liberty: My Father's Business, 1994), 18; Lauenstein, *Temple Emanuel Greensboro, 1907–2007*, 21, 51.

49. Cheryl Lynn Greenberg, *Troubling the Waters: Black-Jewish Relations in the American Century* (Princeton: Princeton University Press, 2006), 41; Thomas Hanchett, "The Rosenwald Schools and Black Education in North Carolina," *North Carolina Historical Review* 65, no. 4 (Oct. 1988): 398.

50. William S. Powell, ed., *Encyclopedia of North Carolina* (Chapel Hill: University of North Carolina Press, 2006), 527; Milton Ready, *The Tar Heel State: A History of North Carolina* (Columbia: University of South Carolina Press, 2005), 323, 324, 328.

51. Letter from Michael Barker to Mr. Arner, 28 May 1942, JHFNC.

52. Rogoff, *Homelands*, 150; Elaine Simons and Faela Backer, "Bridging the Generation Gap," 6 May 1970, JHFNC.

53. Parramore, "Express Lanes and Country Roads," 487, 510; Ready, *Tar Heel State*, 339.

54. Rogoff, *Homelands*, 152; *Wilmington Morning Star*, 3 June 1938, NHCPL; L. Edward Lashman Jr., Letter to the Editors, *Commentary*, 26 Dec. 1953, HGP, UNC-C.

55. Parramore, "Express Lanes and Country Roads," 500, 501.

56. <http://www.bbc.co.uk/radio4/arts/arthurmiller.shtml>, 12 Oct. 2008.

57. Harry Golden, "Causerie: The Textile Workers and the South," typescript, Harry Golden Papers, Mecklenburg County Public Library, Charlotte, North Carolina; Ned Cline, *Success Is a Team Sport: The Marshall Rauch Story* (Gastonia: Rauch Family Foundation, 2004), 40.

58. Levitt, "The Occupational Distribution of the Jews in North Carolina," 70–71.

59. Ibid., 65.

60. Ibid. 68.

61. Ibid., 75.

62. Ibid., 72; Letter from Michael Barker to Mr. Arner, 28 May 1942, JHFNC.

63. Ed Patterson interview with Jill Savitt, 7 Mar. 1997, Agudas Israel archives, Hendersonville.

64. Horowitz, "The Jewish Community of Greensboro," 33; Wilson Gee, "The 'Drag' of Talent Out of the South," *Social Forces* 15 (March 1937): 343.

65. Rogoff, *Homelands*, 158–59.

66. Rogoff, "A History of Temple Emanu-El," 17–18.

67. Rogoff, *Homelands*, 134; Ned Cline, *Success Is a Team Sport: The Marshall Rauch Family Story* (Gastonia: Rauch Family Foundation, 2004), 63.

68. Arthur Goldberg, "Report from the Campus," *American Jewish Times*, June 1944, 11; *North Carolina Association of Jewish Women Yearbook, 1935–36* (Greensboro, 1936), 51–53.

69. Rogoff, *Homelands*, 159–60.

70. Edward Halperin, "Frank Porter Graham, Isaac Hall Manning, and the Jewish Quota at the University of North Carolina Medical School," *North Carolina Historical Review* 67, no. 4 (Oct. 1990): 393–94.

71. Henry Landsberger and Christoph Schweitzer, eds., *They Fled Hitler's Germany and Found Refuge in North Carolina* (Chapel Hill: Academic Affairs Library, 1996), 51; Marcia Synnott, "Anti-Semitism and American Universities: Did Quotas Follow the Jews?" in David Gerber, ed.,

Anti-Semitism in American History(Urbana: University of Illinois Press, 1992), 263; Rogoff, *Homelands*, 165.

72. Rogoff, *Homelands*, 161.

73. Mrs. Gustav Licthenfels, "As I Look into the New Year, I Have Hope for the Future," *American Jewish Times*, Sept. 1939, 96.

74. Rogoff, *Homelands*, 169–70.

75. "Praeterea Censeo Germaniam Esse Delendam," Purim Sermon, 9 March 1933, AJA; Finkelstein, *Leo Finkelstein's Asheville*, 31; *American Jewish Times*, May,1938, 22; <http://museum.unc.edu/exhibits/jewishlife/robert-rolnik>.

76. David Wyman, *The Abandonment of the Jews* (New York: Pantheon, 1986), 217; Lichtenfels, "As I Look into the New Year, I Have Hope for the Future," 20; Rogoff, *Homelands*, 170.

77. *American Jewish Times*, Apr. 1938, 60; Apr. 1944, 7; Apr. 1941, 16; May 1943, 14; Ronald Schechter, *Obstinate Hebrews: Representations of Jews in France, 1715-1815* (Berkeley: University of California Press, 2003), 252.

78. *American Jewish Times*, Apr. 1941, 16; Rogoff, *Homelands*, 170.

79. *American Jewish Times*, Mar. 1940, 23; Rogoff, *Homelands*, 191; Asheville, Beth Ha-Tephila, Board of Directors Meeting, 9 Nov. 1944, AJA.

80. Paul Ritterband and Harold Wechsler, *Jewish Learning in American Universities* (Bloomington: Indiana University Press, 1994), 127–28; Harvie Branscomb, "A Note on Establishing Chairs of Jewish Studies," in Leon Jick, ed., *The Teaching of Judaica in American Universities* (Waltham: Association for Jewish Studies, 1970), 97–98.

81. *American Jewish Times*, Sept. 1939, 96; Jan. 1944, 5.

82. *North Carolina Association of Jewish Women Yearbook, 1936-1937* (Greensboro, 1937), 10; *American Jewish Times*, June 1944, 5; Dec. 1940, 13; May 1942; Oct. 1941, 13.

83. Emma Edwards, "North Carolina Jewish Women and Their Interests," *American Jewish Times*, Sept. 1939, 19; Moore, *American Jewish Identity Politics*, 14.

84. *Golden Book of Memoirs*, 29.

85. *American Jewish Times*, June 1946, 9; I. H. Jacobson, "Hillel and the Jewish Student," in *North Carolina Association of Jewish Women Yearbook, 1937-1938* (Greensboro, 1938), 44; Goldberg, "Report from the Campus," 11.

86. *American Jewish Times*, June 1941, 6.

87. Evans, *A History of Beth Israel Congregation* 150–51.

88. *Greensboro Federation News*, Jan. 1985, 4, 5.

89. *American Jewish Times*, Oct. 1939, 103.

90. Arthrell Sanders, "Former NCCU Prof. Recounts Odyssey," *North Carolina Central University Newsletter* 1 (Fall 1984): 3, 5; Gabrielle Edgcomb, *From Swastika to Jim Crow: Refugee Scholars at Black Colleges* (Malabar: Krieger, 1993), 132.

91. Landsberger and Schweitzer, *They Fled Hitler's Germany*, 126. See Martin Duberman, *Black Mountain: An Exploration in Community* (New York: Norton, 1993).

92. Schweitzer and Landsberger, *They Fled Hitler's Germany*, 121.

93. *Durham Sun*, 13 June 1943; Powell, *Encyclopedia of North Carolina*, 1231; Cone: *A Century of Excellence; The History of Cone Mills 1891 to 1991* (n.p., n.d.), 27.

94. Pearl Teiser Kahn, "Jewish War Record, 1941–1945," courtesy of David Glass, JHFNC; *American Jewish Times*, July 1946, 22; <www.ridge-inn.com/Pages/Press.html>, 2 June 2007.

95. Sarna, *American Judaism*, 264.

96. *American Jewish Times*, Nov. 1943; Apr. 1944, 34.

97. *American Jewish Times*, Aug. 1946, 10.

98. *American Jewish Times*, Nov. 1943, 33; Dec. 1943, 12.

99. *American Jewish Times*, Nov. 1941.

100. Evans, *A History of Beth Israel Congregation* 101, 123; *American Jewish Times*, Nov. 1943, 33; Nov. 1941, 12; Dec. 1943, 12; Apr. 1940.

101. *American Jewish Times*, Apr. 1940; Oct. 1944, 39.

102. Rogoff, *Homelands*, 194; <http://www.alemannia-judaica.de/images/Noerdlingen/FS-STERNGLANZ-DAVID.pdf>, 20 Oct. 2008.

103. "Shoah: Survivors & Witnesses in Western North Carolina," <http://www.toto.lib.unca.edu/projects/Shoa/hoffman.htm>, 12 Oct. 2008; "Choosing to Remember: From the Shoah to the Mountains," <http://www.toto.lib.unca.edu/projects/Shoa/reich.htm>, 12 Oct. 2008; Lauenstein, *Temple Emanuel Greensboro, 1907-2007*, 39.

104. *American Jewish Times*, May 1943, 6; Rogoff, *Homelands*, 195. Sol Robinowitz to King Farouk, 3 July 1949, JHFNC.

105. Letter from Harry Golden to Noel Houston, 26 Jan. 1956, HGP; "The Governor's Dinner," 16 Mar. 1952, UNC-C; *American Jewish Times*, Aug. 1947, 17. Joseph Morrison, "A Southern Philo-Semite: Josephus Daniels of North Carolina," *American Judaism* 12, no. 1 (Winter 1963): 78.

106. Leonard Dinnerstein, *Anti-Semitism in America* (New York: Oxford University Press, 1994), 188; Rogoff, *Homelands*, 221–22.

107. "The Carolina Story: A Virtual Museum," <http://

museum.unc.edu/exhibits/hans-freistadt>, 19 Oct. 2008; "The Carolina Story," <http://museum.unc.edu/exhibits/jewishlife/leonard-bernstein>, 2 Dec. 2008.

108. William Chafe, *Never Stop Running: Allard Lowenstein and the Struggle to Save American Liberalism* (New York: Basic Books, 1993), 38–39.

109. Eugene Feldman to Harry Golden, 17 Oct. 1955, HGP.

110. Greenberg, *Troubling the Waters*, 186, 196–96; Harry Golden to Rabbi Conrad, 9 Jan. 1956, HGP.

111. Rabbi Sidney Unger to Rev. Mark Jenkins, 9 Feb. 1956; Rabbi Sidney Unger to General John Sloan, 21 Oct. 1953, AJA.

112. Diner, *A Time for Gathering*, 229; *Wilmington Star*, 5 Apr. 1946, Bill Reaves Collection, NHCPL; *Fayetteville Observer-Times*, 17 Jan. 1982.

113. Bonnie Wexler to Editor, *Carolina Alumni Review* 86, no. 5 (Sept.–Oct. 1997): 23; Rogoff, *Homelands*, 197, 215.

114. Barry Farber, "The Cost of Killing Jews," 29 July 2006, <http://archive.newsmax.com/archives/2006>; *Danville Register*, 23 Aug. 1953, UNC-C. *Winston-Salem Journal*, 15 Oct. 1989; Harry Golden to Leo Pfeffer, 19 Oct. 1955, HGP; Hadley Cantril, *Public Opinion, 1935-1946* (Princeton: Princeton University Press, 1951), 384; Rogoff, *Homelands*, 207.

115. Jack Kugelmass, *Jews, Sports, and the Rites of Civilization* (Urbana: University of Illinois Press, 2007), 21.

116. *Raleigh News & Observer*, 5 June 2005; Herbert Drooz to Sidney Unger, 24 May 1961, AJA.

117. See Zweigenhaft and Domhoff, *Jews in the Protestant Establishment*.

118. Ibid., 80; Ned Cline, *Frankly Speaking* (Greensboro: Stanley and Dorothy Frank Family Foundation, 2001), 184.

119. *Carolina Israelite*, May–June 1964; Bobby Patterson to Mr. Diamond, 24 June 1995, AJA; Jonathan Sarna, "The 'Mythical Jew' and the 'Jew Next Door,'" in David Gerber, ed., *Anti-Semitism in American History* (Urbana: University of Illinois Press, 1986), 57–78.

120. Rogoff, *A History of Temple Emanu-El*, 62.

121. Leonard Rogoff, interview with Zelda Bernard; *Raleigh News & Observer*, 1 Mar. 1970; Zweigenhaft and Domhoff, *Jews in the Protestant Establishment*, 78, 79.

122. Marc Lee Raphael, *Profiles in American Judaism* (San Francisco: Harper and Row, 1984), 72; Arthur Hertzberg, *Jews in America: Four Centuries of an Uneasy Encounter* (New York: Simon and Schuster, 1989), 323.

123. Walter Shapiro, Temple of Israel oral history, CJHS.

124. Rogoff, *Homelands*, 235.

125. Rogoff, *A History of Temple Emanu-El*, 45; *Golden Book of Memoirs*, 7.

126. Leah and Morris Karpen interview with Dorothy Joynes, 15 May 2002, Voices of Asheville, UNC-A. <http://www.toto.lib.unca.edu/findingaids/oralhistory/VO>, 25 July 2009.

127. "Migrations: the Jewish Settlers of Eastern North Carolina," *NC Crossroads* 5, no. 2 (Apr.–May 2001).

128. Sarna, *American Judaism*, 222; *American Jewish Times*, Sept. 1937, 94; David Schulman, "Mr. Horowitz's Holiday," *Our State*, Aug. 2002, 65–66; Agudas Israel archives, Hendersonville.

129. Maxine Sellers, AMJHISTORY Query on Jewish Debutantes, 19 Jan. 2007.

130. Rogoff, *A History of Temple Emanu-El*, 56.

131. Farber, "The Cost of Killing Jews"; Don Michalove interview with Jill Savitt, 3 Mar. 1995, Agudas Israel archive, Hendersonville.

132. North Carolina Jewish Education Conference, 20 Nov. 1952; North Carolina Association of Jewish Women, 8 Aug., 1955, NCSA.

133. "Report of the Divine Service Committee," Beth Ha-Tephila, 1951, AJA; "Some Highlights of the Circuit Riding Rabbi Program," n.d., JHFNC; Rogoff, *Homelands*, 202; Chazzan Robert Shapiro, Temple Israel interview; Shel Goldstein, Temple Israel interview, CJHS; Report of the Religious School Committee, Temple Beth Ha-Tephilia, 25 June 1960, UNC-A.

134. "Just an Average Hadassah Family," *Hadassah's Planned Giving and Estates Newsletter* 12, no. 1 (Spring 2008): 1.

135. "Circuit Riding Rabbi," North Carolina Association of Jewish Men brochure, JHFNC.

136. Rogoff, *A History of Temple Emanu-El*, 43.

137. Harold Friedman to I. D. Blumenthal, 13 Dec. 1953, JHFNC; "Synagogue on Wheels," *Eternal Light*, 30 Sept. 1956, Jewish Theological Seminary of America, AJA.

138. "Some Highlights of the Circuit Riding Rabbi and Mobile Synagogue," 18 Nov. 1955; Reuben Kesner, "Short Circuit," *Women's League Outlook* 41, no. 1 (Fall 1970): 12.

139. Rogoff, *A History of Temple Emanu-El*, 47–48.

140. Marimar McNaughton, "Aging Gracefully Her Way: The Hannah Block Story," *Wrightsville Beach Magazine*, June 2006, 114; *High Point Enterprise*, 31 Aug. 1980.

141. Mimi Cunningham, *The Joys of Politics: A Biography of B. D. Schwartz* (Wilmington, 1989), 311, Southeastern

North Carolina Collection, William Madison Randall Library, University of North Carolina at Wilmington; Eli Evans, *The Provincials: A Personal History of Jews in the South* (Chapel Hill: University of North Carolina Press, 2005), 321.

142. Cline, *Success Is a Team Sport*, 140–41.

143. City of Charlotte, North Carolina, City Council Resolution, 1 Oct. 1958, HGP; Albert Vorspan to I. Cyrus Gordon, 3 Mar. 1958, AJA; David Cunningham, "Truth, Reconciliation, and the Ku Klux Klan," *Southern Cultures*, Fall 2008, 70.

144. Harry Golden Memo to Dr. George Mitchell, 23 May 1956, HGP; Raymond Arsenault, *Freedom Riders: 1961 and the Struggle for Racial Justice* (New York: Oxford, 2006), 4.

145. "Freedom Day Celebration" program, 1 May 1966, AJA; Arsenault, *Freedom Riders*, 53; Harry Golden, "Incident on a Southern Campus," *Congress Weekly* 22, no. 17 (May 2, 1955): 11.

146. Speizman, *Jews of Charlotte*, 90; Greenberg, *Troubling the Waters*, 128; Arsenault, *Freedom Riders*, 6, 28. The most ardent and bloodied architect of the Freedom Rider movement since 1947 was Jim Peck, from a wealthy Episcopalian family of Jewish origin.

147. Albert Vorspan to I. Cyrus Gordon, 3 Mar. 1958, AJA; *Daily Tar Heel*, 6 Nov. 1958; Greenberg, *Troubling the Waters*, 164.

148. See Mark Bauman and Berkley Kalin, *The Quiet Voices: Southern Rabbis and Black Civil Rights, 1880 to 1990s* (Tuscaloosa: University of Alabama Press, 1997); Resolution of the North Carolina Association of Rabbis adopted at Little Switzerland, 18 Aug. 1955, JHFNC; Golden, "Incident on a Southern Campus," 11.

149. Leonard Rogoff, "Rabbis and Race in North Carolina," Southern Rabbis and Black Civil Rights symposium, University of Memphis, 31 Mar. 1995; Greenberg, *Troubling the Waters*, 99; Rabbi Simcha Kling letter to Jacob R. Marcus, AJA; Rogoff, *Homelands*, 226; Rabbi Simcha Kling letter to Jacob R. Marcus, 20 Mar. 1957.

150. Joseph Asher to Albert Vorspan, 27 May 1963, AJA.

151. Rogoff, "Rabbis and Race."

152. Lauenstein, *Temple Emanuel Greensboro, 1907–2007*, 52; Rogoff, "Rabbis and Race"; Speizman, *Jews of Charlotte*, 91.

153. Harry Golden to Dr. George S. Mitchell, 2 Feb. 1956, HGP.

154. *Seventy Fifth Anniversary Celebration, 1929–2004,*

Temple Emanuel, Gastonia, North Carolina. April 16 & 17, 2004; American Jewish Times, Dec. 1954, 10.

155. Albert Vorspan to I. Cyrus Gordon, Commission on Social Action of Reform Judaism, 3 Mar. 1958, AJA.

156. Rogoff, "Rabbis and Race"; Arnold Schiffman interview with Eugene Pfaff, 11 Apr. 1979, <http://library.uncg.edu/depts/archives/civrights/detail-iv.asp?iv=119>, Greensboro Voices, Greensboro Public Library.

157. Frye Gaillard, *The Dream Long Deferred* (Columbia: University of South Carolina Press, 2006), 12; Cline, *Success Is a Team Sport*, 136.

158. Clive Webb, *Fight against Fear: Southern Jews and Black Civil Rights* (Athens: University of Georgia Press, 2001), 219.

159. *Chapel Hill Newspaper*, 12 Nov. 2008.

160. Edgcomb, *From Swastika to Jim Crow*, 66–67.

161. Rogoff, "Rabbis and Race," 1995.

162. Rogoff, *A History of Temple Emanu-El*, 79; Rogoff, *Homelands*, 230–31; Lauenstein, *Temple Emanuel Greensboro, 1907–2007*, 51.

163. Greenberg, *Troubling the Waters*, 158; Ron Levin, "Letters," *Carolina Alumni Review*, May–June 2006, 16.

164. John Ehle, *The Free Men* (New York: Harper and Row, 1965), 276, 287.

165. Quoted in John Kobler, "Why They Don't Hate Harry," *Saturday Evening Post*, 20 Sept. 1958, 124.

166. Chafe, *Never Stop Running*, 38–40, 178–79.

167. *Carolina Israelite*, Jan.–Feb., 1968.

168. *American Jewish Times*, Sept. 1937, 9.

169. *American Jewish Times*, May 1942, 13; Jonathan Sarna, "The Cult of Synthesis in American Jewish Culture," *Jewish Historical Studies* 5, nos. 1 and 2 (Fall 1998): 52, 74–75.

CHAPTER 6

1. Abraham Karp, *Haven and Home: A History of Jews in America* (New York: Schocken, 1985), 310.

2. C. Vann Woodward, *The Burden of Southern History* (Baton Rouge: Louisiana State University Press, 1960), 3; Milton Ready, *The Tar Heel State: A History of North Carolina* (Columbia: University of South Carolina Press, 2005), 373.

3. *Durham Sun*, 10 Jan. 1975.

4. Tom Hanchett, *Sorting Out the New South City: Race, Class, and Urban Development in Charlotte, 1875–1975* (Chapel Hill: University of North Carolina Press, 1998), 244.

5. Leonard Rogoff, *A History of Temple Emanu-El: An*

Extended Family, Weldon, North Carolina (Durham: Jewish Heritage Foundation of North Carolina, 2007), 89; *Hickory News*, 7 Jan. 1999; Jan Schochet and Sharon Fahrer, eds., *The Man Who Lived on Main Street: Stories by and about Sol Schulman* (Asheville: History@Hand, 2003).

6. *Lasting Impressions*, a film by Drew Levinson and Melinda Weinstein, 2007.

7. <http:///www.tangeroutlet.com/company/history/>, 25 Sept. 2008.

8. *Raleigh News & Observer*, 1 Dec., 2002.

9. Barry Kosmin, Paul Ritterband, and Jeffrey Scheckner, "Jewish Population in the United States," in David Singer, ed., *American Jewish Yearbook, 1987* (Philadelphia: Jewish Publication Society, 1987), 170; Barry Kosmin et al., *Highlights of the CJF 1990 National Jewish Population Survey* (New York: Council of Jewish Federations, 1991), 25; Egon Mayer, Barry Kosmin, and Ariela Keysar, *American Jewish Identity Survey, 2001* (New York: Center for Cultural Judaism, 2003), 28.

10. The figures are not exactly comparable. The Jewish statistics are for Jews older than eighteen; the U.S. statistics for those older than twenty-five. The Charlotte poll was taken in 1997; the others in 1990. Ira Sheskin, *How Jewish Communities Differ: Variations in the Findings of Local Jewish Population Studies* (New York: North American Jewish Data Bank, 2001), 58–59; <http://shalomdch.org/section.aspx?id=5>, 20 Oct. 2008; Jason Black, "A History of High Point Jews," research paper for Southern Jewish History and Culture, Duke University, 22 Apr. 2004, JHFNC.

11. Larry Griffin, Ranae Evenson, and Ashley Thompson, "Southerners All?" *Southern Cultures*, Spring 2005, 9, 14, 19, 21. That southern Jews, at 3 percent, had the lowest rate of regional identification among religious groups is less relevant given the numbers of south Floridians. See also John Shelton Reed, "Shalom Y'All: Jewish Southerners," in *One South: An Ethnic Approach to Regional Culture* (Baton Rouge: Louisiana State University Press, 1982). *Down Home: Jewish Life in North Carolina* (documentary film produced by Steven Channing and Henry A. Greene, 2009).

12. <bbqjew.com>, 18 Mar. 2009.

13. *Raleigh News & Observer*, 20 Nov. 2001; 1 Dec. 2002.

14. <http://quickfacts.census.gov/qfd/states/37000.html>, 25 Sept. 2008.

15. Ronald Schechter, *Obstinate Hebrews: Representations of Jews in France, 1715–1815* (Berkeley: University of California Press, 2003), 259; Sylvia Barack Fishman, "Relatively Speaking: Constructing Identity in America and Mixed Married Families," in Deborah Dash Moore, ed., *American Jewish Identity Politics* (Ann Arbor: University of Michigan Press, 2008), 316.

16. Leonard Rogoff, *Homelands: Southern Jewish Identity in Durham and Chapel Hill, North Carolina* (Tuscaloosa: University of Alabama Press, 2001), 272; Gabrielle Edgcomb, *From Swastika to Jim Crow: Refugee Scholars at Black Colleges* (Malabar: Krieger, 1993), 67–68.

17. *New York Times*, 28 Apr. 1970.

18. *Raleigh News & Observer*, 11 Feb. 2007; <http://www.topix.com/forum/city/morganton-nc/T3EJD-KHA1O4J80Q5T>, 17 Oct. 2008; Sarah Wilkinson-Freeman, untitled typescript, 11, JHFNC.

19. Paul Luebke, *Tar Heel Politics: Myths and Realities* (Chapel Hill: University of North Carolina Press, 1990), 71.

20. Mimi Cunningham, *The Joy of Politics: A Biography of B. D. Schwartz* (Wilmington, 1989), Southeastern North Carolina Collection, William Madison Randall Library, University of North Carolina at Wilmington, 209; *Raleigh News and Observer*, 2 Apr. 1972.

21. *New York Times*, 10 Apr. 1988; North Carolina Collection Clipping File, 1967–89 (0630), NCC.

22. <http://1stroughdraft.blogspot.com/2007/10/morgantons-mayoral-race-pits-2-strong.html>, 17 Oct. 2008; *Bladen Daily Journal*, 19 Oct. 1992.

23. Cunningham, *Joy of Politics*, 211, 221, 259; *Charlotte Observer*, 6 Nov. 1989, 12 Jan. 1990.

24. Morris Speizman, *The Jews of Charlotte, North Carolina* (Charlotte: McNally & Loftin, 1978),136–37; *Charlotte Observer*, 1 Dec. 1988.

25. *Statesville Record & Landmark*, 4 Dec. 1988; Joseph Asher, "A Rabbi Asks: Isn't It Time We Forgave the Germans," *Look*, Apr. 1965.

26. Alvin Rosenfeld, "The Americanization of the Holocaust," in Deborah Dash Moore, ed., *American Jewish Identity Politics* (Ann Arbor: University of Michigan Press, 2008), 55; Hasia Diner, "Before 'The Holocaust': American Jews Confront Catastrophe, 1945–62," in Moore, *American Jewish Identity Politics*, 112; <http://www.dpi.state.nc.us/holocaust_council>, 2 Feb. 2009.

27. University Newswire at UNC-Pembroke, 20 Oct. 2006; *Salisbury Post*, 15 Mar. 2009; <http://www.toto.lib.unca.edu/projects/Shoa>, 12 Oct. 2008.

28. Jonathan Sarna, *American Judaism* (New Haven:

Yale University Press, 1994), 315, 316; Kurt Lauenstein, *Temple Emanuel Greensboro 1907–2007*, 71, JHFNC.

29. Rogoff, *Homelands*, 282–83.

30. "Cooperation between Israel and the State of North Carolina," <http://www.jewishvirtuallibrary.org/jsource/states/NC.html>, 21 Oct. 2008.

31. *Wall Street Journal*, 5 July 2008.

32. Ibid.; <http://www.beth-elsa.org/be_so419a.htm>, 19 Oct. 2008; *The Independent*, 27 Aug. 2008; <http://www.humankindness.org>, 18 Oct. 2008; <http://www.richheartmusic.com/aboutrichard.html>, 20 Oct. 2008.

33. Speizman, *Jews of Charlotte*, 143; Mark Bernstein to Marvin Bienstock, 28 Oct. 1985; Charlotte Jewish Federation, Community Relations Committee, 12 July 1982, Blumenthal Papers, UNC-C.

34. <http://news.duke.edu/mmedia/features/psm/psmends.htnl>, 17 Oct. 2004.

35. <http://www.dukenews.duke.edu/mmedia/features/psm/psmends.html> 21 Oct. 2008; *Raleigh News & Observer*, 21, 23 Mar. 2006; *New York Times*, 10 Mar. 2006; *Hendersonville Times-News*, 21 Jan. 2006.

36. *Raleigh News & Observer*, 14 Dec. 2008; *Families of Abraham*, <http://www.museumofthenewsouth.org/exhibits/detail/?ExhibitId=82>, 4 Feb. 2009.

37. David Goldfield, "Urbanization in a Rural Culture: Suburban Cities and Country Cosmopolites," in Paul Escott and David Goldfield, eds., *The South for New Southerners* (Chapel Hill: University of North Carolina Press, 1991), 67; *75 Years: Temple Emanuel, Winston-Salem, NC* (n.p., n.d. [2007]), JHFNC.

38. Lee Shai Weissbach, *Jewish Life in Small-Town America* (New Haven: Yale University Press, 2005), 306.

39. <http://shalomdch.org/section.aspx?id=5>, 26 Sept. 2008.

40. <http://www.bslkn.org/>, 27 Sept. 2008; <j.weekly.com 5/26/2009>, 3 July 2009.

41. Quoted in Rogoff, *Homelands*, 232.

42. Sarna, *American Judaism*, 307.

43. *Free Jewish University of North Carolina Catalogue*, Fall 1973, Duke.

44. Rogoff, *Homelands*, 285–86.

45. Sarna, *American Judaism*, 326, 330.

46. Ibid., 354–55.

47. Rogoff, *Homelands*, 81; Sheskin, *How Jewish Communities Differ*, 92. The figures are not exactly comparative, given that some places, like Phoenix and Washington, reported numbers dating to 1983; <http://www.bethdavidsynagogue.org>; <http:>, 2 Feb. 2009.

48. Sheskin, *How Jewish Communities Differ*, 92; Sarna, *American Judaism*, 360; <www.interfaithfamily.com/relationships/Parenting-Romm_for_Eveyone>.

49. <http://www.ujc.org/ir_LL_category.html?state=nc>, 9 Oct. 2008.

50. "Live Generously," Jewish Federation of Greater Charlotte, n.d., JHFNC.

51. Stephen Cohen and Lauren Blitzer, *Belonging without Believing: Jews and Their Distinctive Patterns of Religiosity—and Secularity* (Florence G. Heller–JCC Association Research Center, 2008), accessible at <http://www.jewishdatabank.org/Archive/N-Pew-2007-Report_Belonging_Without_Believing_Cohen_2008.pdf>.

52. *Forward*, 1 June 2007.

53. Emily Rotberg, "'Jew-Camp': The Role of Camp Judea in the South," research paper for Southern Jewish History and Culture, Duke University, 23 Apr. 2004, JHFNC; *Young Judaea Alumni Study*, <http://youngjudaea.org/html./full_study.html 8>, Oct. 2008.

54. "History of Maccabi Academy," <http://www.maccabiacademy.org/index.php?submenu=History>, 19 Oct. 2008.

55. Jonathan Sarna, "American Judaism in Historical Perspective," in Moore, *American Jewish Identity Politics*, 140; Sheskin, *How Jewish Communities Differ*, 72; <http://www.or-olam.org>, 20 Mar. 2009; *Raleigh News & Observer*, 4 Sept. 2000.

56. Cohen and Blitzer, *Belonging without Believing*, 11; Sarna, *American Judaism*, 356.

57. *75 Years*, 24.

58. J. J. Goldberg, "Conservative Judaism's 'Vision Thing,'" 11 Feb. 2009, <http:www.forward.com/articles/15176>.

59. Sarna, *American Judaism*, 323; <http://www.hjnc.org/index.html> 24 Mar. 2009.

60. Quoted in Leonard Rogoff, "Synagogue and Jewish Church: A Congregational History of North Carolina," *Southern Jewish History* 1 (1998): 43, 70.

61. *75 Years: Temple Emanuel, Winston-Salem* (2007); Kurt Lauenstein, *Temple Emanuel Greensboro, 1907–2007*, 56, JHFNC.

62. *Raleigh News & Observer*, 19 Sept. 2008.

63. Rogoff, *A History of Temple Emanu-El*, 84; *Raleigh Spectator*, 9 Dec. 1993.

64. Rogoff, *Homelands*, 303; *Raleigh Spectator*, 9 Dec. 1993.

65. *75 Years*, 29.

66. *Forward*, 6 Feb. 2004.

67. <www.boonejewishcommunity.com/havurah .htm>, 17 Oct. 2008.

68. <www.lakenormanjc.org>, 1 Oct. 2008.

69. *Raleigh News & Observer*, 10 Oct. 1997.

70. *Raleigh News & Observer*, 6 May 2006; Rogoff, *Homelands*.

71. Christian Life Council of the Baptist State Convention of North Carolina in sessions September 30, 1980, AJA; David Goldfield, *Still Fighting the Civil War: The American South and Southern History* (Baton Rouge: Louisiana State University Press, 2002), 82; *The (Duke) Chronicle*, 16 Feb. 1983.

72. Cheryl Loflin (Granddaughter of Elizabeth Janie Marks), NC Jewish Descendant, <deereolframer@yahoo .com>, 3 July 2008.

73. Fishman, "Relatively Speaking," 309; Walter Klein, *The Bridge Table: A Love Story*, 84, JHFNC.

74. <http://shamah-elim.info/p_regwhite.htm>, 21 Oct. 2008.

75. *Charlotte Observer*, 4 Nov. 1985.

76. Kim Koster, "An Emerging Presence," *Duke Magazine* 86, no. 2 (Jan.-Feb. 2000): 7.

77. *New York Times*, 1 May 1977.

78. *Chapel Hill Herald*, 19 June 1991.

79. Rogoff, *Homelands*, 262.

80. Jonathan Yardley, "An Interview with Jonathan Yardley," *Carolina Alumni Review* 7, no. 82 (Summer 1989): 40–41. Yardley specifically mentioned students Eli Evans, Joel Fleishman, and Allard Lowenstein, but the generalization holds. Yardley held to stereotypes: Evans and Fleishman were small-town southerners.

81. Paula Hyman, "Forum Response," *AJS Perspectives* (2006): 22–23.

82. *The Independent*, 19 Mar. 2003; <http://www.sfgate .com/cgi-bin/article.cgi?f=/c/a/2003/03/19/DD262218. DTL>, 17 Feb. 2009.

83. Richard Chess, *Third Temple* (Tampa: University of Tampa Press, 2007), 44, 37.

84. *Raleigh News & Observer*, 23 Dec. 2005; *Preview: The Magazine of the North Carolina Museum of Art*, July–August 2006, 6.

85. See Cohen and Blitzer, *Belonging without Believing*, 10; *High Point Enterprise*, 2 Feb. 1958.

86. "Brody Family's Philanthropy to Medical School Spans Decades," 7 Dec. 1999, JHFNC; "The Brenner Family," 8 Sept. 1989, updated 17 Nov. 2006, JHFNC.

87. Schochet and Fahrer, *The Man Who Lived on Main Street*, 18, 19, 37–38; *Raleigh News & Observer*, 1 Feb. 2005; "The Brenner Family."

88. David Goldfield, *Region, Race, and Cities: Interpreting the Urban South* (Baton Rouge: Louisiana State University Press, 1997), 290.

INTERVIEWS

Adler, Hanna and Howard. Interview with Leonard Rogoff, 20 Aug. 2007.

Bernard, Zelda. Interview with Leonard Rogoff, 8 Mar. 2006.

Bernstein, William and Katherine. Interview with Leonard Rogoff, 16 Aug. 2007.

Bloom, Betty. Interview with Leonard Rogoff, 12 July 2005.

Bluethenthal, Arthur and Joanne. Interview with Sarah Malino, 21 June 2005.

Blumenthal, Philip. Interview with Leonard Rogoff, 13 June 2007.

Bossert, Norman. Interview with Leonard Rogoff, 21 June 2005.

Brenner, Abe. Interview with Leonard Rogoff, 24 Apr. 2006.

Chenkin, Suly. Interview with Leonard Rogoff, 13 June 2007.

Cone, Benjamin, Jr. Interview with Leonard Rogoff, 26 Nov. 2007.

Diamond, Ruth. Interview with Leonard Rogoff, 1 June 2007.

D'Lugin, Ben. Interview with Leonard Rogoff, 4 June 2007.

Dickman, Harriet Bloom. Interview with Leonard Rogoff, 25 July 2005.

Ehrlich, Alice. Interview with Leonard Rogoff, 7 Sept. 2007.

Eisenberg, Barry. Interview with Leonard Rogoff, 16 Aug. 2007.

Evans, Eli. Interview with Robin Gruber, 9 March 1986.

Evans, Emanuel J. Interview with Rabbi Steven Sager and Beth-El Confirmation Class, 25 March n.d.

Evans, Sara. Interview with Rabbi Steven Sager and Beth-El Confirmation Class, 25 March n.d.

Farber, Maralyn. Self-interview, 2 May 2006.

Farber, Morton. Interview with Maralyn Farber, 2 May 2006.

Fox, Stan. Interview with Leonard Rogoff, 20 July 2006.

Frazier, Bill. Interview with Leonard Rogoff, 1 June 2007.

Gelfand, Eve Dorra. Interview with Leonard Rogoff, 8 June 2007.

Glass, David. Interview with Leonard Rogoff, 8 Sept. 2007.

Gordon, Barry. Interview with Liz Baker, 17 Feb. 2008.

Gordon, Gene. Interview with Leonard Rogoff, 20 Aug. 2007.

Gordon, Kalman. Interview with Leonard Rogoff, 16 Aug. 2007.

Gordon, Richard. Interview with Leonard Rogoff, 20 Aug. 2007.

Gorelick, William. Interview with Leonard Rogoff, 22 Nov. 2006.

Gordon, Saul. Interview with Leonard Rogoff, 18 June 2007.

Holtzman, Sylvia and Abe. Interview with Leonard Rogoff, 30 Aug. 2007.

Horwitz, Burton. Interview with Leonard Rogoff, 8 Sept. 2007.

Israel, Adelaide and Archie. Interview with Leonard Rogoff, 3 Mar. 2006.

Kanter, Jerry and Sharon. Interview with Leonard Rogoff, 5 Dec. 2005.

Kaplan, Leonard. Interview with Leonard Rogoff, 6 May 2008.

Kaplan, Morris. Interview with Leonard Rogoff, 21 June 2005.

Kiel, David. Interview with Leonard Rogoff, 3 Nov. 2007.

Kittner, Harry. Interview with Leonard Rogoff, 8 Sept. 1997.

Kittner, Harry and Sarah. Interview with David Cecelski, 22, 25 Jan., 22 Feb. 1999.

Kittner, William. Interview with Leonard Rogoff, 11 July 2005.

Klein, Walter. Interview with Leonard Rogoff, 13 June 2007.

Kligerman, Vickie Popkin. Interview with Leonard Rogoff, 16 Aug. 2007.

Kramer, Vivian. Interview with Leonard Rogoff, 7 Apr. 2006.

Krumbein, Amy Meyers. Interview with Leonard Rogoff, 19 Aug. 1999.

Kuttler, Miles. Interview with Leonard Ropgoff, 16 Aug. 2007.

Labell, Nat. Interview with Natalie Mapon, 19 Apr. 2005.

LeBauer, Eugene. Interview with Leonard Rogoff, 1 Jan. 2008.

LeBauer, Joe. Interview with Leonard Rogoff, 1 Jan. 2008.

LeBauer, Sam. Interview with Leonard Rogoff, 1 Jan. 2008.

Leder, Steven. Interview with Leonard Rogoff, 22 Mar. 2007.

Levin, Jerome. Interview with Leonard Rogoff, 2 June 2005.

Levin, Richard. Interview with Leonard Rogoff, 10 Mar. 2006.

Levin, Seymour. Interview with Leonard Rogoff, 24 Dec. 2007.

Levine, Leah. Interview with Leonard Rogoff, 1 May 2006.

Levine, Leon and Sandra. Interview with Leonard Rogoff, 22 Nov. 2006.

Lipman, Elbert. Interview with Leonard Rogoff, 12 Aug. 1995.

Litwack, Charlotte. Interview with Leonard Rogoff, 27 June 2007.

Liverman, Robert. Interview with Leonard Rogoff, 15 Sept. 2005.

Lurey, Milton. Interview with Sharon Fahrer, 6 Aug. 2003.

Mowshowitz, Israel. Self-interview, Mar. 1987.

Norris, Pastor Pete. Interview with Leonard Rogoff, 21 March 2007.

Novey, Bari. Interview with Leonard Rogoff, 25 July 2005.

Offerman, Muriel Kramer. Interview with Leonard Rogoff, 7 Apr. 2006.

Parish, Lucy Goldsmith. Interview with Leonard Rogoff, 29 Apr. 2005.

Patton, Marilyn Blomberg. Interview with Sharon Fahrer, 23 Feb. 2004.

Popkin, Rodger. Interview with Leonard Rogoff, 16 Aug. 2007.

Popkin, Rosalie. Interview with Leonard Rogoff, 16 Aug. 2007.

Rauch, Marshall. Interview with Leonard Rogoff, 18 Apr. 2006.

Reznick, Joseph. Interview with Leonard Rogoff, 21 Jan. 2007.

Robinson, Michael. Interview with Sharon Fahrer, 3 Oct. 2003.

Rosenberg, Thomas. Interview with Leonard Rogoff, 13 June 2007.

Rosenberg, Zahava. Interview with Leonard Rogoff, 13 June 2007.

Roth, Betty. Interview with Natalie Mapou, 28 Apr. 2005.

Sabbah, Maurice. Interview with Leonard Rogoff, n.d.

Samet, Elsie. Interview with Leonard Rogoff, 15 Nov. 2006.

Samet, Harry. Interview with Leonard Rogoff, 17 July 2006.

———. Interview with Leonard Rogoff, 20 Sept. 2007.

Samet, Joan. Interview with Leonard Rogoff, 17 July 2006.

Samet, Leonard. Interview with Leonard Rogoff, 20 Sept. 2007.

Samet, Norman. Interview with Leonard Rogoff, 20 Sept. 2007.

Satisky, Alice and Daniel. Interview with Leonard Rogoff, 1 May 2006.

Scheer, George Moses III. Interview with Leonard Rogoff, 18 June 2007.

Schindler, Rabbi Judy. Interview with Leonard Rogoff, 18 Apr. 2006.

Schochet, Jan. Interview with Leonard Rogoff, 17 Aug. 2007.

Schwartz, Nathan. Interview with Leonard Rogoff, 13 June 2007.

Silver, Louis. Interview with Leonard Rogoff, 11 Dec. 2007.

Sloan, Frank. Interview with Leonard Rogoff, 14 Dec. 2007.

Sloan, Tom. Interview with Leonard Rogoff, 14 Dec. 2007.

Solomon, Walter. Interview with Leonard Rogoff, 16 Aug. 2007.

Stadiem, Abe. Interview with Leonard Rogoff, 8 Apr. 1992.

Stang, Amanda. Interview with Leonard Rogoff, 5 June 2008.

Sternberg, Jerry. Interview with Leonard Rogoff, 21 Oct. 2007.

Straus, Karl and Sylvia. Interview with Leonard Rogoff, 17 Aug. 2007.

Todd, Jeff and Yaffa. Interview with Leonard Rogoff, 16 Aug. 2007.

Warshauer, Sam and Miriam. Interview with Leonard Rogoff, 4 June 2007.

Weinstein, David. Interview with Leonard Rogoff, 5 Aug. 2008.

Winner, Julienne. Interview with Leonard Rogoff, 17 Aug. 2007.

Wojnowich, Simon and Mary. Interview with Leonard Rogoff, 13 June 2007.

Yoffie, Eric. Interview with Leonard Rogoff, 21 July 1986.

ACKNOWLEDGMENTS

A book is a community. Many, many took responsibility for telling, recording, and researching the stories told here. Unfortunately, the spine is not thick enough to list all those deserving people. Credit for *Down Home: Jewish Life in North Carolina* belongs to very many, even as its faults are my own.

This book is but one part of a multimedia project of the Jewish Heritage Foundation of North Carolina. It complements a documentary film, a public-school curriculum, and a traveling museum exhibition. This book is not a catalog but attempts to complete the narrative that could not be told in other formats.

Down Home would not have come to fruition without the vision, commitment, and tenacity of Henry A. Greene, president of the Jewish Heritage Foundation of North Carolina. He persisted when others of us grew fainter of heart. Will Grossman, operations director of JHFNC, brought together the many facets of *Down Home* with a steady hand and good humor. Eric Meyers contributed sound judgment and provided both learning and perspective to all things Jewish. Lyn Slome of the American Jewish Historical Society not only brought professionalism to our collection but discovered new sources. This book would not have been realizable without her. Roberta Morris also helped prepare the way. Rebecca Cerese contributed her expertise and enthusiasm in assembling *Down Home*'s graphics, and she lightened the work with good cheer.

I apologize that I cannot include every story worth retelling or photograph worth reprinting. The hardest part of assembling this book was less so in the writing than in the editing. Space allows but so much. I only hope that *Down Home* inspires communities to compile local histories of their own. All the material collected, all the stories told, will be archived in our North Carolina Jewish Heritage Collection and be accessible to those interested in scholarly research or family history. For reasons of length, references to oral histories cited in the text can be found in the list of interviews.

The research in this book has been supported by The Rabbi Harold D. Hahn Memorial Fellowship from the American Jewish Archives, and I thank Nancy and Jerry Klein for underwriting it. The AJA is exceptional not just for its resources but for its handsome reading room and welcoming ambience. I thank the AJA's executive director Rabbi Gary Zola and archivists Kevin Proffitt and Vicki Lipski for making my research there both pleasant and rewarding. A Harry S. Golden Visiting Scholar grant introduced me to the J. Murrey Atkins Library Special Collections of the University of North Carolina at Charlotte, and I especially thank the exceedingly knowledgeable Robin Brabham and his helpful, efficient staff. Duke University, through the Judaic Studies Program, provided office space and research support, and their contribution has been "in kind," both literally and figuratively.

Down Home is built on the efforts of many local archivists, librarians, and local historians, whom I have found invariably to be as cordial as they are professional. Foremost are the North Carolina Collection and Southern Historical Collection at Wilson Library, the University of North Carolina at Chapel Hill, and the North Carolina State Archives in Raleigh. I thank Robert Anthony, Jerry and Alice Cotten, Keith Longiotti, Eileen McGrath, and Harry McKown of the North Carolina Collection and Tim West and his staff at the Southern Historical Collection. Earl Ijames, Mary Barnes, and Kim Cumber at the North Carolina State Archives have been especially helpful among its welcoming staff. The Duke Rare Books, Manuscripts, and Special Collections Library has been most accommodating. Coordinator Helen Wykle and her assistant Jamie Patterson of Special Collections of Ramsey Library at the University of North Carolina at Asheville were also most patient when I explored their exemplary Jewish Life in Western North Carolina Collection. The R. G. Dun & Co. Collection in the Historical Collections at Baker Library of the Harvard Business School was also an indispensable resource, and I thank its staff.

Local historians laid the foundations of *Down Home*, and North Carolina is fortunate to have excellent ones. First, Beverly Tetterton, senior local history librarian of the New Hanover County Public Library, has taken Wilmington's Jewish history as her theme, and her extraordinary archive is a model. I have benefited from her help, insights, and knowledge and have enjoyed the hospitality of Beverly and her husband, Glenn. Folklorists Sharon Fahrer and Jan Schochet of History@Hand have scrupulously documented Asheville's religious and mercantile Jewish history. As public historians, they brought social history to life in "The Family Store." Monika Fleming of Edgecombe Community College has limned Jewish Tarboro. Charlotte Litwack has collected Raleigh's history, and Jill Savitt created an extraordinary oral-history archive of Hendersonville's pioneer Jews. Robin Gruber and Sigmund Meyer mined Durham's Jewish history. Amalia Warshenbrot of the Levine-Sklut Judaic Library and Resource Center was a capable and personable guardian of the Charlotte Jewish Historical Society archive. Cynthia Chapman assisted ably. Peggy Gartner has been a helpful guide to the Blumenthal legacy. Greensboro has been central to the state's Jewish community development, and its history has capable guardians in Marcia Horowitz, who researched Greensboro Jewry and helped organize an oral-history program; Brenda Henly, who maintains the Temple archives; and Kurt Lauenstein, who compiled them. Marilyn Stern has indefatigably documented New Bern's rich Jewish heritage. Anton Hieke has explored the German legacy with Teutonic thoroughness and shared his scholarship. Walter Klein has faithfully guarded the state's Jewish heritage.

Through the Southern Jewish Historical Society I have benefited from acquaintance with some extraordinary scholars whom I now count as friends as well as colleagues: Eric Goldstein, Scott Langston, Stuart Rockoff, Deb Weiner, and Hollace Weiner. Lee Shai Weissbach is an invaluable resource of small-town Jewry. Mark Bauman and Stephen Whitfield especially have framed the issues and wisely critiqued my own work. Marcie Cohen Ferris and Adam Mendelsohn are founts of new sources and insights. Dale Rosengarten, curator of the Jewish Heritage Collection at the College of Charleston, inspired us as creator of "A Portrait of the People: Three Hundred Years of Southern Jewish Life." Bernie Wax, Cathy Kahn, Barbara Tashler, Beryl Weiner, Les Bergen, and Sumner Levine have kept the Southern Jewish Heritage Society ship afloat. As he did for many, Eli Evans first lit my enthusiasm for southern Jewry with *The Provincials: A Personal History of Jews in the South.*

A pleasure of writing this book was enjoying the hospitality of its subjects. I thank Wendy and Frank Block, Ben Cone, Bob and Sally Cone, Henry Farber, John and Jerry Stein Gimesh, Sandy and Erwin Goldman, Saul and Kalman Gordon, David and Emily Weil, Leslie and Julienne Winner, Faith and Stanley Pearson, Phillip Blumenthal and the Wildacres staff, and Elaine, Howard, and Marvin Zerden. Al G. Taylor generously brought to life the social and material culture of a "Jew store."

I thank, too, Elaine Maisner, Rich Hendel, Ron Maner, Tema Larter, and Brian MacDonald of the University of North Carolina Press for making the publication process a humane one. In diverse ways I have benefited from the assistance and friendship of Howard and Hanna Adler, Emily Bingham, Steve Channing, Rick Chess, Cece Conway, Bob Drake, Jack Frisch, Warren Gentry, Harlan Gradin, Sidney Gray, Stan Greenspon, Tom Hanchett, Charlot Marks Karesh, Arnold Leder, Michelle Leder, Jennie Malcolm, Sarah Malino, Robert Marcus, Jim Martin Jr., David and Bunny Moff, Gail Parrish, Dan Patterson, Al Rogat, Joe Rubin, Lue Simopoulos, Albrecht and Nancy Strauss, and Leslie Winner.

The primary pleasure of this book was meeting its subjects, North Carolinians whose Jewish heritage and southern breeding so warmly blended. Harry and Sarah Kittner embrace the graciousness of small-town Jewish life. I remember especially those whom I met but who did not live to see our conversations bear fruit. Lena Gordon Goldman, a beloved friend to everyone, lived well and wisely for more than a century. Art Shain was both southern gentleman and Jewish mensch. The same was true of Harry Freid, who, as his community died, was concerned: "I thought we were going to be forgotten." I also remember Eugene Bloom, Monroe Evans, Archie and Adelaide Israel, Gibby Katz, Vivian Kramer, Leah Levine, Martin Lipman, Sam Margolis, Sigmund Meyer, Lucy Goldsmith Parish, Dan Satisky, Lou Silver, Leah Tannenbaum, and Julienne Winner. Their passing reminds us of the urgency of recording these stories.

For diversions gustatory, social, and intellectual, I thank Amanda Stang and Howard Weinberg, Ben and Maya Stang-Weinberg, Barry and Sonya Fine, Barbara, JJ, and Les Lang, Paula Press and John Rosenthal, John and Grace Curry, Bill and Marcie Ferris, Lynne Gladstein Grossman, Marvin and Shirley Block, Ed Levin, Joe Herzenberg, Simone Lipman, Joel and Myrna Schwartz, Callie Warner, David Winer, Diane Wright, Tom Stern, Manny Stein, Larry Green, and the Kiebers, as well as my extended family, Jeffrey Drexler, Janos Nevai, Stefan and Gail Pasternack, Paul and Tessa Ripper, Debbie and Warren Binnick, and, most of all, Arthur, Carol, Josh, and Jonathan Rogoff. Deborah Hicks has eased the burdens of this endeavor with sweetness and light, and for that I am most grateful.

The Leon Levine Foundation, Sandra and Leon Levine, and the State of North Carolina Department of Cultural Resources have generously supported the Down Home project. Jeffrey Crow of the North Carolina Department of Cultural Resources early recognized the project's significance, and Betsy Buford and Ken Howard, past and present directors of the North Carolina Museum of History, encouraged us to proceed. We especially thank former governor James B. Hunt Jr., honorary chair of the Down Home project, for his advocacy and commitment. Former and present University of North Carolina presidents William Friday and Erskine Bowles brought credibility to our efforts. Stan Fox, Muriel Kramer Offerman, David Weinstein, Rick Glazier, and Jennifer Weiss, who have all lived the experience, were influential in enlisting support. The Jewish Heritage Foundation of North Carolina board has been steadfast in building Down Home's foundations.

This book is dedicated in memory of Anna Lou Doctor Cassell. She was a gracious and elegant matriarch of her family and the North Carolina Jewish community. Descended from pioneering immigrant families, the Doctors and Londons, she was proud of her North Carolina roots, which extended more than a century. Anna Lou Cassell early and firmly recognized the importance of *Down Home*. Her devotion was deeply felt. She personified the "commitment to community" that underlies the larger *Down Home* endeavor. We were scheduled to interview her the very day that she was hospitalized for what proved to be her final illness, but her presence is felt throughout these pages.

Down Home looks forward as well as back. I remember my own parents, Nathan and Selma Drexler Rogoff, who lived in different quarters but whose lives recompensed so much of what is most exemplary in these pages, and my own Tar Heel children, Aaron and Lilah, who will write their own chapters.

INDEX

Page numbers in italics refer to illustrations.

Henderson, 111, 173, 182, 184
Hendersonville: Agudas Israel, 211, 210, 330; commerce, 132, 136, 197, 231–32, 303; community relations, 201, 276; and Judaism, 207, 284; politics, 316; resorts, 272; retirees, 330; and summer camps, 208–9, 279–80, 281, 340; and Zionism, 327
Henry, Amelia, 43
Henry, Esther, 43
Henry, Jacob, 28, 39–44; portrait, 43; text, 42
Henry, Joel, 23, 29, 35, 43
Henry, Sir Philip, 152
Henry, Samuel Whitehurst, 43
Herbst, Rabbi Solomon, 218
Herman, Rabbi Floyd, 353
Herman, Rabbi Pinhas, 347–48
Herzenberg, Joe, 316
Heschel, Abraham, 275, 333
Hexner, Irvin, 247
Heyman, Art, 278
Hickory: commerce, 301; community relations, 187, 266; organizations, 245; settlement in, 87, 111, 124; synagogue, 268, 283, 345, 349, 350
High Point: community relations, 125, 148–49, 185, 204, 219, 265–66, 268; High Point Hebrew Congregation (later B'nai Israel), 175, 176, 270, 335; industry, 110, 262; and Judaism, 182; occupational mobility in, 305; organizations, 272, 276; and philanthropy, 369; peddlers, 128; politics, 285; settlement in, 51, 124, 246, 300; storekeepers, 132; story, 177, 178, 180, 209; Zionism, 258–59
High Point College, 233
Hillel Foundation, 235–36, 246, 252, 261, 264, 268, 329, 332, 340
Hillsboro/Hillsborough, 25, 27, 39, 56, 75, 127, 187
Hindus, 15, 39, 44, 261, 309
Hirshinger, Jay, 116, 168
Hirshinger family, 208
Hispanic Jews, 358
Hispanics, 4, 309, 318
Hobgood, 233
Hochheimer, Rabbi Henry, 66–67
Hockfield, Joe, 202
Hodges, Luther, 286, 288
Hoey, Clyde, 242
Hoffman, Anne, 247
Hoffman, Fred and Hilde, 258
Hoffman, Max, 116
Hoffman, S. W., 281

Hoffman family, 188
Holden, William, 81, 86
Holland, 8, 9, 19, 31, 67, 86, 104, 119, 246
Holly Ridge, 316
Holly Springs, 331
Holman, Libby, 223
Holocaust, 218, 247, 257–58, 321–24, 359, 361; and concentration camps, 3, 66, 248, 258, 319–20
Holtzman, Abe, 264, 358, 359
Holzman, Alfred, 223
Honigman, Hinda, 363
Hope Mills, 137
Hornthal, L. H., and Brother, 54
Horowitz, Rosemary, 361
Horwitz, Burton, 206, 224, 273
Horwitz, Charlotte, 148
Huguenots, 11, 27, 38
Humanistic Judaism, 342, 344–45
Hungary, 19, 46, 54, 68, 108, 253, 320
Hunt, James B., Jr., 4, 312, 313, 313, 322, 325–26, 358–59
Hurwitz, Harry, 156
Hyams, Daniel, 25
Hyams, Isaac, 25, 29
Hyams, John, 120
Hyams, Mordecai, 119
Hyman, Paula, 359
Hymans, Isaac, 72

Identity, 3–5, 377 (n. 5); American, 170, 190, 194; Jewish, 152; southern, 4, 60, 141, 271–72, 307–8, 348
Immigration, 1, 3–4, 11, 17, 46, 48, 63, 85–87, 100–101, 104–5, 108, 116, 124, 182, 195, 239–40, 311
Indians, 309
Industrialization, 51, 87, 108–11, 195–97, 262
Industrial Removal Office (IRO), 107, 116, 182
Inquisition, 8
Interfaith relations, 8, 96, 145–46, 170, 187–88, 192, 202–3, 219, 255, 264–67, 272, 275–76, 280–81, 334–35, 356. See also Brotherhood; National Conference of Christians and Jews
Intermarriage, 34–35, 150, 184, 208, 219, 334–35, 356
Interstate highways, 300–301
Iraqi Jews, 3, 317
Iredell, Hannah, 38
Iredell, James, 12, 39, 40, 44
Iredell County, 227
Ireland, 19

Irish, 57
Iroquois, 10
Isaacs, Abraham, 24–27, 35
Israel, 3, 218, 258, 260, 262, 264, 278, 280, 293, 311–12, 318, 320, 322–27, 345, 356, 359–60, 364, 366. See also Palestine; Zionism
Israel, Adelaide, 212, 221
Israel, Archie, 222
Israelis, 318, 339
Italians, 108–9, 221

Jackson, 205
Jacksonville, 268–69, 328, 353
Jacobi, Nathaniel, 74, 163–64, 167–68, 167, 179
Jacobi, Rosalie, 94
Jacobi, Solomon, 93
Jacobs, Benjamin, 25
Jacobs, Joseph, 25, 34
Jacobs, Louis, 275
Jacobs, Rabbi Robert, 242, 271
Jacobs, Sol, 292
Jacobson, Rabbi Moses, 192, 240, 245
Jaffé, Louis (editor), 107, 155
Jaffe, Louis (baker), 221
Jaffe, Stephen, 363
Jalowetz, Heinrich and Johanna, 250
Jamaica, 12, 14, 21
James City, 164–65
Jamestown, Va., 9
Japan, 305
Jarrell, Tommy, 365
Jarvis, John, 27
Jastrow, Elizabeth, 247
Jastrow, Rabbi Marcus, 94, 96, 173
Jefferson, Thomas, 14, 38, 41, 44
Jenkins, Addie, 150
Jerusalem, 3, 176, 182, 214, 262, 270, 326, 365
Jewish Business Forum, 337
Jewish Community Centers, 245, 336–38
Jewish Community of the Outer Banks, 330, 352
Jewish day schools, 294, 340, 342
Jewish Heritage Foundation of North Carolina, 338
Jewish-Muslim relations, 327–28
Jewish Publication Society, 68, 152
Jewish Renewal, 342
Jewish South, 152
Jewish studies, 338, 359–61
Jewish Theological Seminary, 173–74, 209, 213–14, 216, 243, 344
Jewish War Sufferers, 4, 187–88, 190